THE MYSTICAL ELEMENT OF RELIGION AS STUDIED IN SAINT CATHERINE OF GENOA AND HER FRIENDS

By BARON FRIEDRICH von HÜGEL

MEMBER OF THE CAMBRIDGE PHILOLOGICAL SOCIETY
HON. LL.D. (ST. ANDREWS), HON. D.D. (OXFORD)

VOLUME SECOND
CRITICAL STUDIES

LONDON

J. M. DENT & SONS LTD

JAMES CLARKE & CO. LTD.

Fourth impression 1961
Published by James Clarke & Co. Ltd.,
33, Store Street, London, W.C.1 by
arrangement with J. M. Dent & Sons Ltd.

Printed in Great Britain by
Latimer Trend & Co Ltd Plymouth

PART III
CRITICAL

THE MYSTICAL ELEMENT
OF RELIGION

CONTENTS OF THE SECOND VOLUME

THE frontispiece consists of a reduced facsimile, in photogravure, of a lithograph by F. Scotto, entitled "Ven. Batt. Vernazza," which was printed and owned by the firm of Gervasoni, and which appeared in the large 4to volume, *Ritratti, ed Elogi di Liguri Illustri*, with the text printed by Ponthenier, all in Genoa. This book was published there, in monthly parts, from 1823 to 1830. Scotto's highly characteristic lithograph no doubt reproduces an authentic likeness; and probably the original portrait was, in the first instance, owned by the Canonesses of S. Maria delle Grazie, Battista's own convent in Genoa. The picture now in the possession of the Nuns of S. Maria in Passione, the successors of those Canonesses, is of a quite conventional, secondary type.

PART III.—CRITICAL

vi

CONTENTS

The Venerable Battista Vernazza

1497—1587

THE MYSTICAL ELEMENT
OF RELIGION

CHAPTER IX

PSYCHO-PHYSICAL AND TEMPERAMENTAL QUESTIONS

INTRODUCTORY.

1. *Plan of Part Three.*

The picture of Catherine's life and teaching which was
attempted in the previous volume will, I hope, have been
sufficiently vivid to stimulate in the reader a desire to try and
go deeper, and to get as near as may be to the driving forces,
the metaphysical depths of her life. And yet it is obvious
that, if we would understand something of these, we must proceed slowly and thoroughly, and must begin with comparatively
superficial questions. Or rather, we must begin by studying
her temperamental and psycho-physical endowment and condition, and then the literary influences that stimulated and
helped to mould these things, as though all this were *not*
secondary and but the material and occasion of the forces and
self-determinations to be considered later on.

2. *Defects of ancient psycho-physical theory.*

Now as to those temperamental and neural matters, to
which this chapter shall be devoted, the reader will, no doubt
long ago, have discovered that it is precisely here that not a
little of the *Vita e Dottrina* is faded and withered beyond
recall, or has even become positively repulsive to us. The
constant assumption, and frequent explicit insistence, on the
part of more or less all the contributors, upon the immediate
and separate significance, indeed the directly miraculous
character, of certain psycho-physical states—states which,
taken thus separately, would now be inevitably classed as
most explicable neural abnormalities,—all this atmosphere of
nervous high-pitch and tremulousness has now become a

3

matter demanding a difficult historical imagination and magnanimity, if we would be just to those who held such views, and would thus benefit to the full from these past positions and misconceptions.

Thus when we read the views of perhaps all her educated attendants : " this condition, in which her body remained alive without food or medicine, was a supernatural thing "; " her state was clearly understood to be supernatural when, in so short a time, so great a change was seen "; and " she became yellow all over,—a manifest sign that her humanity was being entirely consumed in the fire of divine love " : [1] we feel indeed that we can no more follow. And when we read, as part of one of the late additions, the worthless legends gathered from, or occasioned by, the uneducated Argentina : " in proof that she bore the stigmata within her,—on putting her hands in a cup of cold water, the latter became so boiling hot that it greatly heated the very saucer beneath it " : [2] we are necessarily disgusted. And when, worst of all, she is made, by a demonstrable, probable double misinterpretation of an externally similar action, to burn her bare arm with a live charcoal or lighted candle, with intent to see which fire, this external one or that interior one of the divine love, were the greater : [3] we can, even if we have the good fortune of being able, by means of the critical analysis of the sources, to put this absurd story to the discredit of her eulogists, but feel the pathos of such well-meant perversity, which took so sure a way for rendering ridiculous one who, take her all in all, is so truly great.[4]

3. *Slow growth of Neurology.*

We should, of course, be very patient in such matters : for psycho-physical knowledge was, as yet, in its very infancy, witness the all-important fact that the nerves were, in our modern sense of the term, still as unknown as they were to the whole of Græco-Roman antiquity, with which " neuron " and "nervus" ever meant "muscle" or "ligament" and, deriva-

---

[1] *Vita*, pp. 143*b*; 149*b*, 159*b*; 153*a*.   [2] *Ibid*. p. 153*c*.

[3] *Ibid*. pp. 129*c*, 134*a*.

[4] I have already traced the steps in the growth of this legend. It is no doubt this element in the biography which irritated John Wesley, the man of absolute judgments; although he himself, with shrewd good sense, indicates its possible secondary origin. " I am sure this was a fool of a Saint; that is, if it was not the folly of her historian, who has aggrandized her into a mere idiot " (*Journal*, ed. P. L. Parker, London, 1903).

tively, " energy," but never consciously what they now mean
in the strict medical sense.   Thus the *Vita* (1551) writes :
" There remained no member or muscle (*nervo*) of her body
that was not tormented by fire within it " ; " one rib was
separated from the others, with great pains in the ligaments
(*nervi*) and bones " ; and " all her body was excruciated and
her muscles (*nervi*) were tormented" : [1] where, in the first and
last case, visible muscular convulsive movements are clearly
meant.   St. Teresa, in her own *Life* (1561 or 1562), writes :
" Nervous pains, according to the physicians, are intolerable ;
and all my nerves were shrunk " ; and " if the rapture lasts,
all the nerves are made to feel it." [2]   Even Fénelon (died 1715)
can still write of the human body :   " The bones sustain the
flesh which envelops them ;   the nerves " (ligaments, minor
muscles) " which are stretched along them, constitute all their
strength ; and the muscles, by inflation and elongation at the
points where the nerves are intertwined with them, produce
the most precise and regular movements." [3]   Here the soul
acts directly upon the muscles, and, through these and their
dependent ligaments, upon the bones and the flesh.

4. *Permanent values of the ancient theory.*

And yet that old position with regard to the rarer psycho-
physical states has a right to our respectful and sympathetic
study.

For one thing, we are now coming again to recognize, more
and more, how real and remarkable are certain psycho-
physical states and facts, whether simply morbid or fruitfully
utilized states, so long derided, by the bulk of Scientists, as
mere childish legend or deliberate imposture ; and to see how
natural, indeed inevitable it was, that these, at that time quite
inexplicable, things should have been attributed to a direct
and discontinuous kind of Divine intervention.   We, on our
part, have then to guard against the Philistinism both of the
Rationalists and of the older Supernaturalists, and will neither
measure our assent to facts by our ability to explain them,
nor postulate the unmediated action of God wherever our
powers of explanation fail us.   On this point we have admirable models of sympathetic docility towards facts, in the
works of Prof. Pierre Janet, in his medico-psychological

---

[1] *Vita*, pp. 127*c*, 143*b*, 144*b*.
[2] *Life*, tr. by D. Lewis, London, ed. 1888, pp. 27, 420.
[3] *Existence de Dieu*, I, 1, 31 : *Œuvres*, ed. Versailles, 1820, Vol. I,
p. 51.

investigations of present-day morbid cases; of Hermann
Gunkel and Heinrich Weinel, in their examination of mostly
healthy psycho-physical phenomena in early Christian times
and writings; and of William James, in his study of instances
of various kinds, both past and present.[1]

And next, these (at first sight physical) phenomena are
turning out, more and more, to be the direct or indirect consequence of the action of mind : no doubt, in the first instance,
of the human mind, but still of mind, both free-willing and
automatically operative. And at the same time this action
is, more and more, seen to be limited and variously occasioned
by the physical organism, and to be accompanied or followed,
in a determinist fashion, by certain changes in that organism.
Yet if we have now immeasurably more knowledge than men
had, even fifty years ago, of this latter ceaselessly active,
limiting, occasioning influence of the body upon the mind, we
have also immeasurably more precise and numerous facts
and knowledge in testimony of the all but boundless effect of
mind over body. Here, again, Prof. Janet's writings, those
of Alfred Binet, and the Dominican Père Coconnier's very
sensible book register a mass of material, although of the
morbid type.[2]

And further, such remarkable peripheral states and
phenomena are getting again to be rightly looked for in at
least some types of unusual spiritual insight and power
(although such states are found to be indicative, in exact
proportion to the spiritual greatness of their subject, of a
substantially different mental and moral condition of soul).
Witness again the Unitarian Prof. James's *Varieties*, and the
Church-Historical works of the Broad Lutheran German
scholars Weinel, Bernouilli, and Duhm.[3]

And lastly, the very closeness with which modern experimental and analytical psychology is exploring the phenomena

---

[1] Pierre Janet, *Automatisme Psychologique*, ed. 1903; *Etat Mental
des Hystériques*, 2 vols., 1892, 1893. Hermann Gunkel, *Die Wirkungen
des heiligen Geistes*, Göttingen, 1899. Heinrich Weinel, *Die Wirkungen
des Geistes und der Geister*, Freiburg, 1899. William James, *The Varieties
of Religious Experience*, London, 1902.

[2] Pierre Janet, *op. cit.* Alfred Binet, *Les Altérations de la Personnalité*,
Paris, 1902. M. Th. Coconnier, *L'Hypnotisme Franc*, Paris, 1897.

[3] W. James, *op. cit.*, especially pp. 1–25. H. Weinel, *op. cit.*, especially
pp. 128–137; 161–208. Bernouilli, *Die Heiligen der Merowinger*,
Tübingen, 1900, pp. 2–6. B. Duhm, *Das Geheimniss in der Religion*,
Tübingen, 1896.

of our consciousness is once more bringing into ever-clearer relief the irrepressible metaphysical apprehensions and affirmations involved and implied by the experience of every human mind, from its first dim apprehension in infancy of a " something," as yet undifferentiated by it into subjective and objective, up to its mature and reflective affirmation of the trans-subjective validity of its " positions," or at least of its negations—pure scepticism turning out to be practically impossible.   Here we have, with respect to that apprehension, such admirable workers as Henri Bergson in France, and Professors Henry Jones and James Ward in England; and, for this affirmation, such striking thinkers as the French Maurice Blondel, and the Germans Johannes Volkelt and Hugo Münsterberg.   And Mgr. Mercier of Louvain, now Cardinal Mercier, has contributed some valuable criticism of certain points in these positions.[1]

5. *Difficulties of this inquiry.*

Now here I am met at once by two special difficulties, the one personal to myself and to Catherine, and the other one of method.   For, with regard to those three first sets of recent explorations of a psycho-physical kind, I am no physician at all, and not primarily a psychologist.   And again, in Catherine's instance, the evidence as to her psycho-physical states is not, as with St. Teresa and some few other cases, furnished by writings from the pen of the very person who experienced them, and it is at all copious and precise only for the period when she was admittedly ill and physically incapacitated.— And yet these last thirteen years of her life occupy a most prominent place in her biography; it is during, and on occasion of, those psycho-physical states, and largely with the materials furnished by them, that, precisely in those years, she built up her noblest legacy, her great Purgatorial teaching; the illness was (quite evidently) of a predominantly psychical type, and concerns more the psychologist than the physician, being closely connected with her particular temperament and type of spirituality, a temperament and type to be found again and again among the Saints.   All this

[1] H. Bergson, *Essai sur les Données Immédiates de la Conscience*, ed. 1898. H. Jones, *The Philosophy of Lotze*, 1895. J. Ward, *Naturalism and Agnosticism*, 2 vols., 1899. M. Blondel, *l'Action*, 1893. J. Volkelt, *Kant's Erkenntnisstheorie*, 1879; *Erfahrung und Denken*, 1886. H. Münsterberg, *Psychology and Life*, 1899. D. Mercier, *Critériologie Générale*, ed. 1900.

and more makes it simply impossible for me to shrink from some study of the matter, and permits me to hope for some success in attempting, slowly and cautiously, to arrive at certain general conclusions of a spiritually important kind.

But then there is also the difficulty of method. For if we begin the study of these psycho-physical peculiarities and states by judging them from the temperamental and psychological standpoint, we can hardly escape from treating them, at least for the moment, as self-explanatory, and hence from using these our preliminary conclusions about such neural phenonema as the measure, type, and explanation of and for all such other facts and apprehensions as our further study of the religious mind and experience may bring before us. In this wise, these our psychological conclusions would furnish not only a negative test and positive material, but also the exclusive standard for all further study. And such a procedure, until and unless it were justified in its method, would evidently be nothing but a surreptitious begging of the question.—Yet to begin with the fullest analysis of the elementary and normal phenomena of consciousness and of its implications and inviolable prerequisites, would too readily land us in metaphysics which have themselves to operate in and with those immediate and continuous experiences; and hence these latter experiences, whether normal and healthy, or, as here, unusual and in part *maladif*, must be carefully studied first. We have, however, to guard most cautiously against our allowing this, our preliminary, analysis and description of psycho-physical states from imperceptibly blocking the way to, or occupying the ground of, our ultimate analysis and metaphysical synthesis and explanation. Only this latter will be able, by a final outward movement from within, to show the true place and worth of the more or less phenomenal series, passed by us in review on our previous inward movement from without.

6. *Threefold division.*

I propose, then, in this chapter, to take, as separately as is compatible with such a method, the temperamental, psycho-physical side of Catherine's life. I shall first take those last thirteen years of admitted illness, as those which are alone at all fully known to us by contemporary evidence.—I shall then make a jump back to her first period,—to the first sixteen years up to her marriage, with the next ten years of relaxation, and the following four years of her conversion and active penitence. I take these next, because, of these thirty years, we have her own late memories, as registered for us by her disciples, at the time of her narration of the facts concerned.—And only then, with these materials and instruments thus gathered from after and before, shall I try to master the (for us very obscure) middle period, and to arrive at some estimate of her temperamental peripheral condition during these twenty years of her fullest expansion.—I shall conclude the chapter by taking Catherine in her general, life-long temperament, and by comparing and contrasting this type and modality of spiritual character and apprehension with the other rival forms of, and approaches to, religious truth and goodness as these are furnished for us by history.

The ultimate metaphysical questions and valuation are reserved for the penultimate chapter of my book.

I. Catherine's Third Period, 1497 to 1510.

1. *Increasing illness of Catherine's last years.*

Beginning with her third and last period (1497–1510), there can be no doubt that throughout it she was ill and increasingly so. Her closest friends and observers attest it. It is presumably Ettore Vernazza who tells us, for 1497, " when she was about fifty years of age, she ceased to be able to attend either to the Hospital or to her own house, owing to her great bodily weakness. Even on Fast-days she was obliged, after Holy Communion, to take some food to sustain her strength." Probably Marabotto it is who tells us that, in 1499, " after twenty-five years she could no further bear her spiritual loneliness, either because of old age or because of her great bodily weakness." We hear from a later Redactor that, " about nine years before her death (*i. e.* about 1501), there came to her an infirmity." And then, especially from November 1509, May 1510, and August 1510 onwards, she is declared and described as more and more ill.[1] Indeed she herself, both by her acts and by her words, emphatically admits her incapacitation. For it is clearly ill-health which drives her to abandon the Matronship and even all minor continuous work for the Hospital. In her Wills we find indeed that, as late as

[1] *Vita*, pp. 96*c*; 117*b*; 127*a*; 97*c*, 133*b* (dated November 11, 1509, in MSS.); 146*b*; 148*a*.

May 21, 1506, she was able to get to the neighbouring Hospital for Incurables; and that even on November 27, 1508, she was " healthy in mind and body." But her Codicil of January 5, 1503, was drawn up in the presence of nine witnesses at midnight,—a sure sign of some acute ill-health. Indeed already on July 23, 1484, she is lying " infirm in bed, in her room in the Women's quarter of the Hospital, oppressed with bodily infirmity." [1]

2. *Abnormal sensations, impressions and moods.*

Her attendants are all puzzled by the multitude and intensity, the mobility and the self-contradictory character of the psycho-physical manifestations. Perhaps already before 1497 " she would press thorny rose-twigs in both her hands, and this without any pain " ; and so late as about three weeks before her death " she remained paralyzed (*manca,*)" and no doubt anaesthetic " in one (the right) hand and in one finger of the other hand."—Probably again before 1497 " her body could not," at times, " be moved from the sitting posture without the application of force." In February or March 1510 " she could not move out of her bed " ; in August " on some occasions she could not move the lips or the tongue, or the arms or legs, unless helped to do so,—especially on the left side,—and this would, at times, last three or four hours."—In December 1509 " she suffered from great cold," as part of her peculiar condition ; on September 4, 1510, " she suffered from great cold in the right arm." [2]

On other occasions she is, on the contrary, intensely hyper-aesthetic. Some time in February or March 1510, " for a day and a night, her flesh could not be touched, because of the great pain that such touching caused her." At the end of August " she was so sensitive, that it was impossible to touch her very bedclothes or the bedstead, or a single hair on her head, because in such case she would cry out as though she had been grievously wounded."—These states seem to have

---

[1] From my authenticated copies of the original wills in the Archivio di Stato, Genoa.

[2] *Vita*, pp. 113*b*, 149*c*; 143*b*, 152*c*; 138*b*, 155*a*. Note the parallels in St. Teresa's *Life*, written by herself, tr. D. Lewis, ed. 1888. P. 234: " When these (spiritual) impetuosities are not very violent, the soul seeks relief through certain penances ; the painfulness of which, and even the shedding of blood, are no more felt than if the body were dead." P. 30 : " I was unable to move either arm or foot, or hand or head, unless others moved me. I could move, however, I think, one finger of my right hand." P. 31 : " I was paralytic, though getting better, for about three years."

been usually accompanied by sensations of great heat : for on the former occasion " she seemed like a creature placed in a great flame of fire "; whilst on the latter " she had her tongue and lips so inflamed, that they seemed as though actual fire."

And movement appears to have been more often increased than diminished. In the last case indeed " she did not move nor speak nor see; but, when thus immovable, she suffered more than when she could cry out and turn about in her bed." But in the former instance " she could not be kept in bed "; and in April 1510 " she cried aloud, and could not keep herself from moving about, on her bed, on hands and feet."— There are curious localizations of apparently automatic movements. During an attack somewhere in March 1510 " her flesh was all in a tremble, particularly the right shoulder "; on later occasions " an arm, a leg, a hand would tremble, and she would seem to have a spasm within her, with all-but-unbroken acute pains in the flanks, the shoulders, the abdomen, the feet and the brain." On an earlier occasion " her body writhed in great distress." On another day " she seemed all on fire and lost her power of speech, and made signs with her head and hands." On one day in February or March 1510 " she lost both speech and sight, though not her intelligence "; and on September 12 " her sight was so weak, that she could hardly any further distinguish or recognize her attendants." —The heat is liable to be curiously localized. Early in September 1510 " she had a great heat situated in and on her left ear, which lasted for three hours; the ear was red and felt very hot to the touch of others."

Various kinds of haemorrhage are not uncommon. On the last-mentioned occasion bloody urine is passed; bleeding of the nose, with loss of bile, occurs in December 1509; very black blood is lost by the mouth, whilst black spots appear all over her person, on September 12, 1510; and more blood is evacuated on the following day. In February or March 1510 " there were in her flesh certain places which had become concave, like as paste looks where a finger has been put into it." At the end of August 1510 " her skin became saffron-yellow all over."

Troubles of breathing and of heart-action are frequently acute. Somewhere about March 1510 " she had such a spasm in her throat and mouth as to be unable, for about an hour, to speak or to open her eyes, and that she could hardly regain her breath." " Cupping-glasses were applied to her side, to ease her heart, and lung-action, but with little effect." On one occasion " she made signs indicative of feeling as though burning pincers were seizing her heart " ; and on a day soon after " she felt like a hard nail at her heart." [1]

Disturbances of the power of swallowing and of nutrition are often grave and sudden, and in curious contradiction to her abnormally acute and shifting longing for and revulsion from certain specific kinds of food. On August 22, 1510, " she was so thirsty that she felt as though she could drink up the very ocean " ; " yet she could not," in fact, "manage to swallow even one little drop of water." On September 10 " her attendants continuously gave her drinking water ; but she would straightway return it from her mouth." And on September 12, "whilst her mouth was being bathed, she exclaimed, ' I am suffocating,'—and this because a drop of water had trickled down her throat—a drop which she was unable to gulp down." And on a day in August " she saw a melon and had a great desire to eat it ; but hardly did she have some of it in her mouth, when she rejected it with intense disgust." So too with odours. A little later, " on one day the smell of wine would please her, and she would bathe her hands and face in it with great relish ; and next day she would so much dislike it, that she could not bear to see or smell it in her room."—And so too with colours. On September 2 " a physician-friend came to visit her in his scarlet robes ; and she bore the sight a little, so as not to pain him." But she then declared that she could no longer bear it ; and he went, and returned to her in his ordinary black

---

[1] Hyper-aesthesia and sensation of heat : *Vita*, pp. 142*a*, 153*a*. Increase of movement : *ibid.* and pp. 145*b*, 143*a*, 153*c*, 141*a*. Loss of speech and sight : pp. 141*b*, 141*c*, 159*c*. Localization of heat : p. 157*b*. Haemorrhages : 138*c*, 159*c*, 160*a*. Concavities and jaundice : pp. 144*a*, 153*a*. Spasms : pp. 143*c*, 71*c*, 141*c*, 142*b*. Cf. St. Teresa, *loc. cit.* p. 30 : " As to touching me, that was impossible, for I was so bruised that I could not endure it. They used to move me in a sheet, one holding one end, and another the other." P. 31 : " I began to crawl on my hands and feet." P. 263 : " I felt myself on fire : this inward fire and despair . . ." P. 17 : " The fainting fits began to be more frequent ; and my heart was so seriously affected, that those who saw it were alarmed." P. 27 : " It seemed to me as if my heart had been seized by sharp teeth." P. 235 : " I saw, in the Angel's hand, a long spear of gold, and at the iron's point there seemed to be a little fire. He appeared to me to be thrusting it at times into my heart, and to pierce my very entrails. . . . The pain is not bodily, but spiritual."

habit. And yet we have seen, from the Inventory of her effects, that she loved to have vermilion colour upon her bed and person.[1]

And her emotional moods are analogously intense and rapidly shifting. In the spring of 1510 " she cried aloud because of the great pain : this attack lasted a day and a night " ; in the night of August 10 " she tossed about with many exclamations " ; and at the beginning of September " she cried out with a loud voice." At other times, she laughs for joy. So at the end of April " she would laugh without speaking " ; on August 11 " she fixed her eyes steadily on the ceiling ; and for about an hour she abode all but immovable, and spoke not, but kept laughing in a very joyous fashion " ; on August 17 great interior jubilation " expressed itself in merry laughter " ; and on the evening of September 7 " her joy appeared exteriorly in laughter which lasted, with but small interruptions, for some two hours."—And her entire apparent condition would shift from one such extreme to the other with extraordinary swiftness. In the autumn of 1509 " she many times remained as though dead ; and at other times she would appear as healthy,—as though she had never anything the matter with her." Already in December 1509 she herself, after much vomiting and loss of blood, had sent for her Confessor and had declared that " she felt as though she must die in consequence of these many accidents." Yet even on September 10, 1510, " when she was not being oppressed and tormented by her accidents (attacks), she seemed to be in good health ; but when she was being suffocated by them, she seemed as one dead." [2]

---

[1] Swallow : *Vita*, pp. 149*c*, 150*a* ; 159*b* ; 159*c* ; 150*a*. Odours and colours : 153*c*, 154*b*. Cf. St. Teresa, *loc. cit.* p. 27 : " I could eat nothing whatever, only drink. I had a great loathing for food." P. 43 : " I have been suffering for twenty years from sickness every morning." P. 30 : " There was a choking in my throat. . . . I could not swallow even a drop of water." P. 263 : " A sense of oppression, of stifling."

[2] Exclamations : *Vita*, pp. 144*a*, 148*b*, 155*a*. Laughter : *ibid.* 145*c*, 148*b*, 149*b*, 157*c*. Sudden changes of condition : 135*b*, 138*c*, 159*b*. Cf. St. Teresa, *loc. cit.* pp. 28, 29 : " That very night," Feast of the Assumption, 1537, " my sickness became so acute that, for about four days, I remained insensible. For a day and a half the grave was open, waiting for my body. But it pleased Our Lord I should come to myself. I wished to go to confession at once. Though my sufferings were unendurable, and my perceptions dull, yet my confession was, I believe, complete. I communicated with many tears."

II.   Conclusions concerning Catherine's Psycho-
physical Condition during this last Period.

1. *Her illness not primarily physical.   Her self-diagnosis.*

Now we saw, at the beginning of this chapter, how readily
her attendants concluded, from all these extreme, multiple,
swift-changing and self-contradictory states, to their directly
and separately supernatural origin.—And indeed the diagnosis
and treatment of her case showed clearly that it was not
primarily physical. So in the case, probably in November
1509, of the cupping-glasses, when " she got medically treated
for a bodily infirmity, whilst her real trouble was fire of the
spirit "; so with a medicine given to her by the resident
Hospital physician, some time in April 1510, " from taking
which she nearly died "; so with Giovanni Boerio's three-
weeks' treatment of her, in May 1510, a treatment which led
to no other results than momentary additional distress; and
so with the declaration of the ten Physicians who, even on
September 10, four days before her death, " could find no
trace of disease in her pulse, secretions, or any other symptom,"
and who consequently abstained from prescribing anything.
And hence, more or less throughout her last nine years, " there
was confusion in the management of her, not on her own part,
but on that of those who served her." [1]

For—and these two further points are of primary importance—the tending of her, as distinct from physic, was
throughout held by herself to be of great importance; and
yet this care was declared by her to be often useless or
harmful, owing to the powers of discrimination possessed by
her attendants being as much below their good-will, as her
own knowledge as to the differences between her healthy and
maladif states exceeded her power of herself acting upon this
knowledge against these sickly conditions. " She would often
appear to be asleep; and would awake from such a state, at
one time, quite refreshed, and, at another time, so limp and
broken down as to be unable to move. Those that served
her knew not how to distinguish one state from the other;

---

[1] *Vita*, pp. 71c; 145c; 147b; 159c, 159a; 127a. Cf. St. Teresa, *loc.
cit.* p. 23 : " I was in my sister's house, for the purpose of undergoing
medical treatment—they took the utmost care of my comfort." P. 27 :
" In two months, so strong were the medicines, my life was nearly worn
out." " The physicians gave me up : they said I was consumptive."

and on recovering from an attack of the latter sort, she would say to them : ' Why did you let me continue in that state of quiet, from which I have all but died ? ' " So, on September 5, " she cried aloud on waking from a state of quiet, which had appeared to be (healthy) quietude, but had not been so." And indeed, already on January 10 previous, she had shut herself off from her Confessor, " because it seemed to her that he bore with her too much in her sayings and doings."

Yet, at least after this time, Marabotto does oppose her sometimes. Thus on two, somewhat later, occasions she respectively makes signs, and asks, that Extreme Unction be given her; but only some four months later did she actually receive it. In these cases, then, she either had not, even at bottom, a correct physical self-knowledge; or her requests had been prompted, at the time, by her secondary, *maladif* consciousness alone.—When first visited by Boerio, she takes pleasure in the thought of getting possibly cured by him; but " in the following night, when great pain came upon her, she reproved herself, saying, ' You are suffering this, because you allowed yourself to rejoice without cause.' " But this declaration distinctly falls short of any necessary implication of a directly supernatural origin of her malady, as the *Vita* here will have it, and but refers, either to the continuance of earthly existence not deserving such joy, or to her persistent fundamental consciousness that the phenomena were partly the fruitful, profitable occasions, and partly the price paid, for the mind's close intercourse with things divine.

Indeed her (otherwise unbroken) attitude is one, both of quiet conviction that physic cannot help her, and of gentle readiness to let the physicians try whatever they may think worth the trying : so with the cupping-glasses, and the various examinations and physickings. Especially is this disposition clear in her short dialogue with Boerio, where, in answer to his assertion that she ought to beware of giving scandal to all the world by saying that her infirmity had no need of remedies, and that she ought to look upon such an attitude as " a kind of hypocrisy," she declares : " I am sorry if any one is scandalized because of me; and I am ready to use any remedy for my infirmity, supposing that it can be found." [1]

---

[1] Self-knowledge as to " quietudes " : *Vita*, pp. 153*b*, 157*a*. Marabotto's attitude : 139*b*; 141*c*, 143*c*, 149*a*. Relations with Boerio : 147*c*, 147*b*. Cf. St. Teresa, *loc. cit.* p. 86 : " My health has been much better since I have ceased to look after my ease and comforts."

2. *Her preoccupation with the spiritual suggestions afforded
by the phenomena.*

It would, indeed, be a grave misreading of her whole
character and habits of mind to think of her as at all
engrossed in her psycho-physical states as such, and as having
ever formally considered and decided that they must either
come directly from God or be amenable to medicine.   On the
contrary, she is too habitually absorbed in the consideration
and contemplation of certain great spiritual doctrines and
realities, to have the leisure or inclination for any such
questions.—Indeed it is this very absorption in those spiritual
realities which has ended by suggesting, with an extraordinary readiness, frequency and vividness, through her mind
to her senses, and by these back to her mind, certain psycho-
physical images and illustrations for those very doctrines,
until her whole psycho-physical organism has been, all but
entirely, modified and moulded into an apt instrument and
manifestation for and of that world unseen.

Thus, after her greatest psycho-physical and spiritual
experience in November 1509, she declares to Vernazza, when
he urges her to let him write down the graces she has received
from God, that "it would, strictly speaking, be impossible to
narrate those interior things; whilst, of exterior ones, few or
none have happened to me."   And she never entirely loses
her mental consciousness in any state not recognized by herself as *maladif*.   So, on a day of great psycho-physical trouble
in February or March 1510, "they thought she must expire;
but, though she lost both sight and speech, she never lost her
intelligence."   And even on September 11 and 12, amidst
foodlessness and suffocations, her intelligence still persists.—
In the March previous "her mind appeared to grow daily
in contentment."   Some days later, her attendants "saw
how, after an hour of spasm and breathlessness, and then a
great restriction of all her being, she returned to her normal
condition, and addressed many beautiful words to them."
And later on, "her attendants were amazed at seeing a body,
which seemed to be healthy, in such a tormented condition."
But "soon after she laughed and spoke as one in health, and
told them not to distress themselves about her, since she was
very contented; but that they should see to it that they did
much good, since the way of God is very narrow." [1]

[1] Remark to Vernazza : *Vita*, pp. 98c, 99a.   Persistence of intelligence :
141c; 159b, c; 143a; 143c; 145b.   Cf. St. Teresa, *loc. cit.* p. 408 ; " She "

3. *Interaction and mutual suggestion of her spiritual and physical states.*

As to the extraordinary closeness and readiness for mutual response between her sensible impressions and her thoughts and emotions—her sensations turning, all but automatically, into religious emotions, and her thoughts and feelings translating themselves into appropriate psycho-physical states—we have a mass of interesting evidence.

Thus when, about the end of November 1509, in response to her seeing, on some wall of the Hospital, a picture of Our Lord at the Well of Samaria, and to her asking Him for one drop of that Divine water, " instantly a drop was given to her which refreshed her within and without."   The spiritual idea and emotion is here accompanied and further stimulated by the keenest psycho-physical impression of drinking.   And such an impression can even become painful through its excessive suggestiveness.   Thus she herself explains to Maestro Boerio, on September 2, 1510, that she cannot long bear the sight of his scarlet robe " because of what it suggests (represents) to my memory,"—no doubt the fire of divine love. Three days later, on the contrary, " she mentally saw herself lying upon a bier, surrounded by many Religious robed in black," and greatly rejoiced at the sight.   Here the very impression of black, the colour of death, will have conveyed, during this special mood of hers, a downright psycho-physical pleasure, somewhat as Boerio's reappearance, on the former occasion, in a black gown, had been a sensible relief to her.

So also with scents.   When, certainly after 1499, " she perceived, on the (right) hand of her Confessor, an odour which penetrated her very heart," and " which abode with her and restored both mind and body for many days," we have again a primarily mental act and state which she herself knows well to be untransferable, even to Don Marabotto himself.   Here the association of ideas was, no doubt, the right hand of the Priest and her daily reception, by means of it, of the Holy Eucharist.   For the latter, " the Bread from heaven, having

(Teresa herself) " never saw anything with her bodily eyes, nor heard anything with her bodily ears." P. 189 : " The words of the divine locutions are very distinctly formed; but by the bodily ear they are not heard." P. 191 : " In ecstasy, the memory can hardly do anything at all, and the imagination is, as it were, suspended." P. 142 : " You see and feel yourself carried away, you know not whither." P. 187 : " I fell into a trance; I was carried out of myself.   It was most plain."

within it all manner of delight," is already connected in her mind with an impression of sweet odour. " One day, on receiving Communion, so much odour and sweetness came to her, that she seemed to herself to be in Paradise." Probably the love for, and then the disgust at, the smell of wine, was also connected with her Eucharistic experiences. Certainly " one day, having received Holy Communion, she was granted so great a consolation as to fall into an ecstasy, so that when the Priest wanted to give her to drink from the Chalice (with unconsecrated wine) she had to be brought back by force to her ordinary consciousness." Vivid memories of both sets of psycho-physical impressions are, I think, at work when she says : " If a consecrated Host were to be given to me amongst unconsecrated ones, I should be able to distinguish it by the very taste, as I do wine from water." And as the sight of red rapidly became painful from the very excess of its mental suggestiveness, so will the smell of wine have been both specially dear and specially painful to her.[1]

Indeed her psycho-physical troubles possess, for the most part, a still traceable, most delicate selectiveness as to date, range, form, combination, and other peculiarities. Thus some of the most acute attacks coincide, in their date of occurrence and general character, as the biographers point out, with special saint's and holy days : so in the night leading into St. Lawrence's day, August 9 and 10, 1510; so on the Vigil of St. Bartholomew's day, August 24; and so in the night previous to and on the Feast (August 28) of St. Augustine, special Patron of her only sister's Order and of the Convent in which her own Conversion had taken place thirty-seven years before. Yet we have also seen how that these synchronisms did not rise to the heights which were soon desired by her biographers, for we know that she died, not (as they would

---

[1] Picture: *Vita*, p. 135a.   Red and black robes : 154b, 156c.   Suggestions of odour : 118c, 119a; 9c, 8a, 9b.   Cf. St. Teresa, *loc. cit.* pp. 57, 58 : " One day, I saw a picture of Christ most grievously wounded : the very sight of it moved me."   P. 247 : " I used to pray much to Our Lord for that living water of which He spoke to the Samaritan woman : I had always a picture of it with this inscription : ' Domine, da mihi aquam.' "   P. 231 : " Once when I was holding in my hand the cross of my rosary, He took it from me into His own hand.   He returned it; but it was then four large stones incomparably more precious than diamonds : the five wounds were delineated on them with the most admirable art.   He said to me that for the future that cross would appear so to me always, and so it did. The precious stones were seen, however, only by myself."

have it) on the Feast of the Exaltation of the Cross, September 14, but early on the day following.

Thus too as to her incapacity to swallow and retain food, we find that, up to the end, with the rarest exceptions of a directly physical kind, she retained the most complete facility in receiving Holy Communion : so on September 2, 1510, when " all ordinary food was returned, but the Holy Eucharist she retained without any difficulty" ; and so too on September 4, when, after " lying for close upon twelve hours with closed eyes, speechless and all but immovable," Marabotto himself feared to communicate her, but "she made a sign to him, with a joyous countenance, to have no fear, and she communicated with ease, and soon after began to speak, owing to the vigour given to her by the Sacrament." Yet here too the abnormality is not complete : some ordinary food is retained, now and then; so, minced chicken, specially mentioned for December 1509, and on September 3, 1510.

As to her heat-attacks and the corresponding extreme—the sense of intense cold,—it is clear how close is their connection with her profound concentration upon the conception of God as Love, and upon the image of Love as fire. It is these sudden and intense psycho-physical, spiritually suggestive because spiritually suggested, heat-attacks which are, I think, always meant by the terms " assault " (*assalto*), " stroke " (*ferita*), and " arrow " (*saetta*) : terms which already indicate the mental quality of these attacks. And these heats are mostly localized in a doctrinally suggestive manner : they centre in and around the heart, or on the tongue and lips, or they envelop the whole person " as though it were placed in a great flame of fire," or "in a glowing furnace." Indeed these heats are often so described, by her attendants or herself, as to imply their predominantly psycho-physical nature : " it was necessary, with a view to prolonging her life, to use many means for lightening the strain of that interior fire upon her mind "; and " I feel," she says herself, on occasion of such an attack, " so great a contentment on the part of the spirit, as to be unutterable; whilst, on the part of my humanity, all the pains are, so to say, no pains."

As to her boundless thirst, her inability to drink, and her sense of strangulation, their doctrinal suggestions are largely clear. Thus when " she was so thirsty as to feel able to drink up all the waters of the sea," and when she calls out " I am suffocating " (drowning, *io affogo*), we are at once reminded of her great saying : " If the sea were all so much love, there would not live man or woman who would not go to drown himself in it (*si affogasse*)." And when, at the end of August 1510, unable to drink, she herself declares "all the water that is on earth could not give me the least refreshment," there is, perhaps, an implied contrast to that " little drop of divine water " which had so much refreshed her a year before.

And finally, the various paralyses and death-like swoons seem, at least in part, to follow from, and to represent, the death of the spirit to the life of the senses, and to mirror the intensity with which perfection has been conceived and practised as " Love going forth out of self, and abiding all in God and separated from man." Thus when, on August 22, 1510, " she had a day of great heat, and abode paralyzed in one hand and in one finger of the other hand for about sixteen hours, and she was so greatly occupied (absorbed), that she neither spoke, nor opened her eyes, nor could take any food."[1]

4. *Only two cases of spiritually unsuggestive impressions.*

It is indeed profoundly instructive to note how that, in exact proportion as a human-mental mediation and suggestion of a religious kind is directly traceable or at least probable in any or all of these things, is that thing also worthy of being considered as having ultimately the Divine Spirit Itself for its first cause as well as last end; and that, in exact proportion as this kind of human mediation and suggestion is impossible or unlikely, the thing turns out to be unworthy of being attributed, in any special sense, to the spirit of God Himself.

Of such spiritually opaque, religiously unused and apparently unuseable, hysteriform impressions, I can, even during the last days of these nine years of admitted infirmity, find but two clear instances,—instances which, by their very

---

[1] Synchronisms: *Vita*, pp. 148*b*; 150*b*; 152*a*, 160*c*, 161*b*. Communion and ordinary food : 154*a*, 154*c*, 138*c*; 154*c*. Heats : " Assalto," *e.g.* 138*b*, *c*; 143*a*, *c*; " ferita " and " saetta," *e.g.* 141*a*, *c*; 145*a*. Their localization : 135*a*, 141*c*; 153*a*; 142*a*, 158*a*. Their psycho-physical character : 135*b*, 144*b*. Thirst and its suggestion : 149*c*, 159*c*; 76*c*; 152*b*, 135*a*. Paralyses : 134*b*; 149*c*. Cf. St. Teresa, *op. cit.* p. 28 : her death-swoon occurs on evening of the Assumption. P. 235 : Heat, piercing of the heart as by a spear, and a spiritual (not bodily) pain, are all united in the experience of the heart-piercing Angel. P. 423 : " Another prayer very common is a certain kind of wounding; for it really seems to the soul as if an arrow were thrust through the heart or through itself. The suffering is not one of sense, nor is the wound physical; it is in the interior of the soul."

unlikeness to the mass of her spiritually transparent, readily used impressions, strongly confirm our high estimate of the all but totality of her psycho-physical states, as experienced and understood and used by herself. On September 7, 1510, after having seen and wisely utilized the spiritually suggestive image of " a great ladder of fire," she ends by having so vivid an hallucination of the whole world being on fire " that she asked whether it were not so, and caused her windows to be opened that the facts might be ascertained; and " she abode the whole night, possessed by that imagination," as the *Vita* itself calls this impression. At night, on September 11, she complained of a very great heat, and cast forth from her mouth very black blood; and black spots came out all over her body. And on the 13th, " she was seen with her eyes fixed upon the ceiling, and with much movement of the lips and hands; and she answered her attendants' queries as to what she was seeing with ' Drive away that beast . . . .' the remaining words being inaudible." [1]

Here we have, I think, the only two merely factual, unsuggestive, and hence simply delusive, impressions really experienced by herself and recorded in the *Vita*, a book whose very eagerness to discover things of this kind and readiness to take them as directly supernatural is a guarantee that no other marked instances of the kind have been omitted or suppressed. And these two impressions both take place within a week of her death, and respectively four days before, and two days after, the first clear case of organic disease or lesion to be found anywhere in the life.

---

[1] *Vita*, pp. 158*a*; 160*a*. Cf. St. Teresa, *op. cit.* p. 41 : " We saw something like a great toad crawling towards us . . . The impression it made on me was such, that I think it must have had a meaning." Contrast with this naïvely sensible sight and the absence of all interior assurance, such a spiritual vision as " Christ stood before me, stern and grave. I saw Him with the eyes of the soul. The impression remained with me that the vision was from God, and not an imagination " (pp. 40, 41). Another quasi-sensible sight, with no interior assurance, or question as to its provenance and value, is given on pp. 248, 249 : " Once Satan, in an abominable shape, appeared on my left hand. I looked at his mouth in particular, because he spoke, and it was horrible. A huge flame seemed to issue out of his body, perfectly bright without any shadow." Another such impression is recorded on p. 252 : " I thought the evil spirits would have suffocated me one night . . . I saw a great troop of them rush away as if tumbling over a precipice."

very scientific lecture

III. Catherine's Psycho-physical Condition, its Likeness and Unlikeness to Hysteria.

Only by a quite unfair magnifying or multiplying of the two incidents just described could we come to hold, with Mr. Baring-Gould, that Catherine was simply a sufferer from hysteria, and that the Roman Church did well to canonize her on the ground of her having, in spite of this malady, managed to achieve much useful work amongst the sick and poor.[1] Here we shall do well to consider three groups of facts.

1. *Misapprehensions as to hysteria.*

The first group gives the reasons why we should try and get rid of the terror and horror still so often felt in connection with the very name of this malady. This now quite demonstrably excessive, indeed largely mythical, connotation of the term springs from four causes.

First, the very name still tends to suggest, as the causes or conditions of the malady, things fit only for discussion in medical reviews. But then, ever since 1855, all limitation to, or special connection with, anything peculiarly female, or indeed generally sexual, has been increasingly shown to be false, until now no serious authority on the matter can be found to espouse the old view. The malady is now well known to attack men as well as women, and to have no special relation to things of sex at all.[2]

Next, probably as a consequence from the initial error, this disorder was supposed to come predominantly from, or to lead to, moral impurity, or at least to be ordinarily accompanied by strong erotic propensions. But here the now carefully observed facts are imperatively hostile : of the 120 living cases most carefully studied by Prof. Janet, only four showed the predominance of any such tendencies, a proportion undoubtedly not above the percentage to be found amongst non-hysterical persons.[3]

And again, the term was long synonymous with untruthfulness and deceit. But here again Prof. Janet shows how unfounded is this prejudice, since it but springs from the mis-

---

[1] *Lives of the Saints*, ed. 1898, Vol. X, September 15.
[2] Pierre Janet, *Etat Mental des Hystériques*, 2 vols., Paris, 1892, 1894 : Vol. II, pp. 260, 261; 280; Vol. I, pp. 225, 63.
[3] *Ibid.* Vol. I, pp. 63, 225, 226.

placed promptitude with which the earlier observers refused to believe what they had not as yet sufficiently examined and could not at all explain, and from the malady being itself equivalent to a more or less extensive breaking-up of the normal inter-connection between the several, successive or simultaneous states, and, as it were, layers of the one personality.   He is convinced that real untruthfulness is no commoner among such patients than it is among healthy persons.[1]

And, finally, it is no doubt felt that, apart from all such specifically moral suspicions, the malady involves all kinds of fancies and inaccuracies of feeling and of perception, and that it frequently passes into downright insanity.   And this is no doubt the one objection which does retain some of its old cogency.   Still, it is well to note that, as has now been fully established, the elements of the human mind are and remain the same throughout the whole range of its conditions, from the sanest to the maddest, whilst only their proportion and admixture, and the presence or absence and the kind of synthesis necessary to hold them together differentiate these various states of mind.   In true insanity there is no such synthesis; in hysteria the synthesis, however slight and peculiar, is always still traceable throughout the widespread disgregation of the elements and states.[2]   And it is this very persistence of the fundamental unity, together with the strikingly different combination and considerable disgregation of its elements, that makes the study of hysteria so fruitful for the knowledge of the fully healthy mind and of its unity; whilst the continuance of all the elements of the normal intelligence, even in insanity, readily explains why it is apparently so easy to see insanity everywhere, and to treat genius and sanctity as but so much degeneracy.

2. *Hysteriform phenomena observable in Catherine's case.*

The second group of facts consists in the phenomena which, in Catherine's case, are like or identical to what is observable in cases of hysteria.

There is, perhaps above all else, the anaesthetic condition, which was presumably co-extensive with her paralytic states. "Anaesthesia," says Prof. Janet, "can be considered as the type of the other symptoms of hysteria; it exists in the great majority of cases, it is thoroughly characteristic of the malady.

---

[1] Pierre Janet, *Etat Mental*, Vol. I, pp. 226, 227.
[2] *Ibid.* Vol. II, pp. 253, 257.

In its most frequent localization (semi-anaesthesia) it affects one of the lateral halves of the body, and this half is usually the left side." Or, " a finger or hand will be affected." Such " insensibility can be very frequent and very profound "; but " it disappears suddenly " and even " varies from one moment to another." [1]

Then there is the corresponding counter-phenomenon of hyper-aesthesia. "The slightest contact provokes great pains, exclamations, and spasms. The painful zones have their seat mostly on the abdomen or on the hips." And " sensation in these states is not painful in itself, by its own intensity, but by its quality, its characteristics; it has become the signal, by association of ideas, for the production of a set of extremely painful phenomena." So, with the colour-sense : "one patient adores the colour red, and sees in its dullest shade ' sparkling rays which penetrate to her very heart and warm her through and through.' " But " another one finds this ' a repulsive colour and one capable of producing nausea.' " And similarly with the senses of taste and odour.[2]

Then, too, the inability to stand or walk, with the conservation, at times, of the power to crawl; the acceptance, followed by the rejection, of food, because of certain spasms in the throat or stomach, and the curious, mentally explicable, exceptions to this incapacity; the sense, even at other times, of strangulation; heart palpitations, fever heats, strange haemorrhages from the stomach or even from the lung; red patches on the skin and emotional jaundice all over it, and one or two other peculiarities.[3]

Then, as to a particular kind of quietude, from which Catherine warns her attendants to rouse her, we find a patient who " ceases her reading, without showing any sign of doing so. She gets taken to be profoundly attentive; it is, however, but one of her attacks of ' fixity.' And she has promptly to be shaken out of this state, or, in a few minutes, there will be no getting her out of it."

As to Catherine's consciousness of possessing an extraordinary fineness of discrimination between sensibly identical

---

[1] Pierre Janet, *Etat Mental*, Vol. I, pp. 7, 8, 11, 12, 57, 21.

[2] *Ibid.* Vol. II, pp. 82, 91; 70, 71.

[3] *Ibid.* Vol. II. Troubles of movement, pp. 105, 106; of nutrition, pp. 285, 70, 71; strangulation, heart palpitation, fever heats, p. 282; haemorrhages and red patches, p. 283; jaundice (*ictère emotionnel*), p. 287; and note the " ischurie," p. 283, top, compared with *Vita*, p. 12a.

objects, we see that " if one points out, to some of these
patients, an imaginary portrait upon a plain white card, and
mixes this card with other similar ones, they will almost
always find again the portrait on the same card." And
similarly as to her attaching a particular quasi-sensible
perception to Marabotto's hand alone, we find that, if M.
Janet touches Léonie's hand, he having suggested a nosegay
to her, she will henceforth, when he touches the hand, see
that nosegay; whereas, if another person touches that same
hand, Léonie will see nothing special.

As to Catherine's feelings of criminality and of being
already dead, M. Janet quotes M., who says, " I am like a
criminal about to be punished " ; and R., who declares, " It
seems to me that I am dead." As to the hallucination of a
Beast, Marcelle suffers from the same impression.[1]

And,—perhaps the most important of all these surface-
resemblances,—there is Catherine's apparent freedom from
all emotion at the deaths of her brothers and sister, and her
extraordinary dependence upon, and claimfulness towards,
her Confessor alone. " These patients rapidly lose the social
feelings : Berthe, who for some time preserved some affection
for her brother, ends by losing all interest in him; Marcelle,
at the very beginning of her illness, separates herself from
every one." " It is always their own personality which
dominates their thoughts." Yet these patients have " an
extraordinary attachment to their physician. For him they
are resolved to do all things. In return, they are extremely
exacting,—he is to occupy himself entirely with each one
alone. Only a very superficial observer would ascribe this
feeling to a vulgar source." [2]

3. *Catherine's personality not disintegrated.*

But a third group of facts clearly differentiates Catherine's
case, even in these years of avowed ill-health, from such
patients; and these facts become clearer and more numerous
in precise proportion as we move away from peripheral,
psycho-physical phenomena and mechanisms, and dwell upon
her practically unbroken mental and moral characteristics,
and upon the use and meaning, the place and context of
these things within her ample life.

For as to her relations with her attendants, even now it
is still she who leads, who suggests, who influences; a strong

---

[1] Pierre Janet, *Etat Mental*, Vol. I, p. 140; Vol. II, pp. 14, 72, 165.
[2] *Ibid.* Vol. I, pp. 218, 219; 158, 159.

and self-consistent will shows itself still, under all this shifting psycho-physical surface.   Thus Don Marabotto now administers, it is true, all her money and charitable affairs for her. But it is she who insists, alone and unaided, upon the true spiritual function of that impression of odour on his hand.— Vernazza, no doubt, has now to help her in the fight against subtle scruples, on occasion of her deepest depressions.   But her far more frequent times of light and joy are in nowise occasions of a simply subjective self-engrossment or of a purely psycho-physical interest, for her mind is absorbed if in but a few, yet in inexhaustibly fruitful and universally applicable ideas and experiences of a spiritual kind, such as helped to urge this friend on to his world-renewing impulses and determinations.—Her closest relations and friends, one must admit, succeed by their action, taken eighteen months and then again two days before her death, in getting her to desist from ordering her burial by the side of her husband.   But we have seen, in the one case, how indirectly, and, in the other case, how suddenly and even then quite informally, they had to gain their point.—Her attendants in general, and Marabotto in particular, certainly paid her an engrossed attention, and the all but endlessness of her superficial fancies and requirements have been chronicled by them with a naïve and wearisome fulness.   But then she herself is well aware that, had they but the requisite knowledge as to how and when to apply them, some sturdy opposition and a greater roughness of handling would, on their part, be of the greatest use to her, in this her psychical infirmity; indeed her shutting herself away from Marabotto, as late as January 1510, is directly caused by her sense and fear of being spoilt by him.

It is true again that, already in 1502, we hear, in a probably exaggerated but still possibly semi-authentic account, of her indifference of feeling with regard to the deaths of two brothers and of her only sister; and that, from January 1510 onwards, she gradually excludes all her attendants from her sick-room, with, eventually, the sole exceptions of Marabotto or Carenzio and Argentina.   But her Wills show conclusively how persistent were her detailed interest in, and dispositions for, the requirements of her surviving brother, nephews, and nieces; of poor Thobia and the girl's hidden mother; of her priest-attendants, and of each and all of her humblest domestics; of the natives in the far-away Greek Island of

Scios; and, above all, of the Hospital and its great work
which she had ever loved so well.

We have indeed found two cases, both from within the
last week of her life, of mentally opaque and spiritually
unsuggestive and unutilized impressions which are truly
analogous to those characteristic of hysteria. But we have
also seen how forcibly these two solitary cases bring out, by
contrast, the spiritual transparency and fruitfulness of her
usual, finely reflective picturings of these last years. For
here it is her own deliberate and spiritual mind which joyously
greets, and straightway utilizes and transcends, the psycho-
physical occurrences; and it does so, not because these
occurrences are, or are taken to be, the causes or requisites
or objects of her faith and spiritual insight, but because, on
the contrary, they meet and clothe an already exuberant faith
and insight—spiritual certainties derived from quite another
source.

And finally, if the monotony and superficial pettiness of
the sick-room can easily pall upon us, especially when presented with the credulities and hectic exaggerations which
disfigure so much of the *Vita's* description of it; we must, in
justice, as I have attempted to do in my seventh and eighth
chapters, count in, as part of her biography, her deep affection
for and persistent influence with Ettore and Battista Vernazza,
and the exemplification of her doctrine by these virile souls,
makers of history in the wide, varied world of men.[1]

In a word, it is plain at once that, given the necessarily
limited number of ways in which the psycho-physical
organism reacts under mental stimulations, certain neural
phenomena may, in any two cases, be, in themselves, perfectly
similar, although their respective mental causes or occasions
may be as different, each from the other, as the Moonlight
Sonata of Beethoven, or the working out of the Law of
Gravitation by Newton, or the elaboration of the implications
of the Categorical Imperative by Kant, are different from the
sudden jumping of a live mouse in the face of an hysterically-
disposed young woman, or as the various causes of tears and
laughter throughout the whole world.

[1] The biographical chapters of Volume I give all the facts and references alluded to in this paragraph. It would be easy to find parallels for
most of these peripheral disturbances and great central normalities in
St. Teresa's life.

IV. First Period of Catherine's Life, 1447 to 1477, in its Three Stages.

If we next go back to the first period of her life, in its three stages of the sixteen years of her girlhood, 1447–1463, the first ten years of her married life, 1463–1473, and the four years of her Conversion and active Penitence, 1473–1477, we shall find, I think, in the matter of temperament and psycho-physical conditions, little or nothing but a rare degree of spiritual sensitiveness, and an extraordinary close-knitted-ness of body and mind.

1. *From her childhood to her conversion.*

Thus, already in her early childhood, that picture of the Pietà seems to have suggested religious ideas and feelings with the suddenness and emotional solidity of a physical seizure—an impression still undimmed when she herself recounted it, some fifty years later, to her two intimates.—It is true that during those first, deeply unhappy ten years of marriage, we cannot readily find more than indications of a most profound and brooding melancholy, the apparent result of but two factors,—a naturally sad disposition and acutely painful domestic circumstances. Yet it is clear, from the sequel, that more and other things lay behind. It is indeed evident that she possessed a congenitally melancholy temperament; that nothing but the rarest combination of conditions could have brought out, into something like elastic play and varied exercise, her great but few and naturally excessive qualities of mind and heart; that these conditions were not only absent, but were replaced by circumstances of the most painful kind; and that she will hardly, at this time, have had even a moment's clear consciousness of any other sources than just those conditions for her deep, keen, and ever-increasing dissatisfaction with all things, her own self included : all peace and joy, the very capacity for either seemed gone, and gone for ever. But it is only the third stage, with its sudden-seeming conversion on March 20, 1473, and the then following four years of strenuously active self-immolation and dedication to the humblest service of others, which lets us see deep into those previous years of sullen gloom and apparently hopeless drift and dreary wastage.

The two stages really belong to one another, and the depth of the former gloom and dreariness stood in direct proportion and relation to the capacities of that nature and to the height of their satisfaction in the later light and vigour brought to and assimilated by them. It was the sense, at that previous time still inarticulate, but none the less mightily operative, of the insufficiency of all things merely contingent, of all things taken as such and inevitably found to be such, that had been adding, and was now discovered to have added, a quite determining weight and poignancy to the natural pressure of her temperament and external lot. And this temperament and lot, which had not alone produced that sadness, could still less of themselves remove it, whatever might be its cause. Her sense of emptiness and impotence could indeed add to her sense of fulness and of power, once these latter had come; but of themselves the former could no more give her the latter, than hunger, which indeed makes bread to taste delicious, can give us real bread and, with it, that delight.

And it was such real bread of life and real power which now came to her. For if the tests of reality in such things are their persistence and large and rich spiritual applicability and fruitfulness, then something profoundly real and important took place in the soul of that sad and weary woman of six-and-twenty, within that Convent-chapel, at that Annunciation-tide. Her four years of heroic persistence; her unbroken Hospital service of a quarter of a century; her lofty magnanimity towards her husband, Thobia and Thobia's mother; her profound influence upon Vernazza, in urging him on to his splendid labours throughout Italy, and to his grand death in plague-stricken Genoa; her daringly original, yet immensely persuasive, doctrine,—nearly all this dates back, completely for her consciousness and very largely in reality, to those few moments on that memorable day.

2. *Her conversion not sudden nor visionary.*

But two points, concerning the manner and form of this experience, are, though of but secondary spiritual interest, far more difficult to decide. There is, for one thing, the indubitable impression, for her own mind and for ours, of complete suddenness and newness in her change. Was this suddenness and newness merely apparent, or real as well? And should this suddenness, if real, be taken as in itself and directly supernatural?

Now it is certain that Catherine, up to ten years before,

had been full of definitely religious acts and dispositions. Had she not, already at thirteen, wanted to be a Nun, and, at eight or so, been deeply moved by a picture of the dead Christ in His Mother's lap? Hence, ideas and feelings of self-dedication and of the Christ-God's hatred of sin and love for her had, in earlier and during longer times than those of her comparative carelessness, soaked into and formed her mental and emotional bent, and will have in so far shaped her will, as to make the later determination along those earlier lines of its operation, comparatively easy, even after those years of relaxation and deviation. Yet it is clear that there was not here, as indeed there is nowhere, any mere repetition of the past. New combinations and an indefinitely deeper apprehension of the great religious ideas and facts of God's holiness and man's weakness, of the necessity for the soul to reach its own true depth or to suffer fruitlessly, and of God having Himself to meet and feed this movement and hunger which He has Himself implanted; new combinations and depths of emotion, and an indefinite expansion and heroic determination of the will: were all certainly here, and were new as compared with even the most religious moments in the past.

As to the suddenness, we cannot but take it as, in large part, simply apparent,—a dim apprehension of what then became clear having been previously quite oppressively with her. And, in any case, this suddenness seems to belong rather to the temperamental peculiarities and necessary forms of her particular experiences than to the essence and content of her spiritual life. For, whatever she thinks, feels, says or does throughout her life, she does and experiences with actual suddenness, or at least with a sense of suddenness; and there is clearly no more necessary connection between such suddenness and grace and true self-renouncement, than there is between gradualness and mere nature; both suddenness and gradualness being but simple modes, more or less fixed for each individual, yet differing from each to each, modes in which God's grace and man's will interact and manifest themselves in different souls.[1]

And then there is the question as to whether or not this

---

[1] Prof. W. James has got some very sensible considerations on the pace of a conversion (as distinct from its spiritual significance, depth, persistence, and fruitfulness) being primarily a matter of temperament: *Varieties of Religious Experience*, 1902, pp. 227–240.

conversion-experience took the form of a vision. We have seen, in the Appendix, how considerable are the difficulties which beset the account of the Bleeding Christ Vision in the Palace; and how the story of the previous visionless experience in the Chapel is free from all such objections. But, even supposing the two accounts to be equally reliable, it is the first, the visionless experience, which was demonstrably the more important and the more abidingly operative of the two. More important, for it is during those visionless moments that her conversion is first effected; and more abiding, for, according to all the ancient accounts, the impression of the Bleeding Christ Vision disappeared utterly at the end of at longest four years, whereas the memory of the visionless conversion moments remained with her, as an operative force, up to the very last. Witness the free self-casting of the soul into painful-joyous Purgation, into Love, into God (without any picturing of the historic Christ), which forms one of the two constituents of her great latter-day teaching; and how entirely free from directly historic elements all her recorded visions of the middle period turn out to be.[1]

3. *Peculiarities of her active penitence.*

As to the four years of Active Penitence, we must beware of losing the sense of the dependence, the simple, spontaneous instrumentality, in which the negative and restrictive side of her action stood towards the positive and expansive one. An immense affirmation, an anticipating, creative buoyancy and resourcefulness, had come full flood into her life; and had shifted her centre of deliberate interest and willing away from the disordered, pleasure-seeking, sore and sulky lesser self in

---

[1] By the term "visionless," I do not mean to affirm anything as to the presence or absence of ideas or mental images during the times so described, but to register the simple fact, that, for her own memory after the event, she was, at the time, without any one persistent, external-seeming image.—Note how St. Ignatius Loyola in his *Testament*, ed. London, 1900, pp. 91, 92, considered the profoundest spiritual experience of his life to have been one unaccompanied or expressed by any vision : " On his way " to a Church near Manresa, " he sat down facing the stream, which was running deep. While he was sitting there, the eyes of his mind were opened," not so as to see any kind of vision, but " so as to understand and comprehend spiritual things . . . with such clearness that for him all these things were made new. If all the enlightenment and help he had received from God in the whole course of his life . . . were gathered together in one heap, these all would appear less than he had been given at this one time."

which her true personality had for so long been enmeshed. Thus all this strenuous work of transforming and raising her lower levels of inclinations and of habit to the likeness and heights of her now deliberate loftiest standard was not taking place for the sake of something which actually was, or which even seemed to be, less than what she had possessed or had, even dimly, sought before, nor with a view to her true self's contraction.   But, on the contrary, the work was for the end of that indefinite More, of that great pushing upwards of her soul's centre and widening out of its circumference, which she could herself confirm and increase only by such ever-renewed warfare against what she now recognized as her false and crippling self.

And it is noticeable how soon and how largely, even still within this stage, her attitude became " passive." She pretty early came to do these numerous definite acts of penance without any deliberate selection or full attention to them. As in her third period her absorption in large spiritual ideas spontaneously suggests certain corresponding psycho-physical phenomena, which then, in return, stimulate anew the apprehensions of the mind; so here, towards the end of the first period, penitential love ends by quite spontaneously suggesting divers external acts of penitence, which readily become so much fresh stimulation for love.

I take this time to have been as yet free from visions or ecstasies—at least of the later lengthy and specific type. For the Bleeding Christ experience, even if fully historical, occurred within the first conversion-days, and only its vivid memory prolonged itself throughout those penitential years; whilst all such other visions, as have been handed down to us, do not treat of conversion and penance, at least in any active and personal sense.   And only towards the end of these years do the psycho-physical phenomena as to the abstention from food begin to show themselves.   The consideration of both the Visions and the Fasts had, then, better be reserved for the great central period.

V. The Second, Great Middle Period of Catherine's Life, 1477 to 1499.

It is most natural yet very regrettable that we should know so little as to Catherine's spiritual life, or even as to her psycho-physical condition, during these central twenty-two years of her life. It is natural, for she had, at this time, neither Physician nor Confessor busy with her, and the very richness and balanced fulness of this epoch of her life may well have helped to produce but little that could have been specially seized and registered by either. Yet it is regrettable, since here we have what, at least for us human observers, constitutes the culmination and the true measure of her life, the first period looking but like the preparation, and the third period, like the price paid for such a rich expansion.—Yet we know something about three matters of considerable psycho-physical and temperamental interest, which are specially characteristic of this time : her attitude towards food; her ecstasies and visions; and certain peculiarities in her conception and practice of the spiritual warfare.

1. *Her extraordinary fasts*.

As to food, it is clear that, however much we may be able or bound to deduct from the accounts, there remains a solid nucleus of remarkable fact. During some twenty years she evidently went, for a fairly equal number of days,—some thirty in Advent and some forty in Lent, seventy in all annually,— with all but no food; and was, during these fasts, at least as vigorous and active as when her nutrition was normal. For it is not fairly possible to make these great fasts end much before 1496, when she ceased to be Matron of the Hospital; and they cannot have begun much after 1475 or 1476 : so that practically the whole of her devoted service and administration in and of that great institution fell within these years, of which well-nigh one-fifth was covered by these all but total abstentions from food. Yet here again we are compelled to take these things, not separately, and as directly supernatural, but in connection with everything else; and to consider the resultant whole as the effect and evidence of a strong mind and will operating upon and through an immensely responsive psycho-physical organism.

For here again we easily find a significant system and delicate selectiveness both in the constant approximate synchronisms—these incapacities occurring about Advent and Lent; and in the foods exempted—since there is no difficulty in connection with the daily Holy Eucharist, with the unconsecrated wine given to her, as to all Communicants in that age at Genoa, immediately after Communion, or with water when seasoned penitentially with salt or vinegar. And if the actual heightening of nervous energy and balance, recorded as having generally accompanied these two fasts, is indeed a striking testimony to the extraordinary powers of her mind and will, we must not forget that these fruitful fasts were accompanied, and no doubt rendered possible, by the second great psychical peculiarity of these middle years, her ecstasies.

2. *Her ecstasies and visions.*

It is indeed remarkable how these two conditions and functions, her fasts and her ecstasies of a definite, lengthy and strength-bringing kind, arise, persist and then fade out of her life together.   And since, in ecstasy, the respiration, the circulation, and the other physical functions are all slackened and simplified; the mind is occupied with fewer, simpler, larger ideas, harmonious amongst themselves; and the emotions and the will are, for the time, saved the conflict and confusion, the stress and strain, of the fully waking moments; and considering that Catherine was peculiarly sensitive to all this flux and friction, and that she was now often in a more or less ecstatic trance from two up to eight hours : it follows that the amount of food required to heal the breach made by life's wear and tear would, by these ecstasies, be considerably reduced.   And indeed it will have been these contemplative absorptions which directly mediated for her those accessions of vigour : and that they did so, in such a soul and for the uses to which she put this strength, is their fullest justification as thoroughly wholesome, at least in their ultimate outcome, in and for this particular life.

And the visions recorded have these two characteristics, that they all deal with metaphysical realities and relations— God as source and end of all things, as Light and food of the soul, and similar conceptions, and never directly with historical persons, scenes, or institutions; and that, whereas the non-ecstatic picturings of her last period are grandly original, and demonstrably based upon her own spiritual experience, these second-period ecstatic visions are readily traceable to New Testament, Neo-Platonist, and Franciscan precursors, and have little more originality than this special selection from amongst other possible literary sources.

3. *Special character of her spiritual warfare.*

Catherine's ecstasies lead us easily on to the special method of her spiritual warfare, which can, I think, be summed up in three maxims : " One thing, and only one at a time "; " Ever

fight self, and you need not trouble about any other foe ";
and " Fight self by an heroic indirectness and by love, for
love,—through a continuous self-donation to Pure Love
alone."

Studying here these great convictions simply in their
temperamental occasions, colouring, and limitations, we can
readily discover how the " one thing at a time " maxim
springs from the same disposition as that which found such
refreshment in ecstasy. For here too, partly from a congenital incapacity to take things lightly, partly from an
equally characteristic sensitiveness to the conflict and confusion incident to the introduction of any fresh multiplicity
into the consciousness, she requires, even in her non-ecstatic
moments, to have her attention specially concentrated upon
one all-important idea, one point in the field of consciousness.
And, by a faithful wholeness of attention to the successive
spiritually significant circumstances and obligations, interior
impressions and lights, which her praying, thinking, suffering,
actively bring round to her notice, she manages, by such
single steps, gradually to go a very long way, and, by such
severe successiveness, to build up a rich simultaneity. For
each of these faithfully accepted and fully willed and utilized
acts and states, received into her one ever-growing and
deepening personality, leave memories and stimulations
behind them, and mingle, as subconscious elements, with the
conscious acts which follow later on.

4. *Two remarkable consequences of this kind of warfare.*

There were two specially remarkable consequences of this
constant watchful fixation of the one spiritually significant
point in each congeries of circumstances, and of the manner
in which (partly perhaps as the occasion, but probably in
great part as the effect of this attention) one interior condition
of apparent fixity would suddenly shift to another condition
of a different kind but of a similar apparent stability. There
was the manner in which, during these years, she appears to
have escaped the committing of any at all definite offences
against the better and best lights of that particular moment;
and there was the way in which she would realize the
faultiness and subtle self-seeking of any one state, only at
the moment of its disappearing to make room for another.

I take the accounts of both these remarkable peculiarities
to be substantially accurate, since, if the first condition had
not obtained, we should have found her practising more or

D

less frequent Confession, as we find her doing in the first and third, but not in this period; and if the second condition had not existed, we should have had, for this period also, some such vivid account of painful scruples arising from the impression of actually present unfaithfulnesses, such as has been preserved for her last years. And indeed, as soon as we have vividly conceived a state in which a soul (by a wise utilization of the quite exceptional successiveness and simplification to which it has been, in great part, driven by its temperamental requirements, and by a constant heroic watchfulness) has managed to exclude from its life, during a long series of years, all fully deliberate resistances to, or lapses from, its contemporaneous better insight : one sees at once that a consciousness of faultiness could come to her only at those moments when, one state and level giving place to another, she could, for the moment, see the former habits and their implicit defects in the clear light of their contrast to her new, deeper insights and dispositions.

Now it is evident that here again we have in part (in the curious quasi-fixity of each state, and then the sudden replacement of it by another) something which, taken alone, is simply psychically peculiar and spiritually indifferent. The persistent sense of gradual or of rapid change in the midst of a certain continuity and indeed abidingness, characteristic of the average moments of the average soul, is, taken in itself, more true to life and to the normal reaction of the human mind, and not less capable of spiritual utilization, than is Catherine's peculiarity. Her heroic utilization of her special psychic life for purposes of self-fighting, and the degree in which, as we shall find in a later chapter, she succeeded in moulding this life into a shape representative of certain great spiritual truths : these things it is which constitute here the spiritually significant element.

And her second peculiarity of religious practice was her great simplification and intensification of the spiritual combat. Simplification : for she does not fight directly either the Devil or the World; she directly fights the " Flesh " alone, and recognizes but one immediate opponent, her own lower self. Hence the references to the world are always simply as to an extension or indefinite repetition of that same self, or of similar lower selves; and those to the devil are, except where she declares her own lower self " a very devil," extraordinarily rare, and, in their authentic forms, never directly and formally connected with her own spiritual interests and struggles. And Intensification : for she conceives this lower self, against which all her fighting is turned, as capable of any enormity, as actually cloaking itself successively in every kind of disguise, and as more or less vitiating even the most spiritual-seeming of her states and acts.

And here again we can, I think, clearly trace the influence of her special temperament and psycho-physical functioning, yet in a direction opposite to that in which we would naturally expect it. For it is not so much that this temperament led her to exaggerate the badness of her false self, or to elaborate a myth concerning its (all but completely separate) existence, as that, owing in large part to that temperament and functioning, her false self *was* both unusually distinct from her true self and particularly clamorous and claimful. It would indeed be well for hagiography if, in all cases, at least an attempt were made to discover and present the precise and particular good and bad selves, worked for and fought by the particular saint : for it is just this double particularization of the common warfare in every individual soul that gives the poignant interest and instructiveness, and a bracing sense of reality to these lonely yet typical, unique yet universal struggles, defeats, and victories.

And in Catherine's case her special temperament ; her particular attitude during the ten years' laxity, and again during the last years' times of obscurity and scruple ; even some of her sayings probably still belonging to this middle period ; but above all the precise point and edge of her counter-ideal and *attrait :* all indicate clearly enough what was her congenital defect. A great self-engrossment of a downrightly selfish kind ; a grouping of all things round such a self-adoring *Ego ;* a noiseless but determined elimination from her life and memory of all that would not or could not, then and there, be drawn and woven into the organism and functioning of this immensely self-seeking, infinitely woundable and wounded, endlessly self-doctoring " I " and " Me " : a self intensely, although not sexually, jealous, envious and exacting, incapable of easy accommodation, of pleasure in half successes, of humour and brightness, of joyous " once-born " creatureliness : all this was certainly to be found, in strong tendency at least, in the untrained parts and periods of her character and life.

And then the same peculiarity and sensitiveness of her

psycho-physical organism which, in her last period, ended by mirroring her mental spiritual apprehensions and picturings in her very body, and which, even at this time, has been traced by us in the curious long fixities and rapid changes of her fields of consciousness, clearly operates also and already here, in separating off this false self from the good one and in heightening the apprehension of that false self to almost a perception in space, or to an all but physical sensation.

We thus get something of which the interesting cases of " doubleness of personality," so much studied of late years, are, as it were, purely psychical, definitely *maladif* caricatures; the great difference consisting in Catherine herself possessing, at all times, the consciousness and memory of both sides, of both " selves," and of each as both actual and potential, within the range of her one great personality.   Indeed it is this very multiplicity thus englobed and utilized by that higher unity, which gives depth to her sanity and sanctity.[1]

5. *Precise object and end of her striving.*

And all this is confirmed and completed, as already hinted, by the precise object of her ideal, the particular means and special end of the struggle.   Here, at the very culmination of her inner life and aim, we find the deepest traces of her temperamental requirements; and here, in what she seeks, there is again an immense concentration and a significant choice.   The distinctions between obligation and supereroga-tion, between merit and grace, are not utilized but tran-scended; the conception of God having anger as well as love arouses as keen a sense of intolerableness as that of God's envy aroused in Plato, and God appears to her as, in Himself, continuously loving.

This love of God, again, is seen to be present everywhere, and, of Itself, everywhere to effect happiness.   The disposi-tions of souls are indeed held to vary within each soul and between soul and soul, and to determine the differences in their reception, and consequently in the effect upon them, of God's one universal love : but the soul's reward and punish-ment are not something distinct from its state, they are but that very state prolonged and articulated, since man can indeed go against his deepest requirements but can never

---

[1] I would draw the reader's attention to the very interesting parallels to many of the above-mentioned peculiarities furnished both by St. Teresa in her *Life, passim,* and by Battista Vernazza in the Autobio-graphical statements which I have given here in Chapter VIII.

finally suppress them. Heaven, Purgatory, Hell are thus not places as well as states, nor do they begin only in the beyond : they are states alone, and begin already here. And Grace and Love, and Love and Christ, and Christ and Spirit, and hence Grace and Love and Christ and Spirit are, at bottom, one, and this One is God. Hence God, loving Himself in and through us, is alone our full true self. Here, in this constant stretching out and forward of her whole being into and towards the ocean of light and love, of God the All in All, it is not hard to recognize a soul which finds happiness only when looking out and away from self, and turning, in more or less ecstatic contemplation and action, towards that Infinite Country, that great Over-Againstness, God.

And, in her sensitive shrinking from the idea of an angry God, we find the instinctive reaction of a nature too naturally prone itself to angry claimfulness, and which had been too much driven out of its self-occupation by the painful sense of interior self-division consequent upon that jealousy, not to find it intolerable to get out of that little Scylla of her own hungry self only to fall into a great Charybdis, an apparent mere enlargement and canonization of that same self, in the angry God Himself.

And if her second peculiarity, the concentration of the fight upon an unusually isolated and intense false self, had introduced an element of at least relative Rigorism and contraction into her spirituality, this third peculiarity brings a compensating movement of quasi-Pantheism, of immense expansion. Here the crushed plant expands in boundless air, light and warmth ; the parched seaweed floats and unfolds itself in an immense ocean of pure waters—the soul, as it were, breathes and bathes in God's peace and love. And it is evident that the great super-sensible realities and relations adumbrated by such figures, did not, with her, lead to mere dry or vague apprehensions. Even in this period, although here with a peaceful, bracing orderliness and harmony, the reality thus long and closely dwelt on and lived with was, as it were, physically seen and felt in these its images by a ready response of her immensely docile psycho-physical organism.

6. *Catherine possessed two out of the three conditions apparently necessary for stigmatization.*

And in this connection we should note how largely reasonable was the expectation of some of her disciples of finding some permanent physical effects upon her body ; and yet why she not only had not the stigmata of the Passion, but why she could not have them.   For, of the three apparently necessary conditions for such stigmatization, she had indeed two—a long and intense absorption in religious ideas, and a specially sensitive psycho-physical temperament and organization of the ecstatic type ; but the third condition, the concentration of that absorption upon Our Lord's Passion and wounds, was wholly wanting—at least after those four actively penitential and during those twenty-two ecstatic years.   We can, however, say most truly that although, since at all events 1477, her visions and contemplations were all concerning purely metaphysical, eternal realities, or certain ceaselessly repeated experiences of the human soul, or laws and types derived from the greatest of Christian institutions, her daily solace, the Holy Eucharist : yet that these verities ended by producing definite images in her senses, and certain observable though passing impressions upon her body, so that we can here talk of sensible shadows or " stigmata " of things purely spiritual and eternal.

And if, in the cases of some ecstatic saints, mental pathologists of a more or less materialistic type have, at times, shown excessive suspicion as to some of the causes and effects of these saints' devotion to Our Lord's Humanity under the imagery and categories of the Canticle of Canticles—all such suspicions, fair or unfair, have absolutely no foothold in Catherine's life, since not only is there here no devotion to God or to Our Lord as Bridegroom of the Bridal soul : there is no direct contemplative occupation with the historic Christ and no figuring of Him or of God under human attributes or relations at all.   I think that her temperament and health had something to do with her habitual dwelling upon Thing-symbols of God : Ocean—Air—Fire—picturings which, conceived with her psycho-physical vividness, must, in their expanse, have rested and purified her in a way that historical contingencies and details would not have done.   The doctrinal and metaphysical side of the matter will be considered later on.

VI. THREE RULES WHICH SEEM TO GOVERN THE RELATIONS BETWEEN PSYCHO-PHYSICAL PECULIARITIES AND SANCTITY IN GENERAL.

If we next inquire how matters stand historically with regard to the relations between ecstatic states and psycho-physical peculiarities on the one hand, and sanctity in general on the other hand, we shall find, I think, that the following three rules or laws really cover, in a necessarily general, somewhat schematic way, all the chief points, at all certain or practically important, in this complex and delicate matter.

1. *Intense spiritual energizing is accompanied by auto-suggestion and mono-ideism.*

It is clear, for one thing, that as simply all and every mental, emotional, and volitional energizing is necessarily and always accompanied by corresponding nerve-states, and that if we had not some neural sensitiveness and neural adaptability, we could not—whilst living our earthly life—think, or feel, or will in regard to anything whatsoever : a certain special degree of at least potential psycho-physical sensitiveness and adaptability must be taken to be, not the productive cause, but a necessary condition for the exercise, of any considerable range and depth of mind and will, and hence of sanctity in general; and that the actual aiming at, and gradual achievement of, sanctity in these, thus merely possible cases, spiritualizes and further defines this sensitiveness, as the instrument, material, and expression of the soul's work.[1] And this work of the heroic soul will necessarily consist, in great part, in attending to, calling up, and, as far as may be, both fixing and ever renovating certain few great dominant ideas, and in attempting by every means to saturate the imagination with images and figures, historical and symbolic, as so many incarnations of these great verities.

We get thus what, taken simply phenomenally and without as yet any inquiry as to an ultimate reality pressing in upon the soul,—a divine stimulation underlying all its sincere and fruitful action,—is a spiritual mono-ideism and auto-suggestion, of a more or less general kind. But, at this stage, these activities and their psycho-physical concomitants and results will, though different in kind, be no more abnormal than is the mono-ideism and auto-suggestion of the mathematician, the tactician, and the constructive statesman. Newton, Napoleon, and Richelieu : they were all dominated by some great central idea, and they all for long years dwelt upon it and worked for it within themselves, till it became alive and

---

[1] The omnipresence of neural conditions and consequences for all and every mental and volitional activity has been admirably brought out by Prof. W. James, in his *Varieties of Religious Experience*, 1902, Vol. I, pp. 1–25.

aflame in their imaginations and their outward-moving wills, before, yet as the means of, its taking external and visible shape. And, in all the cases that we can test in detail, the psycho-physical accompaniments of all this profound mental-volitional energy were most marked. In the cases of Newton and Napoleon, for instance, a classification of their energizings solely according to their neural accompaniments would force us to class these great discoverers and organizers amongst psycho-physical eccentrics. Yet the truth and value of their work and character has, of course, to be measured, not by this its neural fringe and cost, but by its central spiritual truth and fruitfulness.

2. *Such mechanisms specially marked in Philosophers, Musicians, Poets, and Mystical Religionists.*

The mystical and contemplative element in the religious life, and the group of saints amongst whom this element is predominant, no doubt give us a still larger amount of what, again taking the matter phenomenally and not ultimately, is once more mono-ideism and auto-suggestion, and entails a correspondingly larger amount of psycho-physical impressionableness and reaction utilized by the mind. But here also, from the simplest forms of the " prayer of quiet " to absorptions of an approximately ecstatic type, we have something which, though different in kind and value, is yet no more abnormal than are the highest flights and absorptions of the Philosopher, the Musician, and the Poet. And yet, in such cases as Kant and Beethoven, a classifier of humanity according to its psycho-physical phenomena alone would put these great discoverers and creators, without hesitation, amongst hopeless and useless hypochondriacs. Yet here again the truth of their ideas and the work of their lives have to be measured by quite other things than by this their neural concomitance and cost.

3. *Ecstatics possess a peculiar psycho-physical organization.*

The downright ecstatics and hearers of voices and seers of visions have all, wherever we are able to trace their temperamental and neural constitution and history, possessed and developed a definitely peculiar psycho-physical organization. We have traced it in Catherine and indicated it in St. Teresa. We find it again in St. Maria Magdalena dei Pazzi and in St. Marguerite Marie Alacocque, in modern times, and in St. Catherine of Siena and St. Francis of Assisi in mediaeval times. For early Christian times we are too ignorant as regards the psycho-physical organization of St. Ignatius of Antioch, Hermas, and St. Cyprian, to be able to establish a connection between their temperamental endowments and their hearing of voices and seeing of visions—in the last two cases we get much that looks like more or less of a mere conventional literary device.[1]

We are, however, in a fair position for judging, in the typical and thoroughly original case of St. Paul. In 2 Cor. xiii, 7, 8, after speaking of the abundant revelations accorded to him, he adds that " lest I be lifted up, a thorn " (literally, a stake) " in the flesh was given to me, an Angel of Satan to buffet me." And though " I thrice besought the Lord that it might depart from me, the Lord answered me, ' My grace is sufficient for thee ; for grace is perfected in infirmity.' " And he was consequently determined " rather " to " glory in his infirmities, so that the power of Christ may dwell within " him. And in Gal. iv, 14, 15, written about the same time, he reminds his readers how he had " preached to them through the infirmity of the flesh," commending them because they " did not despise nor loathe their temptation in his flesh " (this is no doubt the correct reading), " but had received him as an Angel of God, as Christ Jesus."

Now the most ancient interpretation of this " thorn " or " stake " is some kind of bodily complaint,—violent headache or earache is mentioned by Tertullian de Pudicitia, 13, and by St. Jerome, Comm. in Gal. *loc. cit.* Indeed St. Paul's own description of his " bodily presence " as " weak," and his " spoken word " as " contemptible " (2 Cor. x, 10), points this way. It seems plain that it cannot have been carnal temptations (only in the sixth century did this interpretation become firmly established), for he could not have gloried in these, nor could they, hidden as they would be within his heart, have exposed him to the contempt of others. Indeed he expressly excludes such troubles from his life, where, in advising those who were thus oppressed to marry, he gives the preference to the single life, and declares, " I would that all men were even as I myself " (1 Cor. vii, 7).

The attacks of this trouble were evidently acutely painful : note the metaphor of a stake driven into the live flesh and the Angel of Satan who buffeted him. (And compare St.

---

[1] H. Weinel's *Die Wirkungen des Geistes und der Geister im nacha-postolischen Zeitalter, bis auf Irenäus*, 1899, contains an admirably careful investigation of these things.

Teresa's account : " An Angel of God appeared to me to be thrusting at times a long spear into my heart and to pierce my very entrails " ; " the pain was so great that it made me moan " ; " it really seems to the soul as if an arrow were thrust through the heart or through itself; the suffering is not one of sense, neither is the wound physical " ; and how, on another occasion, she heard Our Lord answer her : " Serve thou Me, and meddle not with this.") [1]

These attacks would come suddenly, even in the course of his public ministry, rendering him, in so far, an object of derision and of loathing.   (Compare here St. Teresa's declaration : " During the rapture, the body is very often perfectly powerless; it continues in the position it was in when the rapture came upon it : if sitting, sitting; if the hands were open, or if they were shut, they will remain open or shut " ; " if the body " was " standing or kneeling, it remains so.") [2]

Yet these attacks were evidently somehow connected, both in fact and in his consciousness, with his Visions ; and they were recurrent.   The vision of the Third Heaven and his apparently first attack seem to have been practically coincident,—about A.D. 44.   We find a second attack hanging about him for some time, on his first preaching in Galatia, about A.D. 51 or 52 (see 1 Thess. ii, 18; 1 Cor. ii, 3).   And a third attack appears to have come in A.D. 57 or 58, when the Second Epistle to the Corinthians and that to the Galatians were written ; note the words (2 Cor. i, 9), " Yea " (in addition to his share in the public persecution), " we ourselves have had the answer of death within ourselves, that we should not trust in ourselves, but in God which raiseth the dead." (And compare here St. Teresa : in July 1547 " for about four days I remained insensible.   They must have regarded me as dead more than once.   For a day and a half the grave was open in my monastery, waiting for my body.   But it pleased Our Lord I should come to myself.") [3]   Dr. Lightfoot gives as a parallel the epileptiform seizures of King Alfred, which, sudden, acutely painful, at times death-like, and protracted, tended to render the royal power despicable in the eyes of the world.[4]   Yet, except for the difference of sex and of

---

[1] *Life*, written by herself, ed. cit. pp. 235, 423; 136.
[2] *Ibid*. pp. 149, 420.   [3] *Ibid*. pp. xxii, 28.
[4] It is to Dr. Lightfoot's fine Excursus in *St. Paul's Epistle to the Galatians*, ed. 1881, pp. 186–191, that I owe all the Pauline texts and most of the considerations reproduced above.

relative privacy, St. Teresa's states, which I have given here, are more closely similar, in so much as they are intimately connected with religious visions and voices.

And, amongst Old Testament figures, we can find a similar connection, on a still larger scale, in the case of Ezekiel, the most definitely ecstatic, though (upon the whole) the least original, of the literary Prophets. For, as to the visionary element, we have his own records of three visions of the glory of Jahve; of five other ecstasies, three of which are accompanied by remarkable telepathic, second-sight activities; and of twelve symbolic (better : representative) prophetic actions, which are now all rightly coming to be considered as having been externally carried out by him.[1] And we get psycho-physical states, as marked as in any other ecstatic saint. For we hear how Jahve on one occasion says to him : " But thou, son of man, lay thyself on thy left side " (*i. e.* according to Jewish orientation, towards the North) " and I shall lay the guilt of the house of Israel " (the Northern Kingdom) " upon thee; the number of days that thou shalt lie upon it, shalt thou bear their guilt. But I appoint unto thee the years of their guilt, as a (corresponding) number of days, (namely) one hundred and fifty days. . . . And, when thou hast done with them, thou shalt lay thyself on thy right side " (*i. e.* towards the South), " and thou shalt bear the guilt of the house of Judah " (the Southern Kingdom); " one day for each year shall I appoint unto thee. And behold I shall lay cords upon thee, that thou shalt be unable to turn from one side to the other, till thou hast ended the days of thy boundness " (iv, 4–8). Krätzschmar, no doubt rightly, finds here a case of hemiplegia and anaesthesia, functional cataleptic paralysis lasting during five months on the left side, and then shifting for about six weeks to the right side. And the *alalia* (speechlessness), which no doubt accompanied this state, is referred to on three other occasions : xxiv, 27; xxix, 31; xxxiii, 22. And note how Jahve's address to Ezekiel, " son of man," which occurs in this book over ninety times, and but once in the whole of the rest of the Old Testament (Dan. viii,

---

[1] Visions of Jahve's glory : i, 1–28; iii, 22–27; xl, 1; xliv, 4. The five other Ecstasies and Visions : viii, 1 foll.; xi, 1 foll.; xxiv, 1 foll.; xxxiii, 22; xxxvii, 1 foll. Second Sight : viii, 16; xi, 13; xxiv, 1. Representative Actions : iv, 1–3, 7; iv, 4–6, 8; iv, 10; ix, 11–15; xii, 1–16; xii, 17–20; xxi, 11, 12; xxi, 23–32; xxiv, 1–14; xxiv, 15–27; xxxiii, 22; xxxvii, 15–28.

17), evidently stands here for the sense of his creaturely nothingness, so characteristic of the true ecstatic.[1]

Now, at this last stage, the analogy of the other non-religious activities of the healthy mind and of their psycho-physical conditions and effects forsakes us; but not the principle which has guided us all along. For here, as from the very first, some such conditions and effects are inevitable; and the simple fact of this occurrence, apart from the question of their particular character, is something thoroughly normal. And here again, and more than ever, the emphasis and decisions have to lie with, and to depend upon, the mental and volitional work and the spiritual truth and reality achieved in and for the recipient, and, through him, in and for others.

Even at the earlier stages, to cling to the form, as distinct from the content and end, of these things was to be thoroughly unfair to this their content and end, within the spacious economy of the spirit's life; at this stage such clinging becomes destructive of all true religion. For if the mere psycho-physical forms and phenomena of ecstasy, of vision, of hearing of voices is, in proportion to their psycho-physical intensity and seeming automatism and quasi-physical objectivity, to be taken as necessarily a means and mark of sanctity or of insight, or, at least, as something presumably sent direct by God or else as diabolical, something necessarily super-or preter-natural: then the lunatic asylums contain more miracles, saints, and sages, or their direct, strangely similar antipodes, than all the most fervent or perverted churches, monasteries, and families upon God's earth. For in asylums we find ecstasies, visions, voices, all more, not less marked, all more, not less irresistibly objective-seeing to the recipient, than anything to be found outside.

Yet apply impartially to both sets the test, not of form, but of content, of spiritual fruitfulness and of many-sided applicability—and this surface-similarity yields at once to a fundamental difference. Indeed all the great mystics, and this in precise proportion to their greatness, have ever taught

---

[1] The above translation and interpretation is based upon Krätzschmar's admirably psychological commentary, *Das Buch Ezechiel*, Göttingen, 1900, pp. v, vi; 45, 49. But I think he is wrong in taking that six months' abnormal condition to have given rise, in Ezekiel's mind, to a belief in a previous divine order and to an interpretation of this order. All the strictly analogical cases of religious ecstasy, not hysteria, point to a strong mental impression, such as that order and belief having preceded and occasioned the peculiar psycho-physical state.

that, the mystical capacities and habits being but means and not ends, only such ecstasies are valuable as leave the soul, and the very body as its instrument, strengthened and improved; and that visions and voices are to be accepted by the mind only in proportion as they convey some spiritual truth of importance to it or to others, and as they actually help it to become more humble, true, and loving.

And there can be no doubt that these things worked thus with such great ecstatic mystics as Ezekiel, the man of the great prophetic schemes and the permanently fruitful picturing of the Good Shepherd; as St. Paul, the greatest missionary and organizer ever given to the Christian Church; as St. Francis of Assisi, the salt and leaven and light of the Church and of society, in his day and more or less ever since; as St. Catherine of Siena, the free-spoken, docile reinspirer of the Papacy; as Jeanne d'Arc, the maiden deliverer of a Nation; as St. Teresa, reformer of a great Order. All these, and countless others, would, quite evidently, have achieved less, not more, of interior light and of far-reaching helpfulness of a kind readily recognized by all specifically religious souls, had they been without the rest, the bracing, the experience furnished to them by their ecstasies and allied states and apprehensions.

VII. Perennial Freshness of the Great Mystics' Main Spiritual Test, in Contradistinction to their Secondary, Psychological Contention. Two Special Difficulties.

1. *A false and a true test of mystical experience.*

Now it is deeply interesting to note how entirely unweakened, indeed how impressively strengthened, by the intervening severe test of whole centuries of further experience and of thought, has remained the main and direct, the spiritual test of the great Mystics, in contradistinction to their secondary psychological contention with respect to such experiences. The secondary, psychological contention is well reproduced by St. Teresa where she says : " When I speak, I go on with my understanding arranging what I am saying; but, if I am spoken to by others, I do nothing else but listen without any labour." In the former case, " the soul," if it be in good faith, " cannot possibly fail to see clearly that itself arranges the words and utters them to itself. How then can the understanding have time enough to arrange these locutions? They require time." [1] Now this particular argument for their supernaturalness derived from the psychological form—from the suddenness, clearness, and apparent automatism of these locutions—has ceased to carry weight, owing to our present, curiously recent, knowledge concerning the subconscious region of the mind, and the occasionally sudden irruption of that region's contents into the field of that same mind's ordinary, full consciousness.   In the Ven. Battista Vernazza's case we have a particularly clear instance of such a long accumulation,—by means of much, in great part full, attention to certain spiritual ideas, words, and images,—in the subconscious regions of a particularly strong and deeply sincere and saintly mind; and the sudden irruption from those regions of certain clear and apparently quite spontaneous words and images into the field of her mind's full consciousness. [2]

But the reference to the great Mystics' chief and direct test, upon which they dwell with an assurance and self-consistency far surpassing that which accompanies their psychological argument,—the spiritual content and effects of such experiences,—this, retains all its cogency.   St. Teresa tells us: " When Our Lord speaks, it is both word and work : His words are deeds."   " I found myself, through these words alone, tranquil and strong, courageous and confident, at rest and enlightened : I felt I could maintain against all the world that my prayer was the work of God."   " I could not believe that Satan, if he wished to deceive me, could have recourse to means so adverse to his purpose as this, of rooting out my faults, and implanting virtues and spiritual strength : for I saw clearly that I had become another person, by means of these visions."   " So efficacious was the vision, and such was the nature of the words spoken to me, that I could not possibly doubt that they came from Him."   " I was in a trance ; and the effects of it were such, that I could have no doubt it came from God."   On another occasion she writes less positively even of the great test : " She never undertook anything merely because it came to her in prayer. For all that her Confessors told her that these things came from

---

[1] *Op. cit.* pp. 190c; 192c, 193a.

[2] See Prof. W. James's admirable account of these irruptions in his *Varieties of Religious Experience*, 1902, pp. 231–237.

God, she never so thoroughly believed them that she could swear to it herself, though it did seem to her that they were spiritually safe, because of the effects thereof." [1] This doctrine is still the last word of wisdom in these matters.

2. *First special difficulty in testing ecstasies.*

Yet it is only at this last stage that two special difficulties occur, the one philosophical, the other moral. The philosophical difficulty is as follows. As long as the earlier stages are in progress, it is not difficult to understand that the soul may be gradually building up for herself a world of spiritual apprehensions, and a corresponding spiritual and moral character, by a process which, looked at merely phenomenally and separately, appears as a simple case of mono-ideism and auto-suggestion, but which can and should be conceived, when studied in its ultimate cause and end, as due to the pressure and influence of God's spirit working in and through the spirit of man,—the Creator causing His own little human creature freely to create for itself some copy of and approach to its own eternally subsisting, substantial Cause and Crown. There the operation of such an underlying Supreme Cause, and a consequent relation between the world thus conceived and built up by the human soul and the real world of the Divine Spirit, appears possible, because the things which the soul is thus made to suggest to itself are ideas, and because even these ideas are clearly recognized by the soul as only instruments and approaches to the realities for which they stand. But here, in this last stage, we get the suggestion, not of ideas, but of psycho-physical impressions, and these impressions are, apparently, not taken as but distantly illustrative, but as somehow one with the spiritual realities for which they stand. Is not, *e. g.*, Catherine's joy at this stage centred precisely in the downright feeling, smelling, seeing, of ocean waters, penetrating odours, all-enveloping light; and in the identification of those waters, odours, lights, with God Himself, so that God becomes at last an object of direct, passive, sensible perception? Have we not then here at last reached pure delusion?

Not so, in proportion as the mystic is great and spiritual, and as he here still clings to the principles common to all true religion. For, in proportion as he is and does this, will he find and regard the mind as deeper and more operative

[1] *Life*, written by Herself, pp. 190*b*; 196*b*; 224*c*; 295*c*; 413*b*.

than sense, and God's Spirit as penetrating and transcending both the one and the other. And hence he will (at least implicitly) regard those psycho-physical impressions as but sense-like and really mental; and he will consider this mental impression and projection as indeed produced by the presence and action of the Spirit within his mind or of the pressure of spiritual realities upon it, but will hold that this whole mental process, with these its spatial- and temporal-seeming embodiments, these sights and sounds, has only a relation and analogical likeness to, and is not and cannot be identical with, those realities of an intrinsically super-spatial, super-temporal order.—And thus here as everywhere, although here necessarily more than ever, we find again the conception of the Transcendent yet also Immanent Spirit, effecting in the human spirit the ever-increasing apprehension of Himself, accompanied in this spirit by an ever-keener sense of His incomprehensibility for all but Himself. And here again the truth, and more especially the divine origin of these apprehensions, is tested and guaranteed on and on by the consequent deepening of that spiritual and ethical fruitfulness and death to self, which are the common aspirations of every deepest moment and every sincerest movement within the universal heart of man.

Thus, as regards the mentality of these experiences, Catherine constantly speaks of seeing " as though with the eyes of the body." And St. Teresa tells us of her visions with " the eyes of the soul "; of how at first she " did not know that it was possible to see anything otherwise than with the eyes of the body "; of how, in reality " she never," in her true visions and locutions, " saw anything with her bodily eyes, nor heard anything with her bodily ears "; and of how indeed she later on, on one occasion, " saw nothing with the eyes of the body, nothing with the eyes of the soul,"—she " simply felt Christ close by her,"—evidently again with the soul. Thus, too, Catherine tells us, that " as the intellect exceeds language, so does love exceed intellection "; and how vividly she feels that " all that can be said of God," compared to the great Reality, " is but tiny crumbs from the great Master's table." [1]

And, as to the inadequacy of these impressions, the classical authority on such things, St. John of the Cross, declares : " He that will rely on the letter of the divine locutions or on the intelligible form of the vision, will of necessity fall into

[1] *Vita*, passim; *Life*, ed. cit. pp. 40, 41; 408; 206. *Vita*, pp. 87c, 77b.

delusion; for he does not yield to the Spirit in detachment from sense." " He who shall give attention to these motes of the Spirit alone will, in the end, have no spirituality at all." " All visions, revelations, and heavenly feelings, and whatever is greater than these, are not worth the least act of humility, bearing the fruits of that charity which neither values nor seeks itself, which thinketh well not of self but of all others." Indeed " virtue does not consist in these apprehensions. Let men then cease to regard, and labour to forget them, that they may be free." For " spiritual supernatural knowledge is of two kinds, one distinct and special," which comprises " visions, revelations, locutions, and spiritual impressions"; " the other confused, obscure, and general," which " has but one form, that of contemplation which is the work of faith. The soul is to be led into this, by directing it thereto through all the rest, beginning with the first, and detaching it from them."

Hence " many souls, to whom visions have never come, are incomparably more advanced in the way of perfection than others to whom many have been given"; and " they who are already perfect, receive these visitations of the Spirit of God in peace; ecstasies cease, for they were only graces to prepare them for this greater grace." Hence, too, " one desire only doth God allow and suffer in His Presence : that of perfectly observing His law and of carrying the Cross of Christ. In the Ark of the Covenant there was but the Book of the Law, the Rod of Aaron, and the Pot of Manna. Even so that soul, which has no other aim than the perfect observance of the Law of God and the carrying of the Cross of Christ, will be a true Ark containing the true Manna, which is God." And this perfected soul's intellectual apprehensions will, in their very mixture of light and conscious obscurity, more and more approach and forestall the eternal condition of the beatified soul. " One of the greatest favours, bestowed transiently on the soul in this life, is to enable it to see so distinctly and to feel so profoundly, that it cannot comprehend Him at all. These souls are herein, in some degree, like the Saints in Heaven, where they who know Him most perfectly perceive most clearly that He is infinitely incomprehensible; for those who have the less clear vision do not perceive so distinctly as the others how greatly He transcends their vision." [1]

[1] *Ascent of Mount Carmel*, ed. cit. pp. 159, 163; 264, 265, 102, 195; *Spiritual Canticle*, ed. cit. p. 238; *Ascent*, pp. 26, 27; *Canticle*, pp. 206, 207.

3. *Second special difficulty in testing ecstasies.*

The second special difficulty is this. Have not at least some of the saints of this definitely ecstatic type shown more psycho-physical abnormality than spiritually fruitful origination or utilization of such things, so that their whole life seems penetrated by a fantastic spirit ?   And have not many others, who, at their best, may not have been amenable to this charge, ended with shattered nerve- and will-power, with an organism apparently incapable of any further growth or use, even if we restrict our survey exclusively to strength-bringing ecstasy and to a contemplative prayer of some traceable significance ?

(1) As a good instance of the apparent predominance of psycho-physical and even spiritual strangeness, we can take the Venerable Sister Lukardis, Cistercian Nun of Ober-Weimar, born probably in 1276.   Her life is published from a unique Latin MS. by the Bollandists (*Analecta*, Vol. XVIII, pp. 305–367, Bruxelles, 1899), and presents us with a mediaevally naïve and strangely unanalytic, yet extraordinarily vivid picture of things actually seen by the writer.   " Although," say the most competent editors, " we know not the name nor profession of the Author, whether he belonged to the Friars or to the Monks,[1] it is certain that he was a contemporary of Lukardis, that he knew her intimately, and that he learnt many details from her fellow-nuns.   And though we shall be slow to agree with him when he ascribes all the strange things which she experienced in her soul and body to divine influence, yet we should beware of considering him to be in bad faith.   For, though he erred perchance in ascribing to a divine operation things which are simply the work of nature, such a vice is common amongst those who transmit such things." [2]   I take the chief points in the order of their narration by the *Vita*.

" Soon after Lukardis had, at twelve years of age, taken the Cistercian habit, her mother died," over twelve English miles away, at Erfurt, yet Lukardis " saw the scene " in such detail " in the spirit," that, when her sister came to tell her, she, Lukardis, " anticipated her with an account of the day, the place and hour of the death, of the clothes then being worn by their mother, of the precise position of the bed and of the hospital, and of the persons present at the time."

---

[1] Two Confessors of hers are mentioned by her, *Vita*, p. 352 : Fathers Henry of Mühlhausen, and Eberhard of the Friars Preachers.

[2] *Analecta*, *loc. cit.* p. 310.

She soon suffered from " stone " in the bladder ; " quartan, tertian, and continuous fevers," and from fainting fits ; also from contraction of the muscles (*nervi*) of the hands, so that the latter were all but useless and could not even hold the staff on which she had to lean in walking, till they had been " tightly wrapped round in certain clothes." Yet " she would, at times, strike her hands so vehemently against each other, that they resounded as though they had been wooden boards." " When lying in bed she would sometimes, as it were, plant her feet beneath her, hang her head down " backwards, " and raise her abdomen and chest, making thus, as it were, a highly curved arch of her person." Indeed sometimes " she would for a long while stand upon her head and shoulders, with her feet up in air, but with her garments adhering to her limbs, as though they had been sewn on to them." " Often, too, by day or night, she was wont to run with a most impetuous course ;—she understood that, by this her course, she was compensating Christ for His earthly course of thirty-three years." [1]

" On one occasion she had a vision of Christ, in which He said to her : ' Join thy hands to My hands, and thy feet to My feet, and thy breast to My breast, and thus shall I be aided by thee to suffer less.' And instantly she felt a most keen pain of wounds," in all three regions, " although wounds did not as yet appear to sight." But " as she bore the memory of the hammering of the nails into Christ upon the Cross within her heart, so did she exercise herself in outward deed. For she was frequently wont, with the middle finger of one hand, impetuously to wound the other in the place appropriate to the stigmata ; then to withdraw her finger to the distance of a cubit, and straightway again impetuously to wound herself. Those middle fingers felt hard like metal. And about the sixth and ninth hour she would impetuously wound herself with her finger in the breast, at the appropriate place for the wound."—After about two years " Christ appeared to her in the night of Blessed Gregory, Pope " (St. Gregory VII, May 26 ?), " pressed her right hand firmly in His, and declared, ' I desire thee to suffer with Me.' On her consenting, a wound instantly appeared in her right hand ; about ten days later a wound in the left hand ; and thus successively the five wounds were found in her body." " The wounds of the scourging

[1] *Analecta*, pp. 311–313.

were also found upon her, of a finger's length, and having a certain hard skin around them." [1]

" At whiles she would lie like one dead throughout the day; yet her countenance was very attractive, owing to a wondrous flushed look. And even if a needle was pressed into her flesh, she felt no pain."—" On one occasion she was carried upon her couch by two sisters into the Lady Chapel, to the very spot where her body now reposes. After having been left there alone for about an hour, the Blessed Virgin appeared to her, with her beloved Infant, Jesus, in her arms, and suckling Him. And Lukardis, contrary to the law of her strength "— she had, by now, been long confined to a reclining posture— " arose from her couch and began to stand upright. And at this juncture one of the Sisters opened the Chapel door a little, and, on looking in, marvelled at Lukardis being able to stand, but withdrew and forbade the other Sisters from approaching thither, since she feared that, if they saw her standing thus, they might declare her to be quite able, if she but chose, to arise and stand at any time. Upon the Blessed Virgin twice insisting upon being asked for some special favour, and Lukardis declaring, ' I desire that thou slake my thirst with that same milk with which I now see thee suckling thy beloved Son,' the Blessed Virgin came up to her, and gave her to drink of her milk." And when later on Lukardis was fetched by the Sisters, she was " found reclining on her couch. And for three days and nights she took neither food nor drink, and could not see the light of day. And as a precaution, since her death was feared, Extreme Unction was administered to her. And, later on, the Sister who had seen her standing in the Chapel, gradually drew the whole story from her." [2]

" After she had lain, very weak, and, as it were, in a state of contracture, for eleven years, it happened that, about the ninth hour of one Good Friday, the natural bodily heat and colour forsook her; she seemed nowise to breathe; her wounds bled more than usual; she appeared to be dead. And her fellow-Sisters wept greatly. Yet about Vesper-time she opened her eyes and began to move; and her companions were wondrously consoled. And then in the Easter night, about the hour of Christ's Resurrection, as, with the other sick Sisters, she lay in her bed placed so as to be able to hear the Divine

---

[1] *Analecta*, pp. 314, 315.   [2] *Vita, loc. cit.* pp. 317, 319.

Office, she felt all her limbs to be as it were suffused with a most refreshing dew. And straightway she saw stretched down to her from Heaven a hand, as it were of the Blessed Virgin, which stroked her wounds and all the painful places, the ligaments and joints of her members, gently and compassionately. After which she straightway felt how that all her members, which before had for so long been severely contracted, and how the knots, formed by the ligaments (*nervi*), were being efficaciously resolved and equally distended, so that she considered herself freed from her hard bondage. She arose unaided from her couch, proceeded to the near-by entrance to the Choir, and prostrated herself there, in fervent orison, with her arms outstretched in cross-form, for a very long hour. And then, commanded by the Abbess to rise, she readily arose without help, stood with pleasure, and walked whithersoever she would." "At all times she ever suffered more from the cold than any of her companions." [1]

"As, during those eleven years that she lay like one paralyzed, she was wont, on every Friday, to lie with her arms expanded as though on the Cross, and her feet one on the top of the other; so, after the Lord had so wonderfully raised her on that Paschal day, she, on every Friday and every Lenten day, would stand erect with her arms outstretched, crosswise, and, without any support, on one foot only, with the other foot planted upon its fellow, from the hour of noon to that of Vespers."—"Whilst she was still uncured, and required some delicate refection which the Convent could not afford, there came to her," one day, "the most loving Infant, bearing in His Hand the leg of a chicken, newly roasted, and begging her to eat it for His sake." She did so, and was wonderfully strengthened. Apparently late on in her life "they procured, with much labour and diligence, all kinds of drinkables from different and even from distant places for her. But she, having tasted any one of them, would straightway shake her head, close her lips, and then declare that she could not drink it up." "However delicious in itself, it seemed to be so much gall-and wormwood when applied to her mouth." [2]

And if we look, not at seemingly childish fantasticalness in certain mystical lives, but at the later state of shattered health and apparently weakened nerve- and will-power which appears

---

[1] *Vita*, pp. 319, 320.   [2] *Ibid., loc. cit.* pp. 327, 334, 352.

so frequently to be the price paid for the definitely ecstatic type of religion, even where it has been spiritually fruitful, our anxiety is readily renewed. Look at the nine, possibly thirteen, last years of Catherine's, or at the last period of St. Margaret Mary's life; note the similar cases of SS. Maria Magdalena de Pazzi and Juliana Falconieri. And we have a figure of all but pure suffering and passivity in St. Lidwina of Schiedam (1380–1433), over which M. Huysmans has managed to be so thoroughly morbid.

(2) And if such lives strike us as too exceptional to be taken, with whatever deductions, as a case in point, we can find a thoroughly fair instance in the life of Father Isaac Hecker. Here we have a man of extraordinary breadth, solidity, and activity of mind and character, and whose mysticism is of the most sober and harmonious kind. Yet his close companion and most faithful chronicler, Father Walter Elliott, tells us : " From severe colds, acute headaches, and weakness of the digestive organs, Father Hecker was at all times a frequent sufferer. But, towards the end of the year 1871, his headaches became much more painful, his appetite forsook him, and sleeplessness and excitability of the nervous system were added to his other ailments. Remedies of every kind were tried, but without permanent relief. By the summer of 1872 he was wholly incapacitated." " The physical sufferings of those last sixteen " (out of the sixty-nine) " years of his life were never such as to impair his mental soundness . . . though his organs of speech were sometimes too slow for his thoughts." His digestion and nervous system had been impaired by excessive abstinence in early manhood, and by excessive work in later life, " till at last the body struck work altogether. During the sixteen years of his illness every symptom of bodily illness was aggravated by the least attention to community affairs or business matters, and also by interior trials," although he still managed, by heroic efforts, at times directly to serve his congregation and to write some remarkable papers. Yet this state continued, practically unbroken, up to the end, on December 22, 1888.[1] And although the various proximate causes, indicated by Father Elliott, had no doubt been operative here, there can, in view of the numerous similar cases, be no question that the most fundamental of the reasons of this general condition of health was his strongly

---

[1] *The Life of Father Hecker*, by the Rev. Walter Elliott, New York, 1894, pp. 371, 372, 418.

mystical type and habit of mind and his corresponding psycho-physical organization.

(3) In view of those fantasticalnesses and of these exhaustions, we cannot but ask whether these things are not a terrible price to pay for such states? whether such states should not be disallowed by all solid morality, and should not prompt men of sense to try and stamp them out? And, above all, we seem placed once more, with added anxiety, before the question whether what is liable to end in such sad general incapacitation was not, from the first, directly productive of, and indeed simply produced by, some merely subjective, simply psycho-physical abnormality and morbidness?

(4) Three points here call for consideration. Let us, for one thing, never forget that physical health is not the true end of human life, but only one of its most important means and conditions. The ideal man is not, primarily and directly, a physical machine, perfect as such in its development and function, to which would be tacked on, as a sort of concomitant or means, the mental, moral, and spiritual life and character. But the ideal man is precisely this latter life and character, with the psycho-physical organism sustained and developed in such, and only such, a degree, direction, and combination, as may make it the best possible substratum, stimulus, instrument, material, and expression for and of that spiritual personality.[1] Hence, the true question here is not whether such a type of life as we are considering exacts a serious physical tribute or not, but whether the specifically human effects and fruits of that life are worth that cost.

No one denies that mining, or warfare, or hospital work, both spiritual and medical, involve grave risks to life, nor that the preparation of many chemicals is directly and inevitably injurious to health. Yet no one thinks of abolishing such occupations or of blaming those who follow them, and rightly so; for instant death may and should be risked, the slow but certain undermining of the physical health may be laudably embarked on, if only the mind and character are not damaged, and if the end to be attained is found

---

[1] Robert Browning, in *Rabbi Ben Ezra*, viii; Matthew Arnold, in *Culture and Anarchy*, 21; Prof. James Seth, in *A Study of Ethical Principles*, 1894, pp. 260–262; and Prof. Percy Gardner, in *Oxford at the Cross Roads*, 1903, pp. 12–14, have all admirably insisted upon this most important point.

to be necessary or seriously helpful, and unattainable by other means.

The simple fact, then, of frequent and subsequent, or even of universal and concomitant ill-health in such mystical cases, or even the proof of this ill-health being a direct consequence or necessary condition of that mystical life, can but push back the debate, and simply raises the question as to the serious value of that habit and activity. Only a decision adverse to that serious value would constitute those facts into a condemnation of that activity itself.

And, next, it must be plain to any one endowed with an appreciable dose of the mystical sense, and with a sufficiently large knowledge of human nature and of religious apprehension in the past and present,—that, if it is doubtless possible quite erroneously to treat all men as having a considerable element of mysticism in them, and hence to strain and spoil souls belonging to one of the other types : it is equally possible to starve those that possess this element in an operative degree. Atrophy is as truly a malady as plethora.

And here the question is an individual one : would that particular temperament and psycho-physical organism congenial to Sister Lukardis, to Catherine Fiesca Adorna, to Marguerite Marie Alacocque, and to Isaac Hecker, have—taking the whole existence and output together—produced more useful work, and have apprehended and presented more of abiding truth, had their ecstatic states or tendencies been, if possible, absent or suppressed? Does not this type of apprehension, this, as it were, incubation, harmonization, and vivifying of their otherwise painfully fragmentary and heavy impressions, stand out,—in their central, creative periods,—as the one thoroughly appropriate means and form of their true self-development and self-expression, and of such an apprehension and showing forth of spiritual truth as to them,—to them and not to you and me,—was possible? And if we are bound to admit that, even in such cases, ecstasy appears, psycho-physically, as a kind of second state, and that these personalities find or regain their fullest joy and deepest strength only in and from such a state; yet we know too that such ecstasy is not, as in the trances of hysteria and of other functional disorders, simply discontinuous from the ordinary, primary state of such souls; and that,—again contrary to those *maladif* trances,—whenever the ecstasy answers to the tests insisted upon by the great mystics, viz. a true and valuable ethico-spiritual content and effect, it also, in the long run, leaves the very body strengthened and improved.

And if, after this, their productive period, some of these persons end by losing their psycho-physical health, it is far from unreasonable to suppose that the actual alternative to those ecstasies and this break-up, would, *for them*, have been a lifelong dreary languor and melancholy self-absorption, somewhat after the pattern of Catherine's last ten pre-conversion years. Thus for her, and doubtless for most of the spiritually considerable ecstatics, life was, taken all in all, indefinitely happier, richer, and more fruitful in religious truth and holiness, with the help of those ecstatic states, than it would have been if these states had been absent or could have been suppressed.

And thirdly, here again, even from the point of view of psycho-physical health and its protection, it is precisely the actual practice and, as interpreted by it, the deepest sayings of the standard Christian mystics which are being most powerfully confirmed,—although necessarily by largely new reasons and with important modifications in the analysis and application of their doctrine,—by all that we have gained, during the last forty years, in definite knowledge of the psycho-physical regions and functions of human nature, and, during two centuries and more, in enlargement and precision of our religious-historical outlook.

If we consider the specific health-dangers of this way, we shall find, I think, that their roots are ever two. These dangers, and with them the probability of delusion or at least of spiritual barrenness, always become actual, and often acute, the minute that we allow ourselves to attach a primary and independent importance to the psycho-physical form and means of these things, as against their spiritual-ethical content, suggestions, and end; or that we take the whole man, or at least the whole of the religious man, to consist of the specifically mystical habits and life alone. Now the first of these dangers has been ceaselessly exposed and fought by all the great ethical and Christian mystics of the past, *e. g.* St. John of the Cross and St. Teresa; and the latter has been ever enforced by the actual practice, as social religionists, of these same mystics, even if and when some of their sayings, or the logical drift of their speculative system, left insufficient room or no intrinsic necessity and function for such things.

(5) And everything that has happened and is happening in the world of psychological and philosophical research, in the world of historico-critical investigation into the past history and modalities of religion, and in the world of our own present religious experience and requirements, has but brought to light fresh facts, forces, and connections, in proof both of the right and irreplaceableness of the Mystical element in life and religion, and of the reality and constant presence of these its two dangers. For, as to these dangers, we now know, with extraordinary clearness and certainty, how necessary, constant and far-reaching is, on its phenomenal surface, the auto-suggestive, mono-ideistic power and mechanism of the mind; yet how easily, in some states, too much can be made of such vivid apprehensions and quasi-sensible imagings of invisible reality,—things admirable as means, ruinous as ends. And we also know, with an astonishing universality of application, how great a multiplicity in unity is necessarily presented by every concrete object and by every mental act and emotional state of every sane human being throughout every moment of his waking life; and how this unity is actually constituted and measured by the multiplicity of the materials and by the degree of their harmonization.—Hence, not the absence of the Mystical element, but the presence both of it and of the other constituents of religion, will turn out to be the safeguard of our deepest life and of its sanity, a sanity which demands a balanced fulness of the soul's three fundamental pairs of activities : sensible perception and picturing memory; reflection, speculative and analytic; and emotion and volition, all issuing in interior and exterior acts, and these latter, again, providing so much fresh material and occasions for renewed action and for a growing unification in an increasing variety, on and on.

The metaphysical and faith questions, necessarily raised by the phenomenal facts and mechanisms here considered, but which cannot be answered at this level, will be discussed in a later chapter. Here we can but once more point out, in conclusion, that no amount of admitted or demonstrated auto-suggestion or mono-ideism in the phenomenal reaches and mechanism of the mind decides, of itself, anything whatsoever about, and still less against, the objective truth and spiritual value of the ultimate causes, dominant ideas, and final results of the process; nor as to whether and how far the whole great movement is, at bottom, occasioned and directed by the

Supreme Spirit, God, working, in and through man, towards
man's apprehension and manifestation of Himself.[1]

[1] I owe much clearness of conception as to the function of auto-suggestion and mono-ideism to the very remarkable paper of Prof. Emile Boutroux, " La Psychologie du Mysticisme," in the *Bulletin de l'Institut Psychologique International*, Paris, 1902, pp. 9–26 : Engl. tr. in the *International Journal of Ethics*, Philadelphia, Jan. 1908. There are also many most useful facts and reflections in Prof. Henri Joly's *Psychology of the Saints*, Engl. tr., 1898, pp. 64–117.

CHAPTER X

THE MAIN LITERARY SOURCES OF CATHERINE'S CONCEPTIONS

INTRODUCTORY.

1. *The main literary sources of Catherine's teaching are four.*

The main literary sources of Catherine's conceptions can be grouped under four heads : the New Testament, Pauline and Johannine writings ; the Christian Neo-Platonist, Areopagite books ; and the Franciscan, Jacopone da Todi's teachings. And here, as in all cases of such partial dependence, we have to distinguish between the apparently accidental occasions (her seemingly fortuitous acquaintance with these particular writings), and the certainly necessary causes (the intrinsic requirements of her own mind and soul, and its special reactions under, and transformations of, these materials and stimulations). And during this latter process this mind's original trend itself undergoes, in its turn, not only much development, but even some modification. She would no doubt owe her close knowledge of the first two sets of writings to the Augustinian Canonesses, (her sister Limbania amongst them,) and to their Augustinian-Pauline tradition ; her acquaintance with the third set, to her Dominican cousin ; and her intimacy with the fourth, to the Franciscans of the Hospital. Yet only her own spiritual affinity for similar religious states and ideals, and her already at least partial experience of them, could ever have made these writings to her what they actually became : direct stimulations, indeed considerable elements and often curiously vivid expressions, of her own immediate interior life.

2. *Plan of the following study of these sources.*

I shall, in this chapter, first try to draw out those characteristics of each group, which were either specially accepted or transformed, neglected or supplanted by her, and carefully to note the particular nature of these her reactions and refashion-

ings. And I shall end up by a short account of what she
and all four sets have got in common, and of what she has
brought, as a gift of her own, to that common stock which had
given her so much. And since her distinct and direct use of
the Pauline and Johannine writings is quite certain, whereas all
her knowledge of Neo-Platonism seems to have been mediated
by pseudo-Dionysius alone, and all her Franciscanism appears,
as far as literary sources go, to take its rise from Jacopone, I
shall give four divisions to her chief literary sources, and a
fifth section to the stream common to them all.[1]

I. THE PAULINE WRITINGS: THE TWO SOURCES OF
THEIR PRE-CONVERSION ASSUMPTIONS; CATHERINE'S
PREPONDERANT ATTITUDE TOWARDS EACH POSITION.

It is well that the chronological order requires us to begin
with St. Paul, for he is probably, if not the most extensive,
yet the most intense of all these influences upon Catherine's
mind. I here take the points of his experience and teaching
which thus concern us in the probable order of their development in the Apostle's own consciousness,—his pre-conversion
assumptions and positions, first, and the convictions gained
at and after his conversion or clarified last;[2] and under each
heading I shall group together, once for all, the chief reactions
of Catherine's religious consciousness.

Now those Pauline pre-conversion assumptions and positions
come from two chief sources—Palestinian, Rabbinical Judaism
(for he was the disciple of the Pharisee, Gamaliel, at Jerusalem),
and a Hellenistic religiousness closely akin to, though not
derived from, Philo (for he had been born in the intensely
Hellenistic Cilician city Tarsus, at that time a most important seat of Greek learning in general and of the Stoic
philosophy in particular). And we shall find that Catherine

[1] In Chapter XII, § iv, I shall show reason for strongly suspecting
that Catherine possessed some knowledge, probably derived from an
intermediate Christian source, of certain passages in Plato's Dialogues.
But the influence of these passages can, in any case, only be traced in
her Purgatorial doctrine, and had better be discussed together with this
doctrine itself.

[2] My chief obligations are here to Prof. H. J. Holtzmann's *Lehrbuch
der Neutestamentlichen Theologie*, 1897, Vol. II, pp. 1–225: "Der
Paulinismus"; but I have also learnt from Estius and Dr. Lightfoot,
and from my own direct studies in St. Paul, Philo, and Plato.

appropriates especially this, his Hellenistic element; indeed, that at times she sympathizes rather with the still more intensely Hellenistic attitude exemplified by Philo, than with the limitations introduced by St. Paul.

1. *St. Paul's Anthropology in general.*

If we take the Pauline Anthropology first, we at once come upon a profoundly dualistic attitude.

(1) There is, in general, "the outer" and "the inner" man, 2 Cor. iv, 16; and the latter is not the exclusive privilege of the redeemed,—the contrast is that between the merely natural individual and the moral personality. And this contrast, foreign to the ancient Hebrews, is first worked out, with clear consciousness, by Plato, who, *e. g.*, in his *Banquet*, causes one of the characters to say : "Socrates has thrown this Silenus-like form around himself externally, as in the case of those Silenus-statues which enclose a statuette of Apollo; but, when he is opened, how full is he found to be of temperance within"; and who treats this contrast as typical of the dualism inherent to all human life here on earth.[1]—This contrast exists throughout Catherine's teaching as regards the thing itself, although her terms are different.   She has, for reasons which will appear presently, no one constant term for "the inner man," but "the outer man" is continuously styled "la umanità."

(2) The "outer man" consists for St. Paul of the body's earthly material, "the flesh"; and of the animating principle of the flesh, "the psyche," which is inseparably connected with that flesh, and which dies for good and all at the death of the latter; whereas the form of "the body" is capable of resuscitation, and is then filled out by a finer material, "glory."[2]— Here Catherine has no precise or constant word for the "psyche"; her "umanità" generally stands for the "psyche" *plus* body and flesh, all in one; and her "anima" practically always means part or the whole of "the inner man," and mostly stands for "mind."   And there is no occasion for her to reflect upon any distinction between the form and the matter of the body, since she nowhere directly busies herself with the resurrection.

The "inner man" consists for St. Paul in the Mind, the Heart, and the Conscience.   The Mind (*noûs*), corresponding roughly to our theoretical and practical Reason, has a certain tendency towards God : "The invisible things of God are

---

[1] *Symposium*, 216*e*.   [2] 1 Cor. xv, 35-53.

seen by the mind in the works of creation," Rom. i, 20; and
there is " a law of the mind " which is fought by " the law of
sin," Rom. vii, 23; and this, although there is also a " mind
of the flesh," Col. ii, 18; " a reprobate mind," Rom. i, 28;
and a " renovation of the mind," Rom. xii, 2.—Catherine
clings throughout most closely to the Pauline use of the term,
as far as that use is favourable : note how she perceives
invisible things " colla mente mia."

The Heart is even more accessible to the divine influence,—
at least, it is to it that God gives " the first fruits of the Spirit "
and " the Spirit of His Son, crying Abba, Father," Gal. iv, 6;
2 Cor. i, 22. As an organ of immediate perception it is so
parallel to the Mind, that we can hear of " eyes of the heart ";
yet it is also the seat of feeling, of will, and of moral consciousness, Eph. i, 18; 2 Cor. ii, 4; 1 Cor. iv, 5; Rom. ii, 15. It
can stand for the inner life generally; or, like the Mind, it
can become darkened and impenitent; whilst again, over the
heart God's love is poured out, God's peace keeps guard, and
we believe with the heart, 1 Cor. xiv, 25; Rom. i, 21; ii, 5;
v, 5; Phil. iv, 7; Rom. x, 9.—All this again, as far as it is
favourable, is closely followed by Catherine; indeed the persistence with which she comes back to certain effects wrought
upon her heart by the Spirit, Christ,—effects which some of
her followers readily interpreted as so many physical miracles,
—was no doubt occasioned or stimulated by 2 Cor. iii, 3, " Be
ye an epistle of Christ, written by the Spirit of the living
God . . . upon the fleshly tables of the heart."

And Conscience, " Syneidēsis "—that late Greek word introduced by St. Paul as a technical term into the Christian
vocabulary—includes our " conscience," but is as comprehensive as our " consciousness."—Catherine practically never
uses the term : no doubt because, in the narrower of the two
senses which had become the ordinary one, it was too
predominantly ethical to satisfy her overwhelmingly religious
preoccupations.

(3) Now, with regard to this whole dualism of the " outer "
and the " inner man," its application to the resurrection of
the body in St. Paul and in St. Catherine shall occupy us in
connection with her Eschatology; here I would but indicate
the two Pauline moods or attitudes towards the earthly body,
and Catherine's continuous reproduction of but one of these.
For his magnificent conception of the Christian society,
in which each person, by a different specific gift and duty,

co-operates towards the production of an organic whole, a whole which in return develops and dignifies those its constituents, is worked out by means of the image of the human earthly body, in which each member is a necessary part and constituent of the complete organism, which is greater than, and which gives full dignity to, each and all these its factors (1 Cor. xii). And he thus, in his most deliberate and systematic mood, shows very clearly how deeply he has realized the dignity of the human body, as the instrument both for the development of the soul itself and for the work of that soul in and upon the visible world.

But in his other mood, which remains secondary and sporadic throughout his writings, his attitude is acutely dualistic. His one direct expression of it occurs in 2 Cor. v, 1–4 : " For we know that, if our earthly house of this tent be dissolved, we have a building of God, a house not made with hands, eternal in the heavens. For in this also we groan, desiring to be clothed upon with our habitation that is from heaven. We who are in this tabernacle do groan, being burthened." Now this passage is undoubtedly modelled by St. Paul upon the Book of Wisdom, ix, 15 : " For the corruptible body is a load upon the soul, and the earthly habitation presseth down the mind that museth upon many things." And this latter saying again is as certainly formed upon Plato (*Phaedo*, 81 c) : " It behoves us to think of the body as oppressive and heavy and earthlike and visible. And hence the soul, being of such a nature as we have seen, when possessing such a body, is both burthened and dragged down again into the visible world." [1] And it is this conception of the Hellenic Athenian Plato (about 380 B.C.) which, passing through the Hellenistic Alexandrian Jewish Wisdom-writer (80 B.C. ?) and then through the Hellenistically tinctured ex-Rabbi, Paul of Tarsus (52 A.D.), still powerfully, indeed all but continuously, influences the mind of the Genoese Christian Catherine, especially during the years from A.D. 1496 to 1510.

Catherine's still more pessimistic figure of the body as a prison-house and furnace of purification for the soul, is no doubt the resultant of suggestions received, probably in part through intermediary literature, from the following three

---

[1] E. Grafe, " Verhältniss der paulinischen Schriften zur Sapientia Salomonis," in *Theol. Abhandlungen Carl von Weizsäcker Gewidmet*, 1892, pp. 274–276.

passages:—(1) Plato, in his *Cratylus* (400 B.C.), makes Socrates say: " Some declare that the body (*sōma*) is the grave (*sēma*) of the soul, as she finds herself at present. The Orphite poets seem to have invented the appellation : they held that the soul is thus paying the penalty of sin, and that the body is an enclosure which may be likened to a prison, in which the soul is enclosed until the penalty is paid." (2) St. Matt. v, 25, 26, gives Our Lord's words : " Be thou reconciled with thine adversary whilst he is still with thee on the way . . . lest the Judge hand thee over to the prison-warder, and thou be cast into prison. . . . Thou shalt not go forth thence, until thou hast paid the uttermost farthing." And (3) St. Paul declares, 1 Cor. iii, 15 : " Every man's work shall be tested by fire. If any man's work shall be burned, he shall suffer loss : but he himself shall be saved; yet so as through fire." These three passages combined will readily suggest, to a soul thirsting for purification and possessed of an extremely sensitive psycho-physical organization with its attendant liability to fever heats, the picture of the body as a flame-full prison-house,—a purgatory of the soul.

2. *St. Paul's conception of " Spirit."*

A very difficult complication and varying element is introduced into St. Paul's Anthropology by the term into which he has poured all that is most original, deepest, most deliberate and abiding in his teaching,—the Spirit, " Pneuma." For somewhat as he uses the term " Sarx," the flesh, both in its loose popular signification of " mankind in general "; and in a precise, technical sense of " the matter which composes the earthly body "; so also he has, occasionally, a loose popular use of the term " spirit," when it figures as but a fourth parallel to " mind," " heart," and " conscience "; and, usually, a very strict and technical use of it, when it designates the Spirit, God Himself.

(1) Now it is precisely in the latter case that his doctrine attains its fullest depth and its greatest difficulty. For here the Spirit, the Pneuma, is, strictly speaking, only one—the Spirit of God, God Himself, in His action either outside or inside the human mind, Noûs. And in such passages of St. Paul, where man seems to possess a distinct pneuma of his own, by far the greater number only apparently contradict this doctrine. For in some, so in 1 Cor. ii, the context is dominated by a comparison between the divine and the human consciousness, so that, in v. 11, man's Noûs is

designated Pneuma, and in v. 16, and Rom. xi, 34, the Lord's
Pneuma is called His Noûs.   And the " spirit of the world "
contrasted here, in v. 11, with the " Spirit of God," is a still
further deliberate laxity of expression, similar to that of
Satan as " the God of this world," 2 Cor. iv, 4.   In other
passages,—so Rom. viii, 16; i, 9; viii, 10, and even in 1 Cor.
v, 5 (the " spirit " of the incestuous Corinthian which is to be
saved),—we seem to have " spirit " either as the mind in so far
as the object of the Spirit's communications, or as the mind
transformed by the Spirit's influence.   And if we can hear of
a " defilement of the spirit," 2 Cor. vii, 1, we are also told
that we can forget the fact of the body being the temple of
the holy Spirit, 1 Cor. vi, 19; and that this temple's profana-
tion " grieves the holy Spirit," Eph. iv, 30. Very few, sporadic,
and short passages remain in which " the spirit of man "
cannot clearly be shown to have a deliberately derivative
sense.

Catherine, in this great matter, completely follows St. Paul.
For she too has loosely-knit moods and passages, in which
" spirito " appears as a natural endowment of her own,
parallel to, or identical with, the " mente."   But when
speaking strictly, and in her intense moods, she means by
"spirito," the Spirit, Christ, Love, God, a Power which, though
in its nature profoundly distinct and different from her entire
self-seeking self, can and does come to dwell within, and to
supplant, this self.   Indeed her highly characteristic saying,
" my Me is God," with her own explanations of it, expresses,
if pressed, even more than this.   In these moods, the term
" mente " is usually absent, just as in St. Paul.

Now in his formally doctrinal *Loci*, St. Paul defines the
Divine Pneuma and the human Sarx, not merely as ontologically contrary substances, but as keenly conflicting, ethically
contradictory principles.   An anti-spiritual power, lust,
possesses the flesh and the whole outer man, whilst, in an
indefinitely higher degree and manner, the Spirit, which finds
an echo in the mind, the inner man, is a spontaneous, counter-
working force; and these two energies fight out the battle in
man, and for his complete domination, Rom. vi, 12–14; vii,
22, 23; viii, 4–13.   And this dualistic conception is in close
affinity to all that was noblest in the Hellenistic world of St.
Paul's own day; but is in marked contrast to the pre-exilic,
specifically Jewish Old Testament view, where we have but
the contrast between the visible and transitory, and the

Invisible and Eternal; and the consciousness of the weakness
and fallibility of " flesh and blood." And this latter is the
temper of mind that dominates the Synoptic Gospels : " The
spirit indeed is willing, but the flesh is weak "; and " Father,
forgive them, for they know not what they do," are here the
divinely serene and infinitely fruitful leading notes.—And
Catherine, on this point, is habitually on the Synoptist side :
man is, for her, far more weak and ignorant than forcibly and
deliberately wicked. Yet her detailed intensity towards the
successive cloaks of self-love is still, as it were, a shadow and
echo of the fierce, and far more massive, flesh-and-spirit
struggle in St. Paul.

3. *The Angry and the Loving God.*

And, as against the intense wickedness of man, we find in
St. Paul an emphatic insistence—although this is directly
derived from the Old Testament and Rabbinical tradition—
upon the anger and indignation of God, Rom. ii, 8, and
frequently.—Here Catherine is in explicit contrast with him,
in so far as the anger would be held to stand for an emotion
not proceeding from love and not ameliorative in its aim and
operation. This attitude sprang no doubt, in part, from the
strong influence upon her of the Dionysian teaching concerning
the negative character of evil; possibly still more from her
continuous pondering of the text, " Like as a father pitieth
his children, so the Lord pitieth them that fear Him.
For He knoweth our frame; He remembereth that we
are dust," Ps. ciii, 13, 14,—where she dwells upon the fact
that we are all His children rather than upon the fact that
we do not all fear Him; but certainly, most of all, from
her habitual dwelling upon the other side of St. Paul's
teaching, that concerning the Love of God.

Now the depth and glow of Paul's faith and love go
clearly back to his conversion, an event which colours and
influences all his feeling and teaching for some thirty-four
years, up to the end. And similarly Catherine's conversion-
experience has been found by us to determine the sequence
and all the chief points of her Purgatorial teaching, some
thirty-seven years after that supreme event.

Already Philo had, under Platonic influence, believed in an
Ideal Man, a Heavenly Man; had identified him with the
Logos, the Word or Wisdom of God; and had held him to be
in some way ethereal and luminous,—never arriving at either
a definitely personal or a simply impersonal conception of

this at one time intermediate Being, at another time this supreme attribute of God. St. Paul, under the profound impression of the Historic Christ and the great experience on the road to Damascus, perceives the Risen, Heavenly Jesus as possessed of a luminous, ethereal body, a body of " glory," Acts xxii, 11. And this Christ is, for St. Paul, identical with " the Spirit " : " the Lord is the Spirit," 2 Cor. iii, 17 ; and " to be in Christ " and " Christ is in us " are parallel terms to those of " to be in the Spirit " and " the Spirit is within us " respectively. In all four cases we get Christ or the Spirit conceived as an element, as it were an ocean of ethereal light, in which souls are plunged and which penetrates them. In Catherine we have, at her conversion, this same perception and conception of Spirit as an ethereal light, and of Christ as Spirit; and up to the end she more and more appears to herself to bathe, to be submerged in, an ocean of light, which, at the same time, fills her within and penetrates her through and through.

But again, and specially since his conversion, St. Paul thinks of God as loving, as Love, and this conception henceforth largely supplants the Old Testament conception of the angry God. This loving God is chiefly manifested through the loving Christ : indeed the love of Christ and the love of God are the same thing. And this Christ-Love dwells within us.[1] And Catherine, since her mind has perceived Love to be the central character of God, and has adopted fire as love's fullest image, cannot but hold,—God and Love and Christ and Spirit being all one and the same thing,—that Christ-Spirit-Fire is in her and she in It. The yellow light-image, which all but alone typifies God's friendliness in the Bible, is thus turned into a red fire-image. And yet this latter in so far retains with Catherine something of its older connotation of anger, that the Fire and Heat appear in her teaching more as symbols of the suffering caused by the opposition of man's at least partial impurity to the Spirit, Christ, Love, God, and of the pain attendant upon that Spirit's action, even where it can still purify; whereas the Light and Illumination mostly express the peaceful penetration of man's spirit by God's Spirit, and the blissful gain accruing from such penetration.

[1] " The love of Christ," Rom. viii, 35, is identical with " the love of God which is in Christ Jesus," Rom. viii, 39. " The Spirit of God dwelleth in you," Rom. viii, 9; 1 Cor. iii, 16. " I live, not I : but Christ liveth in me," Gal. ii, 20.

4. *The Risen Christ and the Heavenly Adam.*

St. Paul dwells continuously upon the post-earthly, the Risen Christ, and upon Him in His identity with the pre-earthly, the Heavenly Man : so that the historical Jesus tends to become, all but for the final acts in the Supper-room and upon the Cross, a transitory episode ;—a super-earthly bio-graphy all but supplants the earthly one, since His death and resurrection and their immediate contexts are all but the only two events dwelt upon, and form but the two constituents of one inseparable whole.—Here Catherine is deeply Pauline in her striking non-occupation with the details of the earthly life (the scene with the Woman at the Well being the single exception), and in her continuous insistence upon Christ as the life-giving Spirit. Indeed, even the death is strangely absent. There is but the one doubtful contrary instance, in any case a quite early and sporadic one, of the Vision of the Bleeding Christ. The fact is that, in her teaching, the self-donation of God in general, in His mysterious love for each individual soul, and of Christ in particular, in His Eucharistic presence as our daily food, take all their special depth of tenderness from her vivid realization of the whole teaching, temper, life, and death of Jesus Christ; and that teaching derives its profundity of feeling only from all this latter complexus of facts and convictions.

S. P.

5. *Reconciliation, Justification, Sanctification.*

(1) St. Paul has two lines of thought concerning Reconciliation. In the objective, juridical, more Judaic conception, the attention is concentrated on the one moment of Christ's death, and the consequences appear as though instantaneous and automatic; in the other, the subjective, ethical, more Hellenistic conception, the attention is spread over the whole action of the Christ's incarnational self-humiliation, and the consequences are realized only if and when we strive to imitate Him,—they are a voluntary and continuous process. Catherine's fundamental conversion-experience and all her later teachings attach her Reconciliation to the entire act of ceaseless Divine " ecstasy," self-humiliation, and redemptive immanence in Man, of which the whole earthly life and death of Christ are the centre and culmination; but though the human soul's corresponding action is conceived as continuous, once it has begun, she loves to dwell upon this whole action as itself the gift of God and the consequence of His prevenient act.

(2) As to Justification, we have again, in St. Paul, a pre-

ponderatingly Jewish juridical conception of adoption, in which a purely vicarious justice and imputed righteousness seem to be taught; and an ethical conception of immanent justice, based on his own experience and expressed by means of Hellenistic forms, according to which " the love of God hath been shed abroad in our hearts," Rom. v, 5. And he often insists strenuously upon excluding every human merit from the moment and act of justification, insisting upon its being a " free gift " of God.—Catherine absorbs herself in the second, ethical conception, and certainly understands this love of God as primarily God's, the Spirit's, Christ's love, as Love Itself poured out in our hearts; and she often breaks out into angry protests against the very suggestion of any act, or part of an act, dear to God, proceeding from her natural or separate self, indeed, if we press her expressions, from herself at all.

(3) As to Sanctification, St. Paul has three couples of contrasted conceptions. The first couple conceives the Spirit, either Old Testament-wise, as manifesting and accrediting Itself in extraordinary, sudden, sporadic, miraculous gifts and doings—e. g. in ecstatic speaking with tongues; or,—and this is the more frequent and the decisive conception,—as an abiding, equable penetration and spiritual reformation of its recipient. Here the faithful " live and walk in the spirit," are " driven by the spirit," " serve God in the spirit," are " temples of the Spirit," Gal. v, 25; Rom. viii, 14; vii, 6; I Cor. vi, 19: the Spirit has become the creative source of a supernatural character-building.[1]—Here Catherine, in contrast to most of her friends, who are wedded to the first view, is strongly attached to the second view, perhaps the deepest of St. Paul's conceptions.

The second couple conceives Sanctification either juridically and moves dramatically from act to act,—the Sacrifice on the Cross and the Resurrection of the Son of God, the sentence of Justification and the Adoption as sons of God; or ethically, and presupposes everywhere continuous processes,—beginning with the reception of the Spirit, and ending with " the Lord is the Spirit."—Here Catherine has curiously little of the dramatic and prominently personal conception: only in the imperfect soul's acutely painful moment, of standing before and seeing God immediately after death, do we get one link in this chain, in a somewhat modified form. For the rest,

---

[1] H. J. Holtzmann, *op. cit.* Vol. II, p. 145.

the ethical and continuous conception is present practically throughout her teaching, but in a curious, apparently paradoxical form, to be noticed in a minute.

And the third couple either treats Sanctification as, at each moment of its actual presence, practically infallible and complete : " We who died to sin, how shall we any longer live therein ? " " Freed from sin, ye became servants of righteousness " ; " now we are discharged from the law, having died, to that wherein we were beholden ; so that we serve in newness of spirit " ; " they that are after the flesh, do mind the things of the flesh ; but they that are after the Spirit, the things of the Spirit," Rom. vi, 2, 18 ; vii, 6 ; viii, 5. Or it considers Sanctification as only approximately complete, so long as man has to live here below, not only in the Spirit, Rom. viii, 9, but also in the flesh, Gal. ii, 20. The faithful have indeed crucified the flesh once for all, Gal. v, 24 : yet they have continually to mortify their members anew, Col. iii, 5, and by the Spirit to destroy the works of the flesh, Rom. viii, 13. The " fear of the Lord," " of God," does not cease to be a motive for the sanctified, 2 Cor. v, 11 ; vii, 1. To " walk in the Spirit," " in the light," has to be insisted on (1 Thess. v, 4–8 ; Rom. xiii, 11–14), as long as the eternal day has not yet arisen for us. And even in Romans, chapter vi, we find admonitions, vv. 12, 13, 19, which, if we press the other conception, are quite superfluous.[1]

And here Catherine, in her intense sympathy with each of these contrasted conceptions, offers us a combination of both in a state of unstable equilibrium and delicate tension. I take it that it is not her immensely impulsive and impatient temperament, nor survivals of the Old Testament idea as to instantaneousness being the special characteristic of divine action, but her deep and noble sense of the givenness and pure grace of religion, and of God's omnipotence being, if possible, exceeded only by His overflowing, self-communicative love, which chiefly determine her curious presentation and emotional experience of spiritual growth and life as a movement composed of sudden shiftings upwards, with long apparently complete pauses in between. For here this form (of so many instants, of which each is complete in itself) stands for her as the least inadequate symbol, as a kind of shattered mirror, not of time at all, but of eternity ; whilst the succession and difference between these instants indicates a growth in

[1] Holtzmann, *op. cit.* Vol. II, pp. 151, 152.

the apprehending soul, which has, in reality, been proceeding also in between these instants and not only during them. And this remarkable scheme presents her conviction that, in principle, the work of the all-powerful, all-loving Spirit cannot, of itself, be other than final and complete, and yet that, as a matter of fact, it never is so, in weak, self-deceptive, and variously resisting man, but ever turns out to require a fresh and deeper application. And this succession of sudden jerks onwards and upwards, after long, apparently complete pauses between them, gives to her fundamentally ethical and continuous conception something of the look of the forensic, dramatic series, with its separate acts,—a series which would otherwise be all but unrepresented in her picture of the soul's life on this side of death and of its life (immediately after its vivid sight of God and itself, and its act of free-election) in the Beyond.

6. *Pauline Social Ethics.*

As to Social Ethics, St. Paul's worldward movement is strongly represented in Catherine's teaching. Her great sayings as to God being servable not only in the married state, but in a camp of (mercenary) soldiers; and as to her determination violently to appropriate the monk's cowl, should this his state be necessary to the attainment of the highest love of God, are full of the tone of Rom. xiv, 14, 20, "nothing is unclean of itself : save that to him who accounteth anything to be unclean, to him it is unclean,"—" all things are clean "; and of I Cor. x, 26, 28, " the earth is the Lord's, and the fulness thereof." And her sense of her soul's positive relation to nature, *e. g.* trees, was no doubt in part awakened by that striking passage, Rom. viii, 19, " the expectation of the creation waiteth the revealing of the sons of God; for the creation was subjected to vanity, not of its own will."

On the other hand, it would be impossible confidently to identify her own attitude concerning marriage with that of St. Paul, since, as we know, her peculiar health and her unhappiness with Giuliano make it impossible to speak here with any certainty of the mature woman's deliberate judgment concerning continence and marriage. Yet her impulsive protestation, in the scene with the monk, against any idea of being debarred by her state from as perfect a love of God as his,—whilst, of course, not in contradiction with the Pauline and generally Catholic positions in the matter, seems to imply an emotional attitude somewhat different from that

of some of the Apostle's sayings. Indeed, in her whole
general and unconscious position as to how a woman should
hold herself in religious things it is interesting to note the
absence of all influence from those Pauline sayings which,
herein like Philo (and indeed the whole ancient world) treat
man alone as " the (direct) image and glory (reflex) of God,"
and the woman as but " the glory (reflex) of the man," 1 Cor.
xi, 7. Everywhere she appears full, on the contrary, of St.
Paul's other (more characteristic and deliberate) strain, according to which, as there is " neither Jew nor Gentile, bond
nor free " before God, so " neither is the woman without the
man, nor the man without the woman, in the Lord," 1 Cor.
xi, 11.—And in social matters generally, Catherine's convert
life and practice shows, in the active mortifications of its first
penitential part, in her persistent great aloofness from all
things of sense as regards her own gratification, and in the
ecstasies and love of solitude which marked the zenith of her
power, a close sympathy with, and no doubt in part a direct
imitation of, St. Paul's Arabian retirement, chastisement of
his body, and lonely concentration upon rapt communion
with God. Yet she as strongly exemplifies St. Paul's other,
the outward movement, the love-impelled, whole-hearted
service of the poorest, world-forgotten, sick and sorrowing
brethren. And the whole resultant rhythmic life has got
such fine spontaneity, emotional and efficacious fulness,
and expansive joy about it, as to suggest at once those
unfading teachings of St. Paul which had so largely occasioned
it,—those hymns in praise of that love " which minds not high
things but condescends to things that are lowly," Rom. xii,
16; " becomes all things to all men," 1 Cor. ix, 22; " rejoices
with them that rejoice, and weeps with them that weep,"
Rom. xii, 15; and which, as the twin love of God and man,
is not only the chief member of the central ethical triad, but,
already here below, itself becomes the subject which exercises
the other two virtues, for it is " love " that " believeth all
things, hopeth all things," even before that eternity in
which love alone will never vanish away, *ibid.* xiii, 7,8 .
Here Catherine with Paul triumphs completely over time :
their actions and teaching are as completely fresh now,
after well-nigh nineteen and four centuries, as when they
first experienced, willed, and uttered them.

7. *Sacramental teachings.*

In Sacramental matters it is interesting to note St. Paul's

close correlation of Baptism and the Holy Eucharist : " All (our fathers) were baptized unto Moses in the cloud and in the sea ; and did all eat the same spiritual meat ; and did all drink the same spiritual drink," 1 Cor. x, 3 ; " in one Spirit were we all baptized into one body, . . . and were all made to drink of one Spirit," Christ, His blood, *ibid*. xii, 13. And Catherine is influenced by these passages, when she represents the soul as hungering for, and drowning itself in, the ocean of spiritual sustenance which is Love, Christ, God : but she attaches the similes, which are distributed by St. Paul among the two Rites, to the Holy Eucharist alone. Baptism had been a grown man's deliberate act in Paul's case,—an act immediately subsequent to, and directly expressive of, his conversion, the culminating experience of his life ; and, as a great Church organizer, he could not but dwell with an equal insistence upon the two chief Sacraments.

Catherine had received baptism as an unconscious infant, and the event lay far back in that pre-conversion time, which was all but completely ousted from her memory by the great experience of some twenty-five years later. And in the latter experience it was (more or less from the first and soon all but exclusively) the sense of a divine encirclement and sustenance, of an addition of love, rather than a consciousness of the subtraction of sins or of a divine purification, that possessed her. In her late, though profoundly characteristic Purgatorial teaching, the soul again plunges into an ocean ; but now, since the soul is rather defiled than hungry, and wills rather to be purified than to be fed, this plunge is indeed a kind of Baptism by Immersion. Yet we have no more the symbol of water, for the long state and effects to which that swift act leads, but we have, instead, fire and light, and, in one place, once again bread and the hunger for bread. And this is no doubt because, in these Purgatorial picturings, it is her conversion-experience of love under the symbols of light and of fire, and her forty years of daily hungering for the Holy Eucharist and Love Incarnate, which furnish the emotional colours and the intellectual outlines.

8. *Eschatological matters*.

In Eschatological matters the main points of contact and of contrast appear to be four ; and three of the differences are occasioned by St. Paul's preoccupation with Christ's Second Coming, with the Resurrection of the body, and with the General Judgment, mostly as three events in close temporal correlation, and likely to occur soon; whilst Catherine abstracts entirely from all three.

(1) Thus St. Paul is naturally busy with the question as to the Time when he shall be with Christ. In 1 Thess. iv, 15, he speaks of " we that are alive, that are left for the coming of the Lord," *i. e.* he expects this event during his own lifetime; whilst in Phil. i, 23, he " desires to depart and be with Christ," *i. e.* he has ceased confidently to expect this coming before his own death. But Catherine dwells exclusively, with this latter conception, upon the moment of death, as that when the soul shall see, and be finally confirmed in its union with, Love, Christ, God; for into her earthly lifetime Love, Christ, God, can and do come, but invisibly, and she may still lose full union with them for ever.

(2) As to the Place, it is notoriously obscure whether St. Paul thinks of it, as do the Old Testament and the Apocalypse, as the renovated earth, or as the sky, or as the intervening space. The risen faithful who " shall be caught up in the clouds to meet the Lord," 1 Thess. iv, 17, seem clearly to be meeting Him, in mid-air, as He descends upon earth; and " Jerusalem above," Gal. iv, 26, may well, as in Apoc. iii, 12; xxi, 2, be conceived as destined to come down upon earth. But Catherine, though she constantly talks of Heaven, Purgatory, Hell, as " places," makes it plain that such " places " are for her but vivid symbols for states of soul. God Himself repeatedly appears in her sayings as " the soul's place "; and it is this " place," the soul's true spiritual birthplace and home which, ever identical and bliss-conferring in itself, is variously experienced by the soul, in exact accordance with its dispositions,—as that profoundly painful, or that joyfully distressing, or that supremely blissful " place " which respectively we call Hell, and Purgatory, and Heaven.

(3) As to the Body, we have already noted St. Paul's doctrine intermediate between the Palestinian and Alexandrian Jewish teaching, that it will rise indeed, but composed henceforth of " glory " and no more of " flesh." It is this his requirement of a body, however spiritual, which underlies his anxiety to be " found clothed, not naked," at and after death, 2 Cor. v, 3. Indeed, in this whole passage, v, 1–4, " our earthly house of this habitation," and " a building of God not made with hands," no doubt mean, respectively, the present body of flesh and the future body of glory; just as the various, highly complex, conceptions of " clothed," " unclothed," " clothed upon,"

refer to the different conditions of the soul with a body of flesh, without a body at all, and with a body of glory.—Now this passage, owing to its extreme complication and abstruseness of doctrine, has come down to us in texts and versions of every conceivable form; and this uncertainty has helped Catherine towards her very free utilization of it.   For she not only, as ever, simply ignores all questions of a risen body, and transfers the concept of a luminous ethereal substance from the body to the soul itself, and refers the " nakedness," " unclothing," " clothing," and " clothing upon " to conditions obtaining, not between the soul and the body, but between the soul and God; but she also, in most cases, takes the nakedness as the desirable state, since typical of the soul's faithful self-exposure to the all-purifying rays of God's light and fire, and interprets the " unclothing " as the penitential stripping from off itself of those pretences and corrupt incrustations which prevent God's blissful action upon it.

(4) And, finally, as to the Judgment, we have in St. Paul a double current,—the inherited Judaistic conception of a forensic retribution; Christ, the divine Judge, externally applying such and such statutory rewards and punishments to such and such good and evil deeds,—so in Rom. ii, 6–10; and the experimental conception, helped on to articulation by Hellenistic influences, of the bodily resurrection and man's whole final destiny as the necessary resultant and manifestation of an internal process, the presence of the Spirit and of the power of God,—so in the later parts of Romans, in Gal. vi, 8, and in 1 Cor. vi, 14; 2 Cor. xiii, 4.—Among Catherine's sayings also we find some passages—but these the less characteristic and mostly of doubtful authenticity,—where reward and punishment, indeed the three " places " themselves, appear as so many separate institutions of God, which get externally applied to certain good and evil deeds.   But these are completely overshadowed in number, sure authenticity, emotional intensity, and organic connection with her other teachings, by sayings of the second type, where the soul's fate is but the necessary consequence of its own deliberate choice and gradually formed dispositions, the result, inseparable since the first from its self-identification with this or that of the various possible will-attitudes towards God.

(5) We can then sum up the main points of contact and of difference between Paul and Catherine, by saying that, in both cases, everything leads up to, or looks back upon, a great

culminating, directly personal experience of shortest clock-time duration, whence all their doctrine, wherever emphatic, is but an attempt to articulate and universalize this original experience; and that if in Paul there remains more of explicit occupation with the last great events of the earthly life of Jesus, yet in both there is the same insistence upon the life-giving Spirit, the eternal Christ, manifesting His inexhaustible power in the transformation of souls, on and on, here and now, into the likeness of Himself.

II. The Johannine Writings.

On moving now from the Pauline to the Johannine writings, we shall find that Catherine's obligations to these latter are but rarely as deep, yet that they cover a wider reach of ideas and images. I take this fresh source of influence under the double heading of the general relations of the Johannine teaching to other, previous or contemporary, conceptions; and of this same teaching considered in itself.[1]

1. *Johannine teaching contrasted with other systems.*

(1) As to the general relations towards other positions, we get here, towards Judaism and Paganism, an emphatic insistence upon the novelty and independence of Christianity as regards not only Paganism, but even the previous Judaism, " The law was given by Moses; grace and truth came by Jesus Christ," i, 17; and upon the Logos, Christ, as " the Light that enlighteneth every man that cometh into the world," " unto his own," *i. e.* men in general; for this Light " was in the world, and the world was made by Him," i, 9–11. There is thus a divinely-implanted, innate tendency towards this light, extant in man prior to the explicit act of faith, and operative outside of the Christian body : " Every one that is of the truth heareth my voice," xviii, 37 : " he that doeth the truth cometh to the light," iii, 21 : " begotten," as he is, not of man but " of God," i, 13; I John iii, 9. And thus Samaritans, Greeks, and Heathens act and speak in the best dispositions, iv, 42; xii, 20–24; x, 16; whilst such terms and sayings as " the Saviour of the World," " God so loved the world," iv, 42,

---

[1] My chief obligations are here again to Dr. H. J. Holtzmann's *Neutestamentliche Theologie*, 1897, Vol. II, pp. 354–390; 394–396; 399–401; 426–430; 447–466; 466–521.

iii, 16, are the most universalistic declarations to be found in the New Testament.—And this current dominates the whole of Catherine's temper and teaching : this certainty as to the innate affinity of every human soul to the Light, Love, Christ, God, gives a tone of exultation to the musings of this otherwise melancholy woman. Whereas the Johannine passages of a contrasting exclusiveness and even fierceness of tone, such as " all that came before Me are thieves and robbers," x, 8; " ye are from your father the devil," viii, 44; " ye shall die in your sin," viii, 21; " your sin remaineth," ix, 41, are without any parallel among Catherine's sayings. Indeed it is plain that Catherine, whilst as sure as the Evangelist that all man's goodness comes from God, nowhere, except in her own case, finds man's evil to be diabolic in character.

(2) With regard to Paulinism, the Johannine writings give us a continuation and extension of the representation of the soul's mystical union with Christ, as a local abiding in the element Christ. Indeed it is in these writings that we find the terms " to abide in " the light, 1 John ii, 10, in God, 1 John iv, 13, in Christ, 1 John ii, 6, 24, 27, iii, 6, 24, and in His love, John xv, 9, 1 John iv, 16; the corresponding expressions, " God abideth in us," 1 John iv, 12, 16, " Christ abideth in us," 1 John iii, 24, and " love abideth in us," 1 John iv, 16; the two immanences coupled together, where the communicant " abideth in Me and I in him," vi, 56, and where the members of His mystical body are bidden to " abide in Me and I in you," xv, 4; and the supreme pattern of all these interpenetrations, " I am in the Father, and the Father in Me," xiv, 10.—And it is from here that Catherine primarily gets the literary suggestions for her images of the soul plunged into, and filled by, an ocean of Light, Love, Christ, God; and again from here, more than from St. Paul, she gets her favourite term μένειν (It. *restare*), around which are grouped, in her mind, most of the quietistic-sounding elements of her teaching.

(3) As to the points of contact between the Johannine teaching and Alexandrianism, we find that three are vividly renewed by Catherine.

Philo had taught : " God ceases not from acting : as to burn is the property of fire, so to act is the property of God," *Legg. Alleg.* I, 3. And in John we find : " God is a Spirit," and " My Father worketh even until now, and I work," iv, 24; v, 17. And God as pure Spiritual Energy, as the *Actus*

Purus, is a truth and experience that penetrates the whole life of Catherine.

The work of Christ is not dwelt on in its earthly beginnings; but it is traced up and back, in the form of a spiritual "Genesis," to His life and work as the Logos in Heaven, where He abides "in the bosom of the Father," and whence He learns what He " hath declared " to us, i, 18; just as, in his turn, the disciple whom Jesus loved " was reclining " at the Last Supper " on the bosom of Jesus," and later on " beareth witness concerning the things " which he had learnt there, xiii, 23; xxi, 24. So also Catherine transcends the early earthly life of Christ altogether, and habitually dwells upon Him as the Light and as Love, as God in His own Self-Manifestation; and upon the ever-abiding sustenance afforded by this Light and Life and Love to the faithful soul reclining and resting upon it.

And the contrast between the Spiritual and the Material, the Abiding and the Transitory, is symbolized throughout John, in exact accord with Philo, under the spatial categories of upper and lower, and of extension : " Ye are from beneath, I am from above," viii, 23; " He that cometh from heaven, is above all," iii, 31; and " in my Father's house," that upper world, " there are many mansions," abiding-places, xiv, 2. Hence all things divine here below have descended from above : regeneration, iii, 3; the Spirit, i, 32; Angels, i, 51; the Son of God Himself, iii, 13 : and they mount once more up above, so especially Christ Himself, iii, 13; vi, 62. And the things of that upper world are the true things : " the true light," " the true adorers," " the true vine," " the true bread from Heaven," i, 9; iv, 23; xv, 1; vi, 32 : all this in contrast to the shadowy semi-realities of the lower world.—Catherine is here in fullest accord with the spatial imagery generally; she even talks of God Himself, not only as in a place, but as Himself a place, as the soul's " loco." But she has, for reasons explained elsewhere, generally to abandon the upper-and-lower category when picturing the soul's self-dedication to purification, since, for this act, she mostly figures a downward plunge into suffering; and she gives us a number of striking sayings, in which she explicitly re-translates all this quantitative spatial imagery into its underlying meaning of qualitative spiritual states.

(4) As to the Johannine approximations and antagonisms to Gnosticism, Catherine's position is as follows. In the Synoptic

accounts, Our Lord makes the acquisition of eternal life
depend upon the keeping of the two great commandments of
the love of God and of one's neighbour, Luke x, 26–28, and
parallels.   In John Our Lord says : " this is life eternal, that
they should know Thee the only true God, and Him Whom
Thou didst send, even Jesus Christ," xvii, 3.   To " know,"
γινώσκειν, occurs twenty-five times in 1 John alone.   Here
the final object of every soul is to believe and to know :
" they received and knew of a truth . . . and believed,"
xvii, 8; " we have believed and know," vi, 69; or "we know
and have believed," 1 John iv, 16.   And Catherine also lays
much stress upon faith ending, even here below, in a certain
vivid knowledge; but this knowledge is, with her, less
doctrinally articulated, no doubt in part because there was
no Gnosticism fronting her, to force on such articulation.

And the Johannine writings compare this higher mental
knowledge to the lower, sensible perception : " He that cometh
from heaven," witnesseth to what he hath " seen and heard,"
iii, 32; " if He shall be manifested, we shall see Him even as
He is," 1 John iii, 2.   And they have three special terms, in
common with Gnosticism, for the object of such knowledge :
Life, Light, and Fulness (Plerōma),—the latter, as a technical
term, appearing in the New Testament only in John i, 16, and
in the Epistles to the Colossians and Ephesians.   Catherine,
also, is ever experiencing and conceiving the mental apprehensions of faith, as so many quasi-sensible, ocular, perceptions; and Life and Light are constantly mentioned, and
Fulness is, at least, implied in the psycho-physical concomitants or consequences of her thinkings.

On the other hand, she does not follow John in the intensely
dualistic elements of his teaching,—the sort of determinist, all
but innate, distinction between " the darkness," " the men who
loved the darkness rather than the light," and the Light itself
and those who loved it, i, 4, 5; iii, 19,—children of God and
children of the devil—the latter all but incapable of being
saved, viii, 38–47; x, 26; xi, 52; xiv, 17.   Rather is she like
him in his all but complete silence as to " the anger of God,"
—a term which he uses once only, iii, 36, as against the twenty-
two instances of it in St. Paul.

And she is full to overflowing of the great central, profoundly un- and anti-Gnostic, sensitively Christian teachings
of St. John : as to the Light, the only-begotten Son, having
been given by God, because God so loved the world; as to

Jesus having loved his own even to the end; as to the object of Christ's manifestation of His Father's name to men, being that God's love for Christ, and indeed Christ Himself, might be within them; and as to how, if they love Him, they will keep His commandments,—His commandment to love each other as He has loved them, iii, 21; iii, 16; xiii, 1; xvii, 26; xiv, 15; xv, 17. In this last great declaration especially do we find the very epitome of Catherine's life and spirit, of her who can never think of Him as Light and Knowledge only, but ever insists on His being Fire and Love as well; and who has but one commandment, that of Love-impelled, Love-seeking loving.

(5) And lastly, in relation to organized, Ecclesiastical Christianity, the Johannine writings dwell, as regards the more general principles, on points which, where positive, are simply pre-supposed by Catherine; and, where negative, find no echo within her.

The Johannine writings insist continually upon the unity and inter-communion of the faithful: "They shall become one fold, one shepherd"; Christ's death was in order " that He might gather the scattered children of God into one "; He prays to the Father that believers " may be one, as we are one "; and He leaves as His legacy His seamless robe, x, 16; xi, 52; xvii, 21; xix, 24. And these same writings have a painfully absolute condemnation for all outside of this visible fold: " The whole world lies in evil "; its " Prince is the Devil "; " the blood of Jesus cleanseth us from all sin," within the community alone; false prophets, those who have gone forth from the community, are not to be prayed for, are not even to be saluted, 1 John v, 19; John xii, 31; John i, 7; v, 16; 2 John, 10. For the great and necessary fight with Gnosticism has already begun in these writings.

But Catherine dies before the unity of Christendom is again in jeopardy through the Protestant Reformation, and she never dwells—this is doubtless a limit—upon the Christian community, as such. And her enthusiastic sympathy with the spiritual teachings of Jacopone da Todi, who, some two centuries before, had, as one of the prophetic opposition, vehemently attacked the intensely theocratic policy of Pope Boniface VIII, and had suffered a long imprisonment at his hands; her tender care for the schismatic population of the far-away Greek island of Chios; and her intimacy with Dre. Tommaso Moro, who, later on, became for a while a

Calvinist; all indicate how free from all suspiciousness towards individual Catholics, or of fierceness against other religious bodies and persons, was her deeply filial attachment to the Church.

In the Synoptists Our Lord declares, as to the exorcist who worked cures in His name, although not a follower of His, that " he that is not against us, is for us," and refuses to accede to His disciples' proposal to interfere with his activity, Mark ix, 38–41; and He points, as to the means of inheriting eternal life, to the keeping of the two great commandments, as these are already formulated in the Old Testament, and insists that this neighbour, whom here we are bidden to love, is any and every man, Luke x, 25–37. The Johannine writings insist strongly upon the strict necessity of full, explicit adhesion : the commandment of love which Our Lord gives is here " My commandment," " a new commandment," one held "from the beginning "—in the Christian community; and the command to " love one another " is here addressed to the brethren in their relations to their fellow-believers only, xiii, 34; xiii, 35; xv, 12, 17. Catherine's feeling, in this matter, is clearly with the Synoptists.

2. *Johannine teaching considered in itself.*

If we next take the Johannine teachings in themselves, we shall find the following interesting points of contact or contrast to exist between John and Catherine.

(1) In matters of Theology proper, she is completely penetrated by the great doctrine, more explicit in St. John even than in St. Paul, that "God is Love," 1 John iv, 8; and by the conceptions of God and of Christ " working always " as Life, Light, and Love.—But whereas, in the first Epistle of John, God Himself is " eternal life " and " light," v, 20; i, 5; and, in the Gospel, it is Christ Who, in the first instance, appears as Life and as Light, xi, 25; viii, 12 : Catherine nowhere distinguishes at all between Christ and God. And similarly, whereas in St. John " God doth not give " unto Christ " the Spirit by measure "; and Christ promises to the disciples " another Paraclete," *i. e.* the Holy Spirit, iii, 34; xiv, 16; and indeed the Son and the Spirit appear, throughout, as distinct from one another as do the Son and the Father : in Catherine we get, practically everywhere, an exclusive concentration upon the fact, so often implied or declared by St. Paul, of Love, Christ, being Himself Spirit.

(2) The Johannine Soteriology has, I think, influenced

Catherine as follows. Christ's redemptive work appears, in the more original current of that teaching, under the symbols of the Word, Light, Bread, as the self-revelation of God. For in proportion that this Logos-Light and Bread enlightens and nourishes, does He drive away darkness and weakness, and, with them, sin, and this previously to any historic acts of His earthly life. And, in this connection, there is but little stress laid upon penance and the forgiveness of sins as compared with the Synoptic accounts, and the term of turning back, στρέφειν, is absent here.—But that same redemptive work appears, in the more Pauline of the two Johannine currents, as the direct result of so many vicarious, atoning deeds, the historic Passion and Death of Our Lord. Here there is indeed sin, a " sin of the world," and specially for this sin is Christ the propitiation : " God so loved the world, as to give His only-begotten Son "—Him " the Lamb of God, that taketh away the sins of the world," i, 29; 1 John ii, 2; John ii, 16; i, 29, 36.

Catherine, with the probably incomplete exception of her Conversion and Penance-period, concentrates her attention, with a striking degree of exclusiveness, upon the former group of conceptions. With her too the God-Christ is—all but solely—conceived as Light which, in so far as it is not hindered, operates the healing and the growth of souls. And in her great picture of all souls inevitably hungering for the sight of the One Bread, God, she has operated a fusion between two of the Johannine images, the Light which is seen and the Bread which is eaten : here the bare sight (in reality, a satiating sight) of the Bread suffices. If, for the self-manifesting God-Christ, she has, besides the Johaninne Light-image, a Fire-symbol, which has its literary antecedents rather in the Old Testament than in the New, this comes from the fact that she is largely occupied with the pain of the impressions and processes undergone by already God-loving yet still imperfectly pure souls, and that fierce fire is as appropriate a symbol for such pain as is peaceful light for joy.

Now this painfulness is, in Catherine's teaching, the direct result of whatever may be incomplete and piecemeal in the soul's state and process of purification. And this her conception, of Perfect Love being mostly attained only through a series of apparently sudden shifts, each seemingly final, is no doubt in part moulded upon the practically identical Johannine teaching as to Faith.

True, we have already seen that her conception of the nature of God's action upon the soul, and of the soul's reaction under this His touch, is more akin to the rich Synoptic idea of a disposition and determination of the soul's whole being, (a cordial trust at least as much as an intellectual apprehension and clear assent), than to the Johannine view, which lays a predominant stress upon mental apprehension and assent. And again, she nowhere presents anything analogous to the Johannine, already scholastic, formulations of the object of this Faith and Trust,—all of them explicitly concerned with the nature of Christ.

But, everywhere in the Johannine writings, the living Person and Spirit aimed at by these definitions is considered as experienced by the soul in a succession of ever-deepening intuitions and acts of Faith.   Already at the Jordan, Andrew and Nathaniel have declared Jesus to be the Christ, the Son of God, i, 41, 49; yet they, His disciples, are said to have believed in Him at Cana, in consequence of His miracle there, ii, 11.   Already at Capernaum Peter asserts for the twelve, " We have believed and know that Thou art the Holy One of God," vi, 69; yet still, at the Last Supper, Christ exhorts them to believe in Him, xiv, 10, 11, and predicts future events to them, in order that, when these predictions come true, their faith may still further increase, xiii, 19; xiv, 29.   And, as far on as after the Resurrection we hear that the Beloved Disciple " saw " (the empty tomb) " and believed," xx, 8, 29.   We thus get in John precisely the same logically paradoxical, but psychologically and spiritually most accurate and profound, combination of an apparent completeness of Faith at each point of special illumination, with a sudden re-beginning and impulsive upward shifting of the soul's Light and Believing, which is so characteristic of Catherine's experience and teaching as to the successive levels of the soul's Fire, Light and Love.   And the opposite movement—of the fading away of the Light and the Faith—can be traced in John, as the corresponding doctrine of the going out of the Fire, Light and Love within the Soul can be found in Catherine.

Again, both John and Catherine are penetrated with the sense that this Faith and Love is somehow waked up in souls by a true touch of God, a touch to which they spontaneously respond, because they already possess a substantial affinity to Him.   " His," the Good Shepherd's, " sheep hear His voice," x, 16; they hear it, because they are already His : the Light solicits and is accepted by the soul, because the soul itself is light-like and light-requiring, and because it proceeds originally from this very Light which would now reinforce the soul's own deepest requirements. This great truth appears also in those profound Johannine passages : " No man can come to Me, unless the Father which sent Me draw him " ; and " I manifested Thy name unto the men whom Thou gavest Me out of the world," vi, 44; xvii, 6.

And this attractive force is also a faculty of Christ : " I will draw all men unto Myself," xii, 32. And note how Catherine, ever completely identifying God, Christ, Light, Love, and, where these work in imperfectly pure souls, Fire, is stimulated by the last-quoted text to extend God's, Christ's, Love's drawing, attraction, to all men; to limit only, in various degrees, these various men's response to it ; and to realize so intensely that a generous yielding to this our ineradicable deepest *attrait* is our fullest joy, and the resisting it is our one final misery, as to picture the soul, penitent for this its mad resistance, plunging itself, now eagerly responsive to that intense attraction, into God and a growing conformity with Him.

(3) As to points concerning the Sacraments where Catherine is influenced by John, we find that here again Baptismal conceptions are passed over by her. She does not allude to the water in the discourse to Nicodemus, iii, 5, although she is full of other ideas suggested there ; but she dwells upon the water in the address to the Woman at the Well, iv, 10–15, that "living water," which is, for her, the spirit's spiritual sustenance, Love, Christ, God, and insensibly glides over into the images and experiences attaching, for her, to the Holy Eucharist.

But, as to this the greatest of the Sacraments and the all-absorbing devotion of her life, her symbols and concepts are all suggested by the Fourth Gospel, in contrast to the Synoptists and St. Paul. For the Holy Eucharist is, with her, ever detached from any direct memory of the Last Supper, Passion, and Death, the original, historical, unique occasions which still form its setting in the pre-Johannine writings, although those greatest proofs of a divinely boundless self-immolation undoubtedly give to her devotion to the Blessed Sacrament its beautiful enthusiasm and tenderness. The Holy Eucharist ever appears with her, as with St. John, attached to the scene of the multiplication of the breads,—a feast of joy and of life, with Christ at the zenith of His earthly hope and power.   For not " a shewing of the death " in " the eating of this bread," I Cor. xi, 26, is dwelt on by John; but we have : " I am the living Bread . . . if any man eat of this bread, he shall live for ever," John vi, 51.

And Catherine follows John in thinking predominantly of the single soul, when dwelling upon the Holy Eucharist.   For if John presents a great open-air Love-Feast in lieu of Paul's Upper Chamber and Supper with the twelve, he, as over against Paul's profoundly social standpoint, has, throughout this his Eucharistic chapter, but three indications of the plural as against some fourteen singulars.

And, finally, John's change from the future tense, with its reference to a coming historic institution, " the meat which . . . the Son of Man shall give unto you," vi, 27, to the present tense, with its declaration of an eternal fact and relation, " I am " (now and always) " the living bread which came down out of heaven," vi, 51, will have helped Catherine towards the conception of the eternal Christ-God offering Himself as their ceaseless spiritual food to His creatures, possessed as they are by an indestructible spiritual hunger for Himself.   For if the Eucharistic food, Bread, Body, has already been declared by St. Paul to be " spiritual," 2 Cor. iii, 17, in St. John also it has to be spiritual, for it is here " the true bread from heaven " and " the bread of life "; and Christ declares here " it is the Spirit that quickeneth, the flesh (alone) profiteth nothing," vi, 32, 63.   Hence Catherine is, again through the Holy Eucharist and St. John, brought back to her favourite Pauline conception of the Lord as Himself " Spirit," " the Life-giving Spirit," 2 Cor. iii, 17 ; I Cor. xv, 45.

(4) And if we conclude with the Johannine Eschatology, we shall find that Catherine has penetrated deep into the following conceptions, which undoubtedly, even in their union, present us with a less rich outlook than that furnished by the Synoptists, but which may be said to constitute the central spirit of Our Lord's teaching.

Like John, who has but two mentions of " the Kingdom of God," iii, 3, 5, and who elsewhere ever speaks of " Life," Catherine has nowhere " the Kingdom," but everywhere " Life."   Like him she conceives the process of Conversion as a " making alive " of the moribund, darkened, cold soul, by the Light, Love, Christ, God, v, 21–29, when He, Who is Himself " the Life," xi, 25, and " the Spirit," iv, 24, speaks to the soul " words " that are " spirit and life," vi, 63 ; for then

the soul that gives ear to His words " hath eternal life,"
v, 24.

Again Catherine, for the most part, appropriates and develops that one out of the two Johannine currents of doctrine
concerning the Judgment, which treats the latter as already
determined and forestalled by Man's present personal attitude
towards the Light.   The judgment is thus simply a discrimination, according to the original meaning of the noun κρίσις—like
when God in the beginning " divided the light from the
darkness," Gen. i, 5 ; a discrimination substantially effected
already here and now, " he that believeth on Him, is not
judged ; he that believeth not hath been judged already,"
iii, 18. But the other current of doctrine, so prominent in
the Synoptists is not absent from St. John,—the teaching
as to a later, external and visible, forensic judgment.
And Catherine has a similar intermixture of two currents,
yet with a strong predominance of the immanental, present
conception of the matter.

And even for that one volitional act in the beyond, which,
according to her doctrine, has a certain constitutive importance
for the whole eternity of all still partially impure souls—for
that voluntary plunge—we can find an analogue in the
Johannine writings, although here there is no reference to the
after life.   For throughout the greater part of his teaching—
from iii, 15, 16, apparently up to the end of the Gospel,—the
possession of spiritual Life is consequent upon the soul's own
acts of Faith, and not, as one would expect from his other,
more characteristic teaching, upon its Regeneration from
above, iii, 3.   And the result of such acts of Faith is a
" Metabasis," a "passing over from death to life," v, 24 ; 1 John
iii, 14.   Catherine will have conceived such an act of Faith as
predominantly an act of Love, and the act as itself already that
Metabasis ; and will, most characteristically, have quickened
the movement, and have altered its direction from the
horizontal to the vertical, so that the " passing, going over,"
becomes a " plunge down into " Life.   For indeed the Fire
she plunges into is, in her doctrine, Life Itself ; since it is
Light, Love, Christ, and God.

Catherine, once more, is John's most faithful disciple, where
he declares that Life to stream out immediately from the life-
giving object of Faith into the life-seeking subject of that
Faith, from the believed God into the believing soul : " I am
the Bread of Life : he that cometh to Me shall not hunger ";

" he that abideth in Me, and I in him, the same beareth much fruit " ; vi, 35 ; xv, 5.

And finally, she follows John closely where he insists upon Simultaneity and Eternity as contrasted with Succession and Immortality, so as even to abstract from the bodily resurrection. He who " hath passed out of death into life " (already) " possesses eternal life " ; " whosoever liveth and believeth on Me, shall never die " (at any time) ; " this," already and of itself, " is life eternal, that they should know Thee, the only true God, and Him Whom Thou didst send, even Jesus Christ ;" and the soul's abiding in such an experience is Christ's own joy, transplanted into it, and a joy which is full, v, 24 ; xi, 26 ; xvii, 3 ; xv, 11. And there is here such an insistence upon an unbroken spiritual life, in spite of and right through physical death, that, to Martha's declaration that her brother will arise at the last day, xi, 24, Jesus answers, " I am the Resurrection and the Life : he that believeth on Me, though he die " the bodily death, " shall live " on in his soul ; indeed " every man who liveth " the life of the body, " and who believeth in Me, shall never die " (at any time) in his soul, xi, 25, 26. John's other line of thought, in which the bodily resurrection is prominent, remains without any definite or systematic response in Catherine's teaching.

(5) We can then summarize the influence exercised by John upon Catherine by saying that he encouraged her to conceive religion as an experience of eternity ; as a true, living knowledge of things spiritual ; indeed as a direct touch of man's soul by God Himself, culminating in man's certainty that God is Love.

III. The Areopagite Writings.

Catherine's close relations to the Areopagite, the Pseudo-Dionysius, are of peculiar interest, in their manifold agreement, difference, or non-responsiveness ; and this although the ideas thus assimilated are mostly of lesser depth and importance than those derived from the New Testament writings just considered. They can be grouped conveniently under the subject-matters of God's creative, providential, and restorative, outgoing, His action upon souls and all things extant, and of the reasons for the different results of this action ; of certain symbols used to characterize that essential action of

God upon His creatures; of the states and energizings of the
soul, in so far as it is responsive to that action; of certain
terms concerning these reactions of the soul; and of the
final result of the whole process.   I shall try and get back,
in most cases, to the Areopagite's Neo-Platonist sources, the
dry, intensely scholastic Proclus, and that great soul, the
prince of the non-Christian Mystics, Plotinus.[1]

1. *God's general action.*

As to God's action, we have in Dionysius the Circle with
the three stages of its movement,—a conception so dear to
Catherine.   " Theologians call Him the Esteemed and the
Loved, and again Love and Loving-kindness, as being a
Power at once propulsive and leading up " and back " to
Himself; a loving movement self-moved, which pre-exists in
the Good, and bubbles forth from the Good to things existing, and which again returns to the Good—as it were a sort
of everlasting circle whirling round, because of the Good, from
the Good, in the Good, and to the Good,—ever advancing and
remaining and returning in the same and throughout the
same."   This is " the power of the divine similitude " present
throughout creation, " which turns all created things to their
cause." [2]   The doctrine is derived from Proclus : " Everything
caused both abides in its cause and proceeds from it and
returns to it " ; and " everything that proceeds from something returns, by a natural instinct, to that from which it
proceeds." [3]   And Plotinus had led the way : " there " in the
super-sensible world, experienced in moments of ecstasy, " in
touch and union with the One, the soul begets Beauty,
Justice and Virtue : and that place and life is, for it, its principle and end : principle, since it springs from thence ; end,
because the Good is there, and because, once arrived there, the
soul becomes what it was at first." [4]

[1] I am much indebted to the thorough and convincing monograph of
the Catholic Priest and Professor Dr. Hugo Koch, *Pseudo-Dionysius Areo-
pagita in seinen Beziehungen zum Neo-Platonismus und Mysterienwesen,*
Mainz, 1900, for a fuller understanding of the relations between Dionysius,
Proclus, and Plotinus.   I have also found much help in H. F. Müller's
admirable German translation of Plotinus, a translation greatly superior
to Thomas Taylor's English or to Bouillet's French translation.   And I
have greatly benefited by the admirable study of Plotinus in Dr. Edward
Caird's *Evolution of Theology in the Greek Philosophers,* 1904, Vol. II,
pp. 210–346.

[2] *The Divine Names,* iii, 1; ix, 4 : English translation by Parker,
1897, pp. 49, 50; 106.

[3] *Institutio Theologica,* c. 35; c. 31.   [4] *Enneads,* vi, ch. ix, 9.

And Dionysius has the doctrine, so dear to Catherine, that
" the Source of Good is indeed present to all, but all are not,"
by their intention, " present to It; yet, by our aptitude for
Divine union, we all," in a sense, " are present to It." " It
shines, on Its own part, equally upon all things capable
of participation in It." [1] Already Plotinus had finely said :
" The One is not far away from any one, and yet is liable to
be far away from one and all, since, present though It be, It
is " efficaciously " present only to such as are capable of receiving It, and are so disposed as to adapt themselves to It
and, as it were, to seize and touch It by their likeness to It,
. . . when, in a word, the soul is in the state in which it was
when it came from It." [2]

We have again in Dionysius the combination, so characteristic of Catherine, of a tender respect for the substance of
human nature, as good and ever respected by God, and of a
keen sense of the pathetic weakness of man's sense-clogged
spirit here below. " Providence, as befits its goodness, pro-
vides for each being suitably : for to destroy nature is not a
function of Providence." " All those who cavil at the Divine
Justice, unconsciously commit a manifest injustice. For they
say that immortality ought to be in mortals, and perfection
in the imperfect . . . and perfect power in the weak, and that
the temporal should be eternal . . . in a word, they assign
the properties of one thing to another." [3]

2. *Symbols of God's action.*

(1) As to the symbols of God's action, we have first the Chain
or Rope, Catherine's " fune," that " rope of His pure Love," of
which " an end was thrown to her from heaven." [4] This
symbol was no doubt suggested by Dionysius : " Let us then
elevate our very selves by our prayers to the higher ascent of
the Divine . . . rays; as though a luminous chain (rope, σειρά)
were suspended from the celestial heights and reached down
hither, and we, by ever stretching out to it up and up . .
were thus carried upwards." [5] And this passage again goes
back to Proclus, who describes the " chain (rope) of love " as
" having its entirely simple and hidden highest point fixed
amongst the very first ranks of the Gods"; its middle effluence

---

[1] *Divine Names*, iii, 1; ix, 4 : Parker, pp. 27, 104.
[2] *Enneads*, vi, ch. ix, 4.
[3] *Divine Names*, viii, 7 : Parker, pp. 98, 99.
[4] *Vita*, pp. 47c, 48a.
[5] *Divine Names*, iii, 1 : Parker, pp. 27, 28.

" amongst the Gods higher than the (sensible) world "; and
its third, lowest, part, as "divided multiformly throughout the
(sensible) world." "The divine Love implants one common
bond (chain) and one indissoluble friendship in and between
each soul (that participates in its power), and between all and
the Beautiful Itself." [1] And this simile of a chain from heaven,
which in Dionysius is luminous, and in Catherine and Proclus
is loving, goes back, across Plato (*Theaetetus* 153c and *Republic*, X, 61b, 99c) to Homer, where it again is luminous
(golden). For, in the *Iliad*, viii, 17–20, Zeus says to the Gods
in Olympus, "So as to see all things, do you, O Gods and
Goddesses all, hang a golden chain from heaven, and do you
all seize hold of it "—so as thus to descend to earth.

(2) We have next the symbol of the Sun and its purifying,
healing Light, under which God and His action are raptur-
ously proclaimed by Dionysius. "Even as our sun, by its
very being, enlightens all things able to partake of its light
in their various degrees, so also the Good, by its very existence, sends unto all things that be, the rays of its entire goodness, according to their capacity for them. By means of
these rays they are purified from all corruption and death . . .
and are separated from instability." "The Divine Goodness,
this our great sun, enlightens . . . nourishes, perfects, renews."
Even the pure can thus be made purer still. "He, the Good,
is called spiritual light . . . he cleanses the mental vision
of the very angels : they taste, as it were, the light." [2] All
this imagery goes back, in the first instance, to Proclus. For
Proclus puts in parallel " sun " and " God," and " to be enlightened " and " to be deified "; makes all purifying forces to
coalesce in the activity of the Sun-God, Apollo Katharsios,
the Purifier, who " everywhere unifies multiplicity . . .
purifying the entire heaven and all living things throughout
the world "; and describes how " from above, from his super-
heavenly post, Apollo scatters the arrows of Zeus,—his rays
upon all the world." [3] The Sun's rays, here as powerful as
the bolts of Zeus, thus begin to play the part still assigned
to them in Catherine's imagery of the " Saëtte " and " Radii "
of the divine Light and Love. And the substance of the
whole symbol goes back, through fine sayings of Plotinus
and through Philo, to Plato, who calls the Sun " the offspring

---

[1] *In Platonis Alcibiadem*, ii, 78 *seq.*
[2] *Divine Names*, iv, 1; iv, 5 : Parker, pp. 32, 33; 38.
[3] *In Parmenidem*, iv, 34. *In Cratylum*, pp. 103; 107.

of the Good and analogous to it," and who (doubtless rightly) takes Homer's " golden chain " to be nothing but the Sun-rays,—thus identifying the two symbols.[1]

(3) Fire, as a symbol for God and His action, is thus praised by Dionysius: " The sacred theologians often describe the super-essential Essence in terms of Fire . . . For sensible fire is, so to say, present in all things, and pervades them all without mingling with them, and is received by all things; . . . it is intolerable yet invisible; it masters all things by its own might, and yet it but brings the things in which it resides to (the development of) their own energy; it has a transforming power; it communicates itself to all who approach it in any degree; . . . it has the power of dividing (what it seizes); it bears upwards; it is penetrating; . . . it increases its own self in a hidden manner; it suddenly shines forth." [2]—All these qualities, and the delicate transitions from fire to light and from light back to fire, and from heat immanent to heat applied from without, we can find again, vividly assimilated and experienced, in Catherine's teaching and emotional life. But the Sun-light predominates in Dionysius, the Fire-heat in Catherine; and whereas the former explicitly attaches purification only to the Sun-light, the latter connects the cleansing chiefly with Fire-heat, no doubt because the Greek man is busy chiefly with the intellectually cognitive, and the Italian woman with the morally ameliorative, activities and interests of the mind and soul.

3. *The soul's reaction.*

(1) As to the soul's reaction under God's action, and its return to Him, we first get, in Dionysius, the insistence upon Mystical Quietude and Silence, which, according to him, are strictly necessary, since only like can know and become one with like, and God is " Peace and Repose " and, " as compared with every known progression, Immobility," and "the one all-perfect source and cause of the Peace of all "; and He is Silence, " the Angels are, as it were, the heralds of the Divine Silence,"—teaching not unlike that of St. Ignatius of Antioch, " Jesus Christ . . . the Word which proceeds from Silence." [3] Hence " in proportion as we ascend to the higher designations of God, do our expressions become more and more circumscribed "; and at last " we shall find, not a little speaking,

[1] *Republic*, VI, 508c. *Theaetetus*, 153c.
[2] *Heavenly Hierarchy*, xv, 2 : Parker, pp. 56, 57.
[3] *Divine Names*, xi, 1; iv, 2 : Parker, pp. 113, 34. *Ad Magnesios*, viii, 2.

but a complete absence of speech and of conception." [1] As Proclus has it : " Let this Fountain of Godhead be honoured on our part by silence and by the union which is above silence." [2] And Plotinus says : " This," the Divine, " Light comes not from anywhere nor disappears any whither, but simply shines or shines not : hence we must not pursue after it, but must abide in quietness till it appears." And when it does appear, " the contemplative, as one rapt and divinely inspired, abides here with quietude in a motionless condition, . . . being entirely stable, and becoming, as it were, stability itself." [3]—All this still finds its echo in Catherine.—But the treble (cognitive) movement of the Angelic and human mind,—the circular, the straight-line, and the spiral,—which Dionysius, in direct imitation of Proclus, carefully develops throughout three sections, is quite absent from Catherine's mind. [4]

(2) We next get, in Dionysius, the following teachings as to Mystical Vision and Union. " The Unity-above-Mind is placed above the minds ; and the Good-above-word is un-utterable by word." " There is, further, the most divine knowledge of Almighty God, which is known through not knowing . . . when the mind, having stood apart from all existing things, and having then also dismissed itself, has been made one with the super-luminous rays." " We must contem-plate things divine by our whole selves standing out of our whole selves, and becoming wholly of God." " By the resistless and absolute ecstasy, in all purity, from out of thyself and all things, thou wilt be carried on high, to the super-essential ray of the divine darkness." " It is during the cessation of every mental energizing, that such a union of the deified minds and of the super-divine light takes place." [5] And the original cause and final effect of such a going forth from self, are indicated in words which were worked out in a vivid fulness by Catherine's whole convert life : " Divine Love is ecstatic, not permitting any lovers to belong to themselves, but only to those beloved by them. And this love, the

---

[1] *Mystic Theology*, iii : Parker, p. 135.

[2] *Platonic Theology*, III, p. 132.

[3] *Enneads*, v, ch. v, 8; vi, ch. ix, 11.

[4] *Divine Names*, iv, 8–10 : Parker, pp. 42–45. *In Parmenidem*, vi, 52 (see Koch, p. 152).

[5] *Divine Names*, i, i; vii, 3; vii, 1; *Mystic Theology*, 1; *Divine Names*, vii. 3 : Parker, pp. 2; 91, 92; 87; 130; 91, 92.

superior beings show by being full of forethought for their
inferiors; those equal in rank, by their mutual coherence;
and the inferior by a looking back and up to the superior
ones." [1]

Dionysius here everywhere follows Proclus. Yet the
noblest Neo-Platonist sayings are again furnished by Plotinus:
" We are not cut off or severed from the Light, but we breathe
and consist in It, since It ever enlightens and bears us, as long
as It is what It is." In the moments of Union, " we are able
to see both Him and ourself,—ourself in dazzling splendour,
full of spiritual light, or rather one with the pure Light
Itself . . . our life's flame is then enkindled." " There the
soul rests, after it has fled up, away from evil, to the place
which is free from evils . . . and the true life is there."
" Arrived there, the soul becomes that which she was at first." [2]
And if Plotinus has thus already got the symbolism of place,
he is as fully aware as Catherine herself that, for purposes of
vivid presentation, he is spatializing spiritual, that is, un-
extended, qualitative states and realities. " Things incorporeal do not get excluded by bodies; they are severed only
by otherness and difference : hence, when such otherness
is absent, they, not differing, are near each other." And
already, as with Catherine, there is the apparent finality, and
yet also the renewed search for more. " The seer and the seen
have become one, as though it were a case not of vision but
of union." " When he shall have crossed over as the image to
its Archetype, then he will have reached his journey's end."
And yet this " ecstasy, simplification, and donation of one's
self," this " quiet," is still also " a striving after contact," " a
musing to achieve union." [3]

4. *Terminology of the soul's reaction.*

(1) Certain terms and conceptions in connection with the
soul's return to God, which are specially dear to Catherine,
already appear, fully developed, in Dionysius, Proclus, and
Plotinus; in part, even in Plato. Her " suddenly " (*subito*)
appears but rarely in Dionysius, *e. g.* in *Heavenly Hierarchy*
xv, 2; but it is carefully explained by him in his Third
Epistle, specially devoted to the subject.[4] It is common in
Plotinus: "Suddenly the soul saw, without seeing how it saw";
"suddenly thou shalt receive light," " suddenly shining."[5] And

---

[1] *Divine Names*, iv, 13 : Parker, p. 48.   [2] *Enneads*, vi, ch. ix, 9.
[3] *Ibid.* vi, ch. ix, 8; ch. vi, 11.   [4] Parker, p. 142.
[5] *Enneads*, vi, ch. vii, 36; v, ch. iii, 17; v, ch. v, 7.

in Plato we find : " He who has learnt to see the Beautiful in
due order and succession, when he comes towards the end, will
suddenly perceive a Nature of wondrous beauty—Beauty alone,
absolute, separate, simple and everlasting " : a passage which
derives its imagery from the Epopteia of the Eleusynian
Mysteries,—the sudden appearance, the curtain being with-
drawn, upon the stage whereon the Heathen Mystery-play
was being performed, under a peculiar fairy-illumination, of
the figures of Demeter, Kore, and Iacchus, as the culmination
of a long succession of purifications and initiations.[1]

Catherine's " wound," or " wounding stroke," (*ferita*), is, in
part, the necessary consequence of the " arrow " conception
already considered; in part, the echo of that group of terms
which, in Dionysius and Proclus even more than in Plotinus,
express the painfully sudden and overwhelming, free-grace
character of God's action upon the soul,—especially of $\dot{\epsilon}\pi\iota\beta o\lambda\dot{\eta}$,
" immissio," a " coming-upon," a " hitting," a very common
word in the Areopagite; $\mu\epsilon\tau o\chi\dot{\eta}$, " communication," and
$\pi a\rho a\delta o\chi\dot{\eta}$, " reception," being the corresponding terms for God's
and the soul's share in this encounter respectively. Thus :
" Unions, whether we call them immissions or receptions from
God." [2]

"Presence," "presenza," $\pi a\rho a\nu\sigma\iota\dot{a}$, is another favourite term,
as with Catherine so also with Dionysius and Proclus. Thus
the Areopagite : " The presence of the spiritual light causes
recollection and unity in those that are being enlightened with
it," " His wholly inconceivable presence." [3] And Proclus :
" Every perfect spiritual contact and communion is owing to
the presence of God." [4] And the conception of a sudden
presence goes back, among the Neo-Platonists, to Plato and
the Greek Mysteries, in which the God was held suddenly to
arrive and to take part in the sacred dance. Such rings of
sacred dancers, "choirs," are still characteristic of Dionysius—
e.g. Heavenly Hierarchy, vii, 4—but they are quite wanting
in Catherine.—But " contact," " touch " $\dot{\epsilon}\pi a\phi\dot{\eta}$,—said of God's
direct action upon the soul,—a conception so intensely active
in Catherine's mind and life, is again a favourite term with
Dionysius and Proclus. The former declares this " touch " to

---

[1] *Symposium*, 210 E. See the admirable elucidations in Rhode's *Psyche*,
ed. 1898, Vol. I, p. 298; Vol. II, pp. 279; 283, 284.

[2] *Divine Names*, i, 5 : Parker, p. 8.

[3] *Divine Names*, iv, 6; *Mystic Theology*, i, iii : Parker, pp. 39, 132.

[4] *In Alcibiadem*, ii, 302.

be neither " sensible " nor " intelligible," and that " we are
brought into contact with things unutterable"; the latter talks
of " perfect spiritual contact." [1]

The symbols of "Nakedness" and "Garments," as indicative
respectively of the soul's purity and impurity or self-delusion,
are, though most prominent in Catherine, rare in Dionysius.
But his declaration : " The nakedness of the (Angels') feet
indicates purification from the addition of all things external,
and assimilation to the divine simplicity " exactly expresses
her idea.[2]   And Proclus has it more fully : The soul, on
descending into the body, forsakes unity, " and around her,
from all sides, there grow multiform kinds of existence
and manifold garments "; " love of honour is the last garment
of souls "; and " when," in mounting up, " we lay aside our
passions and garments which, in coming down, we had put
on, we must also strip off that last garment, in order that,
having become (entirely) naked, we may establish ourselves
before God, having made ourselves like to the divine life." [3]

(2) Again, as to Triads, it is interesting to note that Catherine
has nothing about the three stages or ways of the inner life,
—purgative, illuminative, unitive,—of which Dionysius is full,
and which are already indicated in Proclus; for we can find
but two in her life, the purgative and unitive, and in her teaching
these two alone appear, mostly in close combination, sometimes in strong contrast.   Nor has she anything about the
three degrees or kinds of prayer,—Meditation, Contemplation,
Union,—as indicated in Dionysius : " It behoves us, by our
prayers, to be lifted into proximity with the Divine Trinity;
and then, by still further approaching it, to be initiated . . .;
and (lastly) to make ourselves one with it"; and as taught by
Proclus: "Knowledge leads, then follows proximity, and then
union." [4]   With her we only get Contemplation and Union.—
Nor do we get in her anything about thrice three choirs of
Angels, or three orders of Christian Ministrants, or three
classes of Christian people, or thrice three groups of Sacraments and Sacramental acts.   For she is too intensely bent
upon immediate intercourse with God, and too much absorbed
in the sense of profound unity and again of innumerable

---

[1] *Mystic Theology*, iv, v; *Divine Names*, i, 1 : Parker, pp. 136, 137;
1; *In Alcibiadem*, ii, 302.

[2] *Heavenly Hierarchy*, ch. xv, s. 3 : Parker, p. 60.

[3] *In Alcibiadem*, iii, 75.

[4] *Divine Names*, iii, 1 : Parker, pp. 27, 28.   *In Parmenidem*, iv, 68.

multiplicity, to be attracted by Dionysius's Neo-Platonist ladder of carefully graduated intermediaries, or by his continuous interest in triads of every kind. Catherine thus follows the current in Dionysius which insists upon direct contact between the soul and the transcendent God, and ignores the other, which bridges over the abyss between the two by carefully graduated intermediaries : these intermediaries having become, with her, successive stages of purification and of ever more penetrating union of the one soul with the one God.

5. *Deification, especially through the Eucharist.*

As to the end of the whole process, we find that Deification, so frequently implied or suggested by Catherine, is formally taught by Dionysius : " A union of the deified minds " (ἐκθεουμένων) ; the heavenly and the earthly Hierachy have the power and task " to communicate to their subjects, according to the dignity of each, the sacred deification " (ἐκθέωσις) ; " we are led up, by means of the multiform of sensible symbols, to the uniform Deification." [1] " The One is the very God," says Proclus, " but the Mind (the Noûs) is the divinest of beings, and the soul is divine, and the body is godlike. . . . And every body that is God-like is so through the soul having become divine ; and every soul that is divine, is so through the Mind being very divine ; and every Mind that is thus very divine, is so through participation in the Divine One." [2] There are preformations of this doctrine in Plotinus and echoes of it throughout Catherine's sayings.

And the Areopagite's teaching that the chief means and the culmination of this deification are found and reached in the reception of the Holy Eucharist will no doubt also have stimulated Catherine's mind : " The Communicant is led to the summit of deiformation, as far as this is possible for him." [3] And her soul responds completely to the beautiful Dionysian-Proclian teaching concerning God's presence in all things, as the cause of the profound sympathy which binds them all together. " They say," declares Dionysius, " that He is in minds . . . and in bodies, and in heaven and in earth ; (indeed that He is) sun, fire, water, spirit . . . all things existing, and yet again not one of all things existing." " The

---

[1] *Divine Names*, i, 5 ; *Ecclesiastical Hierarchy*, i, 2 ; *Divine Names*, ix, 5 ; Parker, pp. 8, 69, 104.

[2] *Institutio Theologica*, c. 129.

[3] *Ecclesiastical Hierarchy*, iii, 3, 7 ; Parker, p. 97.

distribution of boundless power passes from Almighty God to all things, and no single being but has intellectual, or rational, or sensible, or vital, or essential power." "The gifts of the unfailing Power pass on to men and (lesser) living creatures, to plants, and to the entire nature of the Universe."[1]   This latter passage was suggested by Proclus : " One would say that, through participation in the One, all things are deified, each according to its rank, inclusive of the very lowest of beings." "The image of the One and the inter-communion existing through it,—this it is that produces the extant sympathy " which permeates all things.[2]—But Catherine has nowhere the term " echo," which is so dear to Dionysius: "His all-surpassing power holds together and preserves even the remotest of its echoes"; "the sun and plants are or hold most distant echoes of the Good and of Life "; indeed even the licentious man still possesses, in his very passion, "as it were a faint echo of Union and of Friendship."[3]

6. *Dionysius and Catherine ; three agreements and differences.*

I conclude with three important points of difference and similarity between Catherine and Dionysius.

(1) Catherine abstains from the use of those repulsive, impossibly hyperbolic epithets such as "the Super-Good," "the Above-Mind," which Dionysius is never weary of applying to God, and is content with ever feeling and declaring how high above the very best conception which she can form of mind and of goodness He undoubtedly is; thus wisely moderated, I take it, by her constant experience and faith as to God's immediate presence within the human soul, which soul cannot, consequently, be presented as entirely remote from the nature of God.

(2) Catherine transforms over-intense and impoverishing insistence upon the pure Oneness of God, such as we find it even in Dionysius and still more in Proclus, into a, sometimes equally over-intense, conception as to the oneness of our union with Him, leaving Him to be still conceived as an overflowing richness of all kinds.

(3) And Catherine keeps, in an interesting manner, the Hellenic, and specifically Platonic, formulation for the deepest of her experiences and teachings, since her standing designation

---

[1] *Divine Names,* i, 6; viii, 3; 5 : Parker, pp. 10, 95, 96.
[2] *In Parmenidem,* iv, 34; v.
[3] *Divine Names,* viii, 2; iv, 4; iv, 20 : Parker, pp. 95, 84, 57.

of God and of Our Lord is never personal, "My Lover" or " My Friend "; but, as it were, elemental, " Love " or " My Love." Her keen self-purifying instinct and reverence for God will have spontaneously inclined her thus to consider Him first as an Ocean of Being in which to quench and drown her small, clamorous individuality, and this as a necessary step towards reconstituting that true personality, which, itself spirit, would be penetrated and sustained by the Spirit, Christ, God. And then the Pauline-Johannine picturings of God as a quasi-place and extended substance (" from Him and in Him and to Him," "in the Spirit," "in Christ," "God is Charity and he that abideth in Charity, abideth in Him ") will have strongly confirmed this trend. Yet Dionysius too must have greatly helped on this movement of her mind. For in Dionysius the standing appellations for God are, in true Neo-Platonist fashion, derived from extended or diffusive material substances or conditions, Light, Fire, Fountain, Ocean; and from that pervasive emotion, Love, strictly speaking Desire, Eros.

Now this, for our modern and Christian feeling, curiously impersonal, general and abstract method goes back, through Proclus and Plotinus, to Plato, who, above all in his *Symposium*, is dominated by the two tendencies and requirements, of identifying the First and Perfect with the most General and the most Abstract; and of making the very pre-requisites and instruments of the search for It,—even the earthly Eros, still so far from the Heavenly Eros and from the Christian Agapē,—into occasions, effects or instalments of and for the great Reality sought by them. And since it is thus the love, the desire, the eros, of things beautiful, and true, and good,—a love first sensible, then intellectual, and at last spiritual, which makes us seek and find It, the Beauty, Truth, and Goodness which is First Cause and Final End of the whole series, this Cause and End will be considered not as a Lover but as Love Itself. It is plain, I think, that it is specially this second motive, this requirement of a pervading organization and circle of and within the life of spirits and of the Spirit, which has also determined Catherine to retain Plato's terminology.

IV. Jacopone da Todi's "Lode."

In the case of Jacopone, the suddenly wife-bereft and converted lawyer, an ardent poet doubled by a soaring, daring mystic, with an astonishing richness of simultaneous symbols and conceptions and rapidity of successive complements and contrasts, it will really be simplest if I take the chief touches which have characteristically stimulated Catherine or have left her unaffected, in the order and grouping in which they appear in his chief "Lode," as these latter are given in the first printed edition, probably the very one used by Catherine.[1]

1. *Lode XIII, XXIII, XXXV, XLV.*

In Loda XIII "the vicious soul is likened unto Hell," vv. 1–7; and "the soul that yesterday was Hell, to-day has turned into Heaven," v. 8. We thus get here, precisely as in Catherine, the spaceless conditions of the soul and their modifications treated under the symbols of places and of the spatial change from one place to the other.

In Loda XXIII we first have five successive purifications and purities of Love, "carnal, counterfeit, self-seeking, natural, spiritual, transformed," vv. 1–6; and then the symbols of spatial location and movement reappear, "if height does not abase itself, it cannot participate with, nor communicate itself to, the lowest grade"; all which is frequent with Catherine. But she nowhere echoes the teaching reproduced here, v. 10, as to the Divine Trinity being figured in man's three faculties of soul.

Loda XXXV gives us a sort of Christian Stoicism very dear to Catherine: "Thou, my soul, hast been created in great elevation; thy nature is grounded in great nobility (*gentilezza*)," v. 7; "thou hast not thy life in created things; it is necessary for thee to breathe in other countries, to mount up to God, thine inheritance, Who (alone) can satisfy thy poverty," v. 10; "great is the honour which thou doest to God, when thou abidest (*stare*) in Him, in thy (true) nobility," v. 11.

---

[1] *Laude de lo contemplativo et extatico B. F. Jacopone de lo Ordine de lo Seraphico S. Francesco.* . . . In Firenze, per Ser Francesco Bonaccorsi, MCCCCLXXXX. Only the sheets are numbered; and two Lode have, by mistake, been both numbered LVIII: I have indicated them by LVIII*a* and LVIII*b* respectively. I have much felt the absence of any monograph on the sources and characters of Jacopone's doctrine.

Loda XLV gives " the Five Modes in which God appears in the Soul "—" the state of fear " ; curative, " healing-love " ; " the way of love " ; " the paternal mode " ; " the mode of espousals." Catherine leaves the last two, anthropomorphic and familial, conceptions quite unused, and passes in her life, at one bound, from the first to the third mode.

2. *Lode LVIIIa, LVIIIb.*

The fine Loda LVIII*a*, " Of Holy Poverty, Mistress of all Things," has evidently suggested much to Catherine. " Waters, rivers, lakes, and ocean, fish within them and their swimming; airs, winds, birds, and all their flying : all these turn to jewels for me," v. 10. How readily the sense of water, and of rapid movement within it, passes here into that of air, and of swift locomotion within *it !* And both these movements are felt to represent, in vivid fashion, certain very different experiences of the soul.—" Moon, Sun, Sky, and Stars,—even these are *not* amongst my treasures : above the very sky those things abide, which are the object of my song," v. 11. The positive, " analogic " method has here turned suddenly into the negative, " apophatic " one; and yet, even here, we still have the spatial symbolism, for the best is the highest up,—indeed it is this very symbolism which is made to add point to the negative declaration, a declaration which nevertheless clearly implies the mere symbolism of that spatialization. All this is fully absorbed by Catherine.— " Since God has my will, . . . my wings have such feathers that from earth to heaven there is no distance for me," v. 12. Here we see how Plato filters through, complete, to Jacopone; but only in his central idea to Catherine. For the *Phaedrus*, 246*b*, *c*, teaches : " The perfect soul then, having become winged, soars upwards, and is the ruler of the universe; whilst the imperfect soul sheds her feathers and is borne downwards, till it settles on the solid ground." Catherine never mentions wings nor feathers, but often dwells upon flying.

The great Loda LVIII*b*, " Of Holy Poverty and its Treble Heaven," (one passage of which is formally quoted and carefully expounded by Catherine), is a combination of Platonism, Paulinism, and Franciscanism, and has specially influenced her through its Platonist element. Verses 1–9 contain a fine apostrophe to Poverty. " O Love of Poverty, Reign of tranquillity ! Poverty, high Wisdom ! to be subject to nothing; through despising to possess all things created ! " v. 1: all this is echoed by Catherine. But the ex-lawyer's

declaration that such a soul " has neither judge nor notary,"
v. 3, did certainly not determine her literally, for we have
had before us some fifteen cases in which she had recourse to
lawyers. " God makes not His abode in a narrow heart;
thou art, oh man, precisely as great as thine affection may be.
The spirit of poverty possesses so ample a bosom, that Deity
Itself takes up its dwelling there," v. 8. Catherine's deepest
self seems to breathe from out of this profound saying.

Verses 10 to 30 describe the three heavens of successive
self-despoilments. The firmamental heaven, which typifies
the four-fold renouncement,—of honour, riches, science, reputation of sanctity, has left no echo in Catherine. The stellar
heaven is " composed of solidified clear waters (*aque solidate*) ";
here " the four winds " cease " that move the sea,—that per-
turb the mind : fear and hope, grief and joy," 11–14. Here
Plato again touches Catherine through Jacopone. For the
Symposium, 197*a*, declares : " Love it is that produces peace
among men and calm on the sea, a cessation of the winds,
and repose and sleep even in trouble "; and Jacopone identi-
fies the middle " crystalline " heaven, (" the waters above " of
Genesis, chap. i,) with Plato's " sea "; takes Plato's (four) winds
as the soul's chief passions; and considers Plato's " peace "
and " windlessness " as equivalent to the " much silence,"
which, says the Apocalypse, " arose in heaven," viii, 1, interpreted here as " in mid-heaven." " Not to fear Hell, nor to
hope for Heaven, to rejoice in no good, to grieve over no
adversity," v. 16, is a formulation unlike Catherine, although
single sayings of hers stand for sentiments analogous to the
first and last.—" If the virtues are naked, and the vices are
not garmented,—mortal wounds get given to the soul," v. 19,
has a symbolism exactly opposite to Catherine's, who, we
know, loves to glorify " nakedness " as the soul's purity.—
" The highest heaven " is " beyond even the imagings of the
mortified fancy "; " of every good it has despoiled thee, and
has expropriated thee from all virtue : lay up as a treasure
this thy gain,—the sense of thine own vileness." " O purified
Love ! it alone lives in the truth ! " These verses, 20–22, have
left a deep impress upon Catherine, although she wisely does
not press that " expropriation from virtue," which goes back
at least to Plotinus, for whom the true Ecstatic is " beyond the
choir of the virtues." [1]

[1] *Enneads*, vi, ch. ix, 11.

" That which appears to thee (as extant), is not truly existent : so high (above) is that which truly is.   True elevation of soul (*la superbia*) dwells in heaven above, and baseness of mind (*humilitade*) leads to damnation," v. 24, is a saying to which we still have Catherine's detailed commentary. In its markedly Platonic distinction between an upper true and a lower seeming world, and in its characteristically mystical love of paradox and a play upon words, it is more curious than abidingly important ; but in its deeply Christian consciousness of " pride " and " humility," in their ordinary ethical sense, being respectively the subtlest vice and the noblest virtue, it rises sheer above all Platonist and Neo-Platonist apprehension.

" Love abides in prison, in that darksome light !   All light there is darkness, and all darkness there is as the day," vv. 26, 27.   Here Catherine no doubt found aids towards her prison-conception,—of the loving soul imprisoned in the earthly body, and of the imperfect, yet loving, disembodied souls imprisoned in Purgatory ; and towards articulating her strong sense of the change in the meaning and value of the same symbols, as the soul grows in depth and experience.   But her symbolization of God, and of our apprehension of Him as Light and Fire, is too solidly established in her mind, to allow her to emphasize the darkness-symbol with any reference to Him.

" There where Christ is enclosed (in the soul), all the old is changed by Him,—the one is transformed into the Other, in a marvellous union.   To live as I and yet not I ; and my very being to be not mine : this is so great a cross-purpose (*traversio*), that I know not how to define it," vv. 28–30.   This vivid description, based of course upon St. Paul, of the apparent shifting of the very centre of the soul's personality, has left clear echoes in Catherine's sayings ; but the explicit reference to Christ is here as characteristically Franciscan as it is unlike Catherine's special habits.—And the great poem ends with a *refrain* of its opening apostrophe.

3. *Lode LXXIV, LXXIX, LXXXI, LXXXIII.*

In the dramatically vivid Dialogue between the Old and the Young Friar " Concerning the divers manners of contemplating the Cross," Loda LXXIV, the elder says to the younger man : " And I find the Cross full of arrows, which issue from its side : they get fixed in my heart.   The Archer

has aimed them at me; He causes me to be pierced," v. 6.
The Cross is here a bow; and yet the arrows evidently issue
not from it, but, as so many rays, from the Sun, the Light-
Christ, Who is laid upon it,—from the heart of the Crucified.
Catherine maintains the rays and arrows, and the Sun and
Fire from which they issue; but the Cross and the Crucified,
presupposed here throughout, appear not, even to this extent,
in her post-conversion picturings.—" You abide by the
warmth, but I abide within the fire; to you it is delight, but
I am burning through and through, I cannot find a place of
refuge in this furnace," v. 13. All this has been echoed
throughout by Catherine.

Loda LXXIX, " Of the Divine Love and its Praises," has
evidently much influenced her. " O joyous wound, delightful
wound, gladsome wound, for him who is wounded by Thee,
O Love! " " O Love, divine Fire! Love full of laughter and
playfulness! " " O Love, sweet and suave; O Love, Thou
art the key of heaven! Ship that Thou art, bring me to port
and calm the tempest," vv. 3, 6, 16. All this we have found
reproduced in her similes and experiences. " Love, bounteous
in spending Thyself; Love with wide-spread tables! " " Love,
Thou art the One that loves, and the Means wherewith the
heart loves Thee! " vv. 24, 26. These verses give us the
wide, wide world outlook, the connection between Love and
the Holy Eucharist, and the identity of the Subject, Means,
and Object of Love, which are all so much dwelt upon by
Catherine.

Loda LXXXI is interesting by the way in which, although
treating of " the love of Christ upon the Cross," it everywhere
apostrophizes Love and not the Lover, and treats the former,
again like Catherine, as a kind of boundless living substance;
indeed v. 17 must have helped to suggest one of her favourite
conceptions: " O great Love, greater than the great sea! Oh!
the man who is drowned within it, under it, and with it all
around him, whilst he knows not where he is! "

Loda LXXXIII has two touches dear to Catherine. " O
Love, whose name is ' I love '—the plural is never found," v. 5,
—a saying which evidently is directed, not against a social
conception of religion, but against a denial of the Divine Love
being Source as well as Object of our love; and " I did not
love Thee with any gain to myself, until I loved Thee for
Thine own sake," v. 15,—a declaration of wondrous depth
and simplicity.

4. *Lode LXXXVIII, LXXXIX, LXXXX, LXXXXVIII, LXXXXIX*.

The great Loda LXXXVIII, " How the soul complains to God concerning the excessive ardours of the love infused into it," contains numerous touches which have been interestingly responded to or ignored by Catherine. " All my will is on fire with Love, is united, transformed (into It) ; who can bear such Love ? Nor fire nor sword can part the loving soul and her Love; a thing so united cannot be divided; neither suffering nor death can henceforth mount up to that height where the soul abides in ecstasy," vv. 5, 6 : a combination of St. Paul and Plotinus, quite after Catherine's heart. But " the light of the sun appears to me obscure, now that I see that resplendent Countenance," v. 7, has an anthropomorphic touch to which she does not respond; and " I have given all my heart, that it may possess that Lover who renews me so,—O Beauty ancient and ever new ! " v. 10, has the personal designation " Lover," which, again, is alien to her vocabulary.

" Seeing such Beauty, I have been drawn out of myself . . . and the heart now gets undone, melted as though it were wax, and finds itself again, with the likeness of Christ upon it," v. 11, must have stimulated, by its first part, some of her own experiences, and will, by its second part, taken literally, have helped on the fantastic expectations of her attendants. " Love rises to such ardour, that the heart seems to be transfixed as with a knife," v. 14, no doubt both expressed an experience of Jacopone and helped to constitute the form of a similar experience on the part of Catherine. " As iron, which is all on fire, as dawn, made resplendent by the sun, lose their own form (nature) and exist in another, so is it with the pure mind, when clothed by Thee, O Love," v. 21, contains ideas, (all but the symbol of clothing), very dear to Catherine. But the astonishingly daring words : " Since my soul has been transformed into Truth, into Thee, O Christ alone, into Thee Who art tender Loving,—not to myself but to Thee can be imputed what I do. Hence, if I please Thee not, Thou dost not please Thine Own Self, O Love ! " v. 22, remain unechoed by her, no doubt because her states shift from one to another, and she wisely abstains from pushing the articulation of any one of them to its own separate logical limit.

" Thou wast born into the world by love and not by flesh, O Love become Man (*humanato Amore*)," v. 27, is like her in its interesting persistence in the "Love" (not "Lover") designation, but is unlike her in its definite reference to the historic Incarnation. "Love, O Love, Jesus, I have reached the haven," v. 32, is closely like her, all but the explicit mention of the historic name; and "Love, O Love, Thou art the full-orbed circle," "Thou art both warp and woof," beginning and end, material and transforming agency, v. 33, is Catherine's central idea, expressed in a form much calculated to impress it upon her.

The daring and profound Loda LXXXIX, "How the soul, by holy self-annihilation and love, reaches an unknowable and indescribable state," contains again numerous touches which have been assimilated by Catherine. So with: "Drawn forth, out of her natural state, into that unmeasurable condition whither love goes to drown itself, the soul, having plunged into the abyss of this ocean, henceforth cannot find, on any side, any means of issuing forth from it," vv. 12, 13. So also with: "Since thou dost no longer love thyself, but alone that Goodness . . . it has become necessary for thee again to love thyself, but with His Love,—into so great an unity hast thou been drawn by Him," vv. 52–54. So too with: "All Faith ceases for the soul to whom it has been given to see; and all Hope, since it now actually holds what it used to seek," v. 70, although this is more absolute than are her similar utterances. —But especially are the startling words interesting: "In this transformation, thou drinkest Another, and that Other drinketh thee (*tu bevi e sei bevuto, in transformazione*)," v. 98, which, in their second part, are identical with R. Browning's "My end, to slake Thy thirst":[1] for they will have helped to support or to encourage Catherine's corresponding inversion— the teaching of an eating, an assimilation, not of God by man, but of man by God. Both sets of images go back, of course, to the Eucharistic reception by the soul of the God-man Christ, under the forms of Bread eaten and of Wine drunk.

The striking Loda LXXXX, "How the soul arrives at a treble state of annihilation," has doubtless suggested much to Catherine. "He who has become the very Cause of all things" (*chi è cosa d'ogni cosa*) "can never more desire anything," v. 4, is, it is true, more daring, because more quietly explicit, than any saying of hers. But v. 13 has been echoed by her throughout: "The heavens have grown stagnant; their

---

[1] *Rabbi Ben Ezra*, XXXI.

silence constrains me to cry aloud : ' O profound Ocean, the
very depth of Thine Abyss has constrained me to attempt and
drown myself within it,'"—where note the interestingly antique
presupposition of the music of the spheres, which has now
stopped, and of the watery constitution of the crystalline
heaven, which allows of stagnation; and the rapidity of the
change in the impressions,—from immobility to silence, and
from air to water.   Indeed that Ocean is one as much of air
as of water, and as little the one as the other ; and its attractive
force is still that innate affinity between the river-soul and its
living Source and Home, the Ocean God, which we have so
constantly found in Plotinus, Proclus, and Dionysius.   " The
land of promise is, for such a soul, no longer one of promise
only : for the perfect soul already reigns within that land.
Men can thus transform themselves, in any and every place,"
v. 18, has, in its touching and lofty Stoic-Christian teaching,
found the noblest response and re-utterance in and by
Catherine's words and life.

Loda LXXXXVIII, " Of the Incarnation of the Divine
Word," full though it is of beautiful Franciscanism, has left
her uninfluenced.   But the fine Loda LXXXXIX, " How true
Love is not idle," contains touches which have sunk deep
into her mind.   " Splendour that givest to all the world its
light, O Love Jesus . . . heaven and earth are by Thee;
Thine action resplends in all things and all things turn to
Thee.   Only the sinner despises Thy Love and severs himself
from Thee, his Creator," v. 6, is, in its substance, taken over
by her.   " O ye cold sinners ! " v. 12, is her favourite epithet.
And vv. 13, 14, with their rapid ringing of the changes on the
different sense-perceptions, will, by their shifting vividness,
have helped on a similar iridescence in her own imagery : " O
Odour, that transcendest every sweetness !   O living river of
Delight . . . that causest the very dead to return to their
vigour !   In heaven Thy lovers possess Thine immense Sweetness, tasting there those savoury morsels."

And finally Loda LXXXVII, " Of true and false discretion,"
which, in vv. 12–20, consists of a dialogue between " the Flesh "
and " the Reason," will have helped to suggest the slight
beginnings of this form of apprehension to Catherine which
we have found amongst her authentic sayings and experiences,
and which were, later on, developed on so large a scale, by
Battista Vernazza, throughout her long *Dialogo della Beata
Caterina.*

5. Jacopone it is, then, who furnished Catherine with much help towards that rare combination of deep feeling with severely abstract thinking which, if at times it somewhat strains and wearies us moderns who would ever end with the concrete, gives a nobly virile, bracing note to even the most effective of her sayings.

V. POINTS COMMON TO ALL FIVE MINDS; AND CATHERINE'S MAIN DIFFERENCE FROM HER FOUR PREDECESSORS.

If we now consider for a moment the general points common to the four writers just considered and to Catherine, we readily note that all five are profoundly reflective and interpretative in their attitude towards the given contingencies of traditional religion; that they all tend to find the Then and There of History still at work, in various degrees, Here and Now, throughout Time and Space, and in the last resort, above and behind both these categories, in a spaceless, timeless Present. And if only three, Paul, Jacopone, and Catherine, bear marks, throughout all they think and feel and do and are, of the cataclysmic conversion-crisis through which they had passed,—the temporally intermediate two, John and Dionysius, have also got, but in a more indirect form, much of a similar Dualism. All five are, in these and other respects, indefinitely closer to each other than any one of them is to the still richer, more complete, and more entirely balanced though less articulated, Synoptic teaching, which enfolds all that is abiding in those other five, whilst they, even if united, do not approximately exhaust the substance of that teaching.

And if we would briefly define the main point on which Catherine holds views additional to, or other than, those other four, we must point to her Purgatorial teaching, which has received but little or no direct suggestion from any one of them, and which, whatever may have been its literary precursors and occasions, gives, perhaps more than anything else, a peculiarly human and personal, original and yet still modern, touch to what would otherwise be, to our feeling, too abstract and antique a spiritual physiognomy.

CHAPTER XI

CATHERINE'S LESS ULTIMATE THIS-WORLD DOCTRINES

INTRODUCTORY : CATHERINE'S LESS ULTIMATE POSITIONS, CONCERNING OUR LIFE HERE, ARE FOUR.

WE have now attempted, (by means of a doubtless more or less artificial distinction between things that, in real life, constitute parts of one whole in a state of hardly separable interpenetration,) a presentation of Catherine's special, mental and psycho-physical, character and temperament, and of the principal literary stimulations and materials which acted upon, and in return were refashioned by, that character ; and we have also given, in sufficient detail, the resultant doctrines and world-view acquired and developed by that deep soul and noble mind. The most important and difficult part of our task remains, however, still to be accomplished,—the attempt to get an (at least approximate) estimate of the abiding meaning, place, and worth of this whole, highly synthesized position, for and within the religious life generally and our present-day requirements in particular. For the general outline of the Introduction, (intended there more as an instrument of research and classification for the literature and history then about to be examined, than as this history's final religious appraisement,) cannot dispense us from now attempting something more precise and ultimate.—I propose, then, to give the next four chapters to an examination of Catherine's principal positions and practices, the first two, respectively, to " the less ultimate This-World Doctrines "; and " the Other-World Doctrines," or " the Eschatology "; and the last two to " the Ultimate Implications and Problems " underlying both. The last chapter shall then sum up the whole book, and consider the abiding place and function of Mysticism, in its contrast to, and supplementation of, Asceticism, Institutionalism, and the Scientific Habit and Activity of the Mind.

Now I think the less ultimate spiritual positions, as far as they concern our life here below, which are specially represented, or at least forcibly suggested by, Catherine, can reasonably be accounted as four : Interpretative Religion ; a strongly Dualistic attitude towards the body ; Quietude and Passivity ; and Pure Love. I shall devote a section to each position.

I. Interpretative Religion.

1. *Difficulties of the Subjective element of Religion.*

Now, by Interpretative Religion, I do not mean to imply that there is anywhere, in *rerum natura*, such a thing as a religion which is not interpretative, which does not consist as truly of a reaction on the part of the believing soul to certain stimulations of and within it, as of these latter stimulations and actions. As every (even but semi-conscious) act and state of the human mind, ever embraces both such action of the object and such reaction of the subject,—a relatively crude fact of sensation or of feeling borne in upon it, and an interpretation, an incorporation of this fact by, and into, the living tissue and organism of this mind : so is it also, necessarily and above all, with the deepest and most richly complex of all human acts and states,—the specifically religious ones. But if this interpretative activity of the mind was present from the very dawn of human reason, and exists in each individual in the precise proportion as mind can be predicated as operative within him at all : this mental activity is yet the last element in the compound process and result which is, or can be, perceived as such by the mind itself. The process is too near to the observer, even when he is once awake to its existence ; he is too much occupied with the materials brought before his mind and with moulding and sorting them out ; and this moulding and sorting activity is itself too rapid and too deeply independent of those materials as to its form, and too closely dependent upon them as to its content, for the observation by the mind of this same mind's contributions towards its own affirmations of reality and of the nature of this reality, not ever to appear late in the history of the human race or in the life of any human individual, or not to be, even when it appears difficult, a fitful and an imperfect mental exercise.

And when the discovery of this constant contribution of the mind to its own affirmations of reality is first made, it can hardly fail, for the time being, to occasion misgivings and anxieties of a more or less sceptical kind. Is not the whole of what I have hitherto taken to be a solid world of sense outside me, and the whole of the world of necessary truth and of obligatory goodness within me,—is it not, perhaps, all a merely individual creation of my single mind—a mind cut off from all effective intercourse with reality,—my neighbour's mind included? For all having, so far, been held to be objective, the mind readily flies to the other extreme, and suspects all to be subjective. Or if all my apprehensions and certainties are the resultants from the interaction between impressions received by my senses and mind and reactions and elaborations on the part of this mind with regard to those impressions, how can I be sure of apprehending rightly, unless I can divide each constituent off from the other? And yet, how can I effect such a continuous discounting of my mind's action by means of my own mind itself?

And this objection is felt most keenly in religion, when the religious soul first wakes up to the fact that itself, of necessity and continuously, contributes, by its own action, to the constitution of those affirmations and certainties, which, until then, seemed, without a doubt, to be directly borne in upon a purely receptive, automatically registering mind, from that extra-, super-human world which it thus affirmed. Here also, all having for so long been assumed to be purely objective, the temptation now arises to consider it all as purely subjective. Or again, if we insist upon holding that, here too, there are both objective and subjective elements, we readily experience keen distress at our inability clearly to divide off the objective, which is surely the reality, from the subjective, which can hardly fail to be its travesty.

And finally, this doubt and trouble would seem to find specially ready material in the mystical element and form of religion. For here, as we have already seen, psycho-physical and auto-suggestive phenomena and mechanisms abound; here especially does the mind cling to an immediate access to Reality; and here the ordinary checks and complements afforded by the Historical and Institutional, the Analytically Rational, and the Volitional, Practical elements of Religion are at a minimum. Little but the Emotional and the Speculatively Rational elements seems to remain; and these, more than any others, appear incapable of admitting that they are anything other than the pure and direct effects and expressions of spiritual Reality.

What, then, shall we think of all this?

2. *Answers to the above difficulties.*

We evidently must, in the first instance, guard against any attempt at doing a doctrinaire violence to the undeniable facts of our consciousness or of its docile analysis, by explaining all our knowledge, or only even all our knowledge of any single thing, as either of purely subjective or of purely objective provenance; for everywhere and always these two elements co-exist in all human apprehension, reason, feeling, will, and faith. We find, throughout, an organization, an indissoluble organism, of subjective and objective, hence a unity in diversity, which is indeed so great that (for our own experience and with respect to our own minds at all events), the Subjective does not and cannot exist without the Objective, nor the Objective without the Subjective.

In the next place, we must beware against exalting the Objective against the Subjective, or the Subjective against the Objective, as if Life, Reality, and Truth consisted in the one rather than the other. Because the subjective element is, on the first showing, a work of our own minds, it does not follow (as we shall see more clearly when studying the ultimate problems) that its operations are bereft of correspondence with reality, or, at least, that they are further from reality than are our sense-perceptions. For just as the degree of worth represented by these sense-perceptions can range from the crudest delusion to a stimulation of primary importance and exquisite precision, so also our mental and emotional reaction and penetration represent almost any and every degree of accuracy and value.

And, above all, as already implied, the true priority and superiority lies, not with one of these constituents against the other, but with the total subjective-objective interaction and resultant, which is superior, and indeed gives their place and worth to, those ever interdependent parts.

Now, in the general human experience, the Objective element is constituted, in the first instance and for clear and ready analysis, by the sense-stimulations; and, after some mental response to and elaboration of these, by the larger psychic moods; and later still, by the examples of great spiritual attitudes and of great personalities offered by other souls to the soul that keeps itself open to such impressions. And though the sense of Reality (as contrasted with Appearance), of the Abiding and Infinite (as different from the Passing and the Finite), are doubtless awakened, however faintly and inarticulately, in the human soul from the first, as the background and presupposition of the foreground and the middle-distances of its total world of perceptions and aspirations : yet all these middle-distances, as well as that great background and groundwork, would remain unawakened but for those humble little sense-perceptions on the one hand, and intercourse with human fellow-creatures on the other. And in such intercourse with the minds and souls, or with the literary remains and other monuments of souls, either still living here or gone hence some two thousand years or more, a mass of mental and moral impressions and stimulations, which, in those souls, were largely their own elaborations, offer themselves to any one human mind, or to the minds of a whole generation or country, with the apparent homogeneity of a purely objective, as it were a sense-impression.

Especially in Religion the Historical and Institutional (as Religion's manifestation in space and time), come down to us thus from the past and surround us in the present, and either press in upon us with a painful weight, or support us with a comforting solidity, thus giving them many of the qualities of things physically seen and touched, say, a mystery play or a vast cathedral. And, on the other hand, the Rational, (whether Analytic or Synthetic,) and the Emotional and Volitional Elements, whenever they are at all preponderant or relatively independent of the other, more objective ones, are liable, in Religion, to look quite exceptionally subjective, —and this in the unfavourable sense of the word, as though either superfluous and fantastic, or as dangerous and destructive.—And yet both that look of the objective elements being, in Religion, more self-sufficing than they appear to be in the ordinary psychic, or the artistic, or social, or scientific life ; and that impression conveyed by the subjective elements in Religion, as being there less necessary or more dangerous than elsewhere, are doubtless deceptive. These impressions are simply caused by two very certain facts. Religion is the deepest and most inclusive of all the soul's energizings and experiences, and hence all its constituents reveal a difference, at least in amount and degree, when compared with the corresponding constituents of the more superficial and more partial activities of the soul; and Religion, just because of this, requires the fullest action and co-operation, the most perfect unity, in and through diversity, of all the soul's powers, and all mere non-use of any of these forces, even any restriction to the use of but one or two, is here, more readily and extensively than elsewhere, detrimental both to the non-exercised and to the exercised forces, and, above all, is impoverishing to the soul itself and to its religion.

Hence, here as elsewhere, but more than anywhere, our ideal standard will be the greatest possible development of, and inter-stimulation between, each and all of the religious elements, with the greatest possible unity in the resulting organism. And yet,—in view of the very greatness of the result aimed at, and of the fact that its even approximate attainment can, even for any one age of the world, be reasonably expected only from the co-operation of the differently endowed and attracted races and nations, social and moral grades, sexes, ages and individuals that make up mankind,—we shall not only be very tolerant of, we shall positively encourage, largely one-sided developments, provided that each keeps some touch with the elements which itself knows not how to develop in abundance, and that it considers its own self, and works out its own special gift and *attrait*, as but one out of many variously gifted and apportioned fellow-servants in the Kingdom, —as only one of the countless, mutually complementary, individually ever imperfect, part-expressions of the manifold greatness, of the rich unity of spiritual humanity as willed by God, and of God Himself.

3. *Partial developments of the full Gospel Ideal.*

Now in the New Testament we have a most instructive, at first sight puzzling phenomenon, illustrative of the positions just taken up. For here it is clear that, with regard to the distinction between richly many-sided but as yet unarticulated religion, and comparatively one-sided and limited but profoundly developed religion, we have two considerably contrasted types of spiritual tone and teaching. We get the predominantly " Objective " strand of life and doctrine, in the pre-Pauline parts and in their non-Pauline echoes, *i. e.* in the substance of the Synoptic tradition, and in the Epistles of St. James and of St. Peter; and we find the predominantly " Subjective " strain in the " Pauline " parts, St. Paul's Epistles and the Johannine Gospel and Letters.—And it has become more and more clear that it is the pre-Pauline

parts which give us the most immediately and literally
faithful, and especially the most complete and many-sided,
picture of Our Lord's precise words and actions; whereas the
Pauline parts give us rather what some of these great creative
forces were and became for the first generations of Christians
and for the most penetrating of Christ's early disciples and
lovers. And yet it is the latter documents which, at first
sight, appear to be the deeper, the wider, and the more profoundly spiritual; whereas the former look more superficial,
more temporal and local, and more simply popular and
material.

And yet,—though this first impression has been held to be
finally true by large masses of Christians; although the Greek
Fathers predominantly, and, in the West, the great soul of an
Augustine, and the powerful but one-sided personalities of a
Luther and a Calvin have, in various degrees and ways, helped
to articulate and all but finally fix it for the general Christian
consciousness : this view is yielding, somewhat slowly but
none the less surely, to the sense that it is the Synoptic, the
pre-Pauline tradition which contains the fuller arsenal of the
spiritual forces which have transfigured and which still inspire
the world of souls. This, of course, does not mean that the
Pauline-Johannine developments were not necessary, or are
not abiding elements towards the understanding of the
Christian spirit.

And, to come to the true answer to our objection, such a
judgment does not mean that the reflective penetration and
reapplication of the original more spontaneous message was,
from the very nature of the case, inferior to the first less
articulated announcement of the Good Tidings. But it merely
signifies that this necessary process of reflection could only
be applied to parts of the original, immensely rich and varied,
because utterly living, divinely spiritual, whole; and that,
thus, the special balance and tension which characterized the
original, complete spirit and temper, could, however profoundly, be reproduced only in part. For the time being
this later penetration and resetting of some elements from
among the whole of Our Lord's divinely rich and simple life
and teaching, necessarily and rightly, yet none the less most
really, ignored, or put for the time into some other context,
certain other sides and aspects of that primitive treasure of
inexhaustible experience. Only the full, equable, and simultaneous unfolding of all the petals could have realized the

promise and content of the bud; whereas the bud, holding enfolded within itself such various elements and combinations of truth, could not expand its petals otherwise than successively, hence, at any one moment only somewhat one-sidedly and partially. Each and all of these unfoldings bring some further insight into, and articulation of, the original spiritual organism; and that they are not more, but less, than the totality of that primitive experience and revelation, does not prove that such reflective work is wrong or even simply dispensable,—for, on the contrary, in some degree or form it was and ever is necessary to the soul's apprehension of that life and truth,—but simply implies the immensity of the spiritual light and impulsion given by Our Lord, and the relative smallness of even the greatest of His followers.

Thus only if it could be shown that those parts of the New Testament which doubtless give us the nearest approach to the actual words and deeds of Our Lord require us to conceive them as having been without the reflective and emotional element; or again that, in the case of the more derivative parts of the New Testament, it is their reflective-ness, and not their relative incompleteness and onesidedness, that cause them to be more readily englobed in the former world, than that former world in the latter : could the facts here found be used as an argument against the importance and strict necessity for religion of the reflective and emotional, the " Subjective " elements, alongside of the " Objective," the Historical and Institutional ones.

It is a most legitimate ground for consolation to a Catholic when he finds the necessities of life and those of learned research both driving us more and more to this conclusion; for it is not deniable that Catholicism has ever refused to do more than include the Pauline and Johannine theologies amongst its earliest and most normative stimulations and expressions; and that it has ever retained, far more than Protestantism, the sense, which (upon the whole) is most unbrokenly preserved by the Synoptists, of, if I may so phrase it, the Christianity of certain true elements in the pre- and extra-Christian religions. For it is in the Synoptists that we get the clear presentation of Our Lord's attitude towards the Jewish Church of His time, as one, even at its keenest, analogous to that of Savonarola, and not to that of a Luther, still less of a Calvin, towards the Christian Church of their day.—Indeed in these documents all idea of limiting Christianity to what He brought of new, appears as foreign to His mind as it ever has been to that of the Catholic Church. Here we get the most spontaneous and many-sided expression of that divinely human, widely tradi- tional and social, all-welcoming and all-transforming spirit, which embraces both grace *and* nature, eternity *and* time, soul *and* body, attachment *and* detachment. The Pauline strain stands for the stress necessary to the full spiritualiza- tion of all those occasions and materials, as against all, mere unregenerate or static, retention of the simple rudiments or empty names of those things; and predominantly insists upon grace, *not* nature; eternity, *not* time; soul, *not* body; the cross and death here, the Crown and Life hereafter. No wonder it is this latter strain that gets repeated, with varying truth and success, in times of acute transition, and by char- acters more antithetic than synthetic, more great at develop- ing a part of the truth than the whole.

Thinkers, of such wide historical outlook and unim- peachable detachment from immediate controversial interest as Prof. Wilhelm Dilthey and Dr. Edward Caird, have brought out, with admirable force, this greater fulness of content offered by the Synoptists, and how the Pauline- Johannine writings give us the first and most important of those concentrations upon, and in part philosophic and mystical reinterpretations of, certain constituents of the original happenings, actions and message, as apprehended and transmitted by the first eye-witnesses and believers.[1]— Here I would but try and drive home the apparently vague, but in reality ever pressing and concrete, lesson afforded by the clear and dominant fact of these two groups within the New Testament itself :—of how no mere accumulation of external happenings, or of external testimony as to their having happened,—no amount of history or of institu- tionalism, taken as sheer, purely positive givennesses,—can anywhere be found, or can anywhere suffice for the human mind and conscience, in the apprehension and embodiment of the truth. For although, in Our Lord's most literally transmitted sayings and doings, this continuous and inalien- able element of the apprehending, organizing, vitalizing mind

[1] E. Caird, "St. Paul and the Idea of Evolution," *Hibbert Journal*, Vol. II, 1904, pp. 1-19. W. Dilthey has shown this by implication, in his studies of Erasmus, Luther, and Zwingli : *Archiv für Geschichte der Philosophie*, Vol. V, 1892, especially, pp. 381-385.

and heart,—on His part above all, but also on the part of His several hearers and chroniclers,—can mostly still be traced and must everywhere be assumed : yet it is in the Pauline-Johannine literature that the ever important, the rightly and fruitfully " subjective," the speculative and emotional, the mystical and the volitional strain can best be studied, both as to its necessity and as to its special character and dangers, because here it is developed to the relative exclusion of the other factors of complete religion.

4. *The exclusive emotionalism of Dionysius and Jacopone.*

Now if even in St. Paul and St. John there is a strong predominance of these reflective-emotional elements, in Dionysius and Jacopone they threaten to become exclusive of everything else. Especially is this the case with the Pseudo-Areopagite, steeped as he is in reflection upon reflections and in emotion upon emotions, often of the most subtle kind : a Christian echo, with curiously slight modifications, of Neo-Platonism in its last stage,—hence, unfortunately, of the over-systematic and largely artificial Proclus, instead of the predominantly experimental and often truly sublime Plotinus. And even Jacopone, although he has distinctly more of the historic element, is still predominantly reflective-emotional, and presents us with many a hardly modified Platonic or Stoic doctrine, derived no doubt from late Graeco-Roman writers and their mediaeval Christian echoes.

5. *Catherine's interpretation of the Gospel Ideal.*

Catherine herself, although delightfully free from the long scale of mediations between the soul and God which forms one of the predominant doctrines of the Areopagite, continues and emphasizes most of what is common, and much of what is special to, all and each of these four writers ; she is a reflective saint, if ever there was one. And of her too we shall have to say that she is great by what she possesses, and not by what she is without : great because of her noble embodiment of the reflective and emotional, the mystical and volitional elements of Christianity and Religion generally. Religion is here, at first sight at least, all but entirely a thought and an emotion; yet all this thought and emotion is directed to, and occasioned by, an abiding Reality which originates, sustains, regulates, and fulfils it. And although this Reality is in large part conceived, in Greek and specially in Neo-Platonist fashion, rather under its timeless and spaceless,

or at least under its cosmic aspect, rather as Law and Substance, than as Personality and Spirit : yet, already because
of the strong influence upon her of the noblest Platonic
doctrine, it is loved as overflowing Love and Goodness, as
cause and end of all lesser love and goodness; and the real,
though but rarely articulated, acceptance and influence of
History and Institutions, above all the enthusiastic devotion
to the Holy Eucharist with all its great implications, gives to
the whole a profoundly Christian tone and temper.

True, the Church at large, indeed the single soul (if we
would take such a soul as our standard of completeness)
requires a larger proportion of those crisp, definite outlines,
of those factual, historical, and institutional elements; a
very little less than what remains in Catherine of these
elements, and her religion would be a simple, even though
deep religiosity, a general aspiration, not a definite finding,
an explicit religion.   Yet it remains certain, although ever
readily forgotten by religious souls, especially by theological apologists, that without some degree and kind of those
outgoing, apprehending, interpreting activities, no religion is
possible.   Only the question as to what these activities should
be, and what is their true place and function within the whole
religious life, remains an open one.   And this question we
can study with profit in connection with such a life and
teaching as Catherine's, which brings out, with a spontaneous, childlike profundity and daring, the elemental religious
passion, the spiritual hunger and thirst of man when he is
once fully awake; the depths within him anticipating the
heights above him; the affinity to and contact with the
Infinite implied and required by that nobly incurable restlessness of his heart, which finds its rest in Him alone Who
made it.

II. DUALISTIC ATTITUDE TOWARDS THE BODY.

And if Catherine is profoundly reflective, that reflection is,
in its general drift, deeply dualistic,—at least in the matter
of body and spirit.   Their difference and incompatibility;
the spirit's fleeing of the body; the spirit's getting outside
of it,—by ecstasy, for a little while, even in this earthly
life, and by this earthly body's death, for good and all; the
body a prison-house, a true purgatory to the soul : all this

hangs well together, and is largely, in its very form, of ultimately Neo-Platonist or Platonic origin.

1. *New Testament valuations of the body.*

Now here is one of the promised instances of a double type—if not of doctrine, yet at least of emotional valuation in the New Testament.

(1) In the Synoptist documents, (with the but apparent, or at least solitary, exceptions, of Jesus' Fasting in the Desert and of His commendation of those who have made themselves eunuchs for the Kingdom of Heaven,)[1] we find no direct or acute antagonism to the body, even to the average earthly human body, in the teaching and practice of Our Lord.   The Second Coming and its proximity do indeed, here also, dwarf all earthly concerns, in so far as earthly.[2]   This background to the teaching and its tradition was, in course of time, in part abstracted from, in part restated.—The entrance into life is through the narrow gate and the steep way; only if a man turn, can he enter into the Kingdom of God; only if he lose his soul, can he find it : [3] this great teaching and example, as to life and joy being ever reached through death to self and by the whole-hearted turning of the soul from its false self to its true source, God : remains, in the very form of its promulgation as given by the Synoptists, the fundamental test and standard of all truly spiritual life and progress.   But as to the body in particular, Jesus here knows indeed that "the flesh is weak," and that we musy pray for strength against its weakness : [4] but He nowhere declares it evil—an inevitable prison-house or a natural antagonist to the spirit.   The beautiful balance of an unbroken, unstrained nature, and a corresponding doctrine as full of sober earnestness as it is free from all concentrated or systematic dualism, are here everywhere apparent.

(2) It is St. Paul, the man of the strongest bodily passions and temptations, he who became suddenly free from them by the all-transforming lightning-flash of his conversion, who, on and on, remained vividly conscious of what he had been and, but for that grace, still would be, and of what, through that grace he had become.   The deepest shadows are thus ever

---

[1] Mark i, 13, and parallels; Matt. xix, 10-12.

[2] Mark vi, 8; Matt. x, 26-38; viii, 19-22; xiii, 30-32; xxvi, 42, and parallels.

[3] Matt. vii, 13, 14; xviii, 1-5; xvi, 24-28.

[4] Mark xiv, 38, and parallels.

kept in closest contrast to the highest lights; and the line
of demarcation between them runs here along the division
between body and soul. " O wretched man that I am! who
shall deliver me out of the body of this death?" "In my
flesh dwelleth no good thing" : [1] are sayings which are both
keener in their tone and more limited in their range than are
Our Lord's. And we have seen how, in one of his most
depressed moods, he transiently adopts and carries on a specifically Platonist attitude towards the body's relation to the
soul, as he finds it in that beautiful, profoundly Hellenistic
treatise, the Book of Wisdom.[2] This attitude evidently represents, in his strenuous and deeply Christian character, only a
passing feeling; for, if we pressed it home, we could hardly
reconcile it with his doctrine as to the reality and nature of
the body's resurrection. It is indeed clear how the Platonist,
and especially the Neo-Platonist, mode of conceiving that
relation excludes any and every kind of body from the soul's
final stage of purification and happiness; and how the
Synoptic, and indeed the generally Christian conception of
it, necessarily eliminates that keen and abiding dualism
characteristic of the late Greek attitude.

2. *Platonic, Synoptic, and Pauline elements in Catherine's
view.*

Now in Catherine we generally find an interesting combination of the Platonic form with the Synoptic substance
and spirit : and this can, of course, be achieved only because
that abiding form itself is made to signify a changed set and
connection of ideas.

(1) We have seen how she dwells much, Plotinus-like, upon
the soul's stripping itself of all its numerous garments, and
exposing itself naked to the rays of God's healing light. Yet
in the original Platonic scheme these garments are put on
by the soul in its descent from spirit into matter, and are
stripped off again in its ascent back out of matter into spirit;
in both cases, they stand for the body and its effects. In
Catherine, even more than in Plotinus, the garments stand
for various evil self-attachments and self-delusions of the
soul; and against these evils and dangers the Synoptists
furnish endless warnings. And yet she insists upon purity,
clear separation, complete abstraction of the soul, in such
terms as still to show plainly enough the originally Neo-

---

[1] Rom. vii, 24, 18.
[2] 2 Cor. v, 1–4 = Wisd. of Sol. ix, 15.

Platonist provenance of much of her form; for in the Neo-Platonists we get, even more markedly than here, a like insistence upon the natural dissimilarity of the body and the soul, and a cognate longing to get away from it in ecstasy and death. But whilst in the Neo-Platonists there is, at the bottom of all this, a predominant belief that the senses are the primary source and occasion of all sin, so that sin is essentially the contamination of spirit by matter : in Catherine, (although she shares to the full Plotinus's thirst for ecstasy, as the escape from division and trouble into unity and peace,) impurity stands primarily for self-complacency,—belief in, and love of, our imaginary independence of even God Himself; and purity means, in the first instance, the loving Him and His whole system of souls and of life, and one's own self only in and as part of that system.

It is very instructive to note, in this connection, how, after her four years of directly penitential and ascetical practice, (an activity which, even then, extended quite as much to matters of decentralization of the self as of bodily mortification,) her warfare is, in the first instance, all but exclusively directed against the successive refuges and ambushes of self-complacency and self-centredness. Thus there is significance in the secondary place occupied, (even in the *Vita*, and doubtless still more in her own mind,) by the question of continence; indeed her great declaration to the Friar indicates plainly her profound concentration upon the continuous practice of, and growth in, Love Divine, and her comparative indifference to the question of the systematic renunciation of anything but sin and selfish attachments and self-centrednesses of any kind. Her conception of sinners as " cold," even more than as dark or stained; of God as Fire, even more than as Light; and of purity as indefinitely increasable, since Love can grow on and on : all similarly point to this finely positive, flame-, not snow-conception, in which purity has ceased to be primarily, as with the Greeks, a simple absence of soiledness, even if it be moral soiledness, and has become, as with the Synoptic teaching, something primarily positive, love itself.

In her occasionally intense insistence upon herself as being all evil, a very Devil, and in some of her picturings of her interior combat, we get, on the other hand, echoes, not of Plato, nor again of the Synoptist teaching, but of St. Paul's " in my flesh there dwelleth no good thing," and of his combat between flesh and spirit.—Yet the evil which she is thus conscious of, is not sensual nor even sensible evil and temptation, but consists in her unbounded natural claimfulness and intense inclination to sensitive self-absorption.—And this gives, indeed, to these feminine echoes of St. Paul a certain thin shrillness which the original tones have not got, standing there for the massive experiences of a man violently solicitated by both sense and spirit. But it leaves her free to note, as regards the flesh, the whole bodily organism, (and this in beautiful sympathy with Our Lord's own genially fervent, homely heroic spirit,) not its wickedness, but its weakness, its short-livedness, and its appeal for merciful allowance to God, " Who knows that we are dust." Instead of a direct and pointed dualism of two distinct substances informed by all but incurably antagonistic principles, we thus get a direct conflict between two dispositions of the soul, and a but imperfect correspondence between the body and that soul.

(2) There is, indeed, no doubt that the very ancient association of the ideas of Fire and of spiritual Purification goes back, in the first instance, to the conception of the soul being necessarily stained by the very fact of its connection with the body, and of those stains being finally removed by the body's death and cremation. We find this severely self-consistent view scattered up and down Hellenic religion and literature.[1] And even in Catherine the fire, a sense of fever-heat, still seizes the body, and this body wastes away, and leaves the soul more and more pure, during those last years of illness.—Yet the striking identity, between that old cluster of ideas and her own forms of thought, brings out, all the more clearly, the immense road traversed by spirituality between the substance of those ideas and the essence of this thought. For in her teaching, which is but symbolized or at most occasioned by those physico-psychical fever-heats, the Fire is, at bottom, so spiritual and so directly busy with the soul alone, that it is ever identical with itself in Heaven, Hell, Purgatory, and on earth, and stands for God Himself; and that its effects are not the destruction of a foreign substance, but the bringing back, wherever and as far as possible, of the fire-like soul's disposition and equality to full harmony with its Fire-source and Parent, God Himself.

[1] See Erwin Rohde's *Psyche*, ed. 1898, Vol. II, p. 101, n. 2.

(3) Only the Prison-house simile for the body, as essentially an earthly purgatory for the soul, must be admitted, I think, to remain a primarily Platonic, not fully Christianizable conception; just as the absence of all reference by her to the resurrection of the body will have been, in part, occasioned by the strong element of Platonism in her general selection and combination of ideas. Yet it would obviously be unfair to press these two points too much, since, as to the resurrection, her long illness and evidently constant physical discomfort must, even of themselves, have disinclined her to all picturing of an abiding, even though highly spiritualized, bodily organization; and as to the likeness of her body to a prison and purgatory of the soul, we are expressly told that it began only with the specially suffering last part of her life.

3. *Dualism pragmatic, not final. Its limits.*

Now, for this whole matter of the right conception as to the relations of body and soul, it is clear that any more than partial and increasingly superable antagonism between body and spirit cannot be accepted.

(1) A final Dualism is unsound in Psychology, since all the first materials, stimulations, and instruments for even our most abstract thinking are supplied to us by our sense-perceptions, hence also through the body. It is narrow in Cosmology, for we do not want to isolate man in this great universe of visible things; and his link with animal- and plant-life, and even with the mineral creation is, increasingly as we descend in the scale of beings, his body. It is ruinous for Ethics, because purity, in such a physical-spiritual being as is man, consists precisely in spiritual standards and laws extending to and transforming his merely physical inclinations. It is directly contradictory of the central truth and temper of Christianity, since these require a full acceptance of the substantial goodness and the thorough sanctifiableness of man's body; of God's condescension to man's whole physico-spiritual organism; and of the persistence or reanimation of all that is essential to man's true personality across and after death. And it is, at bottom, profoundly un-Catholic; the whole Sacramental system, the entire deep and noble conception of the normal relations between the Invisible and the Visible being throughout of the Incarnational type,—an action of the one in the other, which develops the agent and subject at the same time that it spiritualizes the patient, the object, is in direct conflict

with it. Neo-Platonism came more and more to treat the body
and the entire visible creation as an intrinsic obstacle to spirit,
to be eliminated by the latter as completely as possible; at
least this very prominent strain within it was undoubtedly
pushed on to this extreme by the Gnostic sects. But Christianity has ever to come back to its central pre-supposition
—the substantial goodness and spiritual utility and trans-
figurableness of body and matter; and to its final end,—the
actual transformation of them by the spirit into ever more
adequate instruments, materials, and expressions of abiding
ethical and religious values and realities.

(2) The fact is that here, as practically at every chief turn-
ing-point in ethical and religious philosophy, the movement
of the specifically Christian life and conviction is not a circle
round a single centre,—detachment; but an ellipse round
two centres,—detachment and attachment. And precisely in
this difficult, but immensely fruitful, oscillation and rhythm
between, as it were, the two poles of the spiritual life; in this
fleeing and seeking, in the recollection back and away from
the visible (so as to allay the dust and fever of growing distraction, and to reharmonize the soul and its new gains
according to the intrinsic requirements and ideals of the
spirit), and in the subsequent, renewed immersion in the
visible (in view both of gaining fresh concrete stimulation and
content for the spiritual life, and of gradually shaping and
permeating the visible according to and with spiritual ends
and forces) : in this combination, and not in either of these
two movements taken alone, consists the completeness and
culmination of Christianity.[1]

(3) It no doubt looks, at first sight, as though the Church,
by her canonization of the Monastic Ideal, gave us, for the
ultimate pattern and measure of all Christian perfection, as
pure and simple a flight of the soul from the body and the
world, as (short of insanity or suicide) can be made in this
life. But here we have to remember three things.

In the first place, the Church not only forbids all attacks
upon the legitimacy, indeed sanctity, of marriage, or upon its
necessity, indeed duty, for mankind at large ; but St. Augustine
and St. Thomas only articulate her ordinary, strenuously anti-

---

[1] I owe much help towards acquiring this very important conception,
and all the above similes, to Prof. Ernst Troeltsch's admirable exposition
in his " Grundprobleme der Ethik," *Zeitschrift f. Theologie und Kirche*,
1902, pp. 163–178.

Manichean teaching, in declaring that man was originally created by God, in body and in soul, not for celibacy but for marriage; and that only owing to the accidental event of the Fall and of its effects,—the introduction of disorder and excess into human nature, but not any corruption of its substance and foundations,—does any inferiority,—the dispositions, motives, and circumstances being equal,—attach to marriage as compared with virginity.[1] Hence, still, the absolute ideal would be that man could and did use marriage as all other legitimate functions and things of sense, as a necessary, and ever more and more perfected, means and expression of truly human spirituality, a spirituality which ever requires some non-spiritual material in which to work, and by working in which the soul itself, not only spiritualizes it, but increasingly develops its own self.

And secondly, detachment, unification, spiritual recollection is the more difficult, and the less obviously necessary, of the two movements, and yet is precisely the one which (by coming upon the extant or inchoate attachments, and by suppressing or purifying them according as they are bad or good) first stamps any and every life as definitely religious at all. No wonder, then, that it is this sacred detachment and love of the Cross that we notice, first of all, in the life and doctrine of Our Lord and of all His followers, indeed in all truly religious souls throughout the world; and that the Church should by her teaching and selection of striking examples, ever preach and uphold this most necessary test and ingredient, this very salt of all virile and fruitful spirituality.

But, in the third place, a man need only directly attack the family, society, the state; or art, literature, science,—as intrinsically evil or even as, in practice, true hindrances to moral and religious perfection,—and the Church,—both the learning and experimenting, and the official and formulating Church,—will at once disavow him : so strong is, at bottom, the instinct that attachment and variety of interests,—variety both in kind and in degree—that materials, occasions, and objects for spirituality to leaven and to raise, and to work on in order to be itself deepened and developed,—are as truly essential to the spiritual life as are detachment, and unity, and transcendence of ultimate motive and aim; these latter furnishing to the soul the power gradually to penetrate

---

[1] *St. Augustine*, ed. Ben., Vol. X, 590*b*, 613*a*, 1973*c*, etc. St. Thomas, *Summa Theol.*, suppl., qu. 62, art. 2.

all that material, and, in and through this labour, more and more to articulate its own spiritual character.

(4) No man can become, or is proclaimed to have become, a Christian saint, who has not thus achieved a profound spiritualization and unification of a more or less recalcitrant material and multiplicity.   In some cases, it is the unity and detachment that greatly predominate over the multiplicity and attachment,—as, say, in the Fathers of the Desert.   In other cases, it is the variety and attachment that strikes us first of all,—as, for instance, in Sir Thomas More and Edmund Campion.   And, in a third set of cases, it is the depth of the unity and detachment, in the breadth of the variety and attachment, which is the dominant characteristic, so with St. Paul and St. Augustine.   Catherine herself belongs, for her great middle period, rather to the third group than to either of the other two; only during her penitential period and her last long illness does she clearly belong to the group of intensely detached and unified saints.—It is evidently impossible in such a matter to do more than insist upon the necessity of both movements; upon the immensely fruitful friction and tension which their well-ordered alternation introduces into the soul's inner life; and upon the full ideal and ultimate measure for the complete and perfected man, humanity at large, being a maximum of multiplicity and attachment permeated and purified by a maximum of unity and detachment. The life which can englobe and organize both these movements, with their manifold interaction, will have a multitude of warm attachments, without fever or distraction, and a great unity of pure detachment, without coldness or emptiness : it will have the, winning because rich, simplicity and wondrous combination of apparent inevitableness and of seeming paradox furnished by all true life, hence exhibited in its greatest fulness by the religious life which, at its deepest, is deeper than any other kind of life.

III. Quietude and Passivity.   Points in this
tendency to be considered here.

We have inevitably somewhat anticipated another matter, in which Catherine shows all the true Mystic's affinities : the craving for simplification and permanence of the soul's states, —her practice and teaching as to Quietude and Passivity.

Pushed fully home, this tendency involves four closely related, increasingly profound, convictions and experiences. Utter unification of the soul's functions, indeed utter unity of its substance : *i. e.* the soul does one single thing, and seems to do it by one single act; itself is simply one, and expresses itself by one sole act. Passivity of the soul : *i. e.* the soul does not apparently act at all, it simply *is* and receives—it is now nothing but one pure immense recipiency. Immediacy of contact between the soul and God : *i. e.* there seems to be nothing separating, or indeed in any way between, the soul and God. And, finally, an apparent coalescence of the soul and God : *i. e.* the soul *is* God, and God *is* the soul.—Only the first two points, and then the closely related question of Pure Love, shall occupy us here; the last two points must stand over for our penultimate chapter.

1. *Distinction between experiences, their expression, and their analysis.*

We have already studied the psycho-physical occasions, concomitants, and embodiments of Catherine's keen desire for, and profound experience of, spiritual unification and passivity; and we can have no kind of doubt as to the factual reality and the practical fruitfulness of the state so vividly described by her. Here we have only to inquire into the accuracy of the analysis and terminology effected and employed by her, in so far as they seem to claim more than simply to describe the soul's own feeling and impression as to these states thus experienced by itself. We have then to consider the nature and truth of what can roughly be styled Quietism and Passivity.

Now here especially will it be necessary for us carefully to distinguish between the direct experiences, impressions, and instinctive requirements of the soul,—here all souls, in precise proportion to their depth and delicacy of holiness and of self-knowledge are our masters, and furnish us with our only materials and tests; and, on the other hand, the implications and analysis of these states, as, in the first instance, psychological, and then as requiring elucidation with regard to their ontological cause and reality by means of a religious philosophy,—here, psychology, and religious philosophy, especially also the discriminations and decisions of theologians and Church authorities as expressive of these ultimate questions, will be our guides.[1]

[1] My chief authorities throughout this section have been Bossuet's *Instruction sur les Etats d'Oraison* of 1687, with the important documents

(1) If we start from the history of the nomenclature which, (though present only partially in Catherine's sayings, for she nowhere uses the term " passivity "), runs, with however varying a completeness, right through the Christian Mystics more or less from the first, we shall find that it consists, roughly, of three stages, and, throughout, of two currents. There is the Pre-Pauline and Pre-Philonian stage; the stage of Paul, Philo, and John, through Clement and Origen, on to Gregory of Nyssa and St. Augustine; and the stage from the Pseudo-Dionysius onward, down to Nicolas of Coes inclusive, and which, to this hour, still largely influences us all.—And there are the two currents. The one tends so to emphasize the sense and reality of the soul's simple receptivity, and of what the soul receives at such, apparently, purely receptive times, as to ignore, or even practically deny, the undeniable fact that this very receptivity is, inevitably, an act of its own. Its decisive terms are Passivity, Fixedness, Oneness. The other current realizes that Grace does not destroy, violate, or supplant Nature, either entirely or in part, but that it awakens, purifies, and completes it, so that every divine influx is also ever a stimulation of all the good and true energy already, even though latently, present in the soul. And its characteristic terms are " Action " (as distinguished from " Activity "), Growth, Harmony.

(2) And we should note with care that these two currents are not simply Heathen and Christian respectively. For if that great, indeed all but central, term and conception of " Action " has been wisely generalized by most Christian Mystics, as the truly Christian substitute for the strongly Neo-Platonist term " Passivity ": that term and conception of " Action " was first fixed and elucidated by Aristotle, who, as Mr. Schiller well puts it, " has packed into his technical term ' Energeia,' and especially into the combination ' Unmoving Energy,' all that was most distinctive, most original,

---

prefixed and appended to it (*Œuvres de Bossuet*, ed. Versailles, 1817, Vol. XXVII); Fénelon's chief apologetic works, especially his *Instruction Pastorale*, his *Lettres en Réponse à Divers Ecrits ou Mémoires*, his *Lettre sur l'Etat Passif*, and his two Latin Letters to Pope Clement XI (*Œuvres de Fénelon*, ed. Versailles, 1820, Vols. IV, VI, VIII, and IX); and Abbé Gosselin's admirably clear, impartial, cautious, and authoritative *Analyse de la Controverse du Quiétisme*. I have studied these works, and the condemned propositions of the Beghards, of Molinos, and of Fénelon, very carefully, and believe myself to have, in my text, taken up a position identical with M. Gosselin's.

most fundamental, and most profound in his philosophy "; [1] whilst the second term, " Passivity," goes on figuring in Christian Mystics and Mystical Theologies—(in spite of its demonstrably dangerous suggestions and frequently scandalous history)—because the religious, especially the Christian, consciousness requires a term for the expression of one element of all its deepest experiences, that character of " givenness " and of grace, of merciful anticipation by God, which marks all such states, in exact proportion to their depth and to the soul's awakeness.

(3) Now Aristotle's conception of God's Unmoving Energy, is taken over by St. Thomas in the form of God being One Actus Purus,—sheer Energy, His very peace and stillness coming from the brimming fulness of His infinite life. And even finite spirit, whilst fully retaining, indeed deepening, its own character, can and does penetrate finite spirit through and through,—the law of Physics, which does not admit more than one body in any one place, having here no kind of application,—so that the Infinite Spirit is at once conceived unspiritually, if He is conceived as supplanting, and not as penetrating, stimulating, and transforming the finite spirits whom He made into an increasing likeness to Him, their Maker. And hence according to the unanimous teaching of the most experienced and explicit of the specifically Theistic and Christian Mystics, the appearance, the soul's own impression, of a cessation of life and energy of the soul in periods of special union with God or of great advance in spirituality, is an appearance only. Indeed this, at such times strong, impression of rest springs most certainly from an unusually large amount of actualized energy, an energy which is now penetrating, and finding expression by, every pore and fibre of the soul. The whole moral and spiritual creature expands and rests, yes; but this very rest is produced by Action " unperceived because so fleet," so near, so all fulfilling; or rather by a tissue of single acts, mental, emotional, volitional, so finely interwoven, so exceptionally stimulative and expressive of the soul's deepest aspirations, that these acts are not perceived as so many single acts, indeed that their very collective presence is apt to remain unnoticed by the soul itself.

(4) Close parallels to such a state are abundant in all

---

[1] F. C. S. Schiller, Essay " Activity and Substance," pp. 204–227,—an admirably thorough piece of work, in *Humanism*, 1903. See his p. 208.

phases and directions of the soul's life. The happiest and most fruitful moments for our aesthetic sense, those in which our mind expands most and grows most, hence is most active in aesthetic " action " (though not " activity ") are those in which we are unforcedly and massively absorbed in drinking in, with quiet intentness, the contrasts and harmonies, the grand unity in variety, the very presence and spirit of an alpine upland, or of a river's flowing, or of the ocean's outspread, or of the Parthenon sculptures or of Rafael's madonnas. At such moments we altogether cease to be directly conscious of ourselves, of time or of the body's whereabouts ; and when we return to our ordinary psychical and mental condition, we do so with an undeniable sense of added strength and youthfulness,—somewhat as though our face, old and haggard, were, after gazing in utter self-oblivion upon some resplendent youthfulness, to feel, beyond all doubt, all its many wrinkles to have gone. And so too with the mind's absorption in some great poem or philosophy or character.—In all these cases, the mind or soul energizes and develops, in precise proportion as it is so absorbed in the contemplation of these various over-againstnesses, these " countries " of the spirit, as to cease to notice its own overflowing action. It is only when the mind but partially attends that a part of it remains at leisure to note the attention of the other part; when the mind is fully engrossed, and hence most keenly active, there is no part of it sufficiently disengaged to note the fact of the engrossment and action of, now, the whole mind. And, with the direct consciousness of our mind's action, we lose, for the time being, all clear consciousness of the mind's very existence. And let it be carefully noted, this absence of the direct consciousness of the self is as truly characteristic of the deepest, most creative, moments of full external action : the degree of mind and will-force operating in Nelson at Trafalgar and in Napoleon at Waterloo, or again in St. Ignatius of Antioch in the Amphitheatre, and in Savonarola at the stake, was evidently in the precisely contrary ratio to their direct consciousness of it or of themselves at all.

(5) Now if such " Passivity," or Action, is in reality the condition in which the soul attains to its fullest energizing, we can argue back, from this universal principle, to the nature of the various stages and kinds of the Prayer and States of Quiet. In each case, that is, we shall combat the still very common conception that,—though orthodoxy, it is admitted,

requires *some* human action to remain throughout,—such Prayer and States consist (not only as to the immediate feeling of their subjects, but in reality and in their ultimate analysis) in an ever-increasing preponderance of divine action within the soul, and an ever-decreasing remnant of acts of the soul itself. For such a view assumes that God supplants man, and that, so to speak, His Hand appears unclothed alongside of the tissue woven by man's own mind; whereas God everywhere but stimulates and supports man whom He has made, and His Hand moves ever underneath and behind the tissue,—a tissue which, at best, can become as it were a glove, and suggest the latent hand. The Divine Action will thus stimulate and inform the human action somewhat like the force that drives the blood within the stag's young antlers, or like the energy that pushes the tender sap-full fern-buds up through the hard, heavy ground.

Thus a special intensity of divine help and presence, and an unusual degree of holiness and of union, have nothing to do with the fewness of the soul's own acts at such times, but with their quality,—with the preponderance amongst them of divinely informed acts as against merely natural, or wrongly self-seeking, or downrightly sinful acts. And since it is certain that living simplicity is but the harmony and unification, the synthesis, of an organism, and hence is great in precise proportion to the greater perfection of that synthesis, it follows that the living, utterly one-seeming Action or State will, at such times, contain a maximum number of inter-penetrating acts and energies, all worked up into this harmonious whole.

2. *Four causes of inadequate analysis.*

It is plain, I think, that one thoroughly normal, one accidental, and two mischievous, causes have all conspired to arrest or to deflect the analysis of most of the Mystics themselves concerning Simplicity.

For one thing, the soul, as has just been shown, at such moments of harmonious concentration and of willing and thinking in union with God's Light and Will, necessarily ceases, more or less, to be conscious of its own operations, and, in looking back, braced and rested as it now is, it cannot but think that it either did not act at all, or that its action was reduced to a minimum. For how otherwise could it now feel so rested, when, after its ordinary activity, it feels so tired and dissatisfied? and how otherwise could it be so unable to give any clear account of what happened in those minutes of union? Yet it is, on the contrary, the very fulness of the action which has rested, by expanding, the soul; and which has made the soul, returned to its ordinary distractedness, incapable of clearly explaining that, now past, concentration.

The accidental cause has been the fairly frequent, though not necessary, connection of the more pronounced instances of such habits of mind with more or less of the psycho-physical phenomena of ecstasy, in the technical sense of the word. For, in such trances, the breathing and circulation are retarded, and the operation of the senses is in part suspended. And it was easy to reason, from such visible, literal simplification of the physical life, to a similar modification of the soul's action at such times; and, from the assumed desirableness of that psycho-physical condition, to the advantage of the supposed corresponding state of the soul itself. Any tendency to an extreme dualism, as to the relations between body and soul, would thus directly help on an inclination to downright Quietism.—Here it is, on the contrary, certain that only in so far as those psycho-physical simplifications are the results of, or conditions for, a deepening multiplicity in unity, a fuller synthetic action of the soul, or, at least, of a fuller penetration by the soul of even one limited experience or idea—an operation which entails not less, but more, energizing of the soul,—are such psycho-physical simplifications of any spiritual advantage or significance. And in such cases they could not be indications of the cessation or diminution of the deepest and most docile energizing of the soul.

And the mischievous causes were a mistake in Psychology and a mistake in Theology. For, as to Psychology, not only was simplicity assumed, (through a mistaken acceptance of the soul's own feeling, as furnishing the ultimate analysis of its state,) to consist, at any one moment, of an act materially and literally one, instead of a great organism of various simultaneous energizings; but this one act was often held to require no kind of repetition. Since the act was one as against any simultaneous multiplicity, so was it one as against any successive multiplicity, even if this latter were taken as a repetition differentiated by number alone. And yet here again energizing *is* energizing; and though the soul's acts overlap and interpenetrate each other, and though when, by their number and harmony, they completely fill and pacify the soul, many of them are simultaneously or successively

present to the soul in their effects alone : it is nevertheless
the renewal, however peaceful and unperceived, of these acts,
which keeps the state of soul in existence. For these acts
are not simply unowned acts that happen to be present within
the soul; they are the soul's own acts, whether, in addition,
the soul is directly conscious of them or not.

And, theologically, the idea was often at work that it was
more worthy of God to operate alone and, as it were, *in
vacuo ;* and more creaturely of man to make, or try to make,
such a void for Him. Yet this is in direct conflict with the
fundamental Christian doctrine, of the Condescension, the
Incarnation of God to and in human nature, and of the
persistence, and elevation of this humanity, even in the case
of Christ Himself. God's action does not keep outside of,
nor does it replace, man's action ; but it is,—Our Lord Himself has told us,—that of yeast working in meal, which
manifests its hidden power in proportion to the mass of
meal which it penetrates and transforms.

3. *Four Quietistic aberrations.*

Now it is certain that the error of Quietism has, in no
doubt many cases, not remained confined to such mistakes in
psychological analysis and theological doctrine, but that
these have joined hands with, and have furnished a defence
to, sloth and love of dreamy ease, or to some impatience
of the necessary details of life, or to fanatical attachment
to some one mood and form of experience ; and that they
have, thus reinforced, ravaged not a few wills and souls.

Four chief Quietistic aberrations can be studied in history.

(1) The neglect or even contempt of vocal prayer, and of
the historical and institutional elements of religion, at least
in the case of more advanced souls, is one of these abuses.—
Now it is true, and Catherine has been a striking instance,
that the proportion of all these different elements towards
one another vary, and should vary, considerably between soul
and soul, according to the *attrait* and degree of advance of
each ; that the soul's most solid advance is in the direction of
an ever-deepened spiritual devotedness, and not in that of a
multiplication of particular devotions ; that the use of even
the more central of those elements and means may, for souls
called to the prayer of Quiet, become remarkably elastic and
largely unmethodized ; and that, for such souls (and, in various
degrees and ways, sooner or later, for perhaps most other
souls), a prayer of peacefully humble expectation and of all

but inarticulate, practically indescribable, brooding of love, and of dim, expansive trust and conformity is possible, sometimes alone possible, and is proved right and useful, if it leaves them strengthened to act and to suffer, to help and to devote themselves to their fellows, to Christ, and to God.

But it remains equally true, even for these as for all other souls, that the historical and institutional elements must ever remain represented, and sufficiently represented; indeed the persistence in these elements of religion will be one of the chief means for avoiding delusion. We have St. Teresa's experience and teaching here, as a truly classical instance. And if the prayer of Quiet will give a special colour, depth, and unity to those more contingent-seeming practices, these practices will, in return, give a particular definiteness, content, and creaturely quality to that prayer. And thus too the universally and profoundly important union and interchange with souls of other, equally legitimate, kinds and degrees of spirituality will be kept up. Only the sum-total of all these souls, only the complete invisible Church, is the full Bride of Christ; and though the souls composing her may and should each contribute a varying predominance of different elements, no soul should be entirely without a certain amount of each of these constituents.

(2) Another abuse is the neglect, contempt, or misapplied fear of not directly religious occupations and labours which, however otherwise appropriate or even necessary to this soul's growth and destination, tend to disturb its quiet and to absorb a part of its time and attention. Here it is doubtless true that the other elements of religion are also all more or less apprehensive and jealous with regard to actual, or even only possible, non-religious rival interests. And it is certain that they are all right in so far as that a certain interior leisureliness and recollection, a certain ultimate preference for the spiritualizing religious force of the soul as against the materials, non-religious and other, which that force is to penetrate, are necessary to the soul that would advance.

But the fear that characterizes the Historical and Institutional elements is rather a fear, respectively, of error and of disobedience and singularity, whereas on the part of the Mystical element it is a fear of distraction and absorption away from the *Unum Necessarium* of the soul. Perhaps even among the Canonized Mystics there is none that has more impressively warned us, both by word and example, against this insidious danger, than the distinguished Platonist scholar and deep spiritual writer, Père Jean Nicolas Grou, who, right through the long mystical period of his life, alternated his prayer of Quiet with extensive and vigorous critical work on the Graeco-Latin classics, and whose practice only wants further expansion and application, (according to the largely increased or changed conditions of such not directly religious work,) in order to bear much fruit, not only for criticism and science, but, (by the return-effect of such occupations upon the soul's general temper and particular devotional habits,) for spirituality itself. But we must return to this point more fully in our last chapter.

(3) The third abuse is the neglect or contempt of morality, especially on its social, visible, and physical sides. Particular Mystics, and even whole Mystical schools and movements, have undoubtedly in some instances, and have, possibly, in many more cases, been maligned on this point, since even such a spotless life as Fénelon's, and that of such a profoundly well-intentioned woman as Madame Guyon, did not, for a time, escape the most unjust suspicions. It is also true that, as a man advances in spirituality, he lays increasing stress upon the intention and general attitude of the agent, and increasingly requires to be judged by the same interior standard, if he is to be rightly understood at all. God may and does, to humble and purify him, allow painful temptations and trials from within to combine, apparently, against him, with persecutions and much isolation from without. And the difference rather than the similarity, between Religion and Morality,— the sense of pure grace, of free pardon, of the strange profound " givenness " of even our fullest willings and of our most emphatically personal achievements,—can and should grow in him more and more.

And yet it is clear that there must have been some fire to account for all that smoke of accusation; that the material and the effect outwards, the *body* of an action, do matter, as well as does that action's *spirit ;* that this body does not only act thus outwards, but also inwards, back upon the spirit of the act and of the agent; and that temptations and trials are purifying, not by their simple presence but in proportion as they are resisted, or, if they have been yielded to, in proportion as such defeats are sincerely deplored and renounced. Thus everywhere the full development of any one part of life, and the true unity of the whole, have to be achieved through the gradual assimilation of at first largely recalcitrant other elements, and within an ever-abiding multiplicity—a maximum number of parts and functions interacting within one great organism. And hence not the outrage, neglect, or supersession of morality, but, on the contrary, its deeper development, by more precise differentiation from, and more organic integration into, religion proper, must, here again and here above all, be the final aim. Once more again it is the Incarnational type which is the only fully true, the only genuinely Christian one.

(4) And, finally, there are certain hardly classifiable fanaticisms, which are nevertheless a strictly logical consequence from a wrongly understood Quiet and Passivity,—from Quietism in its unfavourable, condemned sense. I am thinking of such a case as that of Margarethe Peters, a young Quietist, who caused herself to be crucified by her girl-companions, at Wildenspuch, near Schaffhausen, in 1823,—in order to carry out, in full literalness and separateness, the utmost and most painful passivity and dependence and resistless self-donation, in direct imitation of the culminating act of Christ's life on earth and of His truest followers.[1] Here, in the deliberate suicide of this undoubtedly noble Lutheran girl, we get an act which but brings out the strength and weakness of Quietism wherever found. For the greatest constituents of the Christian spirit are undoubtedly there : free self-sacrifice, impelled by love of God, of Christ, and of all men, and by hatred of self.—Yet, because they here suppress other, equally necessary, constituents, and are out of their proper context and bereft of their proper checks, they but render possible and actual a deed of piteous self-delusion. How terrible is false simplification, the short cut taken by pure logic, operating without a sufficient induction from facts, and within an ardent self-immolating temperament !

4. *Rome's condemnation of Quietism.*

All this is abundantly sufficient to explain and justify Rome's condemnation of Quietism. The term " Quietists " appears, I think, for the first time,—at least in an invidious sense,—in the Letter which Cardinal Caraccioli, Archbishop

[1] See Heinrich Heppe, *Geschichte der Quietistischen Mystik*, Berlin, 1875, p. 521. The obviously strong partisan bias of the author against Rome, —of which more lower down,—does not destroy the great value of the large collection of now, in many cases, most rare and inaccessible documents given, often *in extenso*, in this interesting book.

of Naples, addressed to Pope Innocent XI (Odescalchi) on
June 30, 1682, and in which he graphically describes the
abuses which, (under pretext or through the misapplication
of spiritual Quiet and Passivity,) had now appeared in his
Diocese : souls apparently incapable of using their beads
or making the sign of the Cross; or which will neither say
a vocal prayer nor go to Confession; or which, when in
this prayer of Quiet, even when at Holy Communion, will
strive to drive away any image, even of Our Lord Himself,
that may present itself to their imagination; or which tear
down a Crucifix, as a hindrance to union with God; or which
look upon all the thoughts that come to them in the quietude
of prayer, as so many rays and effluences from God Himself,
exempting them henceforth from every law.[1]

Yet it is important to bear well in mind, the special circumstances, the admitted limits, and the probable signification of
Rome's condemnations.

(1) As to the circumstances of the time, it appears certain that
it was the ready circulation of the doctrines of the Spanish
priest, Miguel de Molinos in the *Guida Spirituale*, 1675, and
the abuses of the kind we have just now detailed, and that
sprang from this circulation, which formed the primary reason
and motive for the otherwise excessively severe treatment of
a man and a book, which had both received the very highest
and the most deliberate ecclesiastical approbations. That
these two circumstances were the determining causes of at
least the severity of his condemnation is well brought out
by the circumstance that, during his two years' trial (1685–
1687), not only the short *Guida* but his whole obtainable
correspondence (some twenty thousand letters) were examined, and that it is at least as much on such occasional
manuscript material, and on Molinos's own oral admissions,
—in prison and doubtless, in part at least, under torture,—
that the condemnation was based, containing, as it does,
certain revoltingly immoral propositions and confessions,
admittedly absent from his published writings.

But if at least some shadow of doubt rests upon the moral
character of Molinos, not a shadow of such suspicion or of
doubt concerning his perfectly Catholic intentions can, in
justice, be allowed to rest upon his chief follower and the most
distinguished apologist for his doctrine, the saintly Oratorian

---

[1] Heppe, *op. cit.* pp. 130–133.

and Bishop, the much-tried Cardinal Petrucci; any more than Fénelon's moral and spiritual character, or deeply Catholic spirit and intentions, can, (in spite of the painfully fierce and unjust attack upon both by Bossuet in his formally classic invective, *Relation sur le Quiétisme,*) for one moment be called in question.[1]   Other admittedly deeply spiritual and entirely well-intentioned Catholics, whose writings were also condemned during this time when devotional expressions having an at all quietistic tinge or drift were very severely judged, are Mère Marie de l'Incarnation (Marie Guyard), a French Ursuline Religious, who died in Canada in 1672, and the process of whose Beatification has been introduced; the saintly French layman, Jean de Bernières-Louvigny, much admired by Fénelon, who died in 1659; the very interior, though at times somewhat fantastic, Secular Priest, Henri Marie Boudon, who died in 1702; and the very austere but highly experienced ascetical writer, the Jesuit Père Joseph Surin, whom Bossuet had formally approved, and who died in 1668.[2]   But Madame Guyon herself, that much-tried and vehemently opposed woman, was held, by many an undoubtedly Catholic-minded, experienced and close observer, to be (in spite of the largely misleading and indeed incorrect character of many of her analyses and expressions) a truly saintly, entirely filial Catholic.[3]

(2) As to the limits of these condemnations, we must remember that only two of them,—those of Molinos and of Fénelon,—claim to be directly doctrinal at all; and that Fénelon was never really compromised in the question of Quietism proper, but was condemned on questions of Pure Love alone.   Bossuet himself was far less sound as against the central Quietist doctrine of the One Act, which, unless formally revoked, lasts on throughout life, and hence need never be repeated; Fénelon's early criticism of the Molinos propositions remains one of the clearest extant refutations of that error.   Again in the matter of the Passivity of advanced souls, Bossuet was distinctly less normal and sober than Fénelon : for whilst

---

[1] There is a good article on Petrucci in the Catholic Freiburg *Kirchen-lexikon*, 2nd ed., 1895; and Heppe, in his *Geschichte*, pp. 135–144, gives extracts from his chief book.   Bossuet's attack, *Œuvres*, ed. 1817, Vol. XXIX.

[2] Reusch, *Der Index der verbotenen Bücher*, 1885, Vol. II, pp. 611; 622, 623; 625.

[3] Gosselin's *Analyse, Œuvres de Fénelon*, ed. cit. Vol. IV, pp. xci–xcv.

Fénelon taught that in no state does the soul lose all capacity, although the facility may greatly vary, to produce distinct acts of the virtues or vocal prayers and other partially external exercises, Bossuet taught that, in some cases, all capacity of this kind is abolished.[1] " I take," says Fénelon, " the terms ' Passive ' and ' Passivity ' as they actually appear everywhere in the language of the (sound) Mystics, as something opposed to the terms ' active ' and ' activity ' : ' Passivity,' taken in the sense of an entire inaction of the will, would be a heresy." And he then opposes " Passivity," not to " Action," but to that " Activity," which is a merely natural, restless, and hurried excitation.[2]

(3) And as to the abiding significance of the whole anti-quietist decisions and measures, we shall do well to consider the following large facts.   From St. Paul and St. John to Clement of Alexandria and Origen; from these to Dionysius the Areopagite; from the Areopagite to St. Bernard of Clairvaux and then the Franciscan and Dominican Mystics; from these, again, on to the great Renaissance and Counter-Reformation saints and writers of this type,—the German Cardinal Nicolas of Coes and the Italian St. Catherine of Genoa, the Spaniards St. Teresa and St. John of the Cross, and the French Saint Francis de Sales and Saint Jane Frances de Chantal, we get a particular type of religious experience and doctrine, which but unfolds and concentrates, with an unusual articulation, breadth, and depth, what is to be found, on some sides of their spiritual character and teaching, among Saints and religious souls of the more mixed type, such as St. Augustine, St. Anselm, St. Thomas of Aquin, and St. Ignatius Loyola.   And this mixed type, bearing within it a considerable amount of that mystical quiet and emotional-speculative element, is again but a deepening, a purification and a realization of one of the profoundest affinities and constituents of every human heart and will.

Hence, even in the thickest of the quietist controversy, when that mystical element must have seemed, to many, to be discredited once for all, those best acquainted with the rich history of the Church, and with the manifold requirements of the abiding religious consciousness, could not and did not doubt that all that was good, deep, and true in that element

---

[1] Fénelon, *Explication . . . des Propositions de Molinos* (*Œuvres*, Vol. IV, pp. 25–86).   Gosselin, *Analyse* (*ibid.* pp. ccxvi–ccxxiii).
[2] *Œuvres de Fénelon*, Vol. VIII, pp. 6, 7.

would continue to be upheld by, and represented in, the Church.—And it is not difficult to point to the more or less Mystical souls furnished by the Monks, the Friars; the Clerks-Regular, specially the Jesuits; the Secular Clergy; and the Laity, down to the present day. Such writers and Saints as the Père de Caussade (*d.* about 1770) on the one hand, and Père Jean N. Grou (*d.* 1803) and the Curé d'Ars (*d.* 1859) on the other hand, carry on the two streams of the predominantly mystical and of the mixed type,—streams so clearly observable before 1687 and 1699. Quietism, the doctrine of the One Act; Passivity in a literal sense, as the absence or imperfection of the power and use of initiative on the soul's part in any and every state : these doctrines were finally condemned, and most rightly and necessarily condemned; the Prayer of Quiet, and various states and degrees of an ever-increasing predominance of Action over Activity,— an Action which is all the more the soul's very own, because the more occasioned, directed, and informed by God's action and stimulation,—these, and the other chief lines of the ancient experience and practice, remain as true, correct, and necessary as ever.

5. *Rome's alleged change of front.*

And yet it is undeniable that the Roman events between 1675 and 1688 do seem, at first sight, to justify the strongly Protestant Dr. Heppe's contention that those twelve years,— not to speak of the later troubles of Madame Guyon and of Fénelon,—witnessed a complete *volte face*, a formal self-stultification, of the Roman teaching and authority, on these difficult but immediately important matters.

(1) Let us put aside the many passages in Molinos's *Guida* which were but (more or less) literal reproductions of the teachings of such solemnly approved authorities as Saints Teresa, Peter of Alcantara, John of the Cross, Francis de Sales and Jane Frances de Chantal,—passages which, of course, remained uncondemned even in Molinos's pages, but which it would often be difficult to distinguish from the parts of his book that were censured. Yet there still remain such facts as the following.

Juan Falconi's *Alfabeto* and *Lettera* were at their Fifth Italian edition, 1680, and all five editions had been approved by the Master of the Apostolic Palace; but only in 1688 were these writings forbidden. Yet the *Lettera* contains, with unsurpassed directness and clearness, the central doctrine of

Quietism : an exhortation to the production of one single lively Act of Faith, which will then continue uninterruptedly through the whole earthly life into eternity, and which, consequently, is not to be repeated.[1]

Molinos's *Guida* and *Breve Trattato* appeared in Rome, respectively in 1675 and 1681, with the approbations of five theologians, four of whom were Consultors of the Holy Office,—the Archbishop of Reggio; the Minister-General of the Franciscans; the late General of the Carmelites; Father Martin Esparza, the same Jesuit Theologian-Professor of the Roman College who, some years before, had been one of those who had examined and approved St. Catherine's *Vita ed Opere ;* and the actual General of the Carmelites.[2]

Even after these two writings of Molinos had been criticised by the Jesuits Bell Huomo and Segneri and the Clerk Regular Regio, (Segneri enjoying a deservedly immense reputation, and showing in this affair much moderation and a strong sense of the legitimate claims of Mysticism,) the Inquisition examined these criticisms, and forbade, not the incriminated writings of Molinos and Petrucci, but the critique of Bell Huomo *donec corrigatur*, and those of Regio and of Segneri (in his *Lettera* of 1681) absolutely. Segneri's subsequent *Concordia* almost cost him his life, so strong was the popular veneration of Molinos.

Molinos indeed was the guest of Pope Innocent XI himself, and the friend and confidant, amongst countless other spiritually-minded souls, of various Cardinals, especially of the deeply devout Petrucci, Bishop of Jesi, who was raised to the Cardinalate eighteen months after the beginning of Molinos's trial. The imprisonment of Molinos began in May 1685, but the trial did not end till August 1687, when (after nineteen " Principal Errors of the New Contemplation " had been censured by the Holy Office in February 1687) sixty-eight propositions, out of the two hundred and sixty-three which had been urged against him, were solemnly condemned: of these the clearly and directly immoral ones being admittedly not derived from any printed book, or indeed any ever published letter of Molinos.[3]

---

[1] Heppe, *op. cit.* p. 62.   Reusch, *op. cit.* Vol. II, pp. 619, 620.

[2] I write with these approbations before me, as reprinted in the *Recueil de Diverses Pièces concernant le Quiétisme*, Amsterdam, 1688.

[3] *Œuvres de Bossuet*, ed. 1817, Vol. XXVII, pp. 497–502. Heppe, *op. cit.* pp. 278 n.; 273–281. Denzinger, *Encheiridion*, ed. 1888, pp. 266–274.

(2) To estimate Rome's attitude (as far as it concerns the ultimate truth and completeness of these doctrines, taken in their most characteristic and explicit forms) fairly, we shall have to put aside all questions as to the motives that impelled, and the methods that were employed, by either side against the other. Molinos may have been even worse than the condemned propositions represent, and yet Petrucci would remain a saintly soul; and we certainly are driven to ask with Leibniz : " Si Molinos a caché du venin sous ce miel, est-il juste que Petrucci et autres personnes de mérite en soient responsables ? "[1] But neither the wickedness of the one nor the sanctity of the other would make the doctrines propounded by them, objectively, any less solid or more spiritual than they are in themselves. The acutely anti-Roman Anglican Bishop Burnet may not have invented or exaggerated when he wrote from Rome, during those critical years, that one of the chief motives which actuated the opponents of the Quietists was the fact that, though the latter " were observed to become more strict in their lives, more retired and serious in their mental devotions, yet . . . they were not so assiduous at Mass, nor so earnest to procure Masses to be said for their friends : nor . . . so frequently either at Confession or in processions " : and so " the trade of those that live by these things was sensibly sunk." [2] And the cruel injustice of many details and processes of the movement against the Quietists,—a movement which soon had much of the character of a popular scare and panic, in reaction against a previous, in part, heedless enthusiasm,—are beyond dispute or justification. Yet mercenary and ruthless as part of the motives and much of the action of the anti-quietists doubtlessly were, the question as to the worth and wisdom of Quietism, (taken objectively, and not as an excusable counter-excess but as a true synthesis of the spiritual life,) remains precisely where it was before.

(3) Now I think that two peculiarities, most difficult to notice at the time, seriously differentiate the Molinist movement from the great current of fully Catholic Mysticism, even in those points and elements where the two are materially alike or even identical; and yet that these peculiarities are but the caricature (through further emphasis and systematization) of certain elements present, in a more latent and sporadic

[1] Reusch, *op. cit.* Vol. II, p. 618 *n.* 1.   [2] See Heppe, p. 264, n.

manner, in the formulae and philosophic assumptions or explanations of the older Mysticism,—elements which had been borrowed too largely from an, at bottom, profoundly anti-Incarnational philosophy, not to be of far less value and of much greater danger than the profoundly true experiences, nobly spiritual maxims, and exquisite psychological descriptions which that predominantly Neo-Platonist framework handed on.

The first peculiarity is that the older Mystics, especially those of the type of St. Catherine of Genoa and St. John of the Cross, but even also those of the more " mixed " type of Mysticism, such as St. Teresa, had indeed quite freely used terms which are vividly true as descriptions of the prima facie aspect and emotional impression of certain states and experiences of the soul : " empty," " fixed," " motionless," " the reason and the will have ceased to act," " doing nothing," " incapable of doing anything," " moved by irresistible grace," " but one act," " one single desire " : these and equivalent expressions occur again and again. But these sayings do not here lead up to such a deliberate and exclusive rule as is that given by Falconi, and repeated by Molinos in his *Guida*, Nos. 103–106.[1]

This doctrine of the One Act, in this its negative form,— for it is not to be repeated,—and in its application to the whole waking and sleeping life, is first an exclusive concentration upon, and then a wholesale extension of, one out of the several trends of the older teaching, a doctrine which, compared with that teaching in its completeness, is thin and doctrinaire, and as untrue to the full psychological explanation and working requirements of the soul as it is readily abusable in practice and contrary to the Incarnational type of religion. It is impossible not to feel that the manifold great ocean-waters of life, that the diversely blowing winds of God's Spirit are here, somehow, expected to flow and breathe in a little short-cut, single channel, through a tiny pipe; one more infallible recipe or prescription is here offered to us, hardly more adequate than the many similar " sure " roads to salvation, declared by this or that body of devout religionists to attach to the practice or possession of this or that particular prayer or particular religious object.

And the second difference is that the older Catholic Mystics

---

[1] *Recueil de Diverses Pièces*, pp. 61, 62.

LESS ULTIMATE THIS-WORLD DOCTRINES 147

leave less the impression that the external side of religion, its *body*, is of little or no importance, and indeed very readily an obstacle to its interior side, its *soul*. And this, again, for the simple reason that their teaching is, in general, less systematic and pointed, more incidental, and careless of much self-consistency.

(4) Yet these two differences have largely sprung from the simple pressing and further extension of precisely the least satisfactory, the explanatory and systematic side,—the form as against the content,—of the older Mystics. For once the more specifically Neo-Platonist constituent, in those Mystics' explanation and systematization, was isolated from the elements of other *provenance* which there had kept it in check, and now became, as it were, hypostasized and self-sufficient, this constituent could not but reveal, more clearly than before, its inadequacy as a form for the intensely organic and " incarnational " spiritual realities and processes which it attempted to show forth. That Neo-Platonist constituent, always present in those ancient Mystics, had ever tended to conceive the soul's unity, at any one moment, as a something outside of all multiplicity whatsoever. Hence this character of the simultaneous unity had only to be extended to the successive unity,—and the literally One Act, as in the present so throughout the future, became a necessary postulate.

And that same constituent had, even in those great teachers of profound maxims, exquisite religious psychology, and noblest living, tended, (however efficaciously checked by all this their Christian experience and by certain specifically Platonist and Aristotelian elements of their philosophy,) towards depreciating the necessity, importance, indeed even the preponderant utility, of the External, Contingent, Historical and Institutional, and of the interchange, the inter-stimulation between these sides and expressions of religion and its internal centre and spirit.

Perhaps, amongst all the great ecclesiastically authorized Mystics of that past, the then most recent of them all, St. John of the Cross, comes, by his (theoretically continuous though in his practice by no means exclusive) insistence upon the abstractive and universal, the obscure and invisible, the self-despoiling and simplifying element and movement, nearest to an exclusion of the other element and movement. Indeed the Quietists' generally strong insistence upon the necessity of a Director and upon Frequent Communion gives their teaching, when taken in its completeness, a prima facie greater Institutionalism than is offered by the spiritual theory of the great Spaniard. Yet if, even in him, one misses, in his theoretical system, a sufficiently organic necessity for the outgoing movement, a movement begun by God Himself, and which cannot but be of fundamental importance and influence for believers in the Incarnation, there is as complete an absence of the doctrinaire One-Act recipe for perfection as in the most Historical and Institutional of Christian teachers. But more about this hereafter.

6. *Four needs recognized by Quietism.*

Quietism, then, has undoubtedly isolated and further exaggerated certain explanatory elements of the older Mysticism which, even there, were largely a weakness and not a strength; has thus underrated and starved the Particular, Visible, Historical, Institutional constituents of Religion; and has, indeed, misunderstood the nature of true Unity everywhere. Yet the very eagerness with which it was welcomed at the time,—in France and Italy especially,—and this, not only as a fashion by the *Quidnuncs*, but as so much spiritual food and life by many a deeply religious soul; and the difficulty, and not infrequent ruthlessness of its suppression, indicate plainly enough that, with all its faults and dangers, it was divining and attempting to supply certain profound and abiding needs of the soul. I take these needs to be the following four.

(1) Man has an ineradicable, and, when rightly assuaged, profoundly fruitful thirst for Unity,—for Unification, Synthesis, Harmonization; for a living System, an Organization both within and without himself, in which each constituent gains its full expansion and significance through being, and more and more becoming, just *that* part and function of a great, dynamic whole; a sense of the essential and ultimate organic connection of all things, in so far as, in any degree or form, they are fair and true and good. And this sense and inevitable requirement alone explain the surprise and pain caused, at first, to us all, by the actual condition of mutual aloofness and hostility, characteristic of most of the constituents of the world within us, as of the world around us, towards their fellow-constituents. A truly atomistic world, —even an atomistic conception of the world,—of life, as a collection of things one alongside of another, on and on, is utterly repulsive to any deeply religious spirit whose self-

knowledge is at all equal to its aspirations.—No wonder, then, if the Quietists, haunted by the false alternative of one such impenetrable atom-act or of an indefinite number of them, chose the One Act, and not a multitude of them.

(2) Man has a deep-seated necessity to purify himself by detachment, not only from things that are illicit but even from those that are essential and towards which he is bound to practise a deep and warm attachment. There is no shadow of theoretical or ultimate contradiction here : to love one's country deeply, yet not to be a *Chauvinist;* to love one's wife tenderly, yet not to be uxorious; to care profoundly for one's children, yet to train, rebuke, and ever brace them, when necessary, up to suffering and even death itself : these things so little exclude each the other, that each attachment can only rightly grow in and through the corresponding detachment. The imperfection in all these cases, and in all the analogous, specifically religious ones, lies not in the objects to be loved, nor in these objects being many and of various degrees and kinds of lovableness, nor in the right (both effective and affective, appropriately varied) love of them : but simply in our actual manner of loving them.—No wonder then that Quietism, face to face with the false alternative of either Attachment or Detachment, chose Detachment, (the salt and the leaven of life) and not attachment (life's meat and meal).

(3) Man has a profound, though ever largely latent, capacity and need for admiration, trust, faith; and does not by any means improve solely by direct efforts at self-improvement, and by explicit examinations of his efforts and failures; but, (a little from the first, and very soon as much, and later on far more,) he progresses by means of a happy absorption in anything clean and fruitful that can and does lift him out of and above his smaller self altogether.—And such an absorption will necessarily be unaccompanied, at the time, by any direct consciousness on the part of the mind as to this its absorption. And, religiously, such quiet concentrations will, in so far as they are at all analyzable after the event, consist in a quite inarticulate, and yet profound and spiritually renovating, sense of God ; and they will have to be tested, not by their describable content, but by their ethical and religious effects. " Psychology and religion," says that great psychological authority, Prof. William James, " both admit that there are forces, seemingly outside of the conscious individual, that bring

redemption to his life." " A man's conscious wit and will, so far as they strain after the ideal, are aiming at something only dimly and inaccurately imagined, whilst the deeper forces of organic ripening within him tend towards a rearrangement that is pretty surely definite, and definitely different from what he consciously conceives and determines. It may consequently be actually interfered with by efforts of too direct and energetic a kind on our part."[1]—No wonder then that Quietism, finding this element of quiet incubation much ignored and starved in the lives of most religious souls, flew to the other extreme, of making this inarticulateness and wise indirectness of striving into the one test and measure of the perfection of all the constituents of the religious life, instead of insisting upon various degrees and combination of full and direct consciousness and articulation, and of much dimness and indirect alertness, as each requiring the other, and as both required by the complete and normal life of the soul.

(4) And Man has a deep-seated sense of shame, in precise proportion as he becomes spiritually awake, about appropriating to himself his virtues and spiritual insight, even in so much as he perceives and admits his possession of them. Not all his consciousness and conviction of the reality of his own efforts and initiative, can or does prevent a growing sense that this very giving of his is (in a true sense) God's gift,— that his very seeking of God ever implies that he had, in some degree, already found God,—that God had already sought him out, in order that he might seek and find God.—No wonder then that, once more shrinking from a Unity constituted in a Multiplicity, Quietism should, (with the apparently sole choice before it, of God Himself operating literally all, or of man subtracting something from that exclusive action and honour of God,) have chosen God alone and entire, rather than, as it were, a fragmentary, limited, baffled influence and efficiency of the Almighty within His Own creature. Yet here again the greater does not supplant, but informs, the lesser; and the Incarnational action of God is, in this supreme question also, the central truth and secret of Christianity.

7. *Multiplicity and unity, in different proportions, needful for all spiritual life.*

We find, then, that it is essential for even the most advanced souls, that they should keep and increase the sense and the

---

[1] *Varieties of Religious Experience,* 1902, pp. 209, 211.

practice of a right multiplicity, as ever a constituent and
essential condition of every concrete, living unity; of a right
attachment, as ever the necessary material and content for a
fruitful and enriching detachment; of a right consciousness
and articulation of images, thoughts, feelings, volitions, and
external acts, as ever stimulations, restful alternations, and
food for a wise and strengthening prayer or states of Quiet
and inarticulation; and of a right personal initiative and
responsibility, as the most precious means and element
for the operations of God.

epist.

We find, too, that it is equally important, for even the most
imperfect souls, to be helped towards some, (though but ever
semi-conscious and intermittent,) sense of the unity which
alone can give much worth or meaning to their multiplicity;
of the detachment which alone can purify and spiritualize
their attachments; of the self-oblivion, in rapt and peaceful
admiration, which alone can save even their right self-watch-
ings and self-improvements from still further centring them in
themselves; and of the true self-abandonment to pure grace
and the breathing of God's Spirit, which alone can give a
touch of winning freedom and of joyful spaciousness to all
the prudence and right fear and conscious responsibility
which, left alone, will hip, darken and weigh down the
religious soul.

And thus we shall find that there is no degree of perfection for any one set of souls which is not, in some form and
amount, prefigured and required by all other souls of good-
will; and again, that there is no one constituent, to which
any one soul is specially drawn, which does not require the
supplementation and corrective of some other constituents,
more fully represented in other souls of possibly lower
sanctity.

Thus each soul and grade requires all the others; and
thus the measure of a soul's greatness is not its possessing
things which cannot, in any degree or way, be found in, or
expected of, all human souls, in proportion as they are fully
and characteristically human, but, on the contrary, its being
full of a spirit and a force which, in different degrees and
forms, are the very salt and yeast, the very light and life, of
all men in every place and time.

sanctity

The following weighty declaration, long ascribed to St.
Thomas Aquinas, fully covers, I think, the doctrine and
ideal aimed at throughout this section : " Already in this life

we ought continuously to enjoy God, as a thing most fully our own, in all our works. . . . Great is the blindness and exceeding the folly of many souls that are ever seeking God, continuously sighing after God, and frequently desiring God : whilst, all the time, they are themselves the tabernacles of the living God . . . since their soul is the seat of God, in which He continuously reposes.   Now who but a fool deliberately seeks a tool which he possesses under lock and key? or who can use and profit by an instrument which he is seeking? or who can draw comfort from food for which he hungers, but which he does not relish at leisure?   Like unto all this is the life of many a just soul, which ever seeks God and never tarries to enjoy Him; and all the works of such an one are, on this account, less perfect." [1]

IV. Pure Love, or Disinterested Religion : its Distinction from Quietism.

The problem of Pure Love, of Disinterested Religion, can hardly, in practice, be distinguished from that of Quiet and Passivity, if only because Quietists, (those who have considered perfection to diminish more and more the number of the soul's acts, or at least to eliminate more and more the need of distinctness or difference between them,) have, quite inevitably, ever given a special prominence to the question as to what should be the character of those few acts, of that one unbroken act.   For once allow this their main question we should all have to answer in the Quietist's way,—viz. that this single act must, for a perfect soul, be the most perfect of the acts possible to man, and hence must be an act of Pure Love.—Yet it is well to realize clearly that, if Quietism necessitates an even excessive and unreal doctrine of Pure Love, a moderate and solid Pure-Love teaching has no kind of necessary connection with Quietism.   For even though my interior life be necessarily one continuous stream and tissue of acts, countless in their number, variety, and degrees of interpenetration, it in nowise follows that acts of Pure Love are not the best, or are impossible; nor that, in proportion as Pure Love informs the soul's multiform acts, such acts must lose in depth and delicacy of variety and articu-

---

[1] *De Beatitudine*, c. 3, 3.

lation. Indeed here, with regard to the very culmination of the interior life, we shall again find and must again test the two conceptions : the finally abstractive and materially simplifying one, which must ever have any one real thing outside of another; and the incarnational and synthetic one, which finds spiritual realities and forces working the one inside and through the other. And the latter view will appear the true one.

1. *New Testament teaching as to Pure Love.*

Now we must first try and get some clear ideas as to how this difficult matter stands in the New Testament,—in the Synoptic tradition and in the Pauline-Johannine teaching respectively. Here again it is the former which, (though on its surface it appears as the more ordinary and the more locally coloured teaching,) is the richer, in its grandly elastic and manifold simplicity; and it is the latter which has most profoundly penetrated and articulated the ultimate meaning and genius of a part of Our Lord's doctrine, yet at the cost of a certain narrowing of the variety and breadth of that outlook. In both cases I shall move, from the easier and more popular teaching, to the deepest and most original enunciations and explanations.[1]

(1) The Synoptic teaching starts throughout from the ordinary post-exilic Jewish feeling and teaching, which indeed recognizes the ceremonial obligations and the more tangible amongst the ethical demands as standing under the categorical inperative of the Legal " Thou Shalt," but places the large territory of the finer moral precepts outside of the Law. So with the "Zedakah," the " Justice " of almsdeeds, and with the " Gemiluth Chasadim," the " works of mercy," such as visiting the sick, burying the dead, and rejoicing with the joyful and sorrowing with the sorrowful. Thus Rabbi Simon the Just tells us : " The world rests on three things : on the Law (*Thorah*), on Worship (*Abodah*), and on Works of Mercy (*Gemiluth Chasadim*) "; and Rabbi Eleazar declared the "Gemiluth Chasadim " to be above the "Zedakah." [2] And it is especially in view of these works of supererogation that rewards, and indeed a strict scale of rewards, are conceived.

---

[1] I have been much helped in my own direct studies of the sources by W. Bousset's *Die Religion des Judenthums im Neutestamentlichen Zeitalter,* 1903; by H. J. Holtzmann's *Neutestamentliche Theologie,* 1897; and A. Jülicher's *Gleichnissreden Jesu,* Theil 2, 1899.

[2] Bousset, pp. 395, 396.

Thus already in the Book of Tobit, (written somewhere between 175 and 25 B.C.,) we have Tobit instructing his son Tobias that " Prayer is good with Fasting and Alms, more than to buy up treasures of gold. For Alms delivereth from death . . . they that practise Mercy and Justice shall live long."[1]   And one of the sayings of the Jewish Fathers declares : " So much trouble, so much reward."[2]

Now this whole scheme and its spirit seems, at first sight, to be taken over quite unchanged by Our Lord. The very Beatitudes end with : " Rejoice . . . because your reward is great in heaven."   And, in the following Sermon, his hearers are bidden to beware of doing their " Zedakah,"—the " Justice " of Prayer, Fasting, Almsdeeds in order to be seen by men ; since, in that case, " ye shall not have reward from your Father Who is in heaven." And this is driven home in detail : these three kinds of Justice are to be done " in secret," and " thy Father will repay thee." Even Prayer itself thus appears as a meritorious good work, one of the means to " treasure up treasures in heaven." Similarly, the rich man is bid " Go sell whatsoever thou hast and give to the poor ; and thou shalt have a treasure in heaven." Even " he that shall give you a cup of cold water in My name, shall not lose his reward." Indeed we have the general principle, " the labourer is worthy of his hire."[3]

And yet we can follow the delicate indications of the presence, and the transitions to the expression, of the deeper apprehension and truth.   For, on the part of God, the reward appears, in the first instance, as in intrinsic relation to the deed.   The reward is the deed's congenital equivalent: "Blessed are the merciful, for they shall obtain mercy " ; " if ye forgive men their trespasses, your heavenly Father will also forgive you " ; and " everyone who shall confess Me before men, him will I also confess before My Father Who is in heaven."[4]   Or the reward appears as a just inversion of the ordinary results of the action thus rewarded : " Blessed are the meek : for they shall inherit the earth " ; take the highest seat at a banquet, and you will be forced down to the lowest, take the lowest, and you will be moved up to the highest ; and, generally, " he that findeth his life, shall lose it ; and

---

[1] Ch. xii, 8, 9; see too ch. ii, 2, 7.
[2] Pirke Aboth, v, 23.
[3] Matt. v, 12; vi, 4, 6, 18, 20; Mark x, 21; ix, 41; Luke x, 7.
[4] Matt. v, 7; vi, 14; x, 32.

he that loseth his life for My sake shall find it." [1] Or the
reward appears as an effect organically connected with the
deed, as its cause or condition : " Blessed are the pure of
heart : for they shall see God." [2] And then the reward comes
to vary, although the deed remains quantitatively identical,
solely because of that deed's qualitative difference, *i.e.*
according to the variation in its motive : " He that receiveth a
prophet in the name of a prophet shall receive a prophet's
reward ; and he that receiveth a righteous man in the name
of a righteous man shall receive a righteous man's reward." [3]
And then the reward moves up and up and becomes a grace,
through being so far in excess of the work done : " Every one
who hath left houses . . . or father . . . or children, or lands for
My name's sake, shall receive " manifold, indeed " a hundred-
fold "—" a full . . . and overflowing measure shall they pour
into your lap " ; and " whosoever shall humble himself, shall
be exalted,"—not simply back to his original level, but into
the Kingdom of Heaven. So, too, " Thou hast been faithful
over a few things, I will set thee over many things " ; indeed
this faithful servant's master " shall place him over all his
possessions ; " or rather, " blessed are those servants whom the
Lord, when He cometh, shall find watching : verily I say
unto you, that he shall gird himself . . . and shall come and
serve them." [4]

This immense disproportion between the work and its
reward, and the consequent grace-character of the latter, is
driven home with a purposely paradoxical, provocative
pointedness, in the two Parables of the Wedding Garment
and of the Equal Payment of the Unequal Labourers, both of
which are in St. Matthew alone. The former concerns the
soul's call to the kingdom, and that soul's response. The
King here, after having formally invited a certain select
number of previously warned relatives and nobles, who all, as
such, had a *claim* upon him (Matt. xxii, 3), sends out invita-
tions with absolute indiscrimination,—to men with no claims
or with less than none ; to " bad " as well as " good." And
it is the King, again, who gratuitously supplies them each
with the appropriate white wedding-feast garment. He has
thus a double right to expect all his guests to be thus clothed,

---

[1] Matt. v, 5; Luke xiv, 8–11; Matt. x, 39.
[2] Matt. v, 8.   [3] Matt. x, 41.
[4] Matt. xix, 29; Mark x, 23; Luke vi, 38; Matt. xxiii, 12; xxv, 21;
xxiv, 47; Luke xii, 37.

and to punish instantly, not the mere negligence, but the active rejection implied on the part of the man clothed in his ordinary clothing (vv. 11, 12). Both call and investiture have been here throughout pure graces, which rendered possible, and which invited but did not force, an acceptance.[1]

The second Parable describes the " Householder " who hired labourers for his vineyard at the first, third, sixth, ninth, and even eleventh hour,—each and all of them for a penny a day; who actually pays out to them, at the end of the day, this one identical pay; and who, to the labourer of the first shift who complains, " These last have spent but one hour, and thou hast made them equal unto us, which have borne the burden and heat of the day," declares, " Friend, I do thee no wrong : didst thou not agree with me for a penny? Take up that which is thine, and go thy way : it is my will to give unto this last even as unto thee. Is it not lawful for me to do what I will with mine own? or is thine eye evil (art thou envious) because I am good " (because I choose to be bountiful)? (Matt. xx, 1–15). Here again the overflowing generosity of God's grace is brought home to us, as operating according to other standards than those of ordinary daily life : nor is this operation unjust, for the Householder paid their due to the first set of workers, whilst rewarding, far above their worth, those poor labourers of the last hour. But, as Jülicher well points out, " we should not pedantically insist upon finding here a doctrine of the strict equality of souls in the Beyond—a doctrine contradicted by other declarations of Jesus. Only the *claim* of single groups of souls to preferential treatment is combated here . . . : a certain fundamental religious disposition is to be awakened." And, as Bugge rightly notes, " the great supreme conception which lies at the bottom of the parable has, parablewise, remained here unnamed : Paul has found the expressive term for it,—' Grace.' "[2]

And we get corresponding, increasingly spiritual interpretations with regard to man's action and man's merit. First, all ostentation in the doing of the deed cancels all reward in the Beyond; so, in the case of each of the three branches of " Justice."[3] And then the worker is to be satisfied, day by

---

[1] Interesting reasons and parallels for holding the Wedding Garment to have been the gift of the King, in Bugge's *Die Haupt-Parabeln Jesu*, 1900, pp. 316, 317.

[2] Jülicher, *op. cit.* p. 467. Bugge, *op. cit.* p. 277.

[3] Matt. vi, 1, 2, 5, 16.

day, with that day's pay and sustenance : " Give us this day
our daily bread," every soul is to pray; the divine Householder will say, " Didst thou not agree with me for a penny?
Take up that which is thine and go thy way." And even
" when ye shall have done all the things that are commanded
you, say, 'We are unprofitable servants, we have done that
which it was our duty to do.'" They are invited to look away
from self, to " seek ye first His Kingdom and His righteousness," and then " all these things," their very necessaries for
earthly life, " shall be added unto you." Indeed it is the
boundlessly generous self-communicativeness of God Himself
which is to be His disciples' deliberate ideal, " be ye perfect, as
your heavenly Father is perfect " ; and the production of this
likeness within themselves is to be the ultimate end and crown
of their most heroic, most costly acts : " love your enemies, and
pray for them that persecute you : that you may be sons of
your Father which is in Heaven : for He maketh His sun to
rise on the evil and the good, and sendeth rain upon the just
and the unjust." And the more there is of such self-oblivious
love, the more will even the gravest sins be entirely blotted
out, and the more rapid will be the full sanctification of the
soul, as Our Lord solemnly declares concerning the sinful
woman in St. Luke, " her sins, which are many, are forgiven;
because she loved much."[1]

In all this matter it is St. Luke's Gospel which is specially
interesting as showing, so to speak, side by side, an increased
Rabbinical-like preciseness of balance between work and
reward, and yet the adoption, doubtlessly under Pauline
influence, of St. Paul's central term in lieu of the old Jewish
terminology. For, in one of its curious so-called " Ebionite "
passages, this Gospel works up the Parable of the Talents,
with its only approximate relation between the deeds and
their rewards (Matt. xxv, 14–30), into the Parable of the
Pounds (Luke xix, 12–27), with its mathematically sym-
metrical interdependence between the quantities of the merit
and those of this merit's reward : the man who makes ten

---

[1] Matt. vi, 11; xx, 14; Luke xvii, 10; Matt. vi, 33; v, 48, 44. 45; Luke
vii, 47. It seems plain that the Parable of the Two Debtors, which
appears in this last passage, declares how pardon awakens love; and
that the sinful woman's act and Our Lord's direct comment on it, which
are now made to serve as that Parable's frame, demonstrate how love
produces pardon. In my text I have been busy only with the second of
these twin truths.

pounds is placed over ten cities, and he who makes five, over five. And, on the other hand, in a Lukan equivalent for part of the Sermon on the Mount, St. Matthew's " reward " is replaced by " grace " : " If ye do good to them that do good to you, what thank (χάρις) have you? . . . and if ye lend to them of whom ye hope to receive, what thank have you? " [1]

(2) St. Paul indeed it is who, in the specially characteristic portions of his teaching, unfolds, by means of a partly original terminology, the deepest motives and implications of Our Lord's own divinely deep sayings and doings, and never wearies of insisting upon the Grace-character of the soul's call and salvation,—the Free Mercy, the Pure Love which God shows to us, and the sheer dependence and complete self-donation, the pure love which we owe to Him, and which, at the soul's best, it can and does give Him.

It is true that in the contrasting, the traditional layer of his teaching, we find the old Jewish terminology still intact : " God will render unto every man according to his works "; " we must all be made manifest before the Judgment-seat of Christ; that each one may receive . . . according to what he hath done, whether it be good or bad." [2] Indeed it is precisely in St. Paul's pages that we find the two most difficult and, at first sight, least spiritual sayings concerning this matter to be discovered in the whole New Testament : " If in this life only we have hoped in Christ, we are of all men most pitiable." And : " If the dead are not raised . . . let us eat and drink, for to-morrow we die." [3] But these two passages must doubtless be taken partly as arguments adapted to the dispositions of his hearers,—the " Let us eat and drink " conclusion is given in the words of a current Heathen Greek proverb,—and, still more, as expressions not so much of a formal doctrine as of a mood, of one out of the many intense, mutually supplementary and corrective moods of that rich nature.

According to his own deepest, most deliberate, and most systematic teaching, it is the life of Christ, the living Christ, energizing even now within the faithful soul, that constitutes both the primary source and the ultimate motive of Christian sanctity. " I have been crucified with Christ; yet I live; and yet no longer I, but Christ liveth in me." And through this divine-human life within us " we faint not ; but though our outward man is decaying, yet our inward man is renewed day by

[1] Luke vi, 33, 34.   [2] Rom. ii, 6; 2 Cor. v, 10.
[3] 1 Cor. xv, 19, 32.

day." Indeed the Lord Himself said to him : " My grace is sufficient for thee ; for My power is made perfect in weakness "; and hence he, Paul, could declare : " Gladly therefore will I glory in my weaknesses, that the strength of Christ may rest upon me." And thus, with Christ living within him, he can exclaim : " If God is for us, who is against us ? . . . Who shall separate us from the love of Christ ? shall tribulation, or anguish, . . . or the sword ? . . . In all these things we are more than conquerors, through Him that loved us. For I am persuaded that neither death, nor life . . . nor things present nor things to come . . . shall be able to separate us from the love of God." " Whether we live therefore, or die, we are the Lord's." [1] We thus get here a reinsistence upon, and a further deepening of, perhaps the profoundest utterance of the whole Old Testament : " What have I in Heaven besides Thee ? and besides Thee I seek nothing upon earth. Even though my flesh and my heart faint, Thou art my rock and my portion for ever." [2]

And then that deathless hymn to Pure Love, the thirteenth chapter of the First Epistle to the Corinthians, not only culminates with the proclamation that, of all man can hope and wish and will and do, of all his doings and his graces, " but now abideth Faith, Hope, Love, (Charity) these three : and the greatest of these is Love (Charity)." But the Love that has this primacy is Pure Love, for " it seeketh not its own." And though of this Love alone it is said that " it never passeth away," ever persists in the Beyond : yet even here already it can and does get exercised,—and this, not only without any suppression of parallel acts of the other virtues, but with these other virtues and their specific motives now taken over and deepened, each in its special characteristic, by the supreme virtue and motive of Pure Love : " Love beareth all things, believeth all things, hopeth all things." [3] Thus Faith, Hope, Patience, and all the other virtues, they all remain, but it is Love that is now the ultimate motive of all their specific motives. These, his culminating teachings, indicate clearly enough that virtue's rewards are regarded by him, ultimately and substantially, as " the wages of going on and not to die "; or rather that they are, in their essence, manifestations of that Eternal Life which is already energizing within souls that earnestly seek God, even here and now.

[1] Gal. ii, 20; 2 Cor. iv, 16; xii, 9; Rom. viii, 31, 35, 37–39; xiv, 8.
[2] Ps. lxxiii (lxxii), v, 25. I follow Duhm's restoration of the text.
[3] 1 Cor. xiii, 13; 8, 7.

This Life, then, however great may be its further expansion and the soul's consciousness of possessing it, already holds within itself sufficient, indeed abundant motives, (in the fulfilment of its own deepest nature and of its now awakened requirements of harmony, strength, and peace through self-donation,) for giving itself ever more and more to God.

(3) And with regard to the Johannine teaching, it will be enough for us to refer back to the texts discussed in the preceding chapter, and to note how large and specially characteristic is here the current which insists upon the reward being already, at least inchoatively, enclosed in the deed itself, and upon this deed being the result and expression of Eternal Life operating within the faithful soul, even already, Here and Now. Only the declaration that " perfect love casteth out fear," that it does not tolerate fear alongside of itself, 1 John iv, 18, appears to be contrary to the Pauline doctrine that Perfect Love, " Love " itself " beareth all things, believeth, hopeth, endureth all things," 1 Cor. xiii. 7. Love then can animate other virtues : why not then a holy fear ? But this Johannine saying seems in fact modelled upon St. Paul's quotation and use of a passage from the Septuagint : " Cast out the bondwoman (the slave-servant) and her son, for the son of the bondwoman shall not be heir together with the son of the free," Gal. iv, 30 ; and hence this saying will not exclude " children of the free-woman,"—a holy fear as well as faith, hope, patience,—but only " children of the slave-woman," superstition, presumption, weakmindedness, and slavish fear.

2. *The " Pure Love " controversy.*

In turning now to the controversy as to Pure Love (1694–1699) and its assured results, we shall have again to distinguish carefully between the lives and intentions of the writers who were censured, and the doctrines, analytic or systematic, taught or implied by them, which were condemned. This distinction is easier in this case than in that of Quietism, for the chief writer concerned here is Fénelon, as to whose pure and spiritual character and deeply Catholic intentions there never has been any serious doubt.

But in this instance we have to make a further distinction —viz. between the objective drift of at least part of his *Explication des Maximes des Saints sur la Vie Intérieure,* published in 1697, and especially the twenty-three propositions extracted from it which were condemned by Pope Innocent

XII in 1699; and the teaching which he increasingly clarified and improved in his numerous apologetic writings against Bossuet and other opponents in this memorable controversy—especially in his Latin writings, intended for transmission to the Pope, and written as late as 1710 and 1712.[1] It is certain that Bishops and theologians who opposed his *Maximes* were found warmly endorsing such pieces as his wonderfully clear and sober *Première Réponse aux Difficultés de M. l'Evêque de Chartres*. It is these pieces, comprising also his remarkably rich *Instruction Pastorale*, his admirably penetrating *Lettre sur l'Oraison Passive* and *Lettre sur la Charité*, and his extraordinarily compact and balanced Second Epistle to Pope Clement XI, 1712 (where all the censured ambiguities and expressions are carefully avoided), which alone among Fénelon's writings shall be accepted in what follows.[2] Indeed even the earlier of these writings fail in but one thing—in justifying the actual text of the condemned book, as distinguished from the intentions of its writer. Bishop Hedley sums up the real position with the treble authority of a spiritually trained Monk, of a practised theological writer, and of a Catholic Bishop of long experience : " The doctrine intended by Fénelon, in his *Maximes des Saints*, and as explained by him during his controversy with Bossuet, has never been censured, although the opposite party laboured hard for its condemnation. Fifteen years after the condemnation of his book, we find him re-stating to Pope Clement XI (who, as Cardinal, had drawn up the Brief of his condemnations), in careful scholastic language the doctrine intended by himself, but which he himself had mis-stated in his popular treatise. As there were errors, the other side, whatever the crudity or novelty of some of its contentions, whatever its motives or methods—and some of them were far from creditable—was sure in the end to succeed. And it is well that it should have succeeded as far as it did succeed." [3]

In any case, we shall have to beware of considering Bossuet's contentions as to the specific character of Charity, Love, and as to the possibility, for man here below, of single acts of pure love, to be representative of the ordinary Catholic teaching

---

[1] *Œuvres*, ed. Versailles, 1820, Vols. IV to IX.

[2] *Réponse : Œuvres*, Vol. IV, pp. 119–132; *Instruction : ibid.* pp. 181–308; *Lettre sur l'Oraison*, Vol. VIII, pp. 3–82; *Lettre sur la Charité*, Vol. IX, pp. 3–36; *Epistola II, ibid.* pp. 617–677.

[3] *The Spiritual Letters of Fénelon*, London, 1892, Vol. I, pp. xi, xii.

either before or since the condemnation. On both these fundamental points Fénelon's positions are demonstrably, and indeed have been generally admitted to be, a mere re-statement of that teaching, as is shown, for instance, in the Jesuit Father Deharbe's solid and sober, thoroughly traditional and highly authorized essay : *Die vollkommene Liebe Gottes . . . dargestellt nach der Lehre des h. Thomas von Aquin*, Regensburg, 1856. It is this most useful treatise and the admirable *Analyse Raisonnée de la Controverse du Quiétisme* of the Abbé Gosselin,[1] (which has already much helped me in the preceding section,) that have been my chief aids in my careful study, back through Bossuet and Fénelon, to St. Thomas and his chief commentators, Sylvius, who died in 1649, and Cardinal Cajetan, who died in 1534, and to the other chief authorities beyond them.—I group the main points, which alone need concern us here, under three heads : the specific Nature of Pure Love ; single Acts of Pure Love ; a State of Pure Love.

(1) Now as to the specific Nature of Charity, or Pure, Perfect Love, St. Thomas tells us : " One Kind of Love is perfect, the other kind is imperfect. Perfect Love is that wherewith a man is loved for his own sake : as, for instance, when some one wishes well to another person, for that other person's sake, in the manner in which a man loves his friend. Imperfect love is the love wherewith a man loves something, not for its own sake, but in order that this good thing may accrue to himself,—in the manner in which a man loves a thing that he covets. Now the former kind of love pertains to Charity, which clings to God for His own sake, whereas it is Hope that pertains to the second kind of love, since he who hopes aims at obtaining something for himself." [2] And Cardinal Cajetan explains that this wishing well to God, " this good that we can will God to have, is double. The good that is in Him, that (strictly speaking) is God Himself,— we can, by Love, will Him to have it, when we find our delight in God being what He is. And the good that is but referred to God,—His honour and Kingdom and the Obedience we owe him,—this we can will, not only by finding our pleasure in it, but by labouring at its maintenance and increase with all our might." [3]

And, says St. Thomas, such Perfect Love alone is Love in

[1] *Œuvres de Fénelon*, ed. 1820, Vol. IV, pp. lxxix–ccxxxiv.
[2] *Summa Theologica*, II, ii, qu. 17, art. 8, in corp.
[3] Comment in II, ii, qu. 23, art. 1.

its strict sense and " the most excellent of all the virtues " : for " ever that which exists for its own sake is greater than that which exists in view of something else. Now Faith and Hope attain indeed to God, yet as the source from which there accrue to us the knowledge of the Truth and the acquisition of the Good ; whilst Love attains to God Himself, with a view to abide in Him, and not that some advantage may accrue to us from Him." And perhaps still more clearly : " When a man loves something so as to covet it, he apprehends it as something pertaining to his own well-being. The lover here stands towards the object beloved, as towards something which is his property." [1] And note how, although he teaches that whereas " the beatitude of man, as regards its cause and its object, is something increate," _i. e._ God Himself, " the essence of the beatitude itself is something created," for " men are rendered blessed by participation, and this participation in beatitude is something created " : yet he is careful to explain some of his more incidental passages, in which he speaks of this essence of beatitude as itself man's end, by the _ex professo_ declaration : " God " alone " is man's ultimate end, and beatitude is only as it were an end before the very end, an end in immediate proximity to the ultimate end." [2]

(2) And next, as to the possibility, actual occurrence and desirableness of single Acts of such Pure Love, even here below : all this is assumed as a matter of course throughout St. Thomas's _ex professo_ teaching on the matter. For throughout the passages concerning the Nature of Pure Love he is not exclusively, indeed not even primarily, busy with man's acts in the future life, but with the respective characteristics of man's various acts as executed and as analyzable, more or less perfectly, already here below. And nowhere does he warn us against concluding, from his reiterated insistence upon the essential characteristics of Pure Love, that such love cannot, as a matter of fact, be practised, at least in single acts, here below at all. Hence it is clear that, according to him, the soul as it advances in perfection will—alongside of acts of supernatural Faith, Hope, Fear, etc. (and the production of such acts will never cease), produce more and more acts of Pure Love : not necessarily more, as compared

[1] _Summa_, II, ii, qu. 23, art. 6, concl., et in corp.; I, ii, qu. 28, art. 1, in corp., et ad 2. See also II, ii, qu. 17, art. 6, in corp.; qu. 28, art. 1 ad 3; I, ii, qu. 28, art. 1, in corp., et ad 2.
[2] In Libr. sent. IV, dist. 49, art. 2.

with the other kinds of contemporary acts, but certainly more
as compared with its former acts of the same character.

But there is a further, profoundly and delicately experienced
doctrine. Not only can Pure Love be exercised in single and
simple acts, alongside of single and simple acts of other kinds
of virtues, supernatural or otherwise : but Pure Love can itself
come to command or to inform acts which in themselves bear,
and will now bear in increased degree, the characteristics of
the other kinds of acts. St. Thomas tells us, with admirable
clearness : " An act can be derived from Charity in one of two
ways. In the first way, the act is elicited by Charity itself, and
such a virtuous act requires no other virtue beside Charity,—
as in the case of loving the Good, rejoicing in it, and mourning
over its opposite. In the second way, an act proceeds from
Charity in the sense of being commanded by it : and in this
manner,—since Charity" has the full range of and " commands
all the virtues, as ordering them (each and all) to their (ultimate) end,—an act can proceed from Charity whilst nevertheless belonging to any other special virtue."   And he assures us
that : "The merit of eternal life," " the fountain-head of meriting," " pertains primarily to, consists in Charity, and pertains
to and consists in other kinds of supernatural acts in only a
secondary manner,—that is, only in so far as these acts are
commanded or informed by Charity " or Pure Love.[1]

Let us take some instances of such two-fold manifestations
of identical motives and virtues, according as these motives
and virtues operate in simple co-ordination, or within a compound and organic system. In the scholar's life, Greek and
Latin and Hebrew may be acquired, each simply for its own
sake and each alongside of the other; or they can be acquired,
from the immediate motive indeed of knowing each in its own
specific nature as thoroughly as possible, yet with the ultimate,
ever more and more conscious and all-penetrating, motive of
thus acquiring means and materials for the science of language, or for the study of philosophy, or for research into
early phases of the Jewish-Christian religion. In the family
life, a man, woman, or child can live for himself or herself,
and then for his or her other immediate relatives, each
taken as separate alongside of the other, or he or she may
get more and more dominated by the conception and claims
of the family as an organic whole, and may end by working

---

[1] *Summa Theol.*, III, qu. 85, art. 2 ad 1; I, ii, qu. 114, art. 4, in corp.
In Libr. sent. III, dist. 30, art. 5.

largely, even with respect to himself, as but for so many constituents of that larger organism in which alone each part can attain its fullest significance. And especially a young mother can live for her own health and joys, and then, alongside of these, for those of her child, or she can get to the point of sustaining her own physical health and her mental hopes and will to live as so many means and conditions for feeding and fostering the claimful body and soul of her child.

So again, in the creatively artistic life, we can have a Dante writing prose and poetry and painting a picture, and a Rafael painting pictures and writing sonnets; or we can have Wagner bringing all his activities of scholar, poet, painter, musician, stage-manager,—each retaining, and indeed indefinitely increasing, its specific character and capabilities,—to contribute, by endless mutual stimulation and interaction, to something other and greater than any one of them individually or even than the simple addition of them all,—to a great Music-Drama and multiform yet intensely unified image of life itself. And an organist can draw out, as he plays, the *Vox Humana* stop, and then another and another limitedly efficacious organ-stop, whilst each new-comer takes the place of its predecessor or a place beside it; or he can draw out the *Grand Jeu* stop, which sets all the other stops to work in endless interaction, with itself permeating and organizing the whole. We thus, in these and countless other cases, and in every variety of degree within each case, get two kinds of variety, what we may call the simple and the compound diversification. And everywhere we can find that the richest variety not only can coexist with, but that it requires and is required by, indeed that it is a necessary constituent and occasion of, the deepest and most delicate unity.[1]

(3) And finally, as to a State of Pure Love. Only here do we reach the class of questions to which the condemnations of Fénelon really apply.

We shall do well to begin by bearing in mind the very ancient, practically unbroken, very orthodox Christian discrimination of faithful souls,—sometimes into the two classes of Mercenaries (or Slaves) and Friends or Children, the latter

---

[1] Some of the finest descriptions of these profoundly organized states common, in some degrees and forms, to all mankind, are to be found in the tenth and eleventh books of St. Augustine's *Confessions*, A.D. 397, and in Henri Bergson's *Essai sur les Données Immédiates de la Conscience*, 1898.

of whom the great Clement of Alexandria, who died about A.D. 215, called " Gnostics," " Gnosis " being his term for perfection (this scheme is the one to which Catherine's life and teaching conform); or into the three classes of Servants (Slaves); Mercenaries; and Friends (or Children), as is already worked out with full explicitness by Saints Basil, Gregory of Nazianzum, and Gregory of Nyssa, who died in the years 379, 389, and 395 (?) respectively. Now Clement places the Mercenary on the left of the Sanctuary, but the " Gnostic " on the right; and, whilst declaring that the former " are those who, by means of renouncing things perishable, hope to receive the goods of incorruption in exchange," he demands of the "Gnostic" that "he approach the saving word neither from the fear of punishment, nor from the motive of reward, but simply because He is good."[1] And St. Basil, echoed in this by his two contemporaries, teaches that, " We obey God and avoid vices, from the fear of punishment, and in that case we take on the resemblance of Slaves. Or we keep the precepts, because of the utility that we derive from the recompense, thus resembling Mercenaries. Or finally, from love of Him who has given us the law, we obey with joy at having been judged worthy of serving so great and good a God, and thus we imitate the affection of Children towards their parents."[2] And, in the case of all these Fathers, it is clear that, not only single acts, but whole states of soul and life are meant.

But the increased fineness in the analysis of interior experiences and dispositions has since then required, and the Church formulations have most wisely demanded, that these three classes be not so sharply distinguished as to make any one soul seem exclusively and unchangeably to pertain to any one of them; and, still more, that these three divisions be taken to represent, even where and whilst they are most completely realized, only the predominant character of the majority of the acts constituting the respective state of soul. For it is clear that not only is there, and can there be, no such thing, on earth at least, as a state composed of one unrepeated act; but there is no such thing as a condition of soul made up solely of acts of " simple " Pure Love, or even of supernatural acts of all sorts commanded throughout by Charity, or indeed solely of supernatural acts, both simple and commanded. The " One-act " state is a chimera; the state of "simple" acts

[1] *Stromata*, Book **IV**, ch. **vi**, 30, **1**; ch. iv, 15, 6.
[2] Proemium in *Reg. Fus. Tract*, n. 3, Vol. II, pp. 329, 330.

of Pure Love alone would, if possible, involve the neglect of numberless other virtues and duties; and the last two states are indeed highly desirable, but it would be fanaticism to think we could completely attain to them here below.

Yet there is nothing in any Church-censure to prevent, and there is much in the teaching and life of countless saints to invite, our holding the possibility, hence the working ideal and standard, for even here below, of a state in which two kinds of acts, which are still good in their degree, would be in a considerable minority: acts of merely natural, unspiritualized hope, fear, desire, etc.; and acts of supernatural hope, fear, desire, etc., in so far as not commanded by Charity. For even in this state not fully deliberate venial sins would occasionally be committed, far more would a certain number of acts of an unspiritualized, unsupernatural kind occur. And the necessary variety among the supernatural acts would in nowise be impaired,—it would indeed be greatly stimulated, by Pure Love being now, for the most part, the ultimate motive of their exercise.

Sylvius, in his highly authoritative commentary on St. Thomas, puts the matter admirably : " We may not love God in view of reward in suchwise as to make eternal life the true and ultimate end of our love, or to love God because of it, so that without the reward we would not love Him . . . We must love God with reference to the eternal reward in suchwise that we put forth indeed both love and good works in view of such beatitude,—in so far as the latter is the end proposed to these works by God Himself; yet that we subordinate this our beatitude to the love of God as the true and ultimate end," so that " if we had no beatitude to expect at all, we should nevertheless still love Him and execute good works for His own sake alone. In this manner we shall first love God above all things and for His own sake; and we shall next keep the eternal reward before us, for the sake of God and of His honour." [1] A man in these dispositions would still hope, and desire, and fear, and regret, and strive for, and aspire to conditions, things, persons both of earth and of the beyond, both for himself and for others, both for time and for eternity : but all this, for the most part, from the ultimate motive, penetrating, deepening, unifying all the other motives,—of the love of Love, Christ, Spirit, God.

---

[1] *Summa Theol.*, II, ii, qu. 27, art. 3.

Any hesitation to accept the reality or possibility of such a state cannot, then, be based upon such acceptance involving any kind of Quietism, but simply on the admittedly great elevation of such a condition. Yet this latter objection seems to be sufficiently met if we continuously insist that even such a state neither exempts souls from the commission of (more or less deliberate) venial sin; nor is ever entirely equable; nor is incapable of being completely lost; nor, as we have just contended, is ever without more or less numerous acts of an unsupernaturalized kind, and still less without acts of the supernatural virtues other than Love and unprompted by Love.

And all fear of fanaticism will be finally removed by a further most necessary and grandly enlarging insistence upon the Mercenaries and even the Servants having passing moments, and producing varyingly numerous single acts, of Pure Love and of the other supernatural virtues prompted by Pure Love. All souls in a state of Grace throughout God's wide wide world,—every constituent, however slight and recent, of the great soul of the Church throughout every sex, age, race, clime, and external organization, would thus have some touches, some at least incidental beginnings of Pure Love, and of the other supernatural virtues prompted by Pure Love. All souls would thus, in proportion to their degree of grace and of fidelity, have some of those touches; and the progress of all would consist in the degree to which that variety of acts would become informed and commanded by the supreme motive of all motives, Pure and Perfect Love.[1]

And with such an Ideal, required by fundamental Catholic positions, ever increasingly actuating the soul and binding it to all souls beneath, around, above it, what there is of truth in the savage attacks of Spinoza and of Kant and of such recent

---

[1] The obligation for all of acts of Pure Love is clearly taught by the condemnations, passed by Popes Alexander VII and Innocent XI, upon the opposite contention, in 1665 and 1679: " Homo nullo unquam vitae suae tempore tenetur elicere actum Fidei, Spei et Charitatis, ex vi praeceptorum divinorum ad eas virtutes pertinentium." Note here how " Charitas " necessarily means Pure Love, since Imperfect Love has already been mentioned in " Spes."—" Probabile est, ne singulis quidem rigorose quinquenniis per se obligare praeceptum charitatis erga Deum. Tunc solum obligat, quando tenemur justificari et non habemus aliam viam qua justificari possumus." Here Pure Love is undoubtedly meant by " Charitas," since, outside of the use of the sacraments, Pure Love alone justifies.

writers as A. E. Taylor,[1] upon the supposed hypocritical self-seeking in the practice and temper of average Christians, would lose all its force.

3. *Cognate Problems*.

Three much-discussed cognate matters require some elucidation here. They answer to the questions: Does reference to the self, as for instance in acts of gratitude and thanksgiving, prevent an act from being one of Pure Love? Is the pleasurableness, normally ever attached and subsequent to all virtuous acts, to be regarded as part of the reward from which Pure Love abstracts? And finally are, I will not say any technically ecstatic or other in part psycho-physical peculiarities and manifestations, but even active Contemplation or the simple Prayer of Quiet, necessary conditions or expressions of a state of Pure Love,—understood in the sense explained above?

(1) As to reference to the self, it is highly important to distinguish between acts of Pure Love, and attempts, by means of the maximum possible degree of abstraction, to apprehend the absolute character and being of God. For these two things have no necessary connection, and yet they have been frequently confounded. St. Teresa's noble confession of past error, and consequent doubly valuable, amended teaching is perhaps the most classical pronouncement extant upon this profoundly important point.[2] The contingent, spatial and temporal, manifestations and communications of God, above all as we have them in the life of Our Lord and in those who have come nearest to Him, but also, in their several degrees and forms, in the lives of each one of us : all these, in their sacred, awakening and healing, particularity and closeness of contact, can and should be occasions and materials for the most perfect, for the purest Love.

Indeed it is well never to forget that nothing, and least of all God, the deepest of all the realities, is known to us at all, except in and by means of its relation to our own self or to our fellow-creatures. Hence if Love were Pure only in proportion as it could be based upon our apprehension of God as independent of all relation to ourselves, Pure Love would be simply impossible for us.—But, in truth, such a conception would, in addition, be false in itself : it would imply that the

---

[1] *The Problem of Conduct*, 1901, p. 329, n.

[2] *Life, written by Herself*, ch. XXII, tr. by David Lewis, ed. 1888, pp. 162–174.

whole great Incarnation-fact and -doctrine,—the whole of that great root of all religion, the certainty that it is because God has first loved us that we can love Him, that He is a self-revealing God, and One whom we can know and reach because " in Him we live and move and have our being "—was taking us, not towards, but away from, our true goal. There are, surely, few sadder and, at bottom, more deeply uncreaturely, unchristian attitudes, than that which would seek or measure perfection in and by the greatest possible abstraction from all those touching contingencies which God Himself has vouchsafed to our nature,—a nature formed by Himself to require such plentiful contact with the historical and visible. —And if God's pure love for us can and does manifest itself in such contingent acts, then our love can and should become and manifest itself purer and purer by means, not only of the prayer of formless abstraction and expectation, but also by the contemplation of these contingencies and by the production of analogously contingent acts. And if so, then certainly gratitude, in so far as it truly deserves the name, can and does belong to Pure Love, for the very characteristic of such gratitude consists in a desire to give and not to receive.[1]

Not, then, the degree of disoccupation with the Contingent, even of the contingent of our own life, but the degree of freedom from self-seeking, and of the harmonization and subordination of all these contingencies in and under the supreme motive of the Pure Love and service of God in man and of man in God, is the standard and test of Christian perfection.

(2) As to the pleasureableness which, in normal psychic conditions, more or less immediately accompanies or follows the virtuous acts of the soul, the realizations of its own deeper and deepest ideals, we should note that, in its earthly degree and form, it is not included in what theologians mean by the "rewards" of virtuous action. And in this they are thoroughly self-consistent, for they adhere, I think with practical unanimity, to Catherine's doctrine that these immediate consequences of virtuous acts are not to be considered a matter of positive and, as it were, separate divine institution, —as something which, given the fundamental character of

---

[1] Deharbe, *op. cit.* pp. 139–179, has an admirable exposition and proof of this point, backed up by conclusive experiences and analyses of Saints and Schoolmen.

man's spiritual nature, might have been otherwise; but as what,—given the immutable nature of God and of the image of that nature in His creature, man,—follows from an intrinsic, quite spontaneous necessity.—Hence, at this point especially, would it be foolish and fanatical, because contrary to the immanental nature of things, and to the right interplay of the elemental forces of all life, to attempt the suppression even of the several actual irruptions of such pleasure, and still more of the source and recurrence of this delectation. Fortunately success is here as impossible as it would be undesirable,—as much so as, on a lower plane, would be the suppression of the pleasure concomitant with the necessary kinds and degrees of eating. Indeed, it is clear, upon reflection, that unless a man (at least implicitly) accepts and (indirectly) wills that spiritual or physical pleasure, he cannot profitably eat his food or love his God.

But from this in nowise follows what Bossuet tried so hard to prove,—that what is thus necessarily present in man, as a psychical or physical prompting and satisfaction, must also of necessity be willed by him, directly and as his determining reason and justification. In turning to eat, man cannot help feeling a psychic pleasure of an all but purely physical kind; and, if he is wise, he will make no attempt to meddle with this feeling. But he can either deliberately will, as his action's object, that pleasure which is thus inevitably incident to the act, and the more he does so, the more simply greedy and sensual he will become; or he can directly will, as his determining end, that sustenance of life and strength for his work and spiritual growth, which is the justification and ultimate reason of eating (the *rationale* of that very pleasure so wisely attached by nature, as a stimulus, to a process so necessary to the very highest objects), and the more he does so, the more manly and spiritual he will grow.

And so with every one of man's wondrously manifold and different physical, psychical, spiritual requirements and actions, within the wide range of his right nature and ideals. There is not one of them,—not the most purely physical-seeming of these acts,—which he cannot ennoble and spiritualize by, as it were, meeting it,—by willing it, more and more, because of its rational end and justification. And there is not one of them, —not an act which, judged simply by its direct subject-matter and by the soul's faculties immediately engaged, would be the most purely mental and religious of acts,—which man cannot degrade and de-spiritualize, by, as it were, following it, by willing it more and more because of its psychical attraction and pleasurable concomitance alone. For, in the former case, the act, however gross may seem its material, is made the occasion and instrument of spiritual character-building and of the constitution of liberty; in the latter case, the act, however ethereal its body, is but the occasion and means of the soul's dispersion in the mere phenomenal flux of the surface of existence, and of its subjection to the determinism which obtains here.[1]

Catherine's whole convert life is one long series of the most striking examples of an heroic delicacy in self-knowledge and self-fighting in this matter : a delicacy which, as to the degree of its possibility and desirableness in any particular soul, is, however, peculiarly dependent upon that soul's special circumstances, temperament, *attrait*, and degree of perfection reached and to be reached.

(3) And, finally, as to the relations between the Contemplative forms of Prayer, and Acts and variously complete States of Pure Love; and, again, of such Prayer and Love, and Abnormal or Miraculous conditions : it is clear that, if there is no true Contemplation without much Pure Love, there can be much Pure Love without Contemplation.

Abbé Gosselin well sums up the ordinary Catholic teaching. " Meditation consists of discursive acts which are easily distinguished from each other, both because of the kind of strain and shock with which they are produced, and because of the diversity of their objects. It is the ordinary foundation of the interior life and the ordinary prayer of beginners, whose imperfect love requires to be thus excited and sustained by distinct and reflective acts. Contemplation consists, strictly speaking, in direct ' non-reflex ' acts,—acts so simple and peaceful as to have nothing salient by which the soul could distinguish one from the other. It is called by the Mystical Saints ' a simple and loving look,' as discriminating it from meditation and the latter's many methodic and discursive acts, and as limiting it to a simple and loving consideration and view of God and of divine things, certified and rendered present to the soul by faith. It is the ordinary prayer of perfect souls, or at least of those that have already made much progress in the divine love. For the more purely

---

[1] See Deharbe's excellent remarks, *op. cit.* pp. 109, 110, n.

a soul loves God, the less it requires to be sustained by distinct, reflective acts; reasoning becomes a fatigue and an embarrassment to it in its prayer—it longs but to love and to contemplate the object of its love."

Or as Fénelon puts it : " ' Passivity,' ' Action,' is not precisely itself Pure Love, but is the mode in which Pure Love operates. . . . ' Passivity,' 'Action,' is not precisely the purity of Love, but is the effect of that purity." [1] Yet, as M. Gosselin adds, " It must be admitted that without Contemplation the soul can arrive at a very high perfection; and that the most discursive meditation, and hence still more all prayer as it becomes effective, often includes certain direct acts which form an admixture and beginning of contemplation." [2]

And as to any supposed necessary relations between the very highest contemplation and the most complete state of Pure Love on the one hand, and anything abnormal or miraculous on the other hand, Fénelon, in this point remarkably more sober than Bossuet, well sums up the most authoritative and classical Church-teaching on the matter : " ' Passive ' Contemplation is but Pure Contemplation : ' Active ' Contemplation being one which is still mixed with hurried and discursive acts. When Contemplation has ceased to have any remnant of this hurry, of this ' activity,' it is entirely ' Passive,' that is, peaceful, in its acts." " This free and loving look of the soul means acts of the understanding,—for it is a look; and acts of the will, for the look is a loving one; and acts produced by free-will, without any strict necessity, for the look is a free look." " We should not compare Passive Contemplation," as did Bossuet, " to prophecy, or to the gift of tongues or of miracles; nor may we say that this mystical state consists principally in something wrought by God within us without our co-operation, and where, consequently, there neither is nor can be any merit. We must, on the contrary, to speak correctly, say that the substance of such Passive Prayer, taken in its specific acts, is free, meritorious, and operated within us by a grace that acts together with us " " It is the attraction to the acts which the soul now produces which, as by a secondary and counter-effect, occasions a quasi-incapacity for those acts which it does not produce. Now this attraction is not of a

---

[1] *Analyse, loc. cit.* pp. cxxii, cxxiii, *Lettre sur l'Oraison Passive, Œuvres,* Vol. VIII, p. 47.

[2] *Analyse,* p. cxxiii.

kind to deprive the soul of the use of its free-will : we see this from the nature of the acts which this attraction causes the soul to produce.   Whence I conclude that this same attraction does not, again, deprive it of its liberty with regard to the acts which it prevents.   The attraction but prevents the latter in the way it produces the other,—by an efficacious influence that involves no sheer necessity."   "'Passivity,' if it comes from God, ever leaves the soul fully free for the exercise of the distinct virtues demanded by God in the Gospel; the *attrait* is truly divine only in so far as it draws the soul on to the perfect fulfilment of the evangelical counsels and promises concerning all the virtues."   " The inspiration of the Passive state is but an habitual inspiration for the interior acts of evangelical piety.   It renders the Passive soul neither infallible nor impeccable, nor independent of the Church even for its interior direction, nor exempt from the obligation of meriting and growing in virtue. . . . The inspiration of the passive soul differs from that of actively just souls only in being purer ; that is, more exempt from all natural self-seeking, more full, more simple, more continuous, and more developed at each moment.   We have, throughout, ever one and the same inspiration, which but grows in perfection and purity in proportion as the soul renounces itself more, and becomes more sensitive to the divine impressions." [1]

Thus we get an impressive, simple and yet varied, conception of spirituality, in which a real continuity, and a power and obligation of mutual understanding and aid underlies all the changes of degree and form, from first to last.   For from first to last there are different degrees, but of the same supernatural grace acting in and upon the same human nature responsive in different degrees and ways.   From first to last there is, necessarily and at every step, the Supernatural : at no point is there any necessary presence of, or essential connection with, the Miraculous or the Abnormal.

4. *Spinoza, Leibniz, Kant.*

Theology and Philosophy have not ceased to occupy themselves, at least indirectly, with the substance of these great questions, since they furnished the subject-matter to Bossuet and Fénelon in their memorable controversy ; somewhat over-subtle although some of it was in its earlier phases, owing to Fénelon's chivalrous anxiety to defend, as far as possible, the

[1] *Lettre sur l'Oraison Passive, Œuvres,* Vol. VIII, pp. 10; 18, 11, 12; 14, 15; 74.

very expressions, often so nebulous and shifting, of his cousin, Madame Guyon.

(1) Indeed about twenty years before that controversy, Spinoza had, in his *Theologico-Political Treatise*, and then, more impressively still, in his *Ethics*, made a brilliant assault upon all, especially all religious, self-seeking. Also on this point these writings showed that strange, pathetic combination of grandly religious intuitions and instincts with a Naturalistic system which, logically, leaves no room for those deepest requirements of that great soul; and here they revealed, in addition, considerable injustice towards the, doubtless very mixed and imperfect, motives of average humanity.

True intuition speaks in his *Treatise* (published in 1670) in the words : " Since the love of God is man's supreme beatitude and the final end and scope of all human actions : it follows that only that man conforms to the divine law, who strives to love God, not from fear of punishment, nor from the love of some other thing, such as delights, fame, and so forth, but from this motive alone, that he knows God, or that he knows the knowledge and love of God, to be his supreme end." But a little further back we learn that " the more we know the things of Nature, the greater and the more perfect knowledge of God do we acquire "; a frank application of the pure Pantheism of his reasoned system.

In his *Ethics*, again, a noble intuition finds voice where he says : " Even if we did not know our Mind," our individual soul, " to be eternal, we should still put Piety and Religion and, in a word, all those virtues that are to be referred to magnanimity and generosity, first in our esteem." But he is doubtless excessive in his picturing of the downright, systematic immorality of attitude of ordinary men—the " slaves " and " mercenaries." " Unless this hope of laying aside the burdens of Piety and Religion after death and of receiving the price of their service, and this fear of being punished by dire punishments after death were in men, and if they, contrariwise, believed that their minds would perish with their bodies : they would let themselves go to their natural inclination and would decide to rule all their actions according to their lust." And he is doubtlessly, though nobly, excessive in his contrary ideal : " He who loves God cannot strive that God shall love him in return,"—an ideal which is, however, certainly in part determined by his philosophy, which knows no ultimate abiding personality or consciousness either in God or man.

Yet, once again, we have him at his inspiring best when, Catherine-like, he tells us : " The supreme Good of those who pursue virtue is common to them all, and all are equally able to rejoice in it " ; and " this love towards God is incapable of being stained by the passions of envy and bitterness, but is increased in proportion as we figure to ourselves a larger number of men joined to God by the same bonds of love " ; when he declares : " we do not enjoy beatitude because we master our passions ; rather, contrariwise, do we master our passions because we enjoy beatitude " ; and when he insists, with no doubt too indiscriminating, too Jacopone-like, a simplification, upon what, in its substance, is a profound truth: " the intellectual," the pure " love of the soul for God is the very love of God, wherewith God loves Himself." [1]

(2) It was, however, the astonishingly circumspect and many-sided Leibniz who, indefinitely smaller soul though he was, succeeded, perhaps better than any other modern philosopher, in successfully combining the divers constitutive elements of the act and state of Pure Love, when he wrote in 1714: " Since true Pure Love consists in a state of soul which makes me find pleasure in the perfections and the felicity of the object loved by me, this love cannot but give us the greatest pleasure of which we are capable, when God is that object. And, though this love be disinterested, it already constitutes, even thus simply by itself, our greatest good and deepest interest."

Or, as he wrote in 1698 : " Our love of others cannot be separated from our true good, nor our love of God from our felicity. But it is equally certain that the consideration of our own particular good, as distinguished from the pleasure which we taste in seeing the felicity of another, does not enter into Pure Love." And earlier still he had defined the act of loving as "the finding one's pleasure in the felicity of another" ; and had concluded thence that Love is for man essentially an enjoyment, although the specific motive of love is not the pleasure or the particular good of him who loves, but the good or the felicity of the beloved object.[2]

[1] *Tractatus Theologico-Politicus*, c. iv, opening of par. 4, ed. Van Vloten et Land, 1895, Vol. II, p. 4; *ibid.* middle of par. 3, p. 3; *Ethica*, p. v, prop. xli, *ibid.* Vol. I, p. 264; *ibid. Scholion*, p. 265; *ibid.* prop. xix, p. 251; *ibid.* prop. xx, p. 251; *ibid.* prop. xlii, p. 265; *ibid.* prop. xxxvi, p. 261.

[2] *Die Philosophischen Schriften von Leibniz*, ed. Gebhardt, Vol. VI, 1885, pp. 605, 606; and quotation in Gosselin's *Analyse, Œuvres de Fénelon*, 1820, Vol. IV, pp. clxxviii, clxxvii.

(3) Yet it is especially Kant who, with his predominant hostility to all Eudaemonism in Morality and Religion, has, more than all others, renewed the controversy as to the relations between virtue and piety on the one hand, and self-seeking motives on the other, and who is popularly credited with an entirely self-consistent antagonism to even such a wise and necessary attitude as are the amended positions of Fénelon and those of Leibniz. And yet I sincerely doubt whether (if we put aside the question as to the strictly logical consequences of his Critical Idealism, such as that Idealism appears in its greatest purity in the *Critique of Pure Reason*, 1781; and if we neglect the numerous, often grossly unjust, Spinoza-like sallies against the supposed undiluted mercenariness of ordinary piety, which abound in his *Religion within the Limits of Pure Reason*, 1793) we could readily find any explicit pronouncement hopelessly antagonistic to the Catholic Pure-Love doctrine.

Certainly the position taken up towards this point in that very pregnant and curious, largely-overlooked little treatise, *The Canon of Pure Reason*, which (evidently an earlier and complete sketch), has been inserted by him into his later, larger, but materially altered scheme of the *Critique* of 1781, (where it now forms the *Zweite Hauptstück* of the *Transcendentale Methodenlehre*, ed. Kehrbach, Reclam, pp. 603–628), appears to be substantially acceptable.[1] " Happiness consists in the satisfaction of all our inclinations, according to their various character, intensity, and duration. The law of practical action, in so far as it is derived from the motive of happiness, I call Pragmatic, a Rule of Good Sense; the same law, in so far as it has for its motive only the becoming worthy of such happiness, I call Moral, the Moral Law. Now Morality already by itself constitutes a system, but Happiness does not do so, except in so far as Happiness is distributed in exact accordance with Morality. But such a distribution is only possible in the intelligible world,"—the world beyond phenomena which can be reached by our reason alone—" and under a wise Originator and Ruler. Such an One, together with life in such a world—a world which we are obliged to consider as a future one—reason finds itself forced to assume, or else to look upon the moral laws as empty phantoms, since the necessary result of these laws,—a result which that same reason

[1] It is to Schweizer's admirable monograph, *Die Religions-Philosophie Kant's*, 1899, pp. 4–70, that I owe my clear apprehension of this very interesting doubleness in Kant's outlook.

connects with their very idea,—would have to fall away, if that assumption were to go. Hence every one looks upon the moral laws as *commandments*, a thing which they could not be, if they did not conjoin with their rule consequences of *a priori* appropriateness, and hence if they did not carry with them *promises* and *threats*. But this too they can do only if they lie within the compass of a Single Necessary Being, Itself the Supreme Good, Which alone can render possible such a unity embracing both means and end.—Happiness alone is, for our reason, far from being the Complete Good, for reason does not approve of Happiness unless it be united with the being worthy of Happiness, *i. e.* Moral Rectitude. But Morality alone, and with it the simple being worthy of happiness, is also far from the Complete Good. Even if reason, free from any consideration of any interest of its own, were to put itself in the position of a being that had to distribute all happiness to others alone, it could not judge otherwise : for, in the complete idea of practical action, both points are in essential conjunction, yet in suchwise that it is the moral disposition which, as condition, first renders possible a sharing in happiness, and not the prospect of happiness which first gives an opening to the moral disposition. For, in this latter case, the disposition would not be moral, and, consequently, would not deserve that complete happiness to which reason can assign no other limitation than such as springs from our own immoral attitude of will." [1]

In his *Foundation of the Metaphysic of Morals*, 1785, the noble apostrophe to the Good Will no doubt appears formally to proclaim as possible and desirable a complete human disposition, in which no considerations of Happiness play any part : " The good will is good, not through what it effects or produces, not through its utility for the attainment of any intention or end, but it is good through the quality of the volition alone ; that is, it is good in itself. . . ." " If, with its greatest efforts, nothing were to be effected by it, and only the good will itself were to remain, this bare will would yet shine in lonely splendour as a jewel,—as something which has its full value in itself." But further on he shows us how, after all, " this good will cannot, then, be the only and the whole good, but still it is the highest good and the condition for all the rest, even for our desire of happiness." [2] Certain

[1] *Loc. cit.* pp. 611, 614, 615, 616.
[2] Kant's *Werke*, ed. Berlin Academy, Vol. IV, 1903, pp. 393, 394; 396.

exaggerations, which are next developed by him here, shall be considered in a later chapter.

5. *Four important points.*

Here I will but put together, in conclusion, four positions which I have rejoiced to find in two such utterly, indeed at times recklessly, independent writers as Professor Georg Simmel of Berlin and Professor A. E. Taylor.

(1) Dr. Simmel declares, with admirable cogency : " The concept of religion completely loses in Kant, owing to his rationalistic manner of discovering in it a mere compound of the moral interest and the striving after happiness, its most specific and deepest character. No doubt these two apprehensions are also essential to religion, but precisely the direction in which Kant conjoins them,—that duty issues in happiness, is the least characteristic of religion, and is only determined by his Moralism, which refuses to recognize the striving after happiness as a valuable motive. The opposite direction appears to me as far more decisively a part of religion and of its incomparable force : for we thus find in religion precisely that ideal power, which makes it the duty of man to win his own salvation. According to the Kantian Moralism, it is every man's private affair how he shall meet his requirement of happiness; and to turn such a private aspiration into an objective, ideal claim, would be for Kant a contradiction and abomination. In reality, however, religion itself *requires* that man should have a care for his own welfare and beatitude, and in this consists its incomparable force of attraction." [1] Let the reader note how entirely this agrees with, whilst properly safeguarding, the doctrine of Pure Love : it is the precise position of the best critics of the unamended Fénelon.

(2) Professor Taylor insists that " it is possible to desire directly and immediately pleasant experiences which are not my own. . . . Because it is *I* who in every case have the pleasure of the anticipation, it is assumed that it must be I who am to experience the realization of the anticipation." Yet " it is really no more paradoxical that I should anticipate with pleasure some event which is not to form part of my own direct sensible experience, than it is that I should find pleasure in the anticipation at twenty of myself at eighty." " The austerest saints will and can mortify themselves as a thing well-pleasing

---

[1] Kant, 1904, p. 131.

to God." [1] In this way the joy of each constituent of the
Kingdom of God in the joys of all the rest, and in the all-
pervading joy of God, is seen to be as possible as it is
undoubtedly actual : the problem of the relation between
pleasure and egoism is solved.

(3) And Professor Taylor again insists upon how pleasant
experiences, which do not owe their pleasantness to their
relation to a previous anticipation, are not, properly speaking,
good or worthy. It is by " satisfactions " and not by mere
" pleasures " that " even the most confirmed Hedonist must
compute the goodness of a life. . . . Only when the pleasant
experience includes in itself the realization of an idea is it
truly good." [2] But, if so, then the experience will be good,
not in proportion as it is unpleasant, as Kant was so prone
to imply; nor directly in proportion as it is pleasant, although
pleasantness will accompany or succeed it, of a finer quality
if not of a greater intensity, according as the idea which it
embodies is good : but directly in proportion to the goodness
of that idea. Thus all things licit, from sense to spirit, will
find their place and function in such acts, and in a life composed of such acts, spirit expressing itself in terms of sense.
And the purification, continuously necessary for the ever more
adequate expression of the one in and by the other, will be
something different from any attempt at suppressing this
means of expression. Thus here again the great Christian
Incarnation-Doctrine appears as the deepest truth, and as
the solution of the problem as to the relations of pleasure and
duty.[3]

(4) And finally, as to the ever-present need and importance
of a theory concerning these matters, Professor Taylor points
out, not only that some such theory is necessary to the full
human life, but that it must place an infinite ideal before us :
paradox though it may sound, nothing less is truly practical,
for " any end that is to be permanently felt as worth striving
for, must be infinite," and therefore " in a sense infinitely
remote "; and hence " if indifference to the demand for a

---

[1] *The Problem of Conduct*, pp. 336, 337; 329.

[2] *Ibid.* p. 327.

[3] See James Seth, *A Study of Ethical Principles*, 1894, pp. 193–236,
where this position, denominated there " Eudaemonism," is contrasted
with " Hedonism," uniquely or at least predominantly occupied with the
act's sensational materials or concomitances, and " Rigorism," with its
one-sided insistence upon the rational form and end of action.

practicable ideal be the mark of a dreamer or a fanatic, contentment with a finite and practicable ideal is no less undeniably the mark of an *esprit borné*." [1]

Here Fénelon has adequately interpreted the permanent and complete requirements of the religious life and spirit. "You tell me," he says to his adversaries, "that 'Christianity is not a school of Metaphysicians.' All Christians cannot, it is true, be Metaphysicians; but the principal Theologians have great need to be such. It was by a sublime Metaphysic that St. Augustine soared above the majority of the other Fathers, who were, for the rest, as fully versed in Scripture and Tradition. It was by his lofty Metaphysic that St. Gregory of Nazianzum has merited the distinguishing title of *Theologian*. It is by Metaphysic that St. Anselm and St. Thomas have been such great luminaries of the Church. True, the Church is not 'a school of Metaphysicians,' who dispute without docility, as did the ancient sects of philosophers. Yet she is a school in which St. Paul teaches that Charity is more perfect than Hope, and in which the holiest Doctors declare, in accordance with the principles of the Fathers, that Love is more perfect, precisely because it 'abides in God, not in view of any benefit that may accrue to us from so doing.'"

"I know well," Fénelon writes to a friend, "that men misuse the doctrines of Pure Love and Resignation; I know that there are hypocrites who, under cover of such noble terms, overthrow the Gospel. Yet it is the worst of all procedures to attempt the destruction of perfect things, from a fear that men will make a wrong use of them." Notwithstanding all misuse of the doctrine—"the very perfection of Christianity is Pure Love." [2]

[1] Taylor, *op. cit.* p. 901.
[2] *Seconde Lettre à Monsieur de Paris, Œuvres*, Vol. V, pp. 268, 269. *Lettres de M. de Cambrai à un de ses Amis, ibid.*, Vol. IV, p. 168.

CHAPTER XII

THE AFTER-LIFE PROBLEMS AND DOCTRINES

MOVING on now to the questions concerning the After-Life, it will be convenient to consider them under five heads : the chief present-day positions and perplexities with regard to belief in the After-Life in General; the main implications and convictions inherent to an Eschatology such as Catherine's; and then the principal characteristics, difficulties, and helps of her tendencies and teachings concerning Hell, Purgatory, and Heaven. And throughout the Chapter we shall busy ourselves directly only with the After-Life in the sense of a heightened, or at least an equal, consciousness after death, as compared to that which existed before death : the belief in a shrunken state of survival, in non-annihilation, appearing to be as certainly the universal minimum of belief as such a minimum is not Immortality.

I. THE CHIEF PRESENT-DAY PROBLEMS, PERPLEXITIES, AND REQUIREMENTS WITH REGARD TO THE AFTER-LIFE IN GENERAL.

Now I take our chief present-day problems, perplexities, and resultant requirements with regard to the After-Life in general, to fall into three groups, according as those problems are predominantly Historical, or Philosophical, or directly Practical and Ethical.

1. *Three Historical Difficulties.*

The Historical group now brings very clearly and certainly before us the striking non-universality, the startling lateness, and the generally strange fitfulness and apparent unreasonableness characterizing the earliest stage of belief in the soul's heightened, or at least equivalent, consciousness after death.

(1) Now with respect to the Non-Universality of the doctrine, it is true that, in China, Confucianism is full of care for the dead. "Throughout the Empire, the authorities are obliged to

hold three annual sacrifices for the refreshment and rest of the souls of the dead in general." " It is hardly doubtful that the cultus of Ancestors formed the chief institution in classical Confucianism, and constituted the very centre of religion for the people. Even now ancestor-worship is the only form of religion for which rules, applicable to the various classes among the Emperor's subjects, are laid down in the Dynastic Statutes." And Professor De Groot, from whom I am quoting, gives an interesting conspectus of the numberless ways in which the religious service of the dead penetrates Chinese life.[1]—Yet we hear of Kong-Tse (Confucius) himself (551–478 B.C.), that, though he insisted upon the most scrupulous execution of the three hundred rules of the then extant temple-ceremonial, which were no doubt largely busy with the dead, and though he said that one should sacrifice to the spirits as if they were present, he designated, in several of his sayings, occupation with theological problems as useless : " as long as we do not know men, how shall we know spirits ? As long as we do not understand life, how should we fathom death ? " And to questions relative to the spirits and the dead, he would give evasive answers.[2] Thus the founder of the most characteristic of the Chinese religions was without any clear and consistent conviction on the point in question.

In India we find, for Brahmanic religion, certain unmistakable Immortality-Doctrines (in the sense of the survival of the soul's self-consciousness), expressed in the hymns of the *Rig-Veda*.—But already, in the philosophizings of the *Upanishads*, we get a world-soul, and this soul's exclusive permanence : " to attain to true unity, the very duality of subject and object is to disappear. The terms Atman and Brahman here express the true Being which vivifies all beings and appearances, and with which cognizing man reunites himself whilst losing his individual existence." [3]

And if we move on to Buddhism, with its hundreds of millions of adherents in Burmah, Tibet, China, and Japan, we can learn, from the classical work of Oldenberg, how interestingly deep down lies the reason for the long conflict between

---

[1] Chantepie de la Saussaye, *Lehrbuch der Religions-Geschichte*, ed. 1905, Vol. I, pp. 69, 73–83.

[2] Chantepie de la Saussaye, *Lehrbuch der Religions-Geschichte*, ed. 1887, Vol. I, pp. 248, 249.

[3] *Ibid.* pp. 358, 373.

scholars as to whether Nirvana is or is not to be taken for
the complete extinction of the individual soul. " Everything,
in the Buddhist dogmatic system, is part and parcel of a
circle of Becoming and of Dissolution : all things are but a
Dhamma, a Sankhara ; and all Dhamma, all Sankhara are but
temporary. . . . The Mutable, Conditioned is here thinkable
only as conditioned by another Mutable and Conditioned.
If we follow the dialectic consequence alone, there is no seeing
how, according to this system, there can remain over, when a
succession and mutual destruction of things conditioning and
of things conditioned has run its course, anything but a
pure vacuum." And we have also such a saying of the
Buddha as the following. " Now if, O disciples, the Ego
(*atta*) and anything appertaining to the Ego (*attaniya*) cannot
be comprehended with accuracy and certainty, is not then the
faith which declares : ' This is the world, and this is the Ego ;
this shall I become at death,—firm, constant, eternal, un-
changeable,—thus shall I be there, throughout eternity,'—is
not this sheer empty folly ? " " How should it not, O Lord,
be sheer empty folly ? " answer the disciples. " One who
spoke thus," is Oldenberg's weighty comment, " cannot have
been far from the conviction that Nirvana is annihilation.
Yet it is understandable how the very thinkers, who were
capable of bearing this consequence, should have hesitated to
raise it to the rank of an official dogma of the community. . . .
Hence the official doctrine of the Buddhist Church attained
the form, that, on the question of the real existence of the
Ego, of whether or not the perfected saint lives on after death,
the exalted Buddha has taught nothing. Indeed the legally
obligatory doctrine of the old community required of its
votaries an explicit renunciation of all knowledge concerning
the existence or non-existence of completely redeemed souls."

" Buddhism," so Oldenberg sums up the matter, with, I
think, the substantial adhesion of all present-day competent
authorities, " teaches that there is a way out of the world of
created things, out into the dark Infinite. Does this way
lead to new being ? or does it lead to nothingness ? Buddhist
belief maintains itself on the knife's edge of these alternatives.
The desire of the heart, as it longs for the Eternal, is not left
without something, and yet the thinking mind is not given a
something that it could grasp and retain. The thought of
the Infinite, the Eternal, could not be present at all, and yet
vanish further away than here, where, a mere breath and on

the point of sinking into sheer nothingness, it threatens to disappear altogether." [1]   This vast Buddhist community, numbering, perhaps, a third of the human race, should not, then, be forgotten, when we urge the contrary instances of the religions of Assyria and Babylonia; of Egypt; of Greece and Rome; and, above all, of the Jews and Christianity.

Yet it is well to remember that such non-universality of belief is at least as real, to this very hour, for such a fundamental religious truth and practice as Monotheism and Monolatry; such purely Ethical convictions as Monogamy and the Illicitness of Slavery; such a plain dictate of the universal humanitarian ideal as the illegitimacy of the application of physical compulsion in matters of religious conviction; and such directly demonstrable psychical and natural facts as subconsciousness in the human soul, the sexual character of plants, and the earth's rotundity and rotation around the sun. In none of these cases can we claim more than that the higher, truer doctrine,—that is, the one which explains and transcends the element of truth contained in its predecessor and opposite,—is explicitly reached by a part only of humanity, and is but implied and required by other men, at their best. Yet this is clearly enough for leaving us free to decide,—reasonably conclusive evidence for their truth being forthcoming,—in favour of the views of the minority : since the assumption of an equality of spiritual and moral insight and advance throughout mankind is as little based upon fact, as would be the supposition of men's equal physical strength or height, or of any other quality or circumstance of their nature and environment.

(2) The lateness of the doctrine's appearance, precisely in the cases where there can be no doubt of its standing for a conviction of an endless persistence of a heightened consciousness after death,—that is, amongst the Greeks (and Romans) and the Jews (and Christians),—has now been well established by critical historical research.

With regard to the Greeks,[2] the matter is particularly plain,

---

[1] Oldenberg, *Buddha*, ed. 1897, pp. 310–328; especially 313, 314; 316, 317; 327, 328.

[2] My chief authority here has been that astonishingly living and many-sided book, Erwin Rohde's *Psyche*, ed. 1898, especially Vol. II, pp. 263–295 (Plato); Vol. I, pp. 14–90 (Homer); 91–110 (Hesiod); pp. 146–199 (the Heroes); pp. 279–319, and Vol. II, pp. 1–136 (Eleusinian Mysteries, Dionysian Religion, the Orphics). The culminating interest of this great work lies in this last treble section and in the Plato part.

since we can still trace even in Plato, (427 to 347 B.C.), who, next to Our Lord Himself and to St. Paul, is doubtless the greatest and most influential teacher of full individual Immortality that the world has seen, two periods of thought in this matter, and can show that the first was without any such certain conviction. In his *Apology of Socrates*, written soon after the execution in 399 B.C., he makes his great master, close to his end, declare that death would bring to man either a complete unconsciousness, like to a dreamless sleep, or a transition into another life,—a life here pictured like to the Homeric Hades. Both possibilities Socrates made to accept resignedly, in full reliance on the justice of the Gods, and to look no further; how should he know what is known to no man?—And this is Plato's own earlier teaching. For in the very *Republic* which, in its chronologically later constituents, (especially in Book V, 471*c*, to the end of Book VIII, Book IX, 560*d* to 588*a*, and Book X up to 608*b*), so insists upon and develops the truth and importance of Immortality in the strictest, indeed the sublimest sense : we get, in its earlier portions, (especially in Book II, 10*c*, to Book V, 460*c*), no trace of any such conviction. For, in these earlier passages, the Guardians in the Ideal State are not to consider what may come after death : the central theme is the manner in which Justice carries with it its own recompense; and the rewards, that are popularly wont to be placed before the soul, are referred to ironically,—Socrates is determined to do without such hopes. In those later portions, on the contrary, there is the greatest insistence upon the importance of caring, not for this short life alone, but for the soul's " whole time " and for what awaits it after death. And in the still later parts, (as in Books VI and VII,) the sublimest form of Immortality is presupposed as true and actual throughout. Thus in Greece it is not till about 390–380 B.C., and in Plato himself not till his middle life, that we get a quite definite and final doctrine of the Immortality of all souls, and of a blessed after-existence for every just and holy life here below.

For the survival after the body's death, indubitably attributed to the Psyche in the Homeric Poems, is conceived there, throughout, as a miserably shrunken consciousness, and one which is dependent for its continuance upon the good offices bestowed by the survivors upon the corpse and grave. And the translation of the still living Menelaus to Elysium

(Od. IV, 560–568) is probably a later insertion; belongs to a small class of exceptional cases; implies the writer's inability to conceive a heightened consciousness for the soul, after the soul's separation from the body; and is based, not upon any virtue or reward, but upon Menelaus's family-relationship to Zeus. Ganymede gets similarly translated because of his physical beauty (*Il.* XX, 232 *seq.*).

Hesiod, though later than Homer as a writer, gives us, in his account of the Five Ages of the World (*Works and Days,* ll. 109–201), some traces of an Animistic conception of a heightened life of the bodiless soul beyond the grave,—a conception which had been neglected or suppressed by Homer, but which had evidently been preserved alive in the popular religion of, at least, Central Greece. Yet Hesiod knows of such a life only for the Golden and for the Silver Ages, and for some miraculous, exceptional cases of the fourth, the Heroic Age : already in the third, the Bronze Age, and still more emphatically in his own fifth, the Iron Age, there are no such consolations : nothing but the shrunken consciousness of the Homeric after-death Psyche is, quite evidently, felt by him to be the lot of all souls in the hard, iron present.

The Cultus of the Heroes is already registered in Draco's Athenian Laws, in about 620 B.C., as a traditional custom. And these Heroes have certainly lived at one time as men upon earth, and have become heroes only after death; their souls, though severed from the body, live a heightened imperishable life, indeed one that can mightily help men here below and now,—so at Delphi and at Salamis against the Persians. Yet here again each case of such an elevation was felt to be a miracle, an exception incapable of becoming a universal law : not even the germ of a belief in the Immortality of the soul as such seems to be here.

The Cultus of the Nether-World Deities, of the Departed generally, and, as the culmination of all this movement, the Eleusinian Mysteries, must not be conceived as involving or as leading to, any belief in the ecstatic elevation of the soul, or consciousness of its God-likeness; and such unending bliss as is secured, is gained by men, not because they are virtuous and devout, but through their initiation into the Mysteries. Rohde assures us, rightly I think, that " it remains unproved that, during the classical period of Greek culture, the belief in Judges and a Judgment to be held in Hades over the deeds done by men on earth, had struck root among the people ";

Professor Percy Gardner adds his great authority to the same conclusion.[1] Here again it is Plato who is the first to take up a clearly and consistently spiritual and universalistic position.

Indeed it is only in the predominantly neuropathic, indeed largely immoral and repulsive, forms of the Dionysiac sect and movement, (at work, perhaps, already in the eighth century B.C. and which leads on to the formation of the more aristocratic and priestly Orphic communities) that a demonstrable and direct belief arose in the soul's intrinsic Godlikeness, or even divinity, and in its immortality, or even eternity; and that stimulations, materials, and conceptions were furnished to Greek thought, which are traceable wheresoever it henceforth inclines to belief in the soul's intrinsic Immortality.

Yet the leaven spread but slowly into philosophy. For the Ionian philosophers, and among them Heraclitus, the impressive teacher of the flux of all things, flourish from about 600 to 430 B.C.; but, *naïve* Materialists and Pantheists as they are, they frankly exclude all survival of individual consciousness after death. The Eleatic philosophers live between 550 and 450 B.C., and are all busy with *a priori* logical constructions of the physical world, conceived as sole and self-explanatory; and amongst them is Parmenides, the powerful propounder of the complete identity and immutability of all reality. Those transcendent spiritual beliefs appear first as part, indeed as the very foundation, although still rather of a mode of life than of a formal philosophy, in the teaching and community of Pythagoras, who seems to have lived about 580 to 490 B.C., and who certainly emigrated from Asia Minor to Croton in Southern Italy. The soul appears here as intrinsically immortal, indeed without beginning and without end. And then Immortality forms one (the mystical) of the two thoroughly heterogeneous elements of the, otherwise predominantly Ionic and Materialistic, philosophy of Empedocles of Agrigentum in Sicily, about 490 to 435 B.C. In both these cases the Dionysiac-Orphic provenance of the "Immortality"-doctrines is clearly apparent.

And then, among the poets who bridge over the period up to Plato, we find Pindar, who, alongside of reproductions of the ordinary, popular conceptions, gives us at times lofty,

[1] *Psyche*, Vol. I, pp. 308, 312. *New Chapters in Greek History*, 1892, pp. 333, 334.

Orphic-like teachings as to the eternity, the migration, and the eventual persistent rest and happiness of the just Soul, and as to the suffering of the unjust one; Aeschylus, who primarily dwells upon the Gods' judgment in this life, and who makes occasional allusions to the after-life which are partly still of the Homeric type; Sophocles, who indeed refers to the special privileges which, in the after-life, attend upon the souls that have here been initiated into the Eleusinian Mysteries, and who causes Oedipus to be translated, whilst still alive, to Other-World happiness, but who knows nothing of an unceasing heightened consciousness for all men after death; and Euripides, who, showing plainly the influence of the Sophists, gives expression, alongside of Pantheistic identifications of the soul and of the aether, to every kind of misgiving and doubt as to any survival after death.

And as to the appearance of the doctrine among the Jews, we again find a surprising lateness. I follow here, with but minor contributions and modifications from other writers and myself, the main conclusions of Dr. Charles's standard *Critical History of the Doctrine of a Future Life*, London, 1899, whose close knowledge of the subject is unsurpassed, and who finds as many and as early attestations as are wellnigh findable by serious workers.[1]

" The primitive beliefs of the individual Israelite regarding the future life, being derived from Ancestor-worship, were implicitly antagonistic to Yahwism, from its first proclamation by Moses. . . . This antagonism becomes explicit and results in the final triumph of Yahwism." And to the early Israelite, even under Yahwism, " the religious unit was " not the individual but " the family or tribe." Thus, even fully six centuries after Moses, " the message of the prophets of the eighth century," Amos, Hosea, Isaiah, Micah, " is still directed to the nation, and the judgments they proclaim are collective punishment for collective guilt. It is not till late in the seventh century B.C. that the problem of individual retribution really emerged, and received its first solution in the teaching of Jeremiah." And " the further development of these ideas," by the teaching of Ezekiel and of some of the Psalms and Proverbs, as regards individual responsibility and retribution in this life, and by the deep misgivings and keen questionings of Job and Ecclesiastes, as to the adequacy of

[1] See also the important study of the Abbé Touzard, *Le Développement de la Doctrine de l'Immortalité, Revue Biblique*, 1898, pp. 207–241.

this teaching, " led inevitably to the conception of a blessed life beyond the grave."

Yet throughout the Hebrew Old Testament the Eschatology of the Nation greatly predominates over that of the Individual. Indeed in pre-Exilic times " the day of Yahwe," with its national judgments, constitutes the all but exclusive subject of the prophetic teaching as to the future. Only from the Exile, (597 to 538 B.C.), onwards, does the eschatological development begin to grow in complexity, for now the individualism first preached by Jeremiah begins to maintain its claim also. But not till the close of the fourth century, or the beginning of the third century B.C., do the separate eschatologies of the individual and of the nation issue finally in their synthesis : the righteous individual will participate in the Messianic Kingdom, the righteous dead of Israel will arise to share therein,—thus in Isaiah xxvi, 1–19, a passage which it is difficult to place earlier than about 334 B.C. The resurrection is here limited to the just. In Daniel xii, 2, which is probably not earlier than 165 B.C., the resurrection is extended, not indeed to all members of Israel, but, with respective good and evil effects, to its martyrs and apostates.

And the slowness and incompleteness of the development throughout the Hebrew Old Testament is strikingly illustrated by the great paucity of texts which yield, without the application of undue pressure, any clear conviction or hope of a heightened, or even a sheer, maintenance of the soul's this-life consciousness and force after death. Besides the passages just indicated, Dr. Charles can only find Psalms xlix and lxxiii, and Job xix, 25–27, all three, according to him, later than Ezekiel, who died in 571 B.C.[1] The textually uncertain and obscure Job-passage (xix, 25, 26) must be discounted, since it evidently demands interpretation according to the plain presupposition and point of the great poem as a whole.—And the same result is reached by the numerous, entirely unambiguous, passages which maintain the negative persuasion. In the hymn put into the mouth of the sick king Hezekiah, for about 713 B.C., (a composition which seems to be very late, perhaps only of the second century B.C.), we hear : " The grave cannot praise Thee . . . they that go down into the pit cannot hope for truth. The living, the living, he shall praise Thee, as I do this day." And the Psalter contains

---

[1] Charles, *op. cit.* pp. 52, 53; 58; 61; 84; 124, 125; 126–132; 68–77.

numerous similar declarations. Thus vi, 5 : "In death there is no remembrance of Thee : in the grave who shall give Thee thanks? " and cxv, 17 : " The dead praise not the Lord, neither any that go down into silence; but *we* praise the Lord." See also Psalms xxx, 19; lxxxviii, 11.

Indeed the name for the Departed is Rephaim, " the limp, the powerless ones." Stade well says : " According to the ancient Israelitish conception the entire human being, body and soul, outlasts death, whilst losing all that makes life worth living. That which persists in Sheol for all eternity is the form of man, emptied of all content. Antique thought ignores as yet that there exists no such thing as a form without substance. The conception has as little in common with the conviction of the Immortality of the Soul, which found its chief support in Greek ideas, as with the expectation of the Resurrection, which grew out of the Jewish Messianic hope, or with the Christian anticipation of Eternal Life, which is also based upon religious motives." [1]

Yet, with respect to this objection from the lateness of the doctrine, we must not forget that fully consistent Monotheism and Monogamy are also late, but not, on that account, less true or less precious; and indeed that, as a universal rule, the human mind has acquired at all adequate convictions as to most certain and precious truths but slowly and haltingly. This process is manifest even in Astronomy, Geology, Botany, Human Anatomy. It could not fail to be, not less but more the case in a matter like this which, if it concerns us most deeply, is yet both too close to us to be readily appreciated in its true proportions, and too little a matter of mathematical demonstration or of direct experience not to take much time to develop, and not to demand an ever-renewed acquisition and purification, being, as it is, the postulate and completion of man's ethical and spiritual faiths, at their deepest and fullest.

(3) And with regard to the unsatisfactory character of some of the earliest manifestations of the belief, this point is brought home to us, with startling vividness, in the beginnings of the doctrine in ancient Greece. For Rohde's very careful and competent examination of precisely this side of the whole question shows conclusively (even though I think, with Crusius, that he has overlooked certain rudiments of analogous but

[1] B. Stade, *Biblische Theologie des Alten Testaments*, Vol. I, 1905, p. 184.

healthy experiences and beliefs in pre-Dionysiac Greece) how new and permanently effective a contribution to the full doctrine was made, for the Hellenic world and hence indirectly for all Western humanity, by the self-knowledge gained in that wildly orgiastic upheaval, those dervish-like dances and ecstatic fits during the Dionysian night-celebrations on the Thracian mountain-sides. Indeed Rohde traces how from these experiences, partly from the continuation of them, partly from the reaction against them, on the part of the intensely dualistic and ascetic teaching and training of the Orphic sect, there arose, and filtered through to Pythagoras, to Plato, and to the whole Neo-Platonist school, the clear conception and precise terminology concerning ecstatic, enthusiastic states, the divinity and eternity of the human soul, its punitive lapse into and imprisonment within the body, and its need of purification throughout the earthly life and of liberation through death from this its incurably accidental and impeding companion.—Thus we get here, concerning one of the chief sources of at least the formulation of our belief in Immortality, what looks a very nest of suspicious, repulsive circumstances:—psycho-physical phenomena, which, quite explicable to, and indeed explained by, us now as in nowise supernatural, could not fail to appear portentous to those men who first experienced them; unmoral or immoral attitudes and activities of mind and will; and demonstrable excesses of feeling and conception as regards both the static goodness, the downright divinity, eternity, and increateness of the soul, and the unmixed evil of the body with its entirely disconnected alongsideness to the soul. Does not all this spell a mass of wild hallucination, impurity, fanaticism, and superstition?

Yet here again it behoves us, if not to accept, yet also not to reject, in wholesale fashion and in haste. For the profoundly experienced Professor Pierre Janet shows [1] us, what is now assumed as an axiom, and as the ultimate justification of the present widespread interest in the study of Hysteria, that " we must admit for the moral world the great principle universally admitted for the physical world since Claude Bernard,—viz. that the laws of illness are, at bottom, the same as those of health, and that, in the former, there is but the exaggeration or the diminution of phenomena which existed already in the latter."

And if thus our recent studies of morbid mentalities have

---

[1] *L'Automatisme Psychologique*, ed. 1903, p. 5.

been able to throw a flood of light upon the mechanism and character of the healthy mind, a mind more difficult to analyze precisely because of the harmonious interaction of its forces, there is nothing very surprising if man, in the past, learnt to know his own fundamental nature better in and through periods of abnormal excitation than in those of normal balance. And the resultant doctrines in the case in question only required, and demand again and again, a careful pruning and harmonizing to show forth an extraordinary volume of abiding truth. The insuppressible difference between mind and matter, and the distinction between the fully recollected soul (intuitive reason), and explicit reasoning; the immeasurable superiority of mind over matter, and the superiority of that full reason over this "thin" reasoning; the certainty, involved in all our inevitable mental categories and assumptions and in all our motives for action, of this mind and intuition being more like the cause of all things than are those other inferior realities and activities; the indestructibleness of the postulates and standards of objective and infinite Beauty, Truth, Goodness, of our consciousness of being intrinsically bound to them, and of our inmost humanity and its relative greatness being measurable by just this our consciousness of this our obligation, and hence by the keenness of our sense of failure, and by our striving after purification and the realization of our immanental possibilities: all this remains deeply fruitful and true.

And those crude early experiences and analyses certainly point to what, even now, are our most solid reasons for belief in Immortality: for if man's mind and soul can thus keenly suffer from the sense of the contingency and mutability of all things directly observed by it without and within, it must itself be, at least in part or potentially, outside of this flux which it so vividly apprehends as *not* Permanence, *not* Rest, *not* true Life. Let us overlook, then, and forgive the first tumultuous, childishly rude and clumsy, mentally and emotionally hyper-aesthetic forms of apprehension of these great spiritual facts and laws, forms which are not, after all, more misleading than is the ordinary anaesthetic condition of our apprehending faculties towards these fundamental forces and testimonies of our lot and nature. Not the wholesale rejection, then, of even those crude Dionysian witnessings, still less of the already more clarified Orphic teaching, and least of all of Plato's great utilizations and spiritualizations can be required of us, but only a reinterpretation of those first impressions and of mankind's analogous experiences, and a sifting and testing of the latter by the light of all that has been deeply lived through, and seriously thought out, by spiritually awake humanity ever since.—And we should remember that the history of the doctrine among the Jews is, as has already been intimated, grandly free from any such suspicious occasions and concomitances.

2. *Two Philosophical Difficulties*.

Yet it is precisely this latter, social, body-and-soul-survival doctrine which brings the second group of objections, the philosophical difficulties, to clear articulation. For thus we are unavoidably driven to one or other of the equally difficult alternatives, of a bodiless life of the soul, and of a survival or resurrection of the body.

(1) Christianity, by its explicit teachings, and even more by its whole drift and interior affinities, requires the survival of all that is essential to the whole man, and conceives this whole as constituted, not by thought alone but also by feeling and will and the power of effectuation; so that the body, or some unpicturable equivalent to it, seems necessary to this physico-spiritual, ultimately organic conception of what man is and must continue to be, if he is to remain man at all.—And Psychology, on its part, is showing us, more and more, how astonishingly wide and deep is the dependence, at least for their actuation, of the various functions and expressions of man's character and spirit upon his bodily frame. For not only is the reasoning faculty seen, ever since Aristotle, to depend, for its material and stimulation, upon the impressions of the senses, nor can we represent it to ourselves otherwise than as seated in the brain or in some such physical organism, but the interesting Lange-James observations and theory make it likely that also the emotions,—the feelings as distinct from sensations,—ever result, as a matter of fact, from certain foregoing, physico-neural impressions and modifications, which latter follow upon this or that perception of the mind, a perception which would otherwise, as is the case in certain neural lesions and anaesthesias, remain entirely dry and unemotional.[1]—And the sense of the Infinite, which we have had such reason to take as the very centre of religion, arises ever, within man's life here below, in contrast to, and as a con-

[1] W. James, *The Principles of Psychology*, 1891, Vol. II, pp. 442-467.

comitant and supplementation of, his perception of the Finite and Contingent, and hence not without his senses being alive and active.

Now all this fits in admirably with the whole Jewish-Christian respect for, high claims upon, and constant training of the body, the senses, the emotions, and with the importance attached to the Visible and Audible,—History, Institutions, Society.—Yet our difficulties are clear. For however spiritually we may conceive a bodily survival or resurrection; however completely we may place the identity of the various stages of the body in this life, and the sameness between the body before death and after the resurrection, in the identity of its quasi-creator, the body-weaving soul, we can in nowise picture to ourselves such a new, indefinitely more spiritual, incorporation, and we bring upon ourselves acute difficulties, for both before and after this unpicturable event. Before the resurrection there would have to be unconsciousness between death and that event; but thus the future life is broken up, and for no spiritual reason. Or there would be consciousness; but then the substitute for the body, that occasions this consciousness, would, apparently, render all further revivification of the body unnecessary. And if we take the resurrection as effected, we promptly feel how mixed and clumsy, how inadequate, how less, and not more, than the best and noblest elements of our experience and aspirations even here and now, is such a, still essentially temporal and spatial, mode of existence.

I take it that, against all this, we can but continue to maintain two points. The soul's life after bodily death is not a matter of experience or of logical demonstration, but a postulate of faith and a consequence from our realization of the human spirit's worth; and hence is as little capable of being satisfactorily pictured, as are all the other great spiritual realities which can nevertheless be shown to be presupposed and implicitly affirmed by every act of faith in the final truth and abiding importance of anything whatsoever.—And again, it is not worth while to attempt to rescue, Aristotle-wise, just that single, and doubtless not the highest, function of man's spirit and character, his dialectic faculty, or even his intellectual intuitive power, for the purpose of thus escaping, or at least minimizing, the difficulties attendant upon the belief in Immortality. If we postulate, as we do, man's survival, we must postulate, without being able to fill in or to justify any details of the scheme, the survival of all that may and does constitute man's true and ultimate personality. How much or how little this may precisely mean, we evidently know but very imperfectly : but we know enough to be confident that it means more than the abstractive, increasingly dualistic school of Plato, Philo, Plotinus, Proclus would allow.

(2) But speculative reason seems also to raise a quite general objection, based upon man's littleness within the immense Universe, and upon the arbitrariness of excepting those tiny points, those centres of human consciousness, men's souls, from the flux, the ceaseless becoming and undoing, of all the other parts of that mighty whole, immortal, surely, only *as* a whole.

Here we can safely say that, at least in this precise form, the difficulty springs predominantly not from reason or experience, but from an untutored imagination. For all our knowledge of that great external world, which this objection supposes to englobe our small internal world, as a part inferior, or at most but equal, to the other parts of that whole, is dependent upon this interior world of ours ; and however truly inherent in that external world we may hold that world's laws to be, those laws can, after all, be shown to be as truly the result of our own mind's spontaneous work,—an architectonic building up by this mind of the sense-impressions conveyed to it from without. And that whole Universe, in so far as it is material, cannot be compared, either in kind or in dignity, to Mind : only the indications there, parallel in this to our experiences within our own mind, of a Mind and Spirit infinitely greater and nobler than, yet with a certain affinity to, our own,—only these constitute that outer world as great as this our inner world. Indeed it is plain that Materialism is so far from constituting the solution to the problem of existence, that even Psycho-Physical Parallelism, even the attribution of any ultimate reality to Matter, are on their trial. It is anyhow already clear that, of the two, it is easier and nearer to the truth to maintain that Matter and its categories are simply modes in the manifestation of Mind to minds and in the apprehension of Mind by minds, than to declare Mind to be but a function or resultant of Matter.[1]

But if all this is so, then no simply sensible predominance of the sensible Universe, nor even any ascertainment of the

[1] See Prof. James Ward's closely knit proof in his *Naturalism and Agnosticism*, 2nd ed., 1905, and his striking address, " Mechanism and Morals," *Hibbert Journal*, October, 1905.

mere flux and interchange of and between all things material
and their elements, can reasonably affect the question as to
the superiority and permanence of Mind. But we shall
return, in the next chapter, to the difficulties special to the
Immortality of individual human spirits or personalities,—for
this is, I think, the point at which the problem is still acute.

3. *Three Ethico-Practical Difficulties.*

The last group of objections is directly practical and
ethical, and raises three points (the small space and influence
occupied and exercised, apparently, by such a belief, in the
spiritual life of even serious persons; the seemingly selfish,
ungenerous type of religion and of moral tone fostered by
definite belief in, or at least occupation with, the thought of
an individual future life, as contrasted with the nobility of
tone engendered by such denials or abstractions from all such
beliefs as we find in Spinoza and Schleiermacher; and, finally,
the plausibility of the teaching, on the part of some distinguished thinkers and poets, that a positive conviction of
this our short earthly life being the sole span of our individual
consciousness is directly productive of a certain deep tenderness, an heroic concentration of attention, and a virile truthfulness, which are unattainable, which indeed are weakened or
rendered impossible by, the necessarily vague anticipation of
an unending future life ; a hope which, where operative at all,
can but dwarf and deaden all earthly aspiration and endeavour.

(1) As to the first point, which has perhaps never been
more brilliantly affirmed than by Mr. Schiller,[1] I altogether
doubt whether the numerous appearances, which admittedly
seem to point that way, are rightly interpreted by such a
conclusion. For it is, for one thing, most certainly possible
to be deeply convinced of the reality and importance of the
soul's heightened after-life, and to have no kind of belief or
interest in Psychical Research, at least in such Research as
an intrinsically valuable aid to any specifically religious convictions. No aloofness from such attempts to find spiritual
realities at the phenomenal level can, (unless it is clear that
the majority of educated Western Europeans share the naïve
assumptions of this position), indicate negation of, or indifference to, the belief in Immortality.—And next, it is equally
certain that precisely the most fruitful form of the belief is
that which conceives the After-life as already involved in this

---

[1] " The Desire for Immortality," in *Humanism*, 1903, pp. 228–249.

one, and which, therefore, dwells specially, not upon the posteriority in time, but upon the difference in kind of that spiritual life of the soul which, even *hic et nunc*, can be sought after and experienced, in ever imperfect degrees no doubt, yet really and more and more. Here we ever get an approach to Simultaneity and Eternity, instead of sheer succession and clock-time : and here the fundamental attitude of the believer would appear only if pressed to deny or exclude the death-lessness of the spirit and its life,—the usual latency and simple implication of the positive conviction, in nowise diminishing this conviction's reality.—And, finally, it would have to be seen whether those who are indifferent or sceptical as to Immortal or Eternal Life, are appreciably fewer and largely other than those who are careless as to the other deep implications and requirements of spiritual experience. We may well doubt whether they would turn out to be so.

(2) As to the second point, we have already found how utterly insuppressible is the pleasure, normally concomitant upon every act of noble self-conquest; and how, though we can and should perform such and all other acts, as far as possible, from the ultimate, determining motive of thereby furthering the realization of the Kingdom of God, there can be no solid truthfulness or sane nobility in insisting upon attempts at thinking away and denying the fact and utility of that concomitant pleasure. But if so, then a further, other-world extension of that realization and of this con-comitant happiness, and a belief here below in such an eventual extension, cannot of themselves be ignoble or debasing. Occasions for every degree and kind of purely selfish and faultily natural acts, of acts inchoatively supernatural but still predominantly slavish, reappear here, in close parallel to the variety of disposition displayed by men towards every kind of reality and ideal, towards the Family, Science, the State, Humanity, where the same concomitances and the same high uses and mean abuses are ever possible and actual. Neither here nor there should we attempt to impoverish truth and life, in order to exclude the possibility of their abuse.—And it would, of course, be profoundly unfair to contrast such a rarely noble spirit as Spinoza among the deniers with the average mind from among the affirmers. The average or the majority of the deniers would not, I think, appear as more generous and devoted than the corresponding average or majority on the other side.

(3) And as to the supposed directly beneficial effects of a positive denial of Immortality, such as have been sung for us by George Eliot and Giovanni Pascoli, we can safely affirm that the special tendernesses and quiet heroisms, deduced by them from such a negation, are too obviously dependent upon spiritual implications and instincts, for us to be able to put them directly to the credit of that denial. Only in so far as Immortality were not a postulate intrinsically connected with belief in objective and obligatory Beauty, Truth, and Goodness,—in God as our origin and end,—could its persistent and deliberate denial not be injurious to these fundamental convictions and to the ultimate health of the soul's life : and of this intrinsic non-connection there is no sufficient evidence.— Certainly, in such a case as Spinoza's, the same strain of reasoning which makes him abandon individual Immortality ought, in logic, to prevent him, a mere hopelessly determined link in the *Natura Naturata*, from ever attaining to the free self-dedication of himself, as now a fully responsible member of the *Natura Naturans*. And if not all the grand depth of his spiritual instinct and moral nobility, and its persistence in spite of its having no logical room in the fixedly naturalistic element of his teaching, can be urged as an argument in favour of the ultimate truth and ethical helpfulness of that whole element, neither can it be urged with respect to what is presumably one part of that element, his denial of personal Immortality.

II. Catherine's General After-Life Conceptions.

Now Catherine's general After-Life Conceptions in part bring into interesting prominence, in part really meet and overcome, the perplexities and mutually destructive alternatives which we have just considered. I shall here again leave over to the next chapter the simply ultimate questions, such as that of the pure Eternity *versus* the Unendingness of the soul; but shall allow myself, as to one set of her general ideas, a little digression as to the probability of their ultimate literary suggestion by Plato.—These Platonic passages probably reached her too indirectly, and by means and in forms which I have too entirely failed to discover, for me to be able to discuss them in my chapter devoted to her assured and demonstrably direct literary sources. But these sayings of

Plato greatly help to illustrate the meaning of her doctrine.
—I shall group these, her general, positions and implications
under four heads, and shall consider three of these as, in
substance, profoundly satisfactory, but one of them, the
second, as acceptable only with many limitations, although
this second has obviously much influenced the form given by
her to several of those other conceptions.

1. *Forecasts of the Hereafter, based upon present experience.*

First, then, we get, as the fundamental presupposition of the
whole Eschatology, a grandly sane, simple, and profound
doctrine formulated over and over again and applied throughout, with a splendid consistency, as the key and limit to all
her anticipations and picturings. Only because of the fact,
and of our conviction of the fact, of the unbroken continuity
and identity of God with Himself, of the human soul with
itself, and of the deepest of the relations subsisting between
that God and the soul, across the chasm formed by our
body's death, and only in proportion as we can and do
experience and achieve, during this our earthly life, certain
spiritual laws and realities of a sufficiently elemental, universal,
and fruitful, more or less time- and space-less character, can
we (whilst ever remembering the analogical nature of such
picturings even as to the soul's life here) safely and profitably
forecast certain general features of the future which is thus
already so largely a present. But, given these conditions in
the present, we can and should forecast the future, to the
extent implied. And as Plato's great imaginative projection,
his life-work, the *Republic*, achieves its original end, (of
making more readily understandable, by objectivizing, on a
large scale, the life of the inner city of our own soul,) in so
far as he has rightly understood the human soul and has
found appropriate representations of its powers, laws, and
ideals in his future commonwealth, even if we cannot accept
this picture for political purposes and in all its details : so is
it also with Catherine's projection, which, if bolder in its
subject-matter, is, most rightly, indefinitely more general in
its indications than is Plato's great diagram of the soul.
Man's spiritual personality, being held by her to survive
death,—to retain its identity and an at least equivalent consciousness, of that identity,—the deepest experiences of that
personality before the body's death are conceived as re-
experienced by it, in a heightened degree and form, after
death itself. Hence these great pictures, of what the soul will

experience then, would remain profoundly true of what the soul seeks and requires now, even if there were no *then* at all.

And note particularly how only with regard to one stage and condition of the spirit's future life,—that of the purification of the imperfect soul,—does she indulge in any at all direct doctrine or detailed picturing; and this, doubtless, not only because she has experienced much concerning this matter in her own life here, but also because the projection of these experiences would still give us, not the ultimate state, but more or less only a prolongation of our mixed, joy-in-suffering life upon earth. As to the two ultimate states, we get only quite incidental glimpses, although even these are strongly marked by her general position and method.

2. *Catherine's forecasts and present experience correspondingly limited.*

And next, coming to the projection itself, we naturally find it to present all the strength and limitations of her own spiritual experiences which are thus projected : her attitude towards the body and towards human fellowship, (two subjects which are shown to be closely inter-related by the continuous manner in which they stand and fall together throughout the history of philosophy and religion,) thus constitute the second general peculiarity of her Eschatology. We have already noted, in her life, her strongly ecstatic, body-ignoring, body-escaping type of religion ; and how, even in her case, it tended to starve the corporate, institutional conceptions and affections. Here, in the projection, we find both the cause and the effect again, and on a larger scale. Her continuous psycho-physical discomforts and keen thirst for a unity and simplicity as rapid and complete as possible, the joy and strength derived from ecstatic habits and affinities, would all make her, without even herself being aware of it, drop all further thought as to the future fate of that oppressive " prison-house " from which her spirit had at last got free.

Now such non-occupation with the fate of the body and of her fellow-souls may appear quite appropriate in her Purgatorial Eschatology, yet we cannot but find that, even here, it already possesses grave disadvantages, and that it persists throughout all her After-life conceptions. For in all the states and stages of the soul we get a markedly unsocial, a *sola cum solo* picture. And yet there is, perhaps, no more striking difference, amongst their many affinities, between Platonism and Christianity than the intense Individualism which marks the great Greek's doctrine, and the profoundly social conception which pervades Our Lord's own teaching,—in each case as regards the next life as well as this one. Plotinus's great culminating commendation of " the flight of the alone to the Alone " continues Plato's tradition; whereas, if even St. Paul and the Joannine writings speak at times as though the individual soul attained to its full personality in and by direct intercourse with God alone, the Synoptic Gospels, and at bottom also those two great lovers of Our Lord's spirit, never cease to emphasize the social constituent of the soul's life both here and hereafter. The Kingdom of Heaven, the Soul of the Church, as truly constitutes the different personalities, their spirituality and their joy, as they constitute it,—that great Organism which, as such, is both first and last in the Divine thought and love.

Here, in the at least partial ignoring of these great social facts, we touch the main defect of most mystical outlooks; yet this defect does not arise from what they possess, but from what they lack. For solitude, and the abstractive, unifying, intuitive, emotional, mystical element is also wanted, and this element and movement Catherine exemplifies in rare perfection. Indeed, in the great classical, central period of her life she had, as we know, combined all this with much of the outward movement, society, detailed observation, attachment, the morally *en-static*, the immanental type. Unfortunately the same ill-health and ever-increasing predominance of the former element, which turned her, quite naturally, to these eschatological contemplations, and which indeed helped to give them their touching tone of first-hand experience, also tended, of necessity, to make her drop even such slight and lingering social elements as had formerly coloured her thought. It is, then, only towards the understanding and deepening of the former of these two necessary movements of religion, that these, her latter-day enlargements of some of her deepest experiences and convictions will be found true helps.

Yet if the usual *ad extra* disadvantages of such an abstractive position towards the body are thus exemplified by her, in this her unsocial, individualistic attitude, it is most interesting to note how entirely she avoids the usual *ad intra* drawbacks of this same position. For if her whole attention, and, increasingly, even her consciousness are, in true ecstatic guise, absorbed away from her fellows and concentrated

exclusively upon God in herself and herself in God, yet this
consciousness consists not only of *Noûs*, that dry theoretic
reason which, already by Plato, but still more by Aristotle, is
alone conceived as surviving the body, but contains also the
upper range of *Thumos*,—all those passions of the noblest
kind,—love, admiration, gratitude, utter self-donation, joy in
purifying suffering and in an ever-growing self-realization as
part of the great plan of God,—all the highest notes in that
wondrous scale of deep feeling and of emotionally coloured
willing which Plato made dependent, not for its character but
for the possibility of its operation, upon the body's union with
the soul.—And thus we see how, in her conception of the
soul's own self within itself and of its relation to God, the
Christian idea of Personality, as of a many-sided organism in
which Love and Will are the very flower of the whole, has
triumphed over the Platonic presentation of the Spirit, in so
far as this is taken to require and achieve an ultimate sublima-
tion free from all emotive elements.   Thus in her doctrine
the whole Personality survives death, although this Personality
energizes only, as it were upwards, to God alone, and not also
sideways and downwards, towards its fellows and the lesser
children of God.

3. *Catherine's forecast influenced by Plato.*

Catherine's third peculiarity consists in a rich and profound
organization of two doctrines, the one libertarian, the other
determinist; and requires considerable quotation from Plato,
whose teachings, bereft of all transmigration-fancies, seem
clearly to reappear here, (however complex may have been
the mediation,) in Catherine's great conception.

The determinist doctrine maintains that virtue and vice,
in proportion as they are allowed their full development,
spontaneously and necessarily attain to their own congenital
consummation, a consummation which consists, respectively,
in the bliss inseparable from the final and complete identity
between the inevitable results upon itself of the soul's deliberate endeavours, and the indestructible requirements of this
same soul's fundamental nature; and in the misery of the, now
fully felt but only gradually superable, or even, in other cases,
insuperable, antagonism between the inevitable consequences
within its own self of the soul's more or less deliberate
choosings, and those same, here also ineradicable, demands of
its own truest nature.

As Marsilio Ficino says, in his *Theologia Platonica*,

published in Florence in 1482 : " Virtue is reward in its first budding, reward is virtue full-grown. Vice is punishment at the moment of its birth ; punishment is vice at its consummation. For, in each of these cases, one and the same thing is first the simple seed and then the full ear of corn ; and one and the same thing is the full ear of corn and then the food of man. Precisely the very things then that we sow in this our (earthly) autumn, shall we reap in that (other-world) summer-day." [1] It is true that forensic terms and images are also not wanting in Catherine's sayings ; but these, in part, run simply parallel to the immanental conception without modifying it ; in part, they are in its service ; and, in part, they are the work of the theologians' arrangements and glosses discussed in my Appendix

And the libertarian doctrine declares that it is the soul itself which, in the beyond and immediately after death, chooses the least painful, because the most expressive of her then actual desires, from among the states which the natural effects upon her own self of her own earthly choosings have left her interiorly free to choose.

Now it is in this second doctrine especially that we find so detailed an anticipation by Plato of a whole number of highly original and characteristic points and combinations of points, as to render a fortuitous concurrence between Catherine and Plato practically impossible. Yet I have sought in vain, among Catherine's authentic sayings, actions, possessions, or friends, for any trace of direct acquaintance with any of Plato's writings. But Ficino's Latin translation of Plato, published, with immense applause, in Florence in 1483, 1484, must have been known, in those intensely Platonizing times, to even non-professed Humanists in Genoa, long before Catherine's death in 1510, so that one or other of her intimates may have communicated the substance of these Platonic doctrines to her.[2] Plotinus, of whom Ficino published a Latin translation in 1492, contains but a feeble echo of Plato on this point. Proclus, directly known only very little till much after

---

[1] *Op. cit.* Lib. XVIII, c. x, ed. 1559, fol. 3413.

[2] Neither she nor her friends can have derived these doctrines from Ficino's *Theologia Platonica*, Florence, 1482, since precisely the points in question are quite curiously absent from, or barely recognizable in, that book. See its cc. x and xi, Book XVIII, on " the State of the Impure Soul " and " the State of the Imperfect Soul " respectively : ed. 1559, fol. 340, *v. seq.* See also foll. 318*r*, 319*v*.

Catherine's time, is in even worse case. The Areopagite, who has so continuously taken over whole passages from all three writers, although directly almost exclusively from Proclus, contains nothing more immediately to the purpose than his impressive sayings concerning Providence's continuous non-forcing of the human personality in its fundamental constitution and its free elections with their inevitable consequences; hence Catherine cannot have derived her ideas, in the crisp definiteness which they retain in her sayings, from her cousin the Dominican nun and the Areopagite. And it is certain, as we have seen, how scattered and inchoate are the hints which she may have found in St. Paul, the Joannine writings, and Jacopone da Todi. St. Augustine contains nothing that would be directly available,—an otherwise likely source considering Catherine's close connection with the Augustinian Canonesses of S. Maria delle Grazie.

In Plato, then, we get five conceptions and symbolic pictures that are practically identical with those of Catherine.

(1) First we get the conception of souls having each, in exact accordance with the respective differences of their moral and spiritual disposition and character, as these have been constituted by them here below, a " place" or environment, expressive of that character, ready for their occupation after the body's death. " The soul that is pure departs at death, herself invisible, to the invisible world,—to the divine, immortal and rational : thither arriving, she lives in bliss. But the soul that is impure at the time of her departure and is . . . engrossed by the corporeal . . . , is weighed down and drawn back again into the visible place (world)."

And this scheme, of like disposition seeking a like place, is then carried out, by the help of the theory of transmigration, as a re-incarnation of these various characters into environments, bodies, exactly corresponding to them : gluttonous souls are assigned to asses' bodies, tyrannous souls to those of wolves, and so on : in a word, " there is no difficulty in assigning to all ' a whither' (a place) answering to their general natures and propensities." [1] For this corresponds to a law which runs throughout all things,—a determinism of consequences which does not prevent the liberty of causes. " The King of the universe contrived a general plan, by which a thing of a certain nature found a seat and place of a certain

[1] *Phaedo,* 81a–82a.

kind. But the formation of this nature, he left to the wills of individuals."

Or, with the further spatial imagery of movements up, level, or down, we get : " All things that have a soul change . . . and, in changing, move according to law and the order of destiny. Lesser changes of nature move on level ground, but great crimes sink . . . into the so-called lower places . . .; and, when the soul becomes greatly different and divine, she also greatly changes her place, which is now altogether holy."[1] The original, divinely intended " places " of souls are all high and good, and similar to each other though not identical, each soul having its own special " place " ; and for this congenital " place " each soul has a resistible yet ineradicable home-sickness. " The first incarnation " of human souls which " distributes each soul to a star," is ordained to be similar for all. . . . " And when they have been of necessity implanted in bodily forms, should they master their passions . . . they live in righteousness ; if otherwise, in unrighteousness. And he who lived well through his allotted time shall be conveyed once more to a habitation in his kindred star, and there shall enjoy a blissful and congenial life ; but failing this he shall pass into . . . such a form of (further) incarnation as fits his disposition . . . until he shall overcome, by reason, all that burthen that afterwards clung around him."[2]

If from all this we exclude the soul's existence before any beginning of its body, its transmigration into other bodies, and the self-sufficiency of reason ; and if we make it all to be penetrated by God's presence, grace, and love, and by our corresponding or conflicting emotional and volitional as well as intellectual attitude : we shall get Catherine's position exactly.

(2) But again, in at least one phase of his thinking, Plato pictures the purification of the imperfect soul as effected, or at least as begun, not in a succession of " places " of an extensionally small but organic kind, bodies, but in a " place " of an extensionally larger but inorganic sort,—the shore of a lake, where the soul has to wait. " The Acherusian lake is

---

[1] *Laws*, X, 904*a–e*.
[2] *Timaeus*, 41*d, e*; 42*b, d*. I have, for clearness' sake, turned Plato's indirect sentences into direct ones; and have taken the *Timaeus* after the *Laws*, although it is chronologically prior to them, because the full balance of his system, (which requires the originally lofty " place " of each individual soul),—is, I think, abandoned in the *Laws* : see 904*a*.

the lake to the shores of which the many go when they are dead; and, after waiting an appointed time, which to some is longer and to others shorter, they are sent back to be born as animals." Here we evidently get a survival of the conception, predominant in Homer, of a pain-and-joyless Hades, but limited here to the middle, the imperfect class of souls, and followed, in their case, by transmigration, to which alone, apparently, purification is directly attached.

In the same Dialogue we read later on: " Those who appear to have lived neither well nor ill . . . go to the river Acheron, and are carried to the lake; and there they dwell and are purified of their evil deeds . . . and are absolved and receive the rewards of their good deeds according to their deserts." Here we have, evidently, still the same " many " and the same place, the shores of the Acherusian lake, but also an explicit affirmation of purification effected there, for this purification is now followed directly, not by reincarnation, but by the ultimate happiness in the soul's original and fundamentally congenial " place." And this scheme is far more conformable to Plato's fundamental position : for how can bodies, even lower than the human, help to purify the soul which has become impure precisely on occasion of its human body?—We can see how the Christian Purgatorial doctrine derives some of its pictures from the second of these parallel passages; yet that the " longer or shorter waiting " of the first passage also enters into that teaching,—especially in its more ordinary modern form, according to which there is, in this state, no intrinsic purification.

And lower down we find : " Those who have committed crimes which, although great, are not unpardonable,—for these it is necessary to plunge ($\dot{\epsilon}\mu\pi\epsilon\sigma\epsilon\hat{\iota}\nu$) into Tartarus, the pains of which they are compelled to undergo for a year; but at the end of the year they are borne to the Acherusian lake. But those who appear incurable by reason of the greatness of their crimes . . . such their appropriate destiny hurls ($\dot{\rho}\dot{\iota}\pi\tau\epsilon\iota$) into Tartarus, whence they never come forth." Here we get a Purgatory, pictured as a watery substance in which the more gravely impure of the curable souls are immersed before arriving at the easier purification, the waiting on the dry land alongside the lake; this Purgatory is, as a " place " and, in intensity, identical with Hell; and into this place the curable souls " plunge " and the incurable ones are " hurled." Of this third passage Catherine retains the identification of the pains of Purgatory and those of Hell; the " plunge," or " hurling," of two distinct classes of souls into these pains; and the mitigation, after a time, previous to complete cessa- tion, of the suffering in the case of the curable class.   But the " plunge," with her, is common to all degrees of imperfectly pure souls; there is, for all these souls, no change of " place " during their purgation, but only a mitigation of suffering; and this mitigation is at work gradually and from the first. And the ordinary modern Purgatorial teaching is like this passage, in that it keeps the curable souls in Tartarus, say, for one year, and lets them suffer there, apparently without mitigation, throughout that time : and that, in the case of both classes of souls, it conceives the punishment as extrinsic, vindictive, and inoperative.

And a fourth *Phaedo* passage tells us : " Those who are remarkable for having led holy lives are released from this earthly prison, and go to their pure home, which is above, and dwell in the purer earth," the Isles of the Just, in Oceanus. " And those, again, amongst these who have duly purified themselves with philosophy, live henceforth altogether without the body, in mansions fairer far than these."   Here we get, alongside of the two Purgatories and the one Hell, two Heavens, of which the first is but taken over from Homer and Pindar, but of which the second is Plato's own conception. Catherine, in entire accord with the ordinary teaching, has got but one " place " of each kind; and her Heaven corresponds, apart from his formal and final exclusion of every sort of body, to the second of these Platonic Heavens; whilst, here again, the all-encompassing presence of God's love for souls as of the soul's love for God, which, in her teaching, is the beginning, means, and end of the whole movement, effects an indefinite difference between the two positions.[1]

(3) Yet Plato, in his most characteristic moods, explicitly anticipates Catherine as to the intrinsic, ameliorative nature and work of Purgatory : " The proper office of punishment is twofold : he who is rightly punished ought either to become better . . . by it, or he ought to be made an example to his fellows, that they may see what he suffers and . . . become better. Those who are punished by Gods and men and improved, are those whose sins are curable . . . by pain and

---

[1] These four passages are all within pp. 110b–114d of the *Phaedo*.

suffering :—for there is no other way in which they can be
delivered from evil, as in this world so also in the other.   But
the others are incurable—the time has passed at which they
can receive any benefit themselves. . . . Rhadamanthus," the
chief of the three nether-world judges, " looks with admiration
on the soul of some just one, who has lived in holiness and
truth . . . and sends him " without any intervening suffering
" to the Isles of the Blessed. . . . I consider how I shall
present my soul whole and undefiled before the Judge, in that
day." [1] Here the last sentence is strikingly like in form as
well as in spirit to many a saying of St. Paul and Catherine.

(4) But the following most original passages give us a sentiment and an image which, in their special drift, are as opposed
to St. Paul, and indeed to the ordinary Christian consciousness,
as they are dear to Catherine, in this matter so strongly,
although probably unconsciously, Platonist, indeed Neo-
Platonist, in her affinities.   " In the time of Kronos, indeed
down to that of Zeus, the Judgment was given on the day on
which men were to die," *i. e.* immediately *before* their death ;
" and the consequence was, that the judgments were not well
given,—the souls found their way to the wrong places.   Zeus
said : ' The reason is, that the judged have their clothes on,
for they are alive. . . . There are many, having evil souls, who
are apparelled in fair bodies or wrapt round in wealth and
rank. . . . The Judges are awed by them ; and they themselves too have their clothes on when judging : their eyes
and ears and their whole bodies are interposed, as a veil,
before their own souls.   What is to be done ? . . . Men shall
be entirely stript before they are judged, for they shall be
judged when dead ; the Judge too shall be naked, that is,
dead : he, with his naked soul, shall pierce into the other
naked soul immediately *after* each man dies . . . and is
bereft of all his kith and kin, and has left behind him all his
brave attire upon earth, and thus the Judgment will be just.' " [2]
—If we compare this with St. Paul's precisely contrary instinct
and desire to be " clothed upon " at death, " lest we be found
naked," *i. e.* without the protection of any kind of body ; and
then realize Catherine's intense longing for "nudità,"—to strip
herself here, as far as possible, from all imperfection and self-
delusion before the final stripping off of the body in death,
and to appear, utterly naked, before the utterly naked eye of

<hr />

[1] *Gorgias,* pp. 525*b, c*; 526*c, d.*   [2] *Ibid.* p. 523*b–e.*

God, so that no "clothes" should remain requiring to be burnt away by the purifying fires,[1] the profound affinity of sentiment and imagery between Catherine and Plato—and this on a point essentially Platonic,—is very striking.

(5) But, above all, in his deep doctrine as to the soul's spontaneous choice after death of that condition, "place," which, owing to the natural effects within her of her earthly willings and self-formation, she cannot but now find the most congenial to herself, Plato appears as the ultimate source of a literary kind for Catherine's most original view, which otherwise is, I think, without predecessors. "The souls," he tells us in the *Republic*, "immediately on their arrival in the other world, were required to go to Lachesis," one of the three Fates. And "an interpreter, having taken from her lap a number of lots and plans of life, spoke as follows: 'Thus saith Lachesis, the daughter of Necessity. . . . "Your destiny shall not be allotted to you, but you shall choose it for yourselves. Let him who draws the first lot, be the first to choose a life which shall be his irrevocably. . . . The responsibility lies with the chooser, Heaven is guiltless."'" "No settled character of soul was included in the plans of life, because, with the change of life, the soul inevitably became changed itself." "It was a truly wonderful sight, to watch how each soul selected its life. . . . When all the souls had chosen their lives, Lachesis dispatched with each of them the Destiny he had selected, to guard his life and satisfy his choice."[2] And in the *Phaedrus* Plato tells us that "at the end of the first thousand years" (of the first incarnation) "the good souls and also the evil souls both come to cast lots and to choose their second life; and they may take any that they like."[3]

In both the dialogues the lots are evidently taken over from popular mythology, but are here made merely to introduce a certain orderly succession among the spontaneous choosings of the souls themselves, whilst the lap of the daughter of Necessity, spread out before all the choosers previous to their choice, and the separate, specially appropriate Destiny that accompanies each soul after its choice, indicate plainly that, although the choice itself is the free act and pure self-expression of each soul's then present disposition, yet that this disposition is the necessary result of its earthly volitions and

---

[1] 2 Cor. v, 2, 3.—*Vita*, pp. 109b, 66a, 171a.
[2] *Republic*, X, pp. 617e, 619e, 920e.   [3] *Phaedrus*, p. 249b.

self-development or self-deformation, and that the choice now made becomes, in its turn, the cause of certain inevitable consequences,—of a special environment which itself is then productive of special effects upon, and of special occasions for, the final working out of this soul's character.— Plotinus retains the doctrine : " the soul chooses there " in the Other world,—" its Daemon and its kind of life." [1] But neither Proclus nor Dionysius has the doctrine, whilst Catherine, on the contrary, reproduces it with a penetrating completeness.

4. *Simplifications characteristic of Catherine's Eschatology.*

And under our last, fourth head, we can group the simplifications characteristic of Catherine's Eschatology.

(1) One simplification has, of course, for now some fifteen hundred years, been the ordinary Christian conception : I mean the elimination of the time-element between the moment of death and the beginning of the three states. Yet it is interesting to note how by far the greatest of the Latin Fathers, St. Augustine, who died in 430 A.D., still clings predominantly to the older Christian and Jewish conception of the soul abiding in a state of shrunken, joy-and-painless consciousness from the moment of the body's death up to that of the general resurrection and judgment. " After this short life, thou wilt not yet be where the saints will be," *i. e.* in Heaven. " Thou wilt not yet be there : who is ignorant of this ? But thou canst straightway be where the rich man descried the ulcerous beggar to be a-resting, far away," *i. e.* in Limbo. " Placed in that rest, thou canst await the day of judgment with security, when thou shalt receive thy body also, when thou shalt be changed so as to be equal to an Angel." [2] Only with regard to Purgatory, a state held by him, in writings of his last years, 410–430 A.D., to be possible, indeed probable, does he make an exception to his general rule : for such purification would have to take place " in the interval of time between the death of the body and the last day of condemnation and reward." [3]

It is doubtless the still further fading away of the expectation, so vivid and universal in early Christian times, of the proximity of Our Lord's Second Advent, and the tacit

---

[1] *Enneads*, III, 4, 5.

[2] Enarr. in Ps. xxxvi, § 1, n. 10, ed. Ben., col. 375*b*. See also *Enchiridion*, CIX, *ibid.* col. 402*d*.

[3] So in the *De Civitate Dei*, Lib. XXI, c. xxvi, n. 4, *ibid.* col. 1037*d*.

prevalence of Greek affinities and conceptions concerning the bodiless soul, that helped to eliminate, at last universally, this interval of waiting, in the case of souls too good or too bad for purgation, from the general consciousness of at least Western Christendom. The gain in this was the great simplification and concentration of the immediate outlook and interest; the loss was the diminished apprehension of the essentially complex, concrete, synthetic character of man's nature, and of the necessity for our assuming that this characteristic will be somehow preserved in this nature's ultimate perfection.

(2) There is a second simplification in Catherine which, though here St. Augustine leads the way, is less common among Christians : her three other-world " places " are not, according to her ultimate thought, three distinct spatial extensions and localities, filled, respectively, with ceaselessly suffering, temporarily suffering, and ceaselessly blessed souls; but they are, (notwithstanding all the terms necessitated by such spatial picturings as " entering," " coming out," " plunging into,") so many distinct states and conditions of the soul, of a painful, mixed, or joyful character. We shall have these her ultimate ideas very fully before us presently. But here I would only remark that this her union of a picturing faculty, as vivid as the keenest sense-perception, and of a complete non-enslavement to, a vigorous utilization of, these life-like spatial projections, by a religious instinct and experience which never forgets that God and souls are spirits, to whom our ordinary categories of space and extension, time and motion, do not and cannot in strictness apply, is as rare as it is admirable; and that, though her intensely anti-corporeal and non-social attitude made such a position more immediately easy for her than it can be for those who remain keenly aware of the great truths involved in the doctrines of the Resurrection of the Body and the Communion of Saints, this her trend of thought brings into full articulation precisely the deepest of our spiritual apprehensions and requirements, whilst it is not her fault if it but further accentuates some of our intellectual perplexities.

We get much in St. Augustine, which he himself declares to have derived, in the first instance, from " the writings of the Platonists," which doubtless means above all Plotinus, (that keen spiritual thinker who can so readily be traced throughout this part of the great Convert's teaching,) as to this profound incommensurableness between spiritual presence, energizing, and affectedness on the one hand, and spatial position, extension, and movement on the other. "What place is there within me, to which my God can come? . . . I would not exist at all, unless Thou already wert within me." "Thou wast never a place, and yet we have receded from Thee; and we have drawn near to Thee, yet Thou art never a place." "Are we submerged and do we emerge? Yet it is not places into which we are plunged and out of which we rise. What can be more like to places and yet more unlike? For here the affections are in case,—the impurity of our spirit, which flows downwards, oppressed by the love of earthly cares; and the holiness of Thy Spirit, which lifts us upwards with the love of security." [1] For, as he teaches "the spiritual creature can only be changed by times,"—a succession within a duration : "by remembering what it had forgotten, or by learning what it did not know, or by willing what it did not will. The bodily creature can be changed by times and places, by spatial motion, "from earth to heaven, from heaven to earth, from east to west." "That thing is not moved through space which is not extended in space . . . the soul is not considered to move in space, unless it be held to be a body." [2]

In applying the doctrine just expressed to eschatological matters, St. Augustine concludes : "If it be asked whether the soul, when it goes forth from the body, is borne to some corporeal places, or to such as, though incorporeal, are like to bodies, or to what is more excellent than either : I readily answer that, unless it have some kind of body, it is not borne to bodily places at all, or, at least, that it is not borne to them by bodily motion. . . . But I myself do not think that it possesses any body,when it goes forth from this earthly body. . . . It gets borne, according to its deserts, to spiritual conditions, or to penal places having a similitude to bodies." [3]

The reader will readily note a curiously uncertain frame of mind in this last utterance. I take it that Plotinian influences are here being checked by the Jewish conception of certain, definitely located, provision-chambers (*promptuaria*), in which

---

[1] *Confess.*, Lib. I, c. 2, n. 1; X, c. 26; XIII, c. 7.
[2] *De Genesi ad litt.*, Lib. VIII, n. 39, ed. Ben. col. 387b; n. 43, col. 389a.
[3] *Ibid.* Lib. XII, n. 32, col. 507c. He soon after attempts to decide in favour of "incorporeal places," as the other-world destination of all classes of human souls.

all souls are placed for safe keeping, between the time of the body's death and its resurrection. So in the Fourth Book of Esra (of about 90 A.D.), " the souls of the just in their chambers said : ' How long are we to remain here ? ' " ; and in the Apocalypse of Baruch (of about 150–250 A.D.), " at the coming of the Messiah, the provision-chambers will open, in which the " whole, precise " number of the souls of the just have been kept, and they will come forth." [1]

But it is St. Thomas Aquinas who, by the explicit and consistent adoption and classification of these *promptuaria receptacula*, reveals to us more clearly the perplexities and fancifulnesses involved in the strictly spatial conception. " Although bodies are not assigned to souls (immediately) after death, yet certain bodily places are congruously assigned to these souls in accordance with the degree of their dignity, in which places they are, as it were, locally, in the manner in which bodiless things can be in space : each soul having a higher place assigned to it, according as it approaches more or less to the first substance, God, whose seat, according to Scripture, is Heaven." " In the Scriptures God is called the Sun, since He is the principle of spiritual life, as the physical sun is of bodily life ; and, according to this convention, . . . souls spiritually illuminated have a greater fitness for luminous bodies, and sin-darkened souls for dark places." " It is probable that, as to local position, Hell and the Limbo of the Fathers constitute one and the same place, or are more or less continuous." " The place of Purgatory adjoins (that of) Hell." " There are altogether five places ready to receive (*receptanda*) souls bereft of their bodies : Paradise, the Limbo of the Fathers, Purgatory, Hell, and the Limbo of Infants." [2]

No doubt all these positions became the common scholastic teaching. But then, as Cardinal Bellarmine cogently points out : " no ancient, as far as I know, has written that the Earthly Paradise was destroyed . . . and I have read a large number who affirm its existence. This is the doctrine of all the Scholastics, beginning with St. Thomas, and of the Fathers . . . St. Augustine indeed appears to rank this truth amongst the dogmas of faith." [3] We shall do well, then, not to press

---

[1] Esra IV, iv, 35. See also iv, 41 ; vii, 32, 80, 95, 101. Apocalypse of Baruch, xxx, 2.

[2] *Summa Theol.*, suppl., qu. 69, art. 1, in corp. et ad 3 ; art. 6, in corp. ; Appendix de Purgat., art. 2, in corp. ; suppl., qu. 69, art. 7 concl.

[3] *De gratia primi hominis* XIV.

these literal localization-schemes, especially since, according to
St. Augustine's penetrating analysis, our spiritual experiences,
already in this our earthly existence, have a distinctly non-
spatial character. Catherine's position, if applied to the
central life of man here, and hence presumptively hereafter,
remains as true and fresh and unassailable as ever.

(3) And her last simplification consists in taking the Fire
of Hell, the Fire of Purgatory, and the Fire and Light of
Heaven as profoundly appropriate symbols or descriptions of
the variously painful or joyous impressions produced, through
the differing volitional attitudes of souls towards Him, by the
one God's intrinsically identical presence in each and all.   In
all three cases, throughout their several grades, there are ever
but two realities, the Spirit-God and the spirit-soul, in various
states of inter-relation.

Here again it is Catherine's complete abstraction from the
body which renders such a view easy and, in a manner, necessary for her mind.   But here I would only emphasize the
impressive simplicity and spirituality of view which thus, as
in the material world it finds the one sun-light and the one
fire-heat, which, in themselves everywhere the same, vary
indefinitely in their effects, owing to the varying condition of
the different bodies which meet the rays and flames; so, in
the Spiritual World it discovers One supreme spiritual Energy
and Influence which, whilst ever self-identical, is assimilated,
deflected, or resisted by the lesser spirits, with inevitably
joyous, mixed, or painful states of soul, since they can each
and all resist, but cannot eradicate that Energy's impression
within their deepest selves.   And though, even with her, the
Sun-light image remains quasi-Hellenic and Intellectual, and
the Fire-heat picture is more immediately Christian and
Moral : yet she also frequently takes the sunlight as the
symbol of the achieved Harmony and Peace, and the Fire-
heat as that of more or less persisting Conflict and Pain.   She
is doubtless right in keeping both symbols, and in ever thinking of each as ultimately implying the other, for God is Beauty
and Truth, as well as Goodness and Love, and man is made
with the indestructible aspiration after Him in His living
completeness.

And here again Catherine has a complicated doctrinal
history behind her.

We have already considered the numerous Scriptural
passages where God and His effects upon the soul are

symbolized as light and fire; and those again where joy or, contrariwise, trial and suffering are respectively pictured by the same physical properties. And Catherine takes the latter passages as directly explanatory of the first, in so far as these joys and sufferings are spiritual in their causes or effects.

Among the Greek Fathers, Clement of Alexandria tells us that "the Fire" of Purgatory,—for he has no Eternal Damnation,—" is a rational," spiritual, " fire that penetrates the soul"; and Origen teaches that " each sinner himself lights the flame of his own fire, and is not thrown into a fire that has been lit before that moment and that exists in front of him. . . . His conscience is agitated and pierced by its own pricks." Saints Gregory of Nyssa and Gregory of Nazianzum are more or less influenced by Origen on this point. And St. John Damascene, who died in about 750 A.D., says explicitly that the fire of Hell is not a material fire, that it is very different from our ordinary fire, and that men hardly know what it is.[1]

Among the Latins, St. Ambrose declares : " neither is the gnashing, a gnashing of bodily teeth; nor is the everlasting fire, a fire of bodily flames ; nor is the worm, a bodily one."— St. Jerome, in one passage, counts the theory of the non-physical fire as one of Origen's errors; but elsewhere he mentions it without any unfavourable note, and even enumerates several Scripture-texts which favour it, and admits that " ' the worm which dieth not and the fire which is not quenched,' is understood, by the majority of interpreters (a plerisque), of the conscience of sinners which tortures them." [2] —St. Augustine, in 413 A.D., declares : " In the matter of the pains of the wicked, both the unquenchable fire and the intensely living worm are interpreted differently by different commentators. Some interpreters refer both to the body, others refer both to the soul; and some take the fire literally, in application to the body, and the worm figuratively, in application to the soul, which latter opinion appears the more credible." Yet when, during the last years of his life, he came, somewhat tentatively, to hold an other-world Purgatory as well, he throughout assimilated this Purgatory's fire to the

---

[1] Clemens, *Stromata*, VII, 6. Origen, *De Princ.*, II, 10, 4. St. Greg. Nyss., *Orat.*, XL, 36. St. Greg. Nazianz., *Poema de Seipso*, I, 546. St. Joann. Damasc., *De Fide Orthod.*, cap. ult.

[2] St. Ambros., *In Lucam*, VII, 205. St. Hieron., Ep. 124, 7; *Apol. contra Ruf.*, II; in Isa. lxv, 24.

fire of this-world sufferings. Thus in 422 A.D. : " Souls which renounce the wood, hay, straw, built upon that foundation (1 Cor. iii, 11–15), not without pain indeed (since they loved these things with a carnal affection), but with faith in the foundation, a faith operative through love . . . arrive at salvation, through a certain fire of pain. . . . Whether men suffer these things in this life only, or such-like judgments follow even after this life—in either case, this interpretation of that text is not discordant with the truth." " ' He shall be saved yet so as by fire,' because the pain, over the loss of the things he loved, burns him. It is not incredible that some such thing takes place even after this life . . . that some of the faithful are saved by a certain purgatorial fire, more quickly or more slowly, according as they have less or more loved perishable things." [1]

St. Thomas, voicing and leading Scholastic opinion, teaches that the fire of Purgatory is the same as that of Hell; and Cardinal Bellarmine, who died in 1621, tells us : " The common opinion of theologians is that the fire of Purgatory is a real and true fire, of the same kind as an earthly fire. This opinion, it is true, is not of faith, but it is very probable,"— because of the " consent of the scholastics, who cannot be despised without temerity," and also because of " the eruptions of Mount Etna." [2] Yet the Council of Florence had, in 1439, restricted itself to the quite general proposition that " if men die truly penitent, in the love of God, before they have satisfied . . . for their sins . . . their souls are purified by purgatorial pains after death "; thus very deliberately avoiding all commitment as to the nature of these pains.[3] Cardinal Gousset, who died in 1866, tells us : " The more common opinion amongst theologians makes the sufferings of Purgatory to consist in the pain of fire, or at least in a pain analogous to that of fire." [4] This latter position is practically identical with Catherine's.

As to the fire of Hell, although here especially the Scholastics, old and new, are unanimous, it is certain that there is no definition or solemn judgment of the Church declaring it

---

[1] *Liber de Fide* (A.D. 413), 27, 29; ed. Ben., coll. 313*b*, 314*c*. *De octo Dulcit. quaest.* (A.D. 422) 12, 13; *ibid.* coll. 219*d*, 220*a*. Repeated in Enchiridion (? A.D. 423), LXIX; *ibid.* col. 382*b*, *c*.

[2] *De Purgatorio*, II, 11.

[3] Denzinger, *Enchiridion*, ed. 1888, No. LXXIII.

[4] *Theol. Dogm.*, Vol. II, num. 206.

to be material. On this point again we find St. Thomas and those who follow him involved in practically endless difficulties and in, for us now, increasingly intolerable subtleties, where they try to show how a material fire can affect an immaterial spirit. Bossuet, so severely orthodox in all such matters, preaching, before the Court, about sin becoming in Hell the chastisement of the sinner, does not hesitate to finish thus : " We bear within our hearts the instrument of our punishment. ' Therefore have I brought forth a fire from the midst of thee, it hath devoured thee ' (Ezek. xxviii, 18). I shall not send it against thee from afar, it will ignite in thy conscience, its flames will arise from thy midst, and it will be thy sins which will produce it." [1]—And the Abbé F. Dubois, in a careful article in the Ecclesiastical *Revue du Clergé Français* of Paris, has recently expressed the conviction that " the best minds of our time, which are above being suspected of yielding to mere passing fashions, feel the necessity of abandoning the literal interpretation, judged to be insufficient, of the ancient symbols ; and of returning to a freer exegesis, of which some of the Ancients have given us the example." [2] Among these helpful " Ancients " we cannot but count Catherine, with her One God Who is the Fire of Pain and the Light of Joy to souls, according as they resist Him or will Him, either here or hereafter.

III. CATHERINE AND ETERNAL PUNISHMENT

Introductory : four doctrines and difficulties to be considered.
Taking now the three great after-life conditions separately, in the order of Hell, Purgatory, and Heaven, I would first of all note that some readers may be disappointed that Catherine did not, like our own English Mystic, the entirely orthodox optimist, Mother Juliana of Norwich—her *Revelations* belong to the year 1373 A.D.—simply proclaim that, whilst the teaching and meaning of Christ and His Church would come true, all, in ways known to God alone, would yet be well.[3] In this manner, without any weakening of traditional teaching, the

---

[1] *Œuvres*, ed. Versailles, 1816, Vol. XI, p. 376.
[2] *Le feu du Purgatoire est-il un feu corporel ? op. cit.*, 1902, pp. 263–284 ; 270. I owe most of my references on this point to this paper.
[3] *Sixteen Revelations of Mother Juliana of Norwich*, 1373, ed. 1902, pp. 73, 74, 78.

whole dread secret as to the future of evil-doers is left in the hands of God, and a beautifully boundless trust and hope glows throughout those contemplations.

Yet, as I hope to show as we go along, certain assumptions and conceptions, involved in the doctrine of Eternal Punishment, cannot be systematically excluded, or even simply ignored, without a grave weakening of the specifically Christian earnestness; and that, grand as is, in certain respects, the idea of the Apocatastasis, the Final Restitution of all Things and Souls—as taught by Clement and Origen—it is not, at bottom, compatible with the whole drift, philosophy, and tone, (even apart from specific sayings) of Our Lord. And this latter teaching—of the simply abiding significance and effect of our deliberate elections during this our one testing-time,—and not that of an indefinite series of chances and purifications with an ultimate disappearance of all difference between the results of the worst life and the best, answers to the deepest postulates and aspirations of the most complete and delicate ethical and spiritual sense. For minds that can discriminate between shifting fashions and solid growth in abiding truth, that will patiently seek out the deepest instinct and simplest implications underlying the popular presentations of the Doctrine of Abiding Consequences, and that take these implications as but part of a larger whole: this doctrine still, and now again, presents itself as a permanent element of the full religious consciousness.

It would certainly be unfair to press Catherine's rare and incidental sayings on Hell into a formal system. Yet those remarks are deep and suggestive, and help too much to interpret, supplement, and balance her central, Purgatorial teaching, and indeed to elucidate her general religious principles, for us to be able to pass them over. We have already sufficiently considered the question as to the nature of the Fire; and that as to Evil Spirits is reserved for the next Chapter. Here I shall consider four doctrines and difficulties, together with Catherine's attitude towards them: the soul's final fate, dependent upon the character of the will's act or active disposition at the moment of the body's death; the total moral perversion of the lost; the mitigation of their pains; and the eternity of their punishment.

1. *Eternity dependent on the earthly life's last moment.*

Now as to the soul's final fate being made dependent upon the character of that soul's particular act or disposition at the last moment previous to death, this teaching, prominent in parts of the *Trattato* and *Vita*, goes back ultimately to Ezekiel, who, as Prof. Charles interestingly shows, introduces a double individualism into the older, Social and Organic, Eschatology of the Hebrew Prophets. For Man is seen, by him, as responsible for his own acts alone, and as himself working out separately his own salvation or his own doom; and this individual man again is looked at, not in his organic unity, but as repeating himself in a succession of separate religious acts. The individual act is taken to be a true expression of the whole man at the moment of its occurrence: and hence, if this act is wicked at the moment of the advent of the Kingdom, the agent will rightfully be destroyed; but if it be righteous, he will be preserved.[1]—Now the profound truth and genuine advance thus proclaimed, who can doubt them? And yet it is clear that the doctrine here is solidly true, only if taken as the explicitation and supplement, and even in part as the corrective, of the previously predominant teaching. Take the Ezekielian doctrine as complete, even for its own time, or as final over against the later, the Gospel depth of teaching, (with its union of the social body and of individual souls, and of the soul's single acts and of the general disposition produced by and reacting upon these acts), and you get an all but solipsistic Individualism and an atomistic Psychology, and you offend Christianity and Science equally.

It is evident that Catherine, if she can fairly be taxed with what, if pressed, would, in her doctrine rather than in her life, be an excessive Individualism, is, in her general teaching and practice, admirably free from Psychological Atomism; indeed did any soul ever understand better the profound reality of habits, general dispositions, tones of mind and feeling and will, as distinct from the single acts that gradually build them up and that, in return, are encircled and coloured by them all? Her whole Purgatorial doctrine stands and falls by this distinction, and this although, with a profound self-knowledge, she does not hesitate to make the soul express, in one particular act after death,—that of the Plunge,—an even deeper level of its true attitude of will and of its moral character than is constituted by those imperfect habits of the will, habits which it will take so much suffering and acceptance of suffering gradually to rectify.

[1] *Critical History of the Doctrine of a Future Life,* 1899, pp. 63, 64.

Thus the passages in which Catherine seems to teach that God can and does, as it were, catch souls unawares, calling them away, and finally deciding their fate on occasion of any and every *de facto* volitional condition at the instant of death, however little expressive of the radical determination of that soul such an act or surface-state may be, will have, (even if they be genuine, and most of them have doubtlessly grown, perhaps have completely sprung up, under the pen of sermonizing scribes,) to be taken as hortatory, hence as partly hyperbolical. And such an admission will in nowise deny the possibility for the soul to express its deliberate and full disposition and determination in a single act or combination of acts; nor that the other-world effects will follow according to such deep, deliberate orientations of the character : it will only deny that, at any and every moment, any and every act of the soul sufficiently expresses its deliberate disposition. Certainly it is comparatively rarely that the soul exerts its full liberty, in an act of true, spiritual self-realization ; and an analogous rarity cannot but be postulated by religious philosophy for contrary acts, of an approximately equal fulness of deliberation and accuracy of representation, with regard to the soul's volitional state. And yet the operative influence towards such rare, fully self-expressive acts of the right kind, and the aid towards similar, massive, and truly representative volitions of the wrong kind, afforded by even quite ordinary half-awake acts and habits of respectively good or evil quality are so undeniable, and it is so impossible to draw a general line as to where such wishes pass into full willings and deliberate states : that the prevalence of a hortatory attitude towards the whole subject is right and indeed inevitable.

2. *The reprobate will of the lost.*

As to Moral Perversion, the reprobate will of the lost, we find that Catherine approaches the question from two different, and at bottom, on this point, incompatible, systems ; but some incidental and short sayings of hers give us suggestive hints towards a consistent position in this difficult matter.

Catherine has a double approach. For, consistently with the strong Neo-Platonist, Dionysian strain in her mind, she frequently teaches and implies that Evil is the absence of Good, of Love, and nothing positive at all. In this case Evil would not only be less strong than good—only Manichaeans would maintain that they were equal—but, as against the constructive force of good, it would have no kind even of destructive strength. Varying amounts, degrees, and kinds of good, but good and only good, everywhere, would render all, even transitory, pollution of the soul, and all, even passing, purification of it, so much actual impossibility and theoretical superstition. All that survived at all, could but be good; and at most some good might be added, but no evil could be removed, since none would exist.—Yet all this is, of course, strongly denied and supplanted by the, at first sight, less beautiful, but far deeper and alone fully Christian, position of her specifically Purgatorial teaching. Here Evil is something positive, an active disposition, orientation, and attachment of the will; it is not without destructive force; and its cure is a positive change in that will and its habits, and not a mere addition of good. Yet it is plain that, even exclusively within the implications of this deeper conviction, there is no necessity to postulate unmixed evil in the disposition of any soul. In some the evil would be triumphing over the good; in others good would be triumphing over evil,—each over the other, in every degree of good or of evil, up to the all but complete extinction of all inclinations to evil or to good respectively.

And Catherine has suggestive sayings. For one or two of them go, at least in their implications, beyond a declaration as to the presence of God's extrinsic mercy in Hell, a presence indicated by a mitigation of the souls' sufferings to below what these souls deserve; and even beyond the Areopagite's insistence upon the presence of some real good in these souls, since he hardly gets beyond their continuous possession of those non-moral goods, existence, intelligence, and will-power.[1] For when she says, " The ray of God's mercy shines even in Hell," she need not, indeed, mean more than that extrinsic mercy, and its effect, that mitigation. But when she declares : " if a creature could be found that did not participate in the divine Goodness,—that creature would, as it were, be as malignant as God is good," we cannot, I think, avoid applying this to the moral dispositions of such souls.[2]

Now I know that St. Thomas had already taught, in at first sight identical terms : " Evil cannot exist (quite) pure without the admixture of good, as the Supreme Good exists free from all admixture of evil. . . . Those who are detained

---

[1] *Divine Names*, ch. iv, secs. xxiii, xxiv ; Parker, pp. 61–64.
[2] *Vita*, pp. 173*b*; 33*b*.

in Hell, are not bereft of all good " ; [1] and yet he undoubtedly maintained the complete depravation of the will's dispositions in these souls. And, again, after Catherine's first declaration there follow, (at least in the text handed down in the *Vita*,) words which explain that extrinsic mercy, not as mitigating the finite amount of suffering due to the sinner, but as turning the infinite suffering due to the sinner's infinite malice, into a finite, though indefinite amount; and hence, in the second declaration, a corresponding interior mercy may be signified—God's grace preventing the sinner from being infinitely wicked.

But Catherine, unlike St. Thomas, expressly speaks not only of Good and Evil, but of Good and Malignancy; and Malignancy undoubtedly refers to dispositions of the will. And even if the words, now found as the sequel to the first saying, be authentic, they belong to a different occasion, and cannot be allowed to force the meaning of words spoken at another time. In this latter saying the words " as it were " show plainly that she is not thinking of a possible infiniteness of human wickedness which has been changed, through God's mercy, to an actual finitude of evil; but is simply asking herself whether a man could be, not infinitely but wholly, malignant. For she answers that, were this possible, a man would " as it were " be as malignant as God is good, and thus shows that the malignancy, which she denies, would only in a sense form a counterpart to God's benevolence : since, though the man would be as entirely malignant as God is entirely good, God would still remain infinite in His goodness as against the finitude of Man's wickedness.

The difficulties of such a combination of convictions are, of course, numerous and great. Psychologically it seems hard to understand why this remnant of good disposition should be unable to germinate further and further good, so that, at last, good would leaven the whole soul. From the point of view of any Theodicy, it appears difficult to justify the unending exclusion of such a soul from growth in, and the acquirement of, a predominantly good will and the happiness that accompanies such a will. And the testimony of Our Lord Himself and of the general doctrine of the Church appear definitely opposed : for does not His solemn declaration : " Hell, where their worm dieth not " (Mark ix, 48), find

---

[1] *Summa Theol.*, suppl., qu. 69, art. 7 ad 9.

its authoritative interpretation in the common Church teaching as to the utterly reprobate will of the lost? And indeed Catherine herself, in her great saying that if but one little drop of Love could fall into Hell (that is, surely, if but the least beginning of a right disposition towards God could enter those souls) Hell would be turned into Heaven, seems clearly to endorse this position.

And yet, we have full experience in this life of genuinely good dispositions being present, and yet not triumphing or even spreading within the soul; of such conditions being, in various degrees, our own fault; and of such defeat bringing necessarily with it more or less of keen suffering.—There would be no injustice if, after a full, good chance and sufficient aid had been given to the soul to actualize its capabilities of spiritual self-constitution, such a soul's deliberately sporadic, culpably non-predominant, good did not, even eventually, lead to the full satisfaction of that soul's essential cravings.—The saying attributed to Our Lord, which appears in St. Mark alone, is a pure quotation from Isaiah lxvi, 24 and Ecclesiasticus vii, 17, and does not seem to require more than an abiding distress of conscience, an eternal keenness of remorse.

Again, the common Church-teaching is undoubtedly voiced by St. Thomas in the words, " Since these souls are completely averse to the final end of right reason, they must be declared to be without any good will." Yet St. Thomas himself (partly in explanation of the Areopagite's words, " the evil spirits desire the good and the best, namely, to be, to live, and to understand "), is obliged to distinguish between such souls' deliberate will and their " natural will and inclination," and to proclaim that this latter, " which is not from themselves but from the Author of nature, who put this inclination into nature . . . can indeed be good." [1] And, if we would not construct a scheme flatly contradictory of all earthly experience, we can hardly restrict the soul, even in the beyond, to entirely indeliberate, good inclinations, and to fully deliberate, bad volitions, but cannot help interposing an indefinite variety of inchoative energizings, half-wishes, and the like, and thinking of these as mixed with good and evil. Indeed this conclusion seems also required by the common teaching that the suffering there differs from soul to soul, and this because of the different degrees of the guilt: for such degrees depend

[1] Dionysius, *Divine Names*, ch. iv, sec. xxiii: Parker, p. 63. St. Thomas, *Summa Theol.*, suppl., qu. 98, art. 1, in corp.

undoubtedly even more upon the degree of deliberation and massiveness of the will than upon the degree of objective badness in the deed, and hence can hardly fail to leave variously small or large fragments of more or less good and imperfectly deliberate wishings and energizings present in the soul.

And finally Catherine's " little drop of Love " would, she says, " at once " turn Hell into Heaven, and hence cannot mean some ordinary good moral disposition or even such supernatural virtues as theological Faith and Hope, but Pure Love alone, which latter queen of all the virtues she is explicitly discussing there. Thus she in nowise requires the absence from these souls of a certain remnant of semi-deliberate virtue of a less exalted, and not necessarily regenerative kind.

3. *Mitigation of the sufferings of the lost.*

As to the Mitigation of the Suffering, it is remarkable that Catherine, who has been so bold concerning the source of the pains, and the dispositions, of the lost souls, does not more explicitly teach such an alleviation. I say "remarkable," because important Fathers and Churches, that were quite uninfected by Origenism, have held and have acted upon such a doctrine. St. Augustine, in his *Enchiridion* (423 A.D. (?)) tells us that " in so far as " the Offering of the Sacrifice of the Altar and Alms " profit " souls in the beyond, " they profit them by procuring a full remission (of the punishment), or at least that their damnation may become more tolerable." And after warning men against believing in an end to the sufferings of the lost, he adds : " But let them consider, if they like, that the sufferings of the damned are somewhat mitigated during certain intervals of time." [1]—Saints John Chrysostom and John Damascene, thoroughly orthodox Greek Fathers, and the deeply devout hymn-writer Prudentius among the Latins, teach similar doctrine; and in many ancient Latin missals, ranging from the eleventh to the fourteenth century, prayers for the Mitigation of the Sufferings of the Damned are to be found.[2]

Hence the great Jesuit Theologian Petau, though not himself sharing this view, can declare : " Concerning such a breathing-time (*respiratio*) of lost souls, nothing certain has as

---

[1] *Enchiridion*, CX, ed. Ben., col. 403c; CXII, col. 404c.

[2] The passages here referred to will be found carefully quoted and discussed in Petavius's great *Dogmata Theologica*, *De Angelis*, III, viii, 16, 17, with Zaccaria's important note (ed. Fournials, 1866, Vol. IV, pp. 119–121).

yet been decreed by the Catholic Church, so that this opinion of most holy Fathers should not temerariously be rejected as absurd, even though it be foreign to the common opinion of Catholics in our time." [1] And the Abbé Emery, that great Catholic Christian, the second founder of St. Sulpice, who died in 1811, showed, in a treatise *On the Mitigation of the Pains of the Damned*, that this view had also been held by certain Scholastic Theologians, and had been defended, without any opposition, by Mark of Ephesus, in the Sessions of the Council of Florence (1439 A.D.); and concluded that this doctrine was not contrary to the Catholic Faith and did not deserve any censure. The most learned Theologians in Rome found nothing reprehensible in this treatise, and Pope Pius VII caused his Theologian, the Barnabite General, Padre Fontana, to thank M. Emery for the copy sent by him to the Holy Father.[2]

Catherine herself cannot well have been thinking of anything but some such Mitigation when she so emphatically teaches that God's mercy extends even into Hell. Indeed, even the continuation of this great saying in the present *Vita*-text formally teaches such Mitigation, yet practically withdraws it, by making it consist in a rebate and change, from an infinitude in degree and duration into a finitude in degree though not in duration.[3] But, as we have already found, this highly schematic statement is doubtless one of the later glosses, in which case her true meaning must have been substantially that of the Fathers referred to, viz. that the suffering, taken as anyhow finite in its degree, gets mercifully mitigated for these souls.—And, if she was here also faithful to her general principles, she will have conceived the mitigation, not as simply sporadic and arbitrary, but as more or less progressive, and connected with the presence in these souls of those various degrees of semi-voluntary good inclinations and wishes, required by her other saying. Even if these wishings could slowly and slightly increase, and the sufferings could similarly decrease, this would in nowise imply or require a final full rectification of the deliberate will itself, and hence not a complete extinction of the resultant suffering. Hell would still remain essentially

---

[1] *Dogmata Theologica*, Vol. IV, p. 120b. See also the interesting note in the Benedictine Edition of *St. Augustine*, Vol. VI, col. 403.

[2] *Vie de M. Emery*, by M. Gosselin, Paris, 1862, Vol. II, pp. 322–324.

[3] *Vita* (*Trattato*), p. 173b.

distinct from Purgatory; for in Purgatory the deliberate, active will is good from the first, and only the various semi-volitions and old habits are imperfect, but are being gradually brought into full harmony with that will, by the now complete willing of the soul; and hence this state has an end; whereas in Hell the deliberate, active will is bad from the first, and only various partially deliberate wishes and tendencies are good, but cannot be brought to fruition in a full virtuous determination of the dominant character of the soul, and hence *this* state has no end.

4. *The Endlessness of Hell.*

And lastly, as to the Endlessness of this condition of the Lost, it is, of course, plain that Catherine held this defined doctrine; and again, that " the chief weight, in the Church-teaching as to Hell, rests upon Hell's Eternity." [1]

Here I would suggest five groups of considerations :

(1) Precisely this Eternity appears to be the feature of all others which is ever increasingly decried by contemporary philosophy and liberal theology as impossible and revolting. Thus it is frequently argued as though, not the indiscriminate-ness nor the materiality nor the forensic externality nor the complete fixity of the sufferings, nor again the complete malignity of the lost were incredible, and hence the unending-ness of such conditions were impossible of acceptance; but, on the contrary, as though,—be the degree and nature of those sufferings conceived as ever so discriminated, spiritual, interior and relatively mobile, and as occasioned and accompanied by a disposition in which semi-voluntary good is present,—the simple assumption of anything unending or final about them, at once renders the whole doctrine impossible to believe. It is true that Tennyson and Browning take the doctrine simply in its popular Calvinistic form, and then reject it; and even John Stuart Mill and Frederick Denison Maurice hardly consider the eternity separately. But certainly that thoughtful and religious-minded writer, Mr. W. R. Greg, brings forward the eternity-doctrine as, already in itself, " a *curiosa infelicitas* which is almost stupidity on the part of the Church." [2]

(2) Yet it is plain how strongly, even in Mr. Greg's case, the supposed (local, physical, indiscriminate, etc.) nature of the state affects the writer's judgment as to the possibility of its unendingness,—as indeed is inevitable. And it is even

[1] So Atzberger, in Scheeben's *Dogmatik*, Vol. IV (1903), p. 826.
[2] *Enigmas of Life*, ed. 1892, p. 255.

eternity-doctrine

clearer, I think, that precisely this eternity-doctrine stands for a truth which is but an ever-present mysterious corollary to every deeply ethical or spiritual, and, above all, every specifically Christian view of life. For every such view comes, surely, into hopeless collision with its own inalienable requirements if it *will* hold that the deepest ethical and spiritual acts and conditions are,—avowedly performed though they be in time and space—simply temporary in their inmost nature and effects; whereas every vigorously ethical religion, in so far as it has reached a definite personal-immortality doctrine at all, cannot admit that the soul's deliberate character remains without any strictly final and permanent results. The fact is that we get here to a profound ethical and spiritual postulate, which cannot be adequately set aside on the ground that it is the product of barbarous ages and vindictive minds, since this objection applies only to the physical picturings, the indiscriminateness, non-mitigation, and utter reprobation; or on the ground that a long, keen purification, hence a temporally finite suffering, would do as well, since, when all this has completely passed away, there would be an entire obliteration of all difference in the consequences of right and wrong; or that acts and dispositions built up in time cannot have other than finite consequences, since this is to naturalize radically the deepest things of life; or finally that " Evil," as the Areopagite would have it, " is not,"[1] since thus the very existence of the conviction as to free-will and sin becomes more inexplicable than the theoretical difficulties against Libertarianism are insoluble.—Against this deep requirement of the most alert and complete ethical and spiritual life the wave of any Apocatastasis-doctrine or -emotion will, in the long run, ever break itself in vain.

(3) The doctrine of Conditional Immortality has, I think, many undeniable advantages over every kind of Origenism. This view does not, as is often imputed to it, believe in the annihilation by Omnipotence of the naturally immortal souls of impenitent grave sinners; but simply holds that human souls begin with the capacity of acquiring, with the help of God's Spirit, a spiritual personality, built up out of the mere possibilities and partial tendencies of their highly mixed natures, which, if left uncultivated and untranscended, become definitely fixed at the first, phenomenal, merely individual

---

[1] *Divine Names*, ch. iv, secs. 23, 24 : Parker, pp. 70, 71.

level,—so that spiritual personality alone deserves to live on
and does so, whilst this animal individuality does not deserve
and does not do so. The soul is thus not simply born as, but
can become more and more, that " inner man " who alone
persists, indeed who " is renewed day by day, even though our
outward man perish."[1]

This conception thus fully retains, indeed increases, the
profound ultimate difference between the results of spiritual
and personal, and of animal and simply individual life respectively,—standing, as it does, at the antipodes to Origenism;
it eliminates all unmoralized, unspiritualized elements from
the ultimate world, without keeping souls in an apparently
fruitless suffering; and it gives full emphasis to a supremely
important, though continually forgotten fact,—the profoundly
expensive, creative, positive process and nature of spiritual
character. No wonder, then, that great thinkers and scholars,
such as Goethe, Richard Rothe, Heinrich Holtzmann, and
some Frenchmen and Englishmen have held this view.[2]

Yet the objections against this view, taken in its strictness,
are surely conclusive. For how can an originally simply
mortal substance, force, or entity become immortal, and a
phenomenal nature be leavened by a spiritual principle
which, *ex hypothesi*, is not present within it? And how
misleadingly hyperbolical, according to this, would be the
greatest spiritual exhortations, beginning with those of Our
Lord Himself!

(4) And yet the conception of Conditional Immortality
cannot be far from the truth, since everything, surely, points
to a lowered consciousness in the souls in question, or at
least to one lower than that in the ultimate state of the saved.
This conception of the shrunken condition of these souls was
certainly held by Catherine, even if the other, the view of a
heightened, consciousness, appears in hortatory passages which
just *may* be authentic; and indeed only that conception is
conformable with her fundamental position that love alone is
fully positive and alone gives vital strength, and that all fully
deliberate love is absent from the lost souls. And if we

---

[1] 2 Cor. iv, 16.
[2] See H. J. Holtzmann, Richard Rothe's *Speculatives System*, 1899,
pp. 110, 111; 123, 124;—Georg Class, *Phänomenologie und Ontologie des
Menschlichen Geistes*, 1896, pp. 220, 221;—and that strange mixture of
stimulating thought, deep earnestness, and fantastic prejudice, Edward
White's *Life of Christ*, ed. 1876.

consider how predominantly hortatory in tone and object the ordinary teaching on this point cannot fail to be; and, on the other hand, how close to Manichaeism, any serious equating of the force and intensity of life and consciousness between the Saved and the Lost would be, we can hardly fail to find ourselves free, indeed compelled, to hold a lesser consciousness for the Lost than for the Saved. Whilst the joyful life of the Saved would range, in harmonious intensity, beyond all that we can experience here, the painful consciousness of the Lost would be, in various degrees, indefinitely less. The Saved would thus not be only *other* than the Lost, they would actually be *more*: for God is Life supreme, and, where there is more affinity with God, there is more life, and more consciousness.

(5) But, if the view just stated is the more likely one, then we cannot soften the sufferings of those souls, by giving them a sense of Eternity, of one unending momentary Now, instead of our earthly sense of Succession, as Cardinal Newman and Father Tyrrell have attempted to do, in a very instructive and obviously orthodox manner.[1] I shall presently argue strongly in favour of some consciousness of Eternity being traceable in our best moments here, and of this consciousness being doubtless more extended in the future blessed life. But here I have only to consider whether for one who, like Catherine, follows the analogy of earthly experience, the Lost should be considered nearer to, or further from, such a *Totum-Simul* consciousness than we possess now, here below, at our best? And to this the answer must, surely, be that they are further away from it. Yet God in His Mercy may allow this greater successiveness, if unaccompanied by any keen memory or prevision, to help in effecting that mitigation of the suffering which we have already allowed.

IV. CATHERINE AND PURGATORY.

1. *Introductory.*

(1) *Changed feeling concerning Purgatory.*

In the matter of a Purgatory, a very striking return of religious feeling towards its normal equilibrium has been occurring in the most unexpected, entirely unprejudiced

---

[1] *Grammar of Assent,* 1870 p. 417. *Hard Sayings,* 1898, p. 113.

quarters, within the last century and a half. In Germany we have Lessing, who, in the wake of Leibniz, encourages the acceptance of " that middle state which the greater part of our fellow-Christians have adopted " : Schleiermacher, who calls the overpassing of a middle state by a violent leap at death " a magical proceeding "; David F. Strauss, who entirely agrees; Carl von Hase, who, in his very Manual of Anti-Roman Polemics admits that " most men when they die are probably too good for Hell, but they are certainly too bad for Heaven "; the delicately thoughtful philosopher Fechner who, in the most sober-minded of his religious works, insists upon our " conceiving the life beyond according to the analogy of this-life conditions," and refers wistfully to " the belief which is found amongst all peoples and is quite shrunken only among Protestants—that the living can still do something to aid the dead "; and Prof. Anrich, probably the greatest contemporary authority on the Hellenic elements incorporated in Christian doctrine, declares, all definite Protestant though he is, that " legitimate religious postulates underlie the doctrine of Purgatory." [1] And in England that sensitively religious Unitarian, W. R. Greg, tells us " Purgatory, ranging from a single day to a century of ages, offers that borderland of discriminating retribution for which justice and humanity cry out "; and the Positivist, John Stuart Mill, declares at the end of his life : " All the probabilities in case of a future life are that such as we have been made or have made ourselves before the change, such we shall enter into the life hereafter. . . . To imagine that a miracle will be wrought at death . . . making perfect every one whom it is His will to include among His elect . . . is utterly opposed to every presumption that can be adduced from the light of nature." [2]

(2) *Causes of the previous prejudice.*

Indeed the general principle of ameliorative suffering is so

[1] G. E. Lessing, " Leibniz von den Ewigen Strafen," in Lessing's *Sämmtliche Werke*, ed. Lachmann-Muncker, 1895, Vol. XI, p. 486.   D. F. Strauss, *Die christliche Glaubenslehre*, 1841, Vol. II, pp. 684, 685. Carl von Hase, *Handbuch der protestantischen Polemik*, ed. 1864, p. 422. G. T. Fechner, *Die drei Gründe und Motive des Glaubens*, 1863, pp. 146, 147, 177.   G. Anrich, " Clemens und Origenes, als Begründer der Lehre vom Fegfeuer," in *Theologische Abhandlungen für H. J. Holtzmann*, 1902, p. 120.

[2] W. R. Greg, *Enigmas of Life*, ed. 1892, pp. 256, 257, 259.   J. S. Mill, *Three Essays on Religion*, ed. 1874, p. 211.

obviously true and inexhaustibly profound that only many, long-lived abuses in the practice, and a frequent obscuration in the teaching, of the doctrine, can explain and excuse the sad neglect, indeed discredit, into which the very principle and root-doctrine has fallen among well-nigh one-half of Western Christendom. As to the deplorably widespread existence, at the time of the Protestant Reformation, of both these causes, which largely occasioned or strengthened each other, we have the unimpeachable authority of the Council of Trent itself : for it orders the Bishops " not to permit that uncertain doctrines, or such as labour under the presumption of falsity, be propagated and taught," and " to prohibit, as so many scandals and stones of stumbling for the faithful, whatever belongs to a certain curiosity or superstition or savours of filthy lucre." [1] The cautious admissions of the strictly Catholic scholar-theologian, Dr. N. Paulus, and the precise documentary additions and corrections to Paulus furnished, directly from the contemporary documents, by the fair-minded Protestant worker at Reformation History, Prof. T. Brieger, now furnish us, conjointly, with the most vivid and detailed picture of the sad subtleties and abuses which gave occasion to that Decree.[2]

(3) *Catherine's purgatorial conceptions avoid those causes. Her conceptions harbour two currents of thought.*

It is surely not a small recommendation of Catherine's mode of conceiving Purgatory, that it cuts, as we shall see, at the very root of those abuses. Yet we must first face certain opposite dangers and ambiguities which are closely intertwined with the group of terms and images taken over, for the purpose of describing an immanental Purgation, by her and her great Alexandrian Christian predecessors, from the Greek Heathen world. And only after the delimitation of the defect in the suggestions which still so readily operate from out of these originally Hellenic ideas, can we consider the difficulties and imperfections peculiar to the other, in modern times the predominant, element in the complete teaching as to the Middle State, an element mostly of Jewish and Roman provenance, and aiming at an extrinsically punitive conception. Both currents can be properly elucidated only if we first take them historically.

---

[1] Sess. XXV, Decret. de Purgatorio, med.

[2] N. Paulus, *Johann Tetzel*, 1899. Brieger's review, *Theologische Literatur-Zeitung*, 1900, coll. 117, 118.

1. *Jewish prayers for the dead.*

It is admitted on all hands that, in the practical form of Prayers for the Dead, the general doctrine of a Middle State can be traced back, in Judaism, up to the important passage in the Second Book of Maccabees, c. xii, vv. 43–45, where Judas Maccabaeus sends about two thousand drachms of silver to Jerusalem, in order that a Sin-Offering may be offered up for the Jews fallen in battle against Gorgias, upon whose bodies heathen amulets had been found. " He did excellently in this . . . it is a holy and devout thought. Hence he instituted the Sin-Offering for the dead, that they might be loosed from their sins." That battle occurred in 166 B.C., and this book appears to have been written in 124 B.C., in Egypt, by a Jew of the school of the Pharisees.

Now it is difficult not to recognize, in the doctrinal comment upon the facts here given, rather as yet the opinions of a Judaeo-Alexandrian circle, which was small even at the time of the composition of the comment, than the general opinion of Judaism at the date of Judas's act. For if this act had been prompted by a clear and generally accepted conviction as to the resurrection, and the efficacy of prayers for the dead, the writer would have had no occasion or inclination to make an induction of his own as to the meaning and worth of that act ; and we should find some indications of such a doctrine and practice in the voluminous works of Philo and Josephus, some century and a half later on. But all such indications are wanting in these writers.

And in the New Testament there is, with regard to helping the dead, only that curious passage : " If the dead are not raised at all, why then are they baptized for them? "[1] where St. Paul refers, without either acceptance or blame, to a contemporary custom among Christian Proselytes from Paganism, who offered up that bath of initiation for the benefit of the souls of deceased relatives who had died without any such purification. Perhaps not till Rabbi Akiba's time, about 130 A.D., had prayers for the dead become part of the regular Synagogue ritual. By 200 A.D. Tertullian speaks of the practice as of an established usage among the Christian communities : " we make oblations for the Dead, on their anniversary, every year " ; although " if you ask where is the law concerning this custom in Scripture, you cannot read of

[1] I Cor. xv, 29.

any such there. Tradition will appear before you as its initiator, custom as its confirmer, and faith as its observer." [1]

It is interesting to note how considerably subsequent to the practice is, in this instance also, its clear doctrinal justification. Indeed the Jews are, to this hour, extraordinarily deficient in explicit, harmonious conceptions on the matter. Certainly throughout Prof. W. Bacher's five volumes of Sayings of the Jewish Rabbis from 30 B.C. to 400 A.D., I can only find the following saying, by Jochanan the Amoraean, who died 279 A.D.: "There are three books before God, in which men are inscribed according to their merit and their guilt : that of the perfectly devout, that of the perfect evil-doers, and that of the middle, the uncertain souls. The devout and the evil-doers receive their sentence on New Year's day . . . the first, unto life; the second, unto death. As to middle souls, their sentence remains in suspense till the day of Atonement : if by then they have done penance, they get written down alongside of the devout; if not, they are written down alongside of the evil-doers." [2]

2. Alexandrine Fathers on Purgatory.

Yet it is the Platonizing Alexandrian Fathers Clement and Origen (they died, respectively, in about 215 A.D. and in 254 A.D.), who are the first, and to this hour the most important, Christian spokesmen for a state of true intrinsic purgation. We have already deliberately rejected their Universalism; but this error in no way weakens the profound truth of their teaching as to the immanental, necessary interconnection between suffering and morally imperfect habits, and as to the ameliorative effects of suffering where, as in Purgatory, it is willed by a right moral determination. Thus Clement : " As children at the hands of their teacher or father, so also are we punished by Providence. God does not avenge Himself, for vengeance is to repay evil by evil, but His punishment aims at our good." " Although a punishment, it is an emendation of the soul." " The training which men call punishments." [3] And Origen : " The fury of God's vengeance profits unto the purification of souls; the punishment is unto purgation."

---

[1] *De Corona*, III, IV. See M. Salomon Reinach's interesting paper, " l'Origine des Prières pour les Morts," in *Cultes, Mythes, et Religions*, 1905, pp. 316–331.

[2] W. Bacher, *Die Agada der palästinenischen Amoräer*, Vol. I, 1892, p. 331.

[3] *Strom.*, VII, 26 (Migne, *Ser. Graec*, Vol. IX, col. 541); I, 26 (*ibid.* Vol. VIII, col. 916); VII, 26 (*ibid.* Vol. IX, col. 540).

" These souls receive, in the prison, not the retribution of
their folly, but a benefaction in the purification from the
evils contracted in that folly,—a purification effected by
means of salutary troubles." [1]

Now Clement is fully aware of the chief source for his
formulation of these deeply spiritual and Christian instincts
and convictions. " Plato speaks well when he teaches that
' men who are punished, experience in truth a benefit : for
those who get justly punished, profit through their souls
becoming better.' " [2] But Plato, in contradistinction from
Clement, holds that this applies only to such imperfect souls
as " have sinned curable sins "; he has a Hell as well as a
Purgatory : yet his Purgatory, as Clement's, truly purges : the
souls are there because they are partially impure, and they
cease to be there when they are completely purified.

And Plato, in his turn, makes no secret as to whence he got
his suggestions and raw materials, *viz.* the Orphic priesthood
and its literature, which, ever since the sixth century B.C., had
been succeeding to and supplanting the previous Orgiastic
Dionysianism. [3] Plato gives us vivid pictures of their doings
in Athens, at the time of his writing, in about 380 B.C.
" Mendicant prophets go to rich men's doors, and persuade
these men that they have a power committed to them of
making an atonement for their sins, or for those of their
fathers, by sacrifices and incantations . . . and they persuade
whole cities that expiations and purifications of sin may be
made by sacrifices and amusements which fill a vacant hour,
and are equally at the service of the living and the dead." [4]—
Yet from these men, thus scorned as well-nigh sheer impostors,
Plato takes over certain conceptions and formulations which
contribute one of the profoundest, still unexhausted elements
to his teaching,—although this element is, at bottom, in
conflict with that beautiful but inadequate, quite anti-Orphic,
conception of his—the purely negative character of Evil.
For the Orphic literary remains, fragmentary and late though
they be, plainly teach that moral or ritual transgressions are
a defilement of the soul, an infliction of positive stains upon
it ; that these single offences and " spots " produce a generally

---

[1] *De Princ.*, II, 10, 6. *De Orat.*, XXIX, p. 263.

[2] *Paedag.*, I, 8, p. 51; and Plato, *Gorgias*, p. 477a.

[3] I owe here almost everything to the truly classical account in Rohde's
Psyche, ed. 1898, Vol. II, pp. 1–136.

[4] *Republic*, II, p. 364b, c, e.

sinful and " spotted " condition ; and that this condition is
amenable to and requires purification by suffering,—water, or
more frequently fire, which wash or burn out these stains of
sin. So Plutarch (who died about 120 A.D.) still declares that
the souls in Hades have stains of different colours according
to the different passions ; and the object of the purificatory
punishment is " that, these stains having been worn away,
the soul may become altogether resplendent."   And Virgil,
when he declares " the guilt which infects the soul is washed
out or burnt out . . . until a long time-span has effaced the
clotted stain, and leaves the heavenly conscience pure " : is
utilizing an Orphic-Pythagorean Hades-book.[1]

This conception of positive stains is carefully taken over
by the Alexandrian Fathers : Clement speaks of " removing,
by continuous prayer, the stains ($\kappa\eta\lambda\iota\delta\alpha s$) contracted through
former sins," and declares that " the Gnostic," the perfect
Christian, " fears not death, having purified himself from all
the spots ($\sigma\pi\iota\lambda o\upsilon s$) on his soul."   And Origen describes " the
pure soul that is not weighed down by leaden weights of
wickedness," where the spots have turned to leaden pellets
such as were fastened to fishing-nets.   Hence, says Clement,
" post-baptismal sins have to be purified out " of the soul ;
and, says Origen, " these rivers of fire are declared to be of
God, who causes the evil that is mixed up with the whole
soul to disappear from out of it." [2]

In Pseudo-Dionysius the non-Orphic, purely negative, view
prevails : " Evil is neither in demons nor in us as an existent
evil, but as a failure and dearth in the perfection of our own
proper goods."   And St. Thomas similarly declares that
" different souls have correspondingly different stains, like
shadows differ in accordance with the difference of the bodies
which interpose themselves between the light." [3]

But Catherine, in this inconsistent with her own general
Privation-doctrine, again conceives the stain, the " macchia
del peccato," as Cardinal Manning has acutely observed, not
simply as a deprivation of the light of glory, but " as the cause,
not the effect, of God's not shining into the soul " : it includes

[1] I take these passages from Anrich's *Clemens und Origenes, op. cit.*
p. 102, n. 5.

[2] Clemens, *Strom.*, V, 3, p. 236.   Origen, *Contra Cels.*, VII, 13.   Clemens,
Strom., IV, 24.   Origen, *Contra Cels.*, IV, 13.

[3] Dionysius, *Divine Names*, ch. iv, sec. 24 : Parker, p. 64.   St. Thomas,
Summa Theol., I, ii, qu. 86, art. 1 ad 3 et concl.

in it the idea of an imperfection, weakness with regard to virtue, bad (secondary) dispositions, and unheavenly tastes.[1]

3. *The true and the false in the Orphic conception.*

Now precisely in this profoundly true conception of Positive Stain there lurk certain dangers, which all proceed from the original Orphic diagnosis concerning the source of these stains, and these dangers will have to be carefully guarded against.

(1) The conviction as to the purificatory power of fire was no doubt, originally, the direct consequence from the Orphic belief as to the intrinsically staining and imprisoning effect of the body upon the soul. " The soul, as the Orphics say, is enclosed in the body, in punishment for the punishable acts " ; " liberations " from the body, and " purifications " of the living and the dead, ever, with them, proceed together. And hence to burn the dead body was considered to purify the soul that had been stained by that prison-house : the slain Clytemnestra, says Euripides, " is purified, as to her body, by fire," for, as the Scholiast explains, " fire purifies all things, and burnt bodies are considered holy." [2] And such an intensely anti-body attitude we find, not only fully developed later on into a deliberate anti-Incarnational doctrine, among the Gnostics, but, as we have already seen, slighter traces of this same tone may be found in the (doubtless Alexandrian) Book of Wisdom, and in one, not formally doctrinal passage, a momentary echo of it, in St. Paul himself. And Catherine's attitude is generally, and often strongly, in this direction.

(2) A careful distinction is evidently necessary here. The doctrine that sin defiles,—affects the quality of the soul's moral and spiritual dispositions, and that this defilement and perversion, ever occasioned by the search after facile pleasure or the flight from fruitful pain, can normally be removed, and corrected only by a long discipline of fully accepted, gradually restorative pain, either here, or hereafter, or both : are profound anticipations, and have been most rightly made integral parts, of the Christian life and conception. The doctrine that the body is essentially a mere accident or superaddition or necessary defilement to the soul, is profoundly untrue, in its exaggeration and one-sidedness : for if the body is the occasion of the least spiritual of our sins, it can and should become the

---

[1] *Treatise on Purgatory*, by St. Catherine of Genoa, ed. 1880, p. 31.

[2] Plato, *Cratylus*, p. 400c. *Republic*, II, p. 364e. Euripides, *Orestes*, XXX, *seq.*, with Schol. Rohde, *op. cit.*, Vol. II, p. 101, n. 2.

chief servant of the spirit; the slow and difficult training of
this servant is one of the most important means of development for the soul itself; and many faults and vices are not
occasioned by the body at all, whilst none are directly and
necessarily caused by it. Without the body, we should not have
impurity, but neither should we have specifically human purity
of soul; and without it, given the persistence and activity of
the soul, there could be as great, perhaps greater, pride and
solipsism, the most anti-Christian of all the vices. Hence if,
in Our Lord's teaching, we find no trace of a Gnostic desire
for purification from all things bodily as essentially soul-
staining, we do find a profound insistence upon purity of
heart, and upon the soul's real, active " turning," conversion,
(an interior change from an un- or anti-moral attitude to an
ethical and spiritual dependence upon God), as a *sine qua non*
condition for entrance into the Kingdom of Heaven. And
the Joannine teachings re-affirm this great truth for us as a
Metabasis, a moving from Death over to Life.

4. *Catherine's conceptions as to the character of the stains and
of their purgation.*

And this idea, as to intrinsic purgation through suffering
of impurities contracted by the soul, can be kept thoroughly
Christian, if we ever insist, with Catherine in her most
emphatic and deepest teachings, that Purgation can and
should be effected in this life, hence in the body,—in and
through all the right uses of the body, as well as in and
through all the legitimate and will-strengthening abstentions
from such uses; that the subject-matter of such purgation are
the habits and inclinations contrary to our best spiritual lights,
and which we have largely ourselves built up by our variously
perverse or slothful acts, but which in no case are directly
caused by the body, and in many cases are not even occasioned by it; and, finally, that holiness consists primarily,
not in the absence of faults, but in the presence of spiritual
force, in Love creative, Love triumphant,—the soul becoming
flame rather than snow, and dwelling upon what to do,
give and be, rather than upon what to shun.—Catherine's
predominant, ultimate tone possesses this profound positiveness, and corrects all but entirely whatever, if taken alone,
would appear to render the soul's substantial purity impossible
in this life; to constitute the body a direct and necessary
cause of impurity to the soul; and to find the ideal of perfection in the negative condition of being free from stain.

In her greatest sayings, and in her actual life, Purity is found
to be Love, and this Love is exercised, not only in the inward,
home-coming, recollective movement,—in the purifying of the
soul's dispositions, but also in the outgoing, world-visiting,
dispersive movement,—in action towards fellow-souls.

5. *Judaeo-Roman conception of Purgatory.*

And this social side and movement brings us to the second
element and current in the complete doctrine of a Middle
State,—a constituent which possesses affinities and advantages,
and produces excesses and abuses, directly contrary to those
proper to the element of an intrinsic purgation.

(1) Here we get early Christian utilizations, for purposes of
a doctrine concerning the Intermediate State, of sayings and
images which dwell directly only upon certain extrinsic
consequences of evil-doing, or which, again, describe a future
historical and social event,—the Last Day. For already
Origen interprets, in his beautiful *Treatise on Prayer*, XXIX,
16, Our Lord's words as to the debtor : " And thou be cast
into prison . . . thou shalt by no means come out thence, till
thou hast paid the last farthing," Matt. v, 25, 26, as
applying to Purgatory. And in his *Contra Celsum*, VII, 13,
he already takes, as the Biblical *locus classicus* for a Purgatory,
St. Paul's words as to how men build, upon the one foundation
Christ, either gold, silver, gems, or wood, hay, stubble; and
how fire will test each man's work; and, if the work remain,
he shall receive a reward, but if it be burnt, he shall suffer
loss and yet he himself shall be saved yet so as by fire, 1 Cor.
iii, 10–15. It appears certain, however, that St. Paul is, in this
passage, thinking directly of the Last Day, the End of the
World, with its accompaniment of physical fire, and as to
how far the various human beings, then on earth, will be able
to endure the dread stress and testing of that crisis ; and he
holds that some will be fit to bear it and some will not.

Such a destruction of the world by fire appears elsewhere in
Palestinian Jewish literature,—in the Book of Enoch and the
Testament of Levi; and in the New Testament, in 2 Peter
iii, 12 : " The heavens being on fire shall be dissolved, and the
elements shall melt with fervent heat." Josephus, *Antiquities*,
XI, ii, 3, teaches a destruction by fire and another by water.
And the Stoics, to whom also Clement and Origen appeal,
had gradually modified their first doctrine of a simply cos-
mological Ekpyrōsis, a renovation of the physical universe by
fire, into a moral purification of the earth, occasioned by, and

applied to, the sinfulness of man. Thus Seneca has the double, water-and-fire, instrument: "At that time the tide" of the sea " will be borne along free from all measure, for the same reason which will cause the future conflagration. Both occur when it seems fit to God to initiate a better order of things and to have done with the old. . . . The judgment of mankind being concluded, the primitive order of things will be recalled, and to the earth will be re-given man innocent of crimes." [1]

(2) It is interesting to note how—largely under the influence of the forensic temper and growth of the Canonical Penitential system, and of its successive relaxations in the form of substituted lighter good works, Indulgences,—the Latin half of Christendom, ever more social and immediately practical than the Greek portion, came, in general, more and more to dwell upon two ideas suggested to their minds by those two, Gospel and Pauline, passages. The one idea was that souls which, whilst fundamentally well-disposed, are not fit for Heaven at the body's death, can receive instant purification by the momentary fire of the Particular Judgment; and the other held that, thus already entirely purified and interiorly fit for Heaven, they are but detained (in what we ought, properly, to term a *Satisfactorium*), to suffer the now completely non-ameliorative, simply vindictive, infliction of punishment,—a punishment still, in strict justice, due to them for past sins, of which the guilt and the deteriorating effects upon their own souls have been fully remitted and cured.

In this way it was felt that the complete unchangeableness of the condition of every kind of soul after death, or at least after the Particular Judgment (a Judgment held practically to synchronize with death), was assured. And indeed how could there be any interior growth in Purgatory, seeing that there is no meriting there? Again it was thought that thus the vision of God at the moment of Judgment was given an operative value for the spiritual amelioration of souls which, already in substantially good dispositions, could hardly be held to pass through so profound an experience without intrinsic improvement, as the other view seemed to hold.— And, above all, this form of the doctrine was found greatly to favour the multiplication among the people of prayers, Masses and good-works for the dead; since the *modus operandi* of

---

[1] *Natur. quaest.* III, 28, 7; 30, 7, 8.

such acts seemed thus to become entirely clear, simple, immediate, and, as it were, measurable and mechanical. For these souls in their " Satisfactorium," being, from its very beginning, already completely purged and fit for Heaven,—God is, as it were, free to relax at any instant, in favour of sufficiently fervent or numerous intercessions, the exigencies of his entirely extrinsic justice.

(3) The position of a purely extrinsic punishment is emphasized, with even unusual vehemence, in the theological glosses inserted, in about 1512 to 1529, in Catherine's *Dicchiarazione*. Yet it is probably the very influential Jesuit theologian Francesco Suarez, who died in 1617, who has done most towards formulating and theologically popularizing this view. All the guilt of sin, he teaches, is remitted (in these Middle souls) at the first moment of the soul's separation from the body, by means of a single act of contrition, whereby the will is wholly converted to God, and turned away from every venial sin. " And in this way sin may be remitted, as to its guilt, in Purgatory, because the soul's purification dates from this moment ";—in strictness, from before the first moment of what should be here termed the " Satisfactorium." As to bad habits and vicious inclinations, " we ought not to imagine that the soul is detained for these " : but " they are either taken away at the moment of death, or expelled by an infusion of the contrary virtues when the soul enters into glory." [1] This highly artificial, inorganic view is adopted, amongst other of our contemporary theologians, by Atzberger, the continuator of Scheeben.[2]

6. *The Judaeo-Roman conception must be taken in synthesis with the Alexandrine.*

Now it is plain that the long-enduring Penitential system of the Latin Church, and the doctrine and practice of Indulgences stand for certain important truths liable to being insufficiently emphasized by the Greek teachings concerning an intrinsically ameliorative *Purgatorium*, and that there can be no question of simply eliminating these truths. But neither are they capable of simple co-ordination with, still less of super-ordination to, those most profound and spiritually central immanental positions. As between the primarily forensic and governmental, and the directly ethical and spiritual, it will be the former that will have to be conceived

---

[1] Disp. XI, Sec. iv, art. 2, §§ 13, 10; Disp. XLVII, Sec. i, art. 6.
[2] Scheeben's *Dogmatik*, Vol. IV, 1903, pp. 856 (No. 93), 723.

and practised as, somehow, an expression and amplification of, and a practical corrective and means to, the latter.[1]

(1) The ordinary, indeed the strictly obligatory, Church teaching clearly marks the suggested relation as the right one, at three, simply cardinal points. We are bound, by the Confession of Faith of Michael Palaeologus, 1267 A.D., and by the Decree of the Council of Florence, 1429 A.D., to hold that these Middle souls " are purged after death by purgatorial or cathartic pains "; and by that of Trent " that there is a Purgatory." [2] Yet we have here a true *lucus a non lucendo*, if this place or state does not involve purgation : for no theologian dares explicitly to transfer and restrict the name " Purgatory " to the instant of the soul's Particular Judgment; even Suarez, as we have seen, has to extend the name somehow.

Next we are bound, by the same three great Decrees, to hold indeed that " the Masses, Prayers, Alms, and other pious offices of the Faithful Living are profitable towards the relief of these pains," yet this by mode of " suffrage," since, as the severely orthodox Jesuit, Father H. Hurter, explains in his standard *Theologiae Dogmaticae Compendium*, " the fruit of this impetration and satisfaction is not infallible, for it depends upon the merciful acceptance of God." [3] Hence in no case can we, short of superstition, conceive such good works as operating automatically : so that the *a priori* simplest view concerning the mode of operation of these prayers is declared to be mistaken. We can and ought, then, to choose among the conceptions, not in proportion to their mechanical simplicity, but according to their spiritual richness and to their analogy with our deepest this-life experiences.

And we are all bound, by the Decree of Trent and the Condemnation of Baius, 1567 A.D., to hold that Contrition springing from Perfect Love reconciles man with God, even before Confession, and this also outside of cases of necessity or of martyrdom.[4] Indeed, it is the common doctrine that one single act of Pure Love abolishes, not only Hell, but Purgatory, so that, if the soul were to die whilst that act was in operation,

---

[1] See Abbé Boudhinon's careful article, " Sur l'Histoire des Indulgences," *Revue d'Histoire et de Littérature Religieuses*, 1898, pp. 435–455, for a vivid illustration of the necessity of explaining the details of this doctrine and practice by history of the most patient kind.

[2] Denzinger, *Enchiridion*, ed. 1888, Nos. 387, 588, 859.

[3] Denzinger, *ibid.*, Hurter, *op. cit.* ed. 1893, Vol. III, p. 591.

[4] Denzinger, *ibid.*, ed. 1888, Nos. 778, 951.

it would forthwith be in Heaven. If then, in case of perfect purity, the soul is at once in heaven, the soul cannot be quite pure and yet continue in Purgatory.

(2) It is thus plain that, as regards Sin in its relation to the Sinner, there are, in strictness, ever three points to consider : the guilty act, the reflex effect of the act upon the disposition of the agent, and the punishment; for all theologians admit that the more or less bad disposition, contracted through the sinful act, remains in the soul, except in the case of Perfect Contrition, after the guilt of the act has been remitted. But whilst the holders of an Extrinsic, Vindictive Purgatory, work for a punishment as independent as possible of these moral effects of sin still present in the pardoned soul, the advocates of an Intrinsic, Ameliorative Purgatory find the punishment to centre in the pain and difficulty attendant upon " getting slowly back to fully virtuous dispositions, through retracing the steps we have taken in departing from it." [1] And the system of Indulgences appears, in this latter view, to find its chief justification in that it keeps up a link with the past Penitential system of the Church; that it vividly recalls and applies the profound truth of the interaction, for good even more than for evil, between all human souls, alive and dead; and that it insists upon the readily forgotten truth of even the forgiven sinner, the man with the good determination, having ordinarily still much to do and to suffer before he is quit of the effects of his sin.

(3) And the difficulties and motives special to those who supplant the Intrinsic, Ameliorating Purgatory by an Extrinsic, Vindicative *Satisfactorium*, can indeed be met by those who would preserve that beautifully dynamic, ethical, and spiritual conception. For we can hold that the fundamental condition,—the particular determination of the active will,—remains quite unchanged, from Death to Heaven, in these souls; that this determination of the active will requires more or less of time and suffering fully to permeate and assimilate to itself all the semi-voluntary wishes and habits of the soul; and that this permeation takes place among conditions in which the soul's acts are too little resisted and too certain of success to be constituted meritorious. We can take Catherine's beautiful Plunge-conception as indicating the kind of operation effected in and by the soul, at and through the momentary vision of God. And we can feel convinced that it is ever, in

[1] Cardinal Manning in *Treatise*, ed. cit. p. 31.

the long run, profoundly dangerous to try to clarify and simplify doctrines beyond or against the scope and direction of the analogies of Nature and of Grace, which are ever so dynamic and organic in type : for the poor and simple, as truly as the rich and learned, ever require, not to be merely taken and left as they are, but to be raised and trained to the most adequate conceptions possible to each.—It is, in any case, very certain that the marked and widespread movement of return to belief in a Middle State is distinctly towards a truly Purgative Purgatory, although few of these sincere truth-seekers are aware, as is Dr. Anrich, that they are groping after a doctrine all but quite explained away by a large body of late Scholastic and Neo-Scholastic theologians.[1]

(4) Yet it is very satisfactory to note how numerous, and especially how important are, after all is said, the theologians who have continued to walk, in this matter, in the footsteps of the great Alexandrines. St. Gregory of Nyssa teaches a healing of the soul in the beyond and a purification by fire.[2] St. Augustine says that " fire burns up the work of him who thinketh of the things of this world, since possessions, that are loved, do not perish without pain on the part of their possessor. It is not incredible that something of this sort takes place after this life." [3]

St. Thomas declares most plainly : " Venial guilt, in a soul which dies in a state of grace, is remitted after this life by the purging fire, because that pain, which is in some manner accepted by the will, has, in virtue of grace, the power of expiating all such guilt as can co-exist with a state of grace." " After this life . . . there can be merit with respect to some accidental reward, so long as a man remains in some manner in a state of probation : and hence there can be meritorious acts in Purgatory, with respect to the remission of venial sin." [4]—Dante (d. 1321) also appears, as Father Faber finely notes, to hold such a voluntary, immanental Purgatory, where the poet sees an Angel impelling, across the sea at dawn, a bark filled with souls bent for Purgatory : for the boat is described as driving towards the shore so lightly as to draw no wake upon the water.[5]

[1] Op. cit. pp. 119, 120 : " The Purgatory of the Catholic Church, in strictness, bears its name without warrant."

[2] Cat., cc. viii, 35.   [3] De octo Dulcitii quaest. 12, 13.

[4] Summa Theol., app., qu. 2, art. 4, in corp. et ad 4.

[5] Divina Commedia, Purg. II, 40–42. See Faber, All for Jesus, ed. 1889, p. 361.

Cardinal Bellarmine, perhaps the greatest of all anti-Protestant theologians (*d.* 1621) teaches that " venial sin is remitted in Purgatory *quoad culpam*," and that " this guilt, as St. Thomas rightly insists, is remitted in Purgatory by an act of love and patient endurance." [1] St. Francis of Sales, that high ascetical authority (*d.* 1622), declares : " By Purgatory we understand a place where souls undergo purgation, for a while, from the stains and imperfections which they have carried away with them from this mortal life." [2]

And recently and in England we have had Father Faber, Cardinal Manning, and Cardinal Newman, although differing from each other on many other points, fully united in holding and propagating this finely life-like, purgative conception of Purgatory. [3]

7. A final difficulty.

One final point concerning a Middle State. In the Synoptic tradition there is a recurrent insistence upon the forgiveness of particular sins, at particular moments, by particular human and divine acts of contrition and pardon. In the Purgatorial teaching the stress lies upon entire states and habits, stains and perversities of soul, and upon God's general grace working, in and through immanently necessary, freely accepted sufferings, on to a slow purification of the complete personality. As Origen says : " The soul's single acts, good or bad, go by ; but, according to their quality, they give form and figure to the mind of the agent, and leave it either good or bad, and destined for pains or for rewards." [4]

The antagonism here is but apparent. For the fact that a certain condition of soul precedes, and that another condition succeeds, each act of the same soul, in proportion as this act is full and deliberate, does not prevent the corresponding, complementary fact that such acts take the preceding condition as their occasion, and make the succeeding condition into a further expression of themselves. Single acts which fully express the character, whether good or bad, are doubtless rarer than is mostly thought. Yet Catherine, in union with the Gospels and the Church, is deeply convinced

---

[1] *De Purgatorio,* Lib. I, c. iv, 6; c. xiv, 22.

[2] *Les Controverses,* Pt. III, ch. ii, art. 1 (end); *Œuvres,* Annecy, 1892 seq., Vol. I, p. 365.

[3] Faber's *All for Jesus,* 1853, ch. ix, sec. 4; Cardinal Manning's Appendix (B) to Engl. tr. of St. Catherine's *Treatise on Purgatory,* 1858; Cardinal Newman's *Dream of Gerontius,* 1865.

[4] *In Rom.,* Tom. i, p. 477.

of the power of one single act of Pure Love to abolish, not of course the effects outward, but the reflex spiritual consequences upon the soul itself, of sinful acts or states.

Catherine's picture again, of the deliberate Plunge into Purgatory, gives us a similar heroic act which, summing up the whole soul's active volitions, initiates and encloses the whole subsequent purification, but which itself involves a prevenient act of Divine Love and mercy, to which this act of human love is but the return and response. Indeed, as we know, this plunge-conception was but the direct projection, on to the other-world-picture, of her own personal experience at her conversion, when a short span of clock-time held acts of love received and acts of love returned, which transformed all her previous condition, and initiated a whole series of states ever more expressive of her truest self.—Act and state and state and act, each presupposes and requires the other: and both are present in the Synoptic pictures, and both are operative in the Purgatorial teaching; although in the former the accounts are so brief as to make states and acts alike look as though one single act; and, in the latter, the descriptions are so large as to make the single acts almost disappear behind the states.

V. CATHERINE AND HEAVEN—THREE PERPLEXITIES TO BE CONSIDERED.

We have found a truly Purgational Middle state, with its sense of succession, its mixture of joy and suffering, and its growth and fruitfulness, to be profoundly consonant with all our deepest spiritual experiences and requirements. But what about Heaven, which we must, apparently, hold to consist of a sense of simultaneity, a condition of mere reproductiveness and utterly uneventful finality, and a state of unmixed, unchanging joy?—Here again, even if in a lesser degree, certain experiences of the human soul can help us to a few general positions of great spiritual fruitfulness, which can reasonably claim an analogical applicability to the Beyond, and which, thus taken as our ultimate ideals, cannot fail to stimulate the growth of our personality, and, with it, of further insight into these great realities. I shall here consider three main questions, which will roughly correspond to the three perplexities just indicated.

1. *Time and Heaven.*

Our first question, then, is as to the probable character of man's happiest ultimate consciousness,—whether it is one of succession or of simultaneity : in other words, whether, besides the disappearance of the category of space (a point already discussed), there is likely to be the lapse of the category of time also.—And let it be noted that the retention of the latter sense for Hell, and even for Purgatory, does not prejudge the question as to its presence or absence in Heaven, since those two states are admittedly non-normative, whereas the latter represents the very ideal and measure of man's full destination and perfection.

(1) Now it is still usual, amongst those who abandon the ultimacy of the space-category, simultaneously to drop, as necessarily concomitant, the time-category also. Tennyson, among the poets, does so, in his beautiful " Crossing the Bar " : " From out our bourne of Time and Place, the flood may bear me far " ; and Prof. H. J. Holtzmann, among speculative theologians, in criticising Rothe's conception of man as a quite ultimately spatial-temporal being, treats these two questions as standing and falling together.[1]—Yet a careful study of Kant's critique of the two categories of Space and Time suffices to convince us of the indefinitely richer content, and more ultimate reality, of the latter. Indeed, I shall attempt to show more fully in the next chapter, with the aid of M. Henri Bergson, that mathematical, uniform clock-time is indeed an artificial compound, which is made up of our profound experience of a duration in which the constituents (sensations, imaginations, thoughts, feelings, willings) of the succession ever, in varying degrees, overlap, interpenetrate, and modify each other, and the quite automatic and necessary simplification and misrepresentation of this experience by its imaginary projection on to space,—its restatement, by our picturing faculty, as a perfectly equable succession of mutually exclusive moments. It is in that interpenetrative duration, not in this atomistic clock-time, that our deeper human experiences take place.

(2) But that sense of duration, is it indeed our deepest apprehension ? Dr. Holtzmann points out finely how that we are well aware, in our profoundest experiences, of " that permanently incomprehensible fact,—the existence of, as it

---

[1] *Richard Rothe's Spekulatives System,* 1899, pp. 123, 124.

were, a prism, through which the unitary ray of light, which fills our consciousness with a real content, is spread out into a colour-spectrum, so that what, in itself, exists in pure unitedness " and simultaneity, " becomes intelligible to us only as a juxtaposition in space and a succession in time. Beyond the prism, there are no such two things." And he shows how keenly conscious we are, at times, of that deepest mode of apprehension and of being which is a Simultaneity, an eternal Here and Now; and how ruinous to our spiritual life would be a full triumph of the category of time.[1]

But it is St. Augustine who has, so far, found the noblest expression for the deepest human experiences in this whole matter of Duration and Simultaneity, as against mere Clock-Time, although, here as with regard to Space, he is deeply indebted to Plotinus. " In thee, O my soul, I measure time,— I measure the impression which passing events make upon thee, who remainest when those events have passed : this present impression then, and not those events which had to pass in order to produce it, do I measure, when I measure time." " The three times," tenses, " past, present, and future . . . are certain three affections in the soul, I find them there and nowhere else. There is the present memory of past events, the present perception of present ones, and the present expectation of future ones." God possesses " the splendour of ever-tarrying Eternity," which is " incomparable with never-tarrying times," since in it " nothing passes, but the content of everything abides simply present." And in the next life " perhaps our own thoughts also will not be flowing, going from one thing to another, but we shall see all we know simultaneously, in one intuition." St. Thomas indeed is more positive: "All things will," in Heaven, " be seen simultaneously and not successively." [2]

(3) If then, even here below, we can so clearly demonstrate the conventionality of mere Clock-Time, and can even conceive a perfect Simultaneity as the sole form of the consciousness of God, we cannot well avoid holding that, in the other life, the clock-time convention will completely cease, and that, though the sense of Duration is not likely completely to disappear (since, in this life at least, this sense is certainly not

[1] *Richard Rothe's Spekulatives System*, 1899, pp. 69; 74, 75.
[2] St. Augustine, *Confessions*, Lib. XI, ch. xxvii, 3; ch. xx; ch. xi. *De Trinit.*, Lib. XV, ch. 16, ed. Ben., col. 1492 D.—St. Thomas, *Summa Theol.*, I, qu. 12, art. 10, in corp.

merely phenomenal for man, and its entire absence would
apparently make man into God), the category of Simultaneity
will, as a sort of strong background-consciousness, englobe
and profoundly unify the sense of Duration. And, the more
God-like the soul, the more would this sense of Simultaneity
predominate over the sense of Duration.

2. *The Ultimate Good, concrete, not abstract.*

Our second question concerns the kind and degree of
variety in unity which we should conceive to characterize
the life of God, and of the soul in its God-likeness. Is this
type and measure of all life to be conceived as a maximum
of abstraction or as a maximum of concretion; as pure
thought alone, or as also emotion and will; as solitary and
self-centred, or as social and outgoing; and as simply
reproductive, or also as operative?

(1) Now it is certain that nothing is easier, and nothing
has been more common, than to take the limitations of our
earthly conditions, and especially those attendant upon the
strictly contemplative, and, still more, those connected with
the technically ecstatic states, as so many advantages, or even
as furnishing a complete scheme of the soul's ultimate life.

As we have already repeatedly seen in less final matters, so
here once more, at the end, we can trace the sad impoverishment to the spiritual outlook produced by the esteem in which
the antique world generally held the psycho-physical peculiarities of trances, as directly valuable or even as prophetic
of the soul's ultimate condition; the contraposition and
exaltation, already on the part of Plato and Aristotle, of a
supposed non-actively contemplative, above a supposed non-
contemplatively active life; the largely excessive, not fully
Christianizable, doctrines of the Neo-Platonists as to the
Negative, Abstractive way, when taken as self-sufficient, and
as to Quiet, Passivity, and Emptiness of Soul, when understood literally; and the conception, rarely far away from the
ancient thinkers, of the soul as a substance which, full-grown,
fixed and stainless at the first, requires but to be kept free
from stain up to the end.

And yet the diminution of vitality in the trance, and even
the inattention to more than one thing at a time in Contemplation, are, in themselves, defects, at best the price paid
for certain gains; the active and the contemplative life are,
ultimately, but two mutually complementary sides of life, so
that no life ever quite succeeds in eliminating either element,

and life, *caeteris paribus*, is complete and perfect, in proportion as it embraces both elements, each at its fullest, and the two in a perfect interaction; the Negative, Abstractive way peremptorily requires also the other, the Affirmative, Concrete way; the Quiet, Passivity, Emptiness are really, when wholesome, an incubation for, or a rest from, Action, indeed they are themselves a profound action and peace, and the soul is primarily a Force and an Energy, and Holiness is a growth of that Energy in Love, in full Being, and in creative, spiritual Personality.

(2) Now on this whole matter the European Christian Mystics, strongly influenced by, yet also largely developing, certain doctrines of the Greeks, have, I think, made two most profound contributions to the truths of the spirit, and have seriously fallen short of reality in three respects.

The first contribution can, indeed, be credited to Aristotle, whose luminous formulations concerning Energeia, Action (as excluding Motion, or Activity), we have already referred to. Here to *be* is to *act*, and Energeia, a being's perfect functioning and fullest self-expression in action, is not some kind of movement or process; but, on the contrary, all movement and process is only an imperfect kind of Energeia. Man, in his life here, only catches brief glimpses of such an Action; but God is not so hampered,—He is ever completely all that He can be, His Action is kept up inexhaustibly and ever generates supreme bliss; it is an unchanging, unmoving Energeia.[1] —And St. Thomas echoes this great doctrine, for all the Christian schoolmen: "A thing is declared to be perfect, in proportion as it is in act,"—as all its potentialities are expressed in action; and hence "the First Principle must be supremely in act," "God's Actuality is identical with His Potentiality," "God is Pure Action (*Actus Purus*)."[2]—Yet it is doubtless the Christian Mystics who have most fully experienced, and emotionally vivified, this great truth, and who cease not, in all their more characteristic teachings, from insisting upon the ever-increasing acquisition of "Action," the fully fruitful, peaceful functioning of the whole soul, at the expense of "activity," the restless, sterile distraction and

[1] I am here but giving an abstract of Mr. F. C. S. Schiller's admirable essay, "Activity and Substance," pp. 204–227 of his *Humanism*, 1903, where all the Aristotelian passages are carefully quoted and discussed. He is surely right in translating ἠρεμία by "constancy," not by "rest."

[2] *Summa Theol.*, I, qu. 4, art. 1, concl. qu. 25, art. 1 ad 2 et concl.

internecine conflict of its powers. And Heaven, for them, ever consists in an unbroken Action, devoid of all " activity," rendering the soul, in its degree, like to that Purest Action, God, who, Himself " Life," is, as our Lord declared, " not the God of the dead, but of the living." [1]

And the second contribution can, in part, be traced back to Plato, who does not weary, in the great middle period of his writings, from insisting upon the greatness of the nobler passions, and who already apprehends a Heavenly Eros which in part conflicts with, in part transcends, the Earthly one. But here especially it is Christianity, and in particular Christian Mysticism, which have fully experienced and proclaimed that " God " is " Love," and that the greatest of all the soul's acts and virtues is Charity, Pure Love. And hence the Pure Act of God, and the Action of the God-like soul, are conceived not, Aristotle-like, as acts of pure intelligence alone, but as tinged through and through with a noble emotion.

(3) But in three matters the Mystics, as such and as a whole, have, here especially under the predominant influence of Greek thought, remained inadequate to the great spiritual realities, as most fully revealed to us by Christianity. The three points are so closely interconnected that it will be best first to illustrate, and then to criticise them, together.

(i) Aristotle here introduces the mischief. For it is he who in his great, simply immeasurably influential, theological tractate, Chapters VI to X of the Twelfth Book of his *Metaphysic*, has presented to us God as " the one first unmoved Mover " of the Universe, but Who moves it as desired by it, not as desiring it, as outside of it, not as also inside it. God here is sheer Pure Thought, Noēsis, for " contemplation is the most joyful and the best " of actions. And " Thought " here " thinks the divinest and worthiest, without change," hence " It thinks Itself, and the Thinking is a Thinking of Thought." [2] We have here, as Dr. Caird strikingly puts it, a God necessarily shut up within Himself, " of purer eyes than to behold, not only iniquity but even contingency and finitude, and His whole activity is one act of pure self-contemplation." "The ideal activity which connects God with the world, appears thus as in the world and not in God." [3]

---

[1] Matt. xxii, 32.   [2] *Metaphysic*, xii, 1072b, 1074b.
[3] E. Caird, *Evolution of Theology in the Greek Philosophers*, 1904, Vol. II, pp. 12, 16. See here, too, the fine discussion of the other, rightly immanental as well as transcendental, teaching of Aristotle, pp. 15, 21.

(ii) Now we have already allowed that the Mystics avoid Aristotle's elimination of emotion from man's deepest action, and of emotion's equivalent from the life of God. But they are, for the most part, much influenced in their speculations by this intensely Greek, aristocratic, intellectualist conception, in the three points of a disdain of the Contingent and Historical; of a superiority to volitional, productive energizing; and of a presentation of God as unsocial, and as occupied directly with Himself alone. We have already studied numerous examples of the first two, deeply un-Christian, errors as they have more or less influenced Christian Mysticism; the third mistake, of a purely Transcendental, Deistic God, is indeed never consistently maintained by any Christian, and Catherine, in particular, is ever dominated by the contrary great doctrine, adumbrated by Plato and fully revealed by Our Lord, of the impulse to give Itself intrinsic to Goodness, so that God, as Supreme Goodness, becomes the Supreme Self-giver, and thus the direct example and motive for our own self-donation to Him. Yet even so deeply religious a non-Christian as Plotinus, and such speculative thinkers as Eriugena and Eckhart (who certainly intended to remain Christians) continue all three mistakes, and especially insist upon a Supreme Being, Whose true centre, His Godhead, is out of all relation to anything but Himself. And even the orthodox Scholastics, and St. Thomas himself, attempt at times to combine, with the noblest Platonic and the deepest Christian teachings, certain elements, which, in strictness, have no place in an Incarnational Religion.

(iii) For, at times, the fullest, deepest Action is still not conceived, even by St. Thomas, as a Harmony, an Organization of all Man's essential powers, the more the better. " In the active life, which is occupied with many things, there is less of beatitude than in the contemplative life, which is busy with one thing alone,—the contemplation of Truth "; " beatitude must consist essentially in the action of the intellect; and only accidentally in the action of the will." [1] God is still primarily intelligence : " God's intelligence is His substance "; whereas " volition must be in God, since there is intelligence in Him," and " Love must of necessity be declared to be in God, since there is volition in Him." [2] God is still, in a certain sense, shut up in Himself : " As He understands things other than

---

[1] *Summa Theol.*, I, ii, qu. 3, art. 2 ad 4; art. 4, concl.

[2] *Ibid.*, I, qu. 14, art. 4, in corp.; qu. 19, art. 1, concl.; qu. 20, art. 1, concl.

Himself, by understanding His own essence, so He wills things other than Himself, by willing His own goodness." " God enjoys not anything beside Himself, but enjoys Himself alone." [1] —And we get, in correspondence to this absorption of God in Himself, an absorption of man in God, of so direct and exclusive a kind, as, if pressed, to eliminate all serious, permanent value, for our soul, in God's actual creation of our fellow-creatures. " He who knoweth Thee and creatures, is not, on this account, happier than if he knows them not; but he is happy because of Thee alone." And " the perfection of Love is essential to beatitude, with respect to the Love of God, not with respect to the Love of one's neighbour. If there were but one soul alone to enjoy God, it would be blessèd, even though it were without a single fellow-creature whom it could love." [2]

(iv) And yet St. Thomas's own deeply Christian sense, explicit sayings of Our Lord or of St. Paul, and even, in part, certain of the fuller apprehensions of the Greeks, can make the great Dominican again uncertain, or can bring him to entirely satisfactory declarations, on each of these points. For we get the declaration that direct knowledge of individual things, and quasi-creative operativeness are essential to all true perfection. " To understand something merely in general and not in particular, is to know it imperfectly "; Our Lord Himself has taught us that " the very hairs of your head are all numbered "; hence God must " know all other individual things with a distinct and proper knowledge."—And " a thing is most perfect, when it can make another like unto itself. But by tending to its own perfection, each thing tends to become more and more like God. Hence everything tends to be like God, in so far as it tends to be the cause of other things." [3]—We get a full insistence, with St. Paul (in 1 Cor. xiii), upon our love of God, an act of the will, as nobler than our cognition of Him; and with Plato and St. John, upon God's forthgoing Love for His creatures, as the very crown and measure of His perfection. " Everything in nature has, as regards its own good, a certain inclination to diffuse itself amongst others, as far as possible. And this applies, in a supreme degree, to the Divine Goodness, from which all perfection is derived."

[1] *Summa Theol.*, I, qu. 9, art. 2, 3; qu. 14, art. 2 ad 2; I, ii, qu. 3, art. 2 ad 4.

[2] *Ibid.*, I, qu. 12, art. 8 ad 4; I, ii, qu. 4, art. 8 ad 3.

[3] *Ibid.*, I, qu. 14, art. 8, in corp.; art. 11, contra et concl.; art 8, concl.— *Contra Gent.*, Lib. III, c. xxi, in fine.

" Love, Joy, Delight can be predicated of God "; Love which, of its very essence, " causes the lover to bear himself to the beloved as to his own self " : so that we must say with Dionysius that " He, the very Cause of all things, becomes ecstatic, moves out of Himself, by the abundance of His loving goodness, in the providence exercised by Him towards all things extant." [1]

(v) And we get in St. Thomas, when he is too much dominated by the abstractive trend, a most interesting, because logically necessitated and quite unconscious, collision with certain sayings of Our Lord. For he then explains Matt. xviii, 10, " their," the children's, " Angels see without ceasing the face of their Father who is in Heaven " as teaching that " the action (*operatio*), by which Angels are conjoined to the increate Good, is, in them, unique and sempiternal "; whereas his commentators are driven to admit that the text, contrariwise, implies that these Angels have two simultaneous " operations," and that their succouring action in nowise disturbs their intellectual contemplation. Hence, even if we press Matt. xxii, 30, that we " shall be as the Angels of God," we still have an organism of peaceful Action, composed of intellectual, affective, volitional, productive acts operating between the soul and God, and the soul and other souls, each constituent and object working and attained in and through all the others.

(vi) Indeed all Our Lord's Synoptic teachings, as to man's ultimate standard and destiny, belong to this God-in-man and man-in-God type of doctrine : for there the two great commandments are strictly inseparable; God's interest in the world is direct and detailed,—it is part of His supreme greatness that He cares for every sparrow that falls to the ground; and man, in the Kingdom of God, will sit down at a banquet, the unmistakable type of social joys.—And even the Apocalypse, which has, upon the whole, helped on so much the conception of an exclusive, unproductive entrancement of each soul singly in God alone, shows the deepest emotion when picturing all the souls, from countless tribes and nations, standing before the throne,—an emotion which can, surely, not be taken as foreign to those souls themselves.[2]

---

[1] *Summa Theol.*, II, ii, qu. 3, art. 4, 4; I, qu. 19, art. 2, in corp.; qu. 20, art. 1 ad 1; ad 3; art. 2 ad 1.

[2] Mark xii, 28–34 and parallels; Matt. x, 29; Luke xii, 6; Matt. xxv, 10; Mark xiv, 25 and parallels, and elsewhere; Apoc. vii, 9.

But, indeed, Our Lord's whole life and message become unintelligible, and the Church loses its deepest roots, unless the Kingdom of God is, for us human souls, as truly a part of our ultimate destiny as is God Himself, that God who fully reveals to us His own deepest nature as the Good Shepherd, the lover of each single sheep and of the flock as a whole.[1]

(4) We shall, then, do well to hold that the soul's ultimate beatitude will consist in its own greatest possible self-realization in its God-likeness,—an Action free from all Activity, but full of a knowing, feeling, willing, receiving, giving, effectuating, all which will energize between God and the soul, and the soul and other souls,—each force and element functioning in its proper place, but each stimulated to its fullest expansion, and hence to its deepest delight, by the corresponding vitalization of the other powers and ends, and of other similar centres of rich action.

3. *The pain-element of Bliss.*

And our third, last question is whether our deepest this-life apprehensions and experiences give us any reason for holding that a certain equivalent for what is noblest in devoted suffering, heroic self-oblivion, patient persistence in lonely willing, will be present in the life of the Blessed. It would certainly be a gain could we discover such an equivalent, for a pure glut of happiness, an unbroken state of sheer enjoyment, can as little be made attractive to our most spiritual requirements, as the ideal of an action containing an element of, or equivalent for, devoted and fruitful effort and renunciation can lose its perennial fascination for what is most Christian within us.

(1) It is not difficult, I take it, to find such an element, which we cannot think away from any future condition of the soul without making that soul into God Himself. The ultimate cause of this element shall be considered, as Personality, in our next chapter : here I can but indicate this element at work in our relations to our fellow-men and to God.—Already St. Thomas, throughout one current of his teaching, is full of the dignity of right individuality. " The Multitude and Diversity of natures in the Universe proceed directly from the intention of God, who brought them into being, in order to communicate His goodness to them, and to have It represented by them. And since It could not be sufficiently represented

[1] Matt. **xviii**, 12–14; Luke **xv**, 1–10; John **x**, 11–16 (Ezekiel xxxiv, 12–19).

by one creature alone, He produced many and diverse ones, so that what is wanting to the one towards this office, should be supplied by the other." [1] Hence the multiplication of the Angels, who differ specifically each from all the rest, adds more of nobility and perfection to the Universe, than does the multiplication of men, who differ only individually.[2] And Cardinal Nicolas of Coes writes, in 1457 A.D., " Every man is, as it were, a separate species, because of his perfectibility." [3] As Prof. Josiah Royce tells us in 1901, " What is real, is not only a content of experience and the embodiment of a type ; but an individual content of experience, and the unique embodiment of a type." [4]

(2) Now in the future beatitude, where the full development of this uniqueness in personality cannot, as so often here, be stunted or misapplied, all this will evidently reach its zenith.   But, if so, then it follows that, although one of the two greatest of the joys of those souls will be their love and understanding of each other,—this love and trust, given as it will be to the other souls, in their full, unique personality, will, of necessity, exceed the comprehension of the giving personalities. Hence there will still be an equivalent for that trust and venture, that creative faith in the love and devotion given by us to our fellows, and found by us in them, which are, here below, the noblest concomitants and conditions of the pain and the cost and the joy in every virile love and self-dedication.— There is then an element of truth in Lessing's words of 1773 : " The human soul is incapable of even one unmixed emotion,— one that, down to its minutest constituent, would be nothing but pleasurable or nothing but painful : let alone of a condition in which it would experience nothing but such unmixed emotions."—For, as Prof. Troeltsch says finely in 1903, " Everything historical retains, in spite of all its relation to absolute values, something of irrationality,"—of impenetrableness to finite minds, " and of individuality.   Indeed just this mixture is the special characteristic of the lot and dignity of man ; nor is a Beyond for him conceivable in which it would altogether cease.   Doubt and unrest can indeed give way to clear sight and certitude : yet this very clarity and assurance

---

[1] *Summa Theol.*, I, qu. 47, art. 1, in corp.

[2] *Ibid.*, I, qu. 50, art. 4 ad 3 ; ad 2 ; in corp.   *Contra Gent.*, Lib. II, c. xciii.

[3] *Excitationum*, Lib. VIII, 604.

[4] *The World and the Individual*, Vol. II, p. 430.

will, in each human soul, still bear a certain individual character," fully comprehensible to the other souls by love and trust alone.[1]

(3) And this same element we find, of course, in a still greater degree,—although, as I shall argue later on, our ex-perimental knowledge of God is greater than is our knowledge of our fellow-creatures,—in the relations between our love of God and our knowledge of Him. St. Thomas tells us most solidly : " Individual Being applies to God, in so far as it implies Incommunicableness." Indeed, " Person signifies the most perfect thing in nature,"—" the subsistence of an indi-vidual in a rational nature." " And since the dignity of the divine nature exceeds every other dignity, this name of Per-son is applicable, in a supreme degree, to God." And again : " God, as infinite, cannot be held infinitely by anything finite " ; and hence " only in the sense in which comprehension is opposed to a seeking after Him, is God comprehended, i.e. possessed, by the Blessed." And hence the texts : " I press on, if so be that I may apprehend that for which also I was apprehended " (Phil. iii, 12) ; " then shall I know even as also I have been known " (1 Cor. xiii, 12) ; and " we shall see Him as He is " (1 John iii, 2) : all refer to such a possession of God. In the last text " the adverb ' as ' only signifies ' we shall see His essence ' and not ' we shall have as perfect a mode of vision as God has a mode of being.' "[2]—Here again, then, we find that souls loving God in His Infinite Individuality, will necessarily love Him beyond their intellectual comprehension of Him; the element of devoted trust, of free self-donation to One fully known only through and in such an act, will thus remain to man for ever. St. John of the Cross proclaimed this great truth : " One of the greatest favours of God, bestowed transiently upon the soul in this life, is its ability to see so distinctly, and to feel so profoundly, that . . . it cannot comprehend Him at all. These souls are herein, in some degree, like to the souls in heaven, where they who know Him most perfectly perceive most clearly that He is infinitely incomprehensible ; for those that have the less clear vision, do not perceive so distinctly as the others how greatly He transcends their

---

[1] G. E. Lessing : *Leibniz von den Ewigen Strafen, Werke*, ed. Lach-mann-Muncker, Vol. XI, 1895, p. 482. E. Troeltsch, *Theologische Rund-schau*, 1893, p. 72.

[2] *Summa Theol.*, I, art. 7, in corp.; art. 6 ad 1.

vision." [1] With this teaching, so consonant with Catherine's experimental method, and her continuous trust in the persistence of the deepest relations of the soul to God, of the self-identical soul to the unchanging God, we can conclude this study of her Eschatology.

[1] " A Spiritual Canticle," stanza vii, 10, in *Works*, transl. by D. Lewis, ed. 1891, pp. 206, 207.

CHAPTER XIII

THE FIRST THREE ULTIMATE QUESTIONS. THE RELATIONS
BETWEEN MORALITY, MYSTICISM, PHILOSOPHY, AND
RELIGION. MYSTICISM AND THE LIMITS OF HUMAN
EXPERIENCE AND KNOWLEDGE. MYSTICISM AND THE
NATURE OF EVIL.

I TAKE the ultimate questions involved in the religious
positions which are taken up by Catherine, and indeed by the
Christian Mystics generally, and which we have studied in the
preceding two chapters, to be four. In the order of their
increasing difficulty they are: the question as to the relations
between Morality, Mysticism, Philosophy, and Religion; that
as to the Limits of Human Knowledge, and as to the special
character and worth of the Mystics' claim to Trans-subjective
Cognition; that as to the Nature of Evil and the Goodness or
Badness of Human Nature; and that as to Personality,—the
character of, and the relations between, the human spirit and
the Divine Spirit. The consideration of these deepest matters
in the next two chapters will, I hope, in spite of its inevitable
element of dimness and of repetition, do much towards binding
together and clarifying the convictions which we have been
slowly acquiring,—ever, in part, with a reference to these
coming ultimate alternatives and choices.

I. THE RELATIONS BETWEEN MORALITY AND MYSTICISM, PHILOSOPHY AND RELIGION.

Now the first of these questions has not, for most of the
more strenuous of our educated contemporaries, become, so
far again, a living question at all. A morally good and pure,
a socially useful and active life,—all this in the sense and with
the range attributed to these terms by ordinary parlance : this
and this alone is, for doubtless the predominant public present-
day consciousness, the true object, end, and measure of all

healthy religion; whatever is alongside of, or beyond, or other than, or anything but a direct and exclusive incentive to this, is so much superstition and fanaticism. According to this view, at least one-half of Catherine's activity at all times, and well-nigh the whole of it during her last period, would be practically worthless. Thus only certain elements of such a life would be retained even for and in religion, and even these would be bereft of all that has hitherto been held to be their specifically religious sense and setting.

1. *Kant's non-mystical religion.*

It is doubtless Kant who, among the philosophers, has been the most consistent and influential in inculcating such non-Mystical Religion. " Religion," he says in 1793, " is, on its subjective side, the cognition of all our duties as so many Divine Commandments." " The delusion that we can effect something, in view of our justification before God, by means of acts of religious worship, is religious superstition; and the delusion that we can effect something by attempts at a supposed intercourse with God, is religious fanaticism. . . . Such a feeling of the immediate presence of the Supreme Being, and such a discrimination between this feeling and every other, even moral, feeling, would imply a capacity for an intuition, which is without any corresponding organ in human nature. . . . If then a Church doctrine is to abolish or to prevent all religious delusion, it must,—over and above its statutory teachings, with which it cannot, for the present, entirely dispense,—contain within itself a principle which shall enable it to bring about the religion of a pure life, as the true end of the whole movement, and then to dispense with those temporary doctrines." [1]

It is deeply instructive to note how thoroughly this, at first sight, solid and triumphant view, has not only continued to be refuted by the actual practice and experience of specifically religious souls, but how explicitly it is being discredited by precisely the more delicately perceptive, the more truly detached and comprehensive, students and philosophers of religion of the present day,—heirs, let us not forget in justice to Kant, of the intervening profound development of the historical sense, and of the history and psychology of religion.—Thus that most vigorous, independent thinker, Prof. Simmel of Berlin, writes in 1904 : " Kant has, I think, simply

[1] *Religion innerhalb der Grenzen der blossen Vernunft*, Werke, ed. Hartenstein, 1868, Vol. VI, pp. 252, 274.

passed by the essentials of religion,—that is to say, of that reality which historically bears the name of religion. Only the reflection, that the harmony of complete happiness with complete morality is producible by a Divine Being alone, is here supposed to lead us to believe in such a Being. There is here a complete absence of that direct laying hold of the Divine by our souls, because of our intrinsic needs, which characterizes all genuine piety. And the religious sense is not recognized as an organism with a unity of its own, as a growth springing from its own root. The entirely specific character of religion, which is resolvable neither into morality nor into a thirst after happiness: the direct self-surrender of the soul to a higher reality, the giving and taking, the unification and differentiation,—that quite organic unity of the religious experience, which we can but most imperfectly indicate by a multiplicity of some such, simultaneously valid, antitheses: this, there is no evidence to show, was ever really known to Kant. What was religion for Augustine and Francis of Assisi, he was unable to reproduce in himself; indeed religion, of this type, he readily rejects as fanaticism. Here lay the limit both of his own nature and of his own times." [1]

The rich mind of Prof. Troeltsch is, perhaps, more entirely just: " As Kant's theory of knowledge is throughout dependent upon the state of contemporary psychology, so also is his theory of religious knowledge dependent upon the psychology of religion predominant in his day. Locke, Leibniz, Pascal had already recognized the essentially practical character of all religion; and since their psychology was unable to conceive the ' practical ' otherwise than as the moral, it had looked upon Religion as Morality furnished forth with its metaphysical concomitants. And as soon as this psychology had become the very backbone of his conception of Religion, Morality gained an entirely one-sided predominance over Kant's mind,—considerably, indeed, beyond his own personal feelings and perceptions." For he remains deeply penetrated by " the conceptions of Regeneration and Redemption; the idea of divine Grace and Wisdom, which accepts the totality of a soul's good disposition in lieu of that soul's ever defective single good works; the belief in a Providence which strengthens the Good throughout the world against Evil; adoring awe in face of the majesty of the

[1] *Kant*, 1904, pp. 129–132.

Supersensible " ; and " all these " conceptions " are no more simply moral, they are specifically religious thoughts." [1]

Such a fuller conception of religion is admirably insisted on by that penetrating philosopher and historian of philosophy, Prof. Windelband : " Actual Religion, in its complete reality, belongs to all the spheres of life, and yet transcends them all, as something new and *sui generis*. It is first an interior life—an apprehending, cognizing, feeling, willing, accomplishing. But this accomplishing leads it on to being also an exterior life ; an acting out, according to their various standards, of such feeling and willing ; and an outward expression of that inner life in general, in ritual acts and divine worship. Yet this worship takes it beyond the little circle of the individual, and constitutes the corporate acts of a community, a social, external organization with visible institutions. And yet Religion ever claims to be more than the whole series of such empirical facts and doings, it ever transcends mere earthly experience, and is an intercourse with the inmost nature and foundation of all reality ; it is a life in and with God, a metaphysical life. All these elements belong to the complete concept of actual religion." [2] I would add, that they each stimulate the other, the external, *e. g.* being not only the expression of the awakened internal, but also the occasion of that awakening.

And the great Dutch scholar, Prof. C. P. Tiele, unexcelled in the knowledge of the actual course taken by the great religions of the world, declares : " All progress, not only in Morality, but also in Science, Philosophy, Art, necessarily exerts an influence upon that of Religion. But . . . Religion is not, on that account, identical with Ethics any more than with Philosophy or Art. All these manifestations of the human spirit respond to certain needs of man ; but none of them, not even Morality, is capable of supplying the want which Religion alone can satisfy. . . . Religion differs from the other manifestations of the human mind " in this, that whereas " in the domain of Art, the feelings and the imagination predominate ; in that of Philosophy, abstract thought is paramount " ; and " the main object of Science is to know accurately, whilst Ethics are chiefly concerned with the emotions and with the fruit they

[1] *Das Historische in Kant's Religions-philosophie, Kant-Studien*, 1904, pp. 43, 44.
[2] " Das Heilige," in *Präludien*, 1903, pp. 356, 357.

yield: in Religion all these factors operate alike, and if their equilibrium be disturbed, a morbid religious condition is the result." [1]

2. *Ritschlian modification of Kant's view.*

It is deeply interesting to note the particular manner in which Kant's impoverishment of the concept of religion has been in part retained, in part modified, by the Ritschlian school,—I am thinking especially of that vigorous writer, Prof. Wilhelm Hermann.

(1) If in Kant we get the belief in God derived from reflection upon Goodness and Happiness, and as the only possible means of their ultimate coalescence: in Hermann we still get the Categorical Imperative, but the thirst for Happiness has been replaced by the historic figure of Jesus Christ. " Two forces of different kinds," he says, " ever produce the certainty of Faith: the impression of an Historic Figure which approaches us in Time; and the Moral Law which, when we have heard it, we can understand in its Eternal Truth. Faith arises, when a man recognizes, in the appearance of Jesus, that symbol of his own existence which gives him the courage to recognize in the Eternal, which claims him in the Moral Imperative, the source of true life for his own self." [2]—And these two sole co-efficients of all entirely living religion are made to exclude, as we have already seen, especially all Mysticism from the life of Faith. " True, outside of Christianity, Mysticism will everywhere arise, as the very flower of the religious development. But a Christian is bound to declare the mystical experience of God to be a delusion. Once he has experienced his elevation, by Christ alone, above his own previous nature, he cannot believe that another man can attain the same result, simply by means of recollection within his own self. . . . We are Christians precisely because we have struck, in the person of Jesus, upon a fact which is incomparably richer in content than the feelings that arise within ourselves." " Only because Christ is present for us can we possess God with complete clearness and certainty." And, with Luther,—who remained, however, thoroughly faithful to the Primitive and Mediæval high esteem for the Mystical element of religion;—" right prayer is a work of faith, and only a Christian can perform it."

---

[1] *Elements of the Science of Religion*, 1897, Vol. I, pp. 274, 275; Vol. II, p. 23.

[2] *Der Verkehr des Christen mit Gott*, ed. 1892, p. 281.

And, more moderately : " We have no desire to penetrate through Christ on to God : for we consider that in God Himself we still find nothing but Christ." [1]

(2) Now it is surely plain that we have here a most understandable, indeed respectable, reaction against all empty, sentimental Subjectivism, and a virile affirmation of the essential importance of the Concrete and Historical. And, in particular, the insistence upon the supreme value and irreplaceable character and function of Christ is profoundly true. —Yet three counter-considerations have ever to be borne in mind. (i) It remains certain that we do not know, or experience anything, to which we can attribute any fuller reality, which is either purely objective or purely subjective ; and that there exists no process of knowing or experiencing such a reality which would exclude either the objective or the subjective factor. " Whatever claims to be fully real," either as apprehending subject or as apprehended object, " must be an individual . . . an organic whole, which has its principle of unity in itself." The truly real, then, is a thing that has an inside ; and the sharp antithesis drawn, although in contrary directions, by Aristotle and by Kant, between the Phenomenal and the Intelligible worlds, does not exist in the reality either of our apprehending selves, or of our apprehended fellow-men, or God.[2]—But Hermann is so haunted by the bogey-fear of the subjective resonance within us being necessarily useless towards, indeed obstructive of, the right apprehension of the object thus responded to, that he is driven to follow the will-o'-the-wisp ideal of a pure, entirely exclusive objectivity.

(ii) Bent on this will-o'-the-wisp quest of an exclusive objectivity, he has to define all Mysticism in terms of Exclusive Mysticism, and then to reject such an aberration. " Wherever the influence of God upon the soul is sought and found solely in an interior experience of the individual soul, in an excitation of the feelings which is supposed directly to reveal the true nature of this experience, viz. in a state of possession by God, and this without anything exterior being apprehended and held fast with a clear consciousness, without the positive content of some mental contemplation setting

[1] *Der Verkehr des Christen mit Gott*, ed. 1892, pp. 27, 28 ; 230, 231 ; 262 ; 23.
[2] E. Caird, *Development of Theology in the Greek Philosophers*, Vol. I, pp. 367, 362. The whole chapter, " Does the Primacy belong to Reason or to Will ? " pp. 350–382, is admirable in its richness and balance.

thoughts in motion and raising the spiritual level of the soul's life; *there* is Mystical Piety." [1]

Now it is, of course, true that false Mysticism does attempt such an impossible feat as the thing at which Hermann is thus aiming. But, even here, the facts and problems are again misstated. Just now the object presented was everything, and the apprehending subject was nothing. Here, on the contrary, the apprehension by the subject is pressed to the degree of requiring the soul to remain throughout reflexly aware of its own processes.

Already in 1798 Kant had, in full acceptance of the great distinction worked out by Leibniz in the years 1701–1709, but not published till 1765, declared: "We can be mediately conscious of an apprehension as to which we have no direct consciousness"; and "the field of our obscure apprehensions,—that is, apprehensions and impressions of which we are not directly conscious, although we can conclude without doubt that we have them,—is immeasurable, whereas clear apprehensions constitute but a very few points within the complete extent of our mental life." [2] This great fact psychologists can now describe with greater knowledge and precision : yet the observations and analyses of Pierre Janet, William James, James Ward and others, concerning Subconsciousness, have but confirmed and deepened the Leibnizian-Kantian apprehensions. Without much dim apprehension, no clear perception; nothing is more certain than this.

And it is certain, also, that this absence of reflex consciousness, of perceiving that we are apprehending, applies not only to impressions of sensible objects, or to apprehensions of realities inferior in richness, in interiority, to our own nature, but also, indeed especially, to apprehensions of realities superior, in dignity and profundity of organization, to our own constitution. When engrossed in a great landscape of Turner, the Parthenon sculptures, a sonata of Beethoven, Dante's *Paradiso;* or when lost in the contemplation of the seemingly endless spaces of the heavens, or of the apparently boundless times of geology; or when absorbed in the mysterious greatness of Mind, so incommensurable with

[1] *Verkehr des Christen mit Gott,* pp. 15, 16.

[2] I. Kant, "Anthropologie," in *Werke,* ed. Berlin Academy, Vol. VII, 1907, pp. 135, 136. G. W. Leibniz, "Nouveaux Essais sur l'Entendement," in *Die philosophischen Schriften von G. W. L.,"* ed. Gerhardt, Vol. V, 1882, pp. 8, 10; 45, 69, 100, 121, 122.

matter, and of Personality, so truly presupposed in all these appreciations yet so transcendent of even their collectivity— we are as little occupied with the facts of our engrossment, our self-oblivion, our absorption, or with the aim and use of such immensely beneficial self-oblivion, as we are, in our ordinary, loosely-knit states, occupied with the impression which, nevertheless, is being produced upon our senses and mind by some small insect or slight ray of light to which we are not giving our attention, or which may be incapable of impressing us sufficiently to be thus attended to and clearly perceived.[1] And, as in the case of these under-impressions, so in that of those over-impressions, we can often judge, as to their actual occurrence and fruitfulness, only from their after-effects, although this indirect proof will, in each case, be of quite peculiar cogency.—All this leaves ample room for that prayer of simple quiet, so largely practised by the Saints, and indeed for all such states of recollection which, though the soul, on coming from them, cannot discover definite ideas or picturings to have been contained in them, leave the soul braced to love, work, and suffer for God and man, beyond its previous level. Prof. William James is too deeply versed a Psychologist not fully to understand the complete normality of such conditions, and the entire satisfactoriness of such tests [2]

(iii) And finally, it is indeed true that God reveals Himself to us, at all fully, in Human History alone, and within this history, more fully still, in the lives and experiences of the Saints of all the stages of religion, and, in a supreme and normative manner, in the life and teaching of Jesus Christ; that we have thus a true immanence of the Divine in the Human; and that it is folly to attempt the finding or the making of any shorter way to God than that of the closest contact with His own con-descensions. Yet such a wisely Historical and fully Christian attitude would be imperilled, not secured, by such an excessive Christocentrism, indeed such *Panchristism*, as that of Prof. Hermann.

We shall indeed beware of all indifferentist levelling-down of the various religions of the world. For, as Prof. Robertson Smith, who knew so well the chief great religions, most wisely said, " To say that God speaks to all men alike,

---

[1] All this first clearly formulated by Leibniz, *op. cit.* pp. 121, 122.

[2] See his *Varieties of Religious Experience*, 1902, pp. 209–211; 242, 243; and elsewhere.

and gives the same communication directly to all without the
use of a revealing agency, reduces religion to Pure Mysticism.
In point of fact it is not true of any man that what he believes
and knows of God, has come to him directly through the voice
of nature and conscience." And he adds : " History has not
taught us anything in true religion to add to the New Testament. Jesus Christ still stands as high above us as He did
above His disciples, the perfect Master, the supreme head of
the fellowship of all true religion." [1]

Yet we must equally guard against making even Our Lord
into so exclusive a centre and home of all that is divine, as to
cause Him to come into an entirely God-forsaken, completely
God-forgetting world, a world which did not and could not,
in any degree or manner whatsoever, rightly know, love, or
serve God at all; and against so conceiving the religion,
taught and practised by Him, as to deprive it of all affinity
with, or room for, such admittedly universal forces and
resultants of the human soul and the religious sense as are
dim apprehension, formless recollection, pictureless emotion,
and the sense of the Hiddenness and Transcendence of the
very God, Who is also Immanent and Self-Revealing, in various
degrees and ways, in every place and time. Indeed, these two
forces : the diffused Religiosity and more or less inchoate
religion, readily discoverable, by a generous docility, more or
less throughout the world of human souls, and the concentrated
spirituality and concrete, thoroughly characteristic Religion,
which has its culmination, after its ample preludings in the
Hebrew Prophets, in the Divine-Human figure and spirit of
Jesus Christ : are interdependent, in somewhat the way in
which vague, widely spread Subconsciousness requires, and is
required by, definite, narrowly localized Consciousness in each
human mind. Precisely because there have been and are
previous and simultaneous lesser communications of, and
correspondences with, the one " Light that enlighteneth every
man that cometh into the world "; because men can and do
believe according to various, relatively preliminary, degrees
and ways, in God and a Providence, in Sin and Contrition,
without a knowledge of the Historic Christ (although never
without the stimulation of some, often world-forgotten, historic
personality, and ever with some real, though unconscious
approximation to His type of life and teaching), therefore can

[1] *The Prophets of Israel*, 1882, pp. 11, 12; 10, 11.

Christ be the very centre, and sole supreme manifestation and measure of all this light. Not only can Christ remain supreme, even though Moses and Elijah, Amos and Isaiah, Jeremiah and Ezekiel; and indeed, in their own other degrees and ways, Plato and Plotinus, Epictetus and Marcus Aurelius, Gautama Buddha and Rabbi Akiba be all revered as God-loved and God-loving, as, in various amounts, truly, spiritually great: but only thus can His central importance be fully realized.

There is certainly much in Our Lord's own attitude, as we have already found, to demand such a view; and Clement of Alexandria, Origen and St. Justin Martyr have emphasized it continually. And there is no necessary Naturalism here— for the position is entirely compatible with the profoundest belief in the great truth that it is Grace which everywhere produces the various degrees of God-pleasing religion to be found scattered throughout the world. Father Tyrrell has admirably said: " God's salutary workings in man's heart have always been directed, however remotely, to the life of Grace and Glory; of 'the Order of mere nature,' and its exigencies, we have no experimental knowledge. . . . In the present order, Theism is but embryonic Christianity, and Christianity is but developed Theism : ' purely natural' religion is what might have been, but never was." [1]

(3) Now this must suffice as a sketch of the relations between (Historical) Religion and Mysticism, and will have shown why I cannot but regret that so accomplished a scholar as Prof. Morris Jastrow should class all and every Mysticism, whether Pure or Mixed, as so far forth a religious malady; why I rejoice that so admirably circumspect an investigator as Prof. C. P. Tiele should, (in the form of a strenuous insistence upon the apprehension, indeed the ontological action of, the Infinite, by and within the human spirit, as the very soul and mainspring of Religion), so admirably reinforce the fundamental importance of the Mystical apprehensions; why I most warmly endorse Prof. Rauwenhoff's presentment of Mysticism as, with Intellectualism and Moralism, one of the three psychological forms of religion, which are each legitimate and necessary, and which each require the check of the other two, if they are not to degenerate each into some corruption special to the exclusive develop-

---

[1] *Lex Orandi,* 1903, pp. xxix, xxxi.

ment of that particular form; and why I cordially applaud the unequalled analysis and description by Prof. Eucken of the manner in which "Universal Religion" is at work, as an often obscure yet (in the long run) most powerful leaven, throughout all specifically human life,—Sciences, Art, Philosophy, and Ethics, calling for, and alone satisfied with, the answering force and articulation of "Characteristic Religion," each requiring and required by the other, each already containing the other in embryo, and both ever operating together, in proportion as Man and Religion attain to their fullness.[1]

3. *Hermann's impossible simplification concerning philosophy.* But what shall we say as to the relations between Religion and Philosophy? Here again Hermann is the vigorous champion of a very prevalent and plausible simplification. "There exists no Theory of Knowledge for such things as we hold to be real in the strength of faith. In such religious affirmations, the believer demolishes every bridge between his conviction and that which Science can recognize as real." Indeed Hermann's attitude is here throughout identical with that of his master, Albrecht Ritschl : Metaphysics of any and every kind appear everywhere, to both writers, as essentially unnecessary, unreal, misleading, as so much inflation and delusion of soul.—Yet this again is quite demonstrably excessive, and can indeed be explained only as an all but inevitable recoil from the contrary metaphysical excesses of the Hegelian school.

(1) Since the culmination of that reaction, "it has," as Prof. H. J. Holtzmann, himself so profoundly historical and so free from all extreme metaphysical bent, tells us, "become quite impossible any further to deny the metaphysical factors which had a share in constituting such types of New Testament doctrine as the Pauline and Johannine. Indeed, not even if we were to reduce the New Testament to the Synoptic Gospels and the Acts on the one hand, and to the Pastoral Epistles, the Epistle of James and the Apocalypse on the other hand, would the elements which spring from speculative sources be entirely eliminated. And since, again, the Old Testament religion, in its last stage, assimilated similarly

---

- M. Jastrow, *The Study of Religion*, 1901, pp. 279–286. C. P. Tiele, *Elements of the Science of Religion*, 1897, Vol. II, pp. 227–234; L. W. E. Rauwenhoff, *Religions-philosophie*, Germ. tr., ed. 1894, pp. 109–124. R. Eucken, *Der Wahrheitsgehalt der Religion*, 1901, pp. 59–238; 303–399. There are important points in pp. 425–438, which I do not accept.

metaphysical materials from the East and from the West; since Mohammedanism, in its Persian and Indian branches, did the same with regard to the older civilized religions of Middle and Eastern Asia; since also these latter religions received a speculative articulation in even the most ancient times, so that they are both Philosophy and Religion simultaneously : we are forced to ask ourselves, whether so frequent a concomitant of religion is satisfactorily explicable as a mere symptom of falsification or decay." And whilst answering that the primary organ for religion is Feeling and Conscience, he points out how large an amount of Speculation was, nevertheless, required and exercised by a St. Augustine, even after his unforgettable experiences of the sufferings attendant upon Sin, and of their cure by Grace alone.[1]

(2) The fact is that, if man cannot apprehend the objects,—the historic and other facts,—of Religion, without certain subjective organs, dispositions, and effects, any more than can all these subjective capacities, without those objects, produce religious convictions and acts, or be waked up into becoming efficient forces : neither can man thus experience and effect the deepest foundations and developments of his own true personality in and through contact with the divine Spirit, without being more or less stimulated into some kind of, at least rudimentary, Philosophy as to these his profoundest experiences of reality, and as to their rights and duties towards the rest of what he is and knows.

(3) Indeed his very Religion is already, in itself, the profoundest Metaphysical Affirmation. As the deeply historical-minded Prof. Tiele admits : " Every man in his sound senses, who does not lead the life of a half-dormant animal, philosophizes in his own way "; and " religious doctrine rests on a metaphysical foundation; unless convinced of the reality of a supersensual world, it builds upon sand." [2] Or as Prof. Eucken, the most eloquent champion of this central characteristic of all vital religion, exclaims : " If we never, as a matter of fact, get beyond merely subjective psychological processes, and we can nowhere trace within us the action of cosmic forces; if we in no case experience through them an enlargement, elevation, and transformation of our nature : then not all the endeavours of its well-meaning friends can preserve religion from sinking to the level of a mere illusion. Without a

---

[1] *Rothe's Spekulatives System*, 1899, pp. 25, 26.
[2] *Elements of the Science of Religion*, 1897, Vol. II, pp. 61, 62.

universal and real principle, without hyper-empirical processes, there can be no permanence for religion." [1]

(4) Some kind of philosophy, then, will inevitably accompany, follow, and stimulate religion, were it only as the, necessarily ever inadequate, attempt at giving a fitting expression to the essentially metaphysical character of belief in a supersensible world, in God, in man's spiritual capacities and in God's redemption of man. Not because the patient analysis of the completer human personalities, (as these are to be found throughout the length and breadth of history,) requires the elimination of a wholesome Mysticism and a sober Metaphysic from among the elements and effects of the fullest Manhood and Religion; but because of the ever serious difficulties and the liability to grave abuses attendant upon both these forces, the inevitably excessive reactions against these abuses, and the recurrent necessity of remodelling much of the theory and practice of both, in accordance with the growth of our knowledge of the human mind, (a necessity which, at first sight, seems to stultify all the hyper-empirical claims of both these forces) : only because of this have many men of sense and goodness come to speak as though religion, even at its fullest, could and should get on without either, contenting itself to be a somewhat sentimental, Immanental Ethics.

(5) Yet, against such misgivings, perhaps the most immediately impressive counter-argument is the procession, so largely made up of men and of movements not usually reckoned as exclusively or directly religious, whose very greatness,—one which humanity will not let die,—is closely interwoven with Mystical and Metaphysical affirmations. There are, among philosophers, a Spinoza and a Leibniz, a Fichte, Hegel, Schopenhauer, a Trendelenburg and a Lotze, with the later stages of a John Mill, a Littré, and a Herbert Spencer; among poets, a Pindar and Aeschylus, a Lucretius and Vergil, a Lessing and a Goethe, a Wordsworth and a Browning; among historians, a Thucydides and a Tacitus, a St. Simon and de Tocqueville, a Carlyle, a Jacob Grimm, a Droysen and a Ranke; among scientists, a Copernicus and a Kepler, a Newton, a Lyell, indeed, largely still, also a Darwin; and among men of action, a Moltke and a Gordon, a Burke and a von Stein. Shear any of these men of their Mystical and

[1] *Der Kampf um einen geistigen Lebensinhalt*, 1896, p. 309.

Metaphysical elements, and you will have shorn Samson of his locks.

And if we can frame a contrary list of men of force and distinction, who have represented an un- or even an anti-Mystical and anti-Metaphysical type : Caesar and Hannibal, Napoleon and Bismarck, Voltaire and Laplace, Hume and Bentham, Huxley and Mommsen, we must ever remember the complex truth as to the Polarity of Life,—the strict necessity of the movement towards an intensely close contact with empirical reality, as well as of the movement back to recollection ; the frequent sickliness of the recollective movement, as found in the average practice of life, which cannot but produce a reaction and contrary excess ; and hence the legitimacy of what this second type has got of positiveness and of corrective criticism. Yet here too the greatness will consist directly in what these men are and have, not in what they are not ; and wherever this their brutal-seeming sense of the apparent brutalities of life is combined with an apprehension of a higher world and of a deeper reality, *there* something fuller and more true has been attained than is reached by such strong but incomplete humanity alone.

4. *Religion and Morality, their kinship and difference.*

And, finally, as to Religion and Morality, we should note how that the men, who deny all essential connection between Religion and Mysticism and Religion and Philosophy, ever, when they do retain Religion at all, tend to identify it with Morality, if not as to the motives, yet as to the contents of the two forces. And yet it is not difficult to show that, if the relation between Religion and Morality is closer than that between Religion and Philosophy, though not as intimate as is that between Historical-Institutional Religion and Mysticism : Religion and Morality are nevertheless not identical.

(1) This non-identity is indicated by the broad historical fact that, though the development of Religion tells upon that of Morality, and *vice versa :* yet that the rate of development of these two forces is practically never the same, even in one and the same soul, still less in any one country or race. In each case we get various inequalities between the two developments, which would be impossible, were the two forces different only in name.

We reach again the same conclusion, if we note, what Dr. Edward Caird has so well pointed out, " the imperfection of the subjective religion of the prophets and psalmists of

Israel,"—who nevertheless already possessed a very advanced
type of profoundly ethical religion,—" shown by its inability
to overcome the legal and ceremonial system of worship to
which it was opposed "; as, " in like manner, Protestantism
. . . has never been able decisively to conquer the system of
Rome." [1] For this, as indeed the failure of Buddhism to
absorb and supersede Hindooism, evidently implies that
Religion cannot find its full development and equilibrium in
an exclusive concentration upon Morality Proper, as alone
essential; and hence that complete Religion embraces other
things besides Morality.

Once more we find non-identity between the very Ethics
directly postulated by Religion at its deepest, and the Ethics
immediately required by the Family, Society, the State, Art,
Science, and Philosophy. As Prof. Troeltsch admirably puts
it, " the special characteristic of our modern consciousness
resides in the insistence both upon the Religious, the That-
world Ends, *and* upon the Cultural, This-world Ends,
which latter are taken as Ends-in-themselves : it is precisely in this combination that this consciousness finds its
richness, power, and freedom, but also its painful interior
tension and its difficult problems." " As in Christian Ethics
we must recognize the predominance of an Objective Religious
End,—for here certain relations of the soul to God are the
chief commandments and the supreme good,—so in the
Cultural Ends we should frankly recognize objective Moral
Ends of an Immanental kind." And in seeking after the
right relation between the two, we shall have to conclude
that " Ethics, for us, are not, at first, a unity but a multiplicity :
man grows up amongst a number of moral ends, the unification of which is his life's task and problem, and not its starting-
point." And this multiplicity " is " more precisely " a polarity
in human nature, for it contains two poles—that of Religious
and that of Humane Ethics, neither of which can be ignored
without moral damage, but which, nevertheless, cannot be
brought under a common formula." " We can but keep a
sufficient space open for the action of both forms, so that from
their interaction there may ever result, with the least possible
difficulty, the deepening of the Humane Ends by the Christian
Ethics, and the humanizing of the Christian End by the
Humane Ethics, so that life may become a service of God

---

[1] *The Evolution of Religion*, 1893, Vol. II, p. 313.

within the Cultural Ends, and that the service of God may transfigure the world." [1]

We can perceive the difference between the two forces most clearly in Our Lord's life and teaching—say, the Sermon on the Mount; in the intolerableness of every exegesis which attempts to reduce the ultimate meaning and worth of this world-renewing religious document to what it has of literal applicability in the field of morality proper. Schopenhauer expressed a profound intuition in the words : " It would be a most unworthy manner of speech to declare the sublime Founder of the Christian Religion, whose life is proposed to us as the model of all virtue, to have been the most reasonable of men, and that his maxims contained but the best instruction towards an entirely reasonable life." [2]

(2) The fact is that Religion ever insists, even where it but seems to be teaching certain moral rules and motives as appropriate to this visible world of ours, upon presenting them in the setting of a fuller, deeper world than that immediately required as the field of action and as the justification of ordinary morality. Thus whilst, in Morality Proper, the concepts of Responsibility, Prudence, Merit, Reward, Irretrievableness, are necessarily primary; in Religious Ethics the ideas of Trust, Grace, Heroism, Love, Free Pardon, Spiritual Renovation are, as necessarily, supreme. And hence it is not accidental, although of course not necessary, that we often find men with a keen religious sense but with a defective moral practice or even conception, and men with a strong moral sense and a want of religious perception ; that Mystics, with their keen sense for one element of religion, so often seem, and sometimes are, careless of morality proper ; and that, in such recent cases (deeply instructive in their very aberrations) as that of Nietzsche, we get a fierce anti-Moralism combined with a thirst for a higher and deeper world than this visible one, which not all its fantastic form, nor even all Nietzsche's later rant against concrete religion, can prevent from being essentially religious. [3]

(3) We have then, here, the deepest instance of the law and

[1] " Grund-probleme der Ethik," in *Zeitschrift für Theologie und Kirche*, 1902, pp. 164; 166, 167; 172.

[2] *Die Welt als Wille und Vorstellung*, I, Anhang, p. 653.

[3] A. E. Taylor's *The Problem of Conduct*, 1901, contains, pp. 469–487, a very vigorous and suggestive study of the similarities and differences between Morality and Religion, marred though it is by paradox and impatience.

necessity which we have, so often, found at the shallower levels of the spirit's life. For here, once more, there is one apprehension, force, life,—This-world Morality,—which requires penetration and development, in nowise destruction, by another, a deeper power, That-world Ethics and Religion. Let the one weaken or blunt the edge and impact of the other, and it has, at the same time, weakened itself. For here again we have, not a Thing which simply exists, by persistence in its dull unpenetratingness and dead impenetrability, but a Life, growing by the incorporation and organization, within its ampler range, of lesser lives, each with its own legitimate autonomy.

II. Mysticism and the Limits of Human Knowledge and Experience.

But have not even the most sober-minded of the Partial Mystics greatly exceeded the limits of human knowledge, more or less continuously, throughout their conclusions? Is Kant completely in the wrong? And are not the Positivists right in restricting all certain cognition to the experiences of the senses and to the Mathematico-Physical Sciences built upon those experiences? And, again, is there such a thing at all as specifically Mystical Experience or Knowledge? And, if so, what is its worth?—I must keep the elaboration of the (ultimately connected) question, as to the nature of the realities experienced or known—as to the human spirit and the Divine Spirit, and their inter-relations, hence as to Pantheism and Personality—for the next chapter, and can here but prepare the ground for it, by the elucidation of certain important points in general Epistemology, and of the more obvious characteristics of Mystical apprehension.

1. *Positivist Epistemology an error.*

As regards general Epistemology, we may well take up the following positions.

(1) We cannot but reject, with Prof. Volkelt, as a mere vulgar error, the Positivist limitation of trans-subjectively valid knowledge to direct sense-perception and to the laws of the so-called Empirical Sciences. For, as he shows conclusively, the only fact which is absolutely indubitable, is that of the bare occurrence of our (possibly utterly misleading) sensations and impressions. Some of these are, it is true,

T

accompanied by a certain pressure upon our minds to credit them with trans-subjective validity; and the fact of this (possibly quite misleading) pressure is itself part of our undeniable experience. Yet we can, if we will, treat this pressure also as no more than a meaningless occurrence, and not as evidencing the trans-subjective reality which it seems to indicate. No man, it is true, has ever succeeded in consistently carrying out such a refusal of assent,—since no scepticism is so thorough but that it derives its very power, against the trans-subjective validity of some of the impressions furnished with trans-subjective pressure, from an utterly inconsistent acceptance, as trans-subjectively valid, of other impressions furnished with a precisely similar trans-subjective intimation. Yet the fact remains that, in all such cases of trans-subjective pressure, the mind has " an immediate experience of which the content is precisely this, that we are justified in proceeding with these concepts into what is absolutely beyond the possibility of being experienced by us." " Positivistic Cognition," to which no man, Positivist included, can systematically restrict himself, " abides absolutely within the immediately experienced. Logical Cognition," which every man practises surreptitiously if not avowedly, " exceeds experience at every step, and conceptually determines what is absolutely incapable of being experienced, yet the justification for this kind of cognition is, here also, an immediately experienced certitude." [1]

We have, " then, immediately experienced presentations which of themselves already constitute a knowledge,—our first knowledge, and the only one possessed of absolute indubitableness." And some of these presentations " are accompanied by a kind of immediate certainty or revelation that, in some way, they reach right into the Thing-in-Itself, that they directly express something objectively valid, present in that Thing-in-Itself "; and " this pressure ever involves, should the contradictory of what it enunciates be admitted as objectively existent, the self-destruction of objective reality."—" And this pressure can, in any one case, be resisted by the mind; an act of endorsement, of a kind of faith, is necessary on the part of the mind: for these presentations, furnished with such pressure, do not transform themselves into the Things-in-Themselves directly,—we do not come to see objective reality simply face to face." [2] And we find thus that " in principle the

[1] J. Volkelt, Immanuel Kant's Erkenntnisstheorie, 1879, pp. 258, 259.
[2] Ibid. pp. 206, 208, 209.

entire range of reality, right down to its last depths, lies open
to cognition, proceeding according to the principle of the
necessities of thought. For he who recognizes this principle,
thereby admits that the necessities of thought have trans-
subjective significance, so that, if any affirmation concerning
the ultimate reasons and depths of Reality can be shown to
be necessary in thought, this affirmation possesses as rightful
a claim to trans-subjective validity, as any determination,
necessary in thought, which concern only such parts of the
Thing-in-Itself as are the nearest neighbours to our sense-
impressions concerning it. Everywhere our principle leaves
us only the question whether thought, as a matter of fact, does
or does not react, under the given problems, with the said
logical constraint and pressure." [1]

(2) We can next insist upon how we have thus already
found that the acquisition of even so rudimentary an outline
of Reality, as to be ever in part presupposed in the attacks
of the most radical sceptics, necessarily involves a certain
emotive disposition and volitional action. And, over and
above this partially withholdable assent such quite elementary thinking will also ever require the concomitant energizing
of the picturing faculty. And again, the more interior and
spiritual are this thinking's subject-matters, the more will it
be permeated by, and be inseparable from, deep feeling. It
is then all man's faculties conjoined, it is the whole man, who
normally thus gives, without reflecting on it, his all, to gain
even this elementary nucleus of certainty as to Reality.
"Even receptivity," as Prof. Ward well says, "is activity"; for
even where non-voluntary, it is never indifferent. "Not mere
receptivity, but conative or selective activity, is the essence
of subjective reality." Or, with Prof. Volkelt: "Purely
isolated thought,"—which, in actual life ever more or less of
a fiction, is not rarely set up by individuals as an ideal,—"is,
however intensified and interiorized, something ever only
formal, something, in the final resort, insignificant and
shadowy."—And, concurrently with the recognition of this
fact, man will come to find that "the ultimate Substance or
Power of and in the world,"—that objective reality which
is the essential counterpart to his own subjective reality,—"is
something possessed of a true, deep content and of a positive
aim, and alive according to the analogy of a willing individual

[1] J. Volkelt, *Immanuel Kant's Erkenntnisstheorie*, 1879, p. 244.

The world would thus be a Logical Process only in the sense that this concrete fundamental Power is bound by the ideal necessity of its own nature." [1]

(3) And again, I would note with Volkelt how Kant, owing to his notoriously intense natural tendency to universal Dualism, never admits, even as a point for preliminary settlement, the possibility that our subjective conceptions of Objective Reality may have some true relation to that Reality. His professed ignorance as to the nature of that Reality changes instantaneously, quite unbeknown to himself, into an absolute unvarying, negative knowledge concerning that Reality,—he simply *knows* that it is *utterly heterogeneous* to our conception of it. Thus he finds the view that " God has implanted into the human mind certain categories and concepts of a kind spontaneously to harmonize with things," to be " the most preposterous solution that we could possibly choose." [2] Thus the epistemological difference between Presentation and Thing-in-Itself becomes a metaphysical exclusion of each by the other. And yet we know of no fact, whether of experience or of thought, to prevent something which is *my* presentation existing also, in so far as it is the content of that presentation, outside of this presentment. Indeed Psychology and Epistemology have, driven by every reason and stopped by none, more and more denied and refuted this excessive, indeed gratuitous, Dualism.

As Prof. Henry Jones well puts it : " The hypothesis that knowledge consists of two elements which are so radically different as to be capable of description only by defining each negatively in terms of the other, the pure manifold or differences of sense, and a purely universal or relative thought," breaks down under the fact that " pure thought and the manifold of sense pass into each other, the one proving meaningless and the other helpless in its isolation." These elements " are only aspects of one fact, co-relates mutually penetrating each other, distinguishable in thought, but not separable as existences." Hence we must not " make logical remnants do the work of an intelligence which is never purely formal, upon a material which is

[1] James Ward, " Present Problems of Psychology," in (American) *Philosophical Review*, 1904, p. 607. J. Volkelt, *Kant's Erkenntnisstheorie*, p. 241.

[2] In a letter of 1772, *Briefe*, ed. Berlin Academy, Vol. I, 1900, p. 126.

nowhere a pure manifold ": for " the difference between
the primary data of thought on the one hand, and the
highest kinds of systematized knowledge on the other, is
no difference . . . between a mere particular and a mere
universal, or a mere content and a mere form; but it is a
difference in comprehensiveness of articulation." However
primary may be the distinction of subjective and objective,
" we are not entitled to forget the unity of the reality in which
the distinction takes place." If we begin with the purely
subjective, we must doubtless end there; but then, in spite
of certain, never self-consistent, philosophical hypotheses,
" the purely subjective is as completely beyond our reach as
the purely objective." [1]

Prof. Ward indeed pushes the matter, I think rightly,
even a step further. He points out how readily, owing to
the ambiguous term "consciousness," "we confound experience
with knowledge"; but holds that experience is the wider term.
"Knowledge must fall within experience, and experience
extend beyond knowledge. Thus I am not left to infer my
own being from my knowing. . . . Objective reality is immediately ' given,' or immediately ' there,' not inferred." But
the subjective reality is not immediately given, immediately
there. "There is no such parallelism between the two. . . .
The subjective factor in experience is not *datum* but *reci-
piens : it is not ' there ' but ' here '; a ' here ' relative to that
' there.' " [2] Nothing of this, I think, really conflicts with the
positions we have adopted from Volkelt, since " experience "
is evidently used here in a sense inclusive of the presentations,
the trans-subjective pressure and the endorsement of the
latter's estimations,—the three elements which, according also
to Volkelt, form an organism which even the most daring
subjectivism can never consistently reject. At most, the
term " experience " is more extended in Prof. Ward, since it
includes all three elements, than in Prof. Volkelt, who restricts
it to the two first.

(4) And further, we must take care to find room for
the only unforced explanation of the wondrous fact that
" although," as Dr. Volkelt strikingly says, " the various
schools of philosophy "—this is largely true of those of theology
also,—are " in part essentially determined by historical

[1] H. Jones, *A Critical Account of the Philosophy of Lotze*, 1895, pp. 102–
104; 106, 107; 108, 111.
[2] *The Present Problems*, pp. 606, 607.

currents, forces which follow other standards than those of logical necessity " : yet " these points of view and modes of thought, thus determined by" apparently non-logical "history, subserve nevertheless logical necessity, indeed represent its " slow, intermittent, yet real " progressive realization." The explanation is that " the forces of history are, unbeknown to themselves, planned, in their depths, for agreement with the necessities and ends of thought and of truth." " And thus the different spheres" and levels "of spiritual life and endeavour appear as originally intended for each other, so that each sphere, whilst consciously striving only after its own particular laws and standards, in reality furthers the objects of the rest." For " only the operative presence of such an original, teleo-logical inter-relation can explain how historic forces, by their influence upon, and determination of, philosophical thinking, can, instead of staining and spoiling it by the introduction of religious, artistic, political, and other motives, actually advance it most essentially." [1]—Here then we get a still further en-largement of the already wide range of interaction, within the human mind, between forces which, at first sight, appear simply external to, indeed destructive of, each other; and a corresponding increase in the indications of the immense breadth, depth, and closeness of inter-penetration characterizing the operative ground-plan, the pre-existing Harmony and Teleology of the fundamental forces of Reality. Thus once more man's spirit appears as possessed of a large interiority; and as met, supported and penetrated, by a Spirit stupend-ously rich in spiritual energy.

(5) And finally, let us never forget that " the only experi-ence immediately accessible to us " men, " is our own: this, in spite of its complexity, is the first we know." [2] And this means that we have direct experience and anything like adequate knowledge, (because knowledge from within,) not of things, but of mind and will, of spiritual life struggling within an animal life; and that in face, say, of plant-life, and still more of a pebble or of a star, we have a difficulty as to an at all appropriate and penetrative apprehension, which, if opposite to, is also in a sense greater than, the difficulty inherent to our apprehension of God Himself. For towards this latter apprehension we have got the convergent testimony

---

[1] J. Volkelt, *Erfahrung und Denken*, 1886, p. 485.
[2] James Ward, " On the Definition of Psychology," in *Journal of Psychology*, Vol. I, 1904, p. 25.

of certain great, never quite obliterable facts without us and within ourselves.

There is the upward trend, the ever-increased complexity of organization, the growing depth and interiority in the animate world,—Plant-Life itself being already, very probably, possessed of a vague consciousness, and Man, at the other end of the scale, summing up the tendency of the whole series in a deep self-consciousness which, at the same time, makes him alone keenly aware of the great difference, in the midst of the true kinship, between himself and the humbler members of that one world. For Natural Selection can but describe the results and explain part of the method of this upward trend, but cannot penetrate to its ultimate cause and end.

There is, again, the great, deep fact of the mutually necessary, mutually stimulating presence and interaction, within our own mental and spiritual life, of sense-impressions, imaginative picturings, rational categories, emotional activities, and volitional acts; and, again, of subject and object; and, once more, of general, philosophic Thought and the contingencies of History. For the immanental inter-adaptation and Teleology, that mysteriously link together all these, profoundly disparate-seeming, realms and forces is far too deep-down, it too much surprises, and exacts too much of us, it too much reveals itself, precisely at the end of much labour of our own and in our truest and most balanced moods, as the mostly unarticulated presupposition and explanation of both the great cost and the rich fruitfulness of every approximately complete actuation of all our faculties, each with and in the others, and in and with their appropriate objects, to be permanently ruled out of court as mere sentimentalism or baseless apologetic.

And there is the deepest fact of all, the one which precisely constitutes the specific characteristic of all true humanity, the sense of mental oppression, of intolerable imprisonment inflicted by the very idea of the merely contingent, the simply phenomenal and Finite, and the accompanying noble restlessness and ready dwarfing of all man's best achievements by the agent's own Ideal of Perfection. For this latter sense is, precisely in the greater souls, so spontaneous and so keen, so immensely operative in never leaving our, otherwise indolent and readily self-delusive, self-complacent race fully and long satisfied with anything that passes entirely away, or that is admittedly merely a subjective fancy, even though this fancy be shared by every member of the human race : and this sense operates so explosively within Sceptics as well as Dogmatists, within would-be Agnostic Scientists as well as in the most Intellectualist Theologians ; it so humbles, startles, and alone so braces, sweetens, widens, indeed constitutes our humanity : as to be unforcedly explicable only by admitting that man's spirit's experience is not shut up within man's own clear analysis or picturing of it ; that it is indefinitely wider, and somehow, in its deepest reaches, is directly touched, affected, in part determined, by the Infinite Spirit Itself. " Man never knows how anthropomorphic he is," says Goethe. Yes, but it was a man, Goethe, it is at bottom all men, in proportion as they are fully, sensitively such, who have somehow discovered this truth ; who suffer from its continuous evidences, as spontaneously as from the toothache or from insomnia ; and whose deepest moments give them a vivid sense of how immensely the Spirit, thus directly experienced by their spirit, transcends, and yet also is required by and is immanent in, their keen sense of the Finitude and Contingency present throughout the world of sense-perception and of clear intellectual formulation.

(6) With Plato and Plotinus, Clement of Alexandria and St. Augustine, St. Bernard, Cardinal Nicolas of Coes and Leibniz in the past ; with Cardinal Newman, Professors Maurice Blondel and Henri Bergson Siegwart, Eucken, Troeltsch and Tiele, Igino Petrone and Edward Caird, in the present ; with the explicit assent of practically all the great Mystics of all ages and countries, and the implicit instinct, and at least partial, practical admission, of all sane and developed human souls ; we will then have to postulate here, not merely an intellectual reasoning upon finite data, which would somehow result in so operative a sense of the Infinite ; nor even simply a mental category of Infinitude which, evoked in man by and together with the apprehension of things finite, would, somehow, have so massive, so explosive an effect against our finding satisfaction in the other categories, categories which, after all, would not be more subjective, than itself : but the ontological presence of, and the operative penetration by the Infinite Spirit, within the human spirit. This Spirit's presence would produce, on occasion of man's apprehension or volition of things contingent and finite, the keen sense of disappointment, of contrast with the Simultaneous,

Abiding, and Infinite.—And let the reader note that this is not Ontologism, for we here neither deduce our other ideas from the idea of God, nor do we argue from ideas and their clarity, but from living forces and their operativeness.

We thus get man's spirit placed within a world of varying degrees of depth and interiority, the different levels and kinds of which are necessary, as so many materials, stimulants, obstacles, and objects, for the development of that spirit's various capacities, which themselves again interact the one upon the other, and react upon and within that world. For if man's experience of God is not a mere discursively reasoned conclusion from the data of sense, yet man's spirit experiences the Divine Spirit and the spirits of his fellow-men on occasion of, and as a kind of contrast, background, and support to, the actuation of his senses, imagination, reason, feeling, and volition, and, at least at first and in the long run, not otherwise.

2. *No distinct faculty of Mystical apprehension.*

Is there, then, strictly speaking, such a thing as a specifically distinct, self-sufficing, purely Mystical mode of apprehending Reality? I take it, *distinctly not ;* and that all the errors of the Exclusive Mystic proceed precisely from the contention that Mysticism does constitute such an entirely separate, completely self-supported kind of human experience. —This denial does not, of course, mean that soul does not differ quite indefinitely from soul, in the amount and kind of the recollective, intuitive, deeply emotive element possessed and exercised by it concurrently or alternately with other elements,—the sense of the Infinite within and without the Finite springing up in the soul on occasion of its contact with the Contingent ; nor, again, that these more or less congenital differences and vocations amongst souls cannot and are not still further developed by grace and heroism into types of religious apprehension and life, so strikingly divergent, as, at first sight, to seem hardly even supplementary the one to the other. But it means that, in even the most purely contingent-seeming soul, and in its apparently but Institutional and Historical assents and acts, there ever is, there never can fail to be, *some,* however implicit, however slight, however intermittent, sense and experience of the Infinite, evidenced by at least some dissatisfaction with the Finite, except as this Finitude is an occasion for growth in, and a part-expression of, that Infinite, our true home. And, again, it means, that even the most exclusively mystical-seeming soul ever depends, for the fulness and healthiness of even the most purely mystical of its acts and states, as really upon its past and present contacts with the Contingent, Temporal, and Spatial, and with social facts and elements, as upon its movement of concentration, and the sense and experience, evoked on occasion of those contacts or of their memories, of the Infinite within and around those finitudes and itself.

Only thus does Mysticism attain to its true, full dignity, which consists precisely in being, not everything in any one soul, but something in every soul of man; and in presenting, at its fullest, the amplest development, among certain special natures with the help of certain special graces and heroisms, of what, in some degree and form, is present in every truly human soul, and in such a soul's every, at all genuine and complete, grace-stimulated religious act and state. And only thus does it, as Partial Mysticism, retain all the strength and escape the weaknesses and dangers of would-be Pure Mysticism, as regards the mode and character of Religious Experience, Knowledge, and Life.

3. *The first four pairs of weaknesses and strengths special to the Mystics.*

I take the Mystic's weaknesses and strengths to go together in pairs, and that there are seven such pairs. Only the first four shall be considered here; the fifth and the last two couples are reserved respectively for the following, and for the last section, of this chapter.

(1) The Mystic finds his joy in the recollective movement and movements of the soul; and hence ever tends, *qua* Mystic, to ignore and neglect, or to over-minimize, the absolutely necessary contact of the mind and will with the things of sense. He will often write as though, could he but completely shut off his mind from all sense-perceptions,—even of grand scenery, or noble works of art, or scenes of human devotedness, suffering, and peace,—it would be proportionately fuller of God.—Yet this drift is ever more or less contradicted by his practice, often at the very moment of such argument : for no religious writers are more prolific in vivid imagery derived from noble sensible objects and scenes than are the Mystics, —whose characteristic mood is an intuition, a resting in a kind of vision of things invisible.—And this contradiction is satisfactory, since it is quite certain that if the mind, heart, and will could be completely absorbed, (from the first or for

any length of time,) in the flight from the sensible, it would become as dangerously empty and languid concerning things invisible themselves as, with nothing but an outgoing occupation with the sensible, it would become distracted and feverish. It is this aversion from Outgoing and from the world of sense, of the contemporaneous contingencies environing the soul, that gives to Mysticism, as such, its shadowy character, its floating above, rather than penetrating into, reality,—in contradiction, where this tendency becomes too exclusive, to the Incarnational philosophy and practice of Christianity, and indeed of every complete and sound psychology.

And yet the Incoming, what the deep religious thinker Kierkegaard has so profoundly analyzed in his doctrine of " Repetition," [1]—recollection and peaceful browsing among the materials brought in by the soul's Outgoing,—is most essential. Indeed it is the more difficult, and, though never alone sufficient, yet ever the more centrally religious, of the two movements necessary for the acquisition of spiritual experience and life.

(2) Again, the Mystic finds his full delight in all that approximates most nearly to Simultaneity, and Eternity; and consequently turns away, qua Mystic, from the Successive and Temporal presented by History.—Yet here also there are two movements, both necessary for man. He will, by the one, once more in fullest sympathy with the grand Christian love of lowliness, strive hard to get into close, and ever closer, touch with the successivenesses of History, especially those of Our Lord's earthly life and of His closest followers. Without this touch he will become empty, inflated, as St. Teresa found to be the case with herself, when following the false principle of deliberate and systematic abstraction from Christ's temporal words and acts : for man's soul, though it does not energize in mere Clock-Time, cannot grow if we attempt to eliminate Duration, that interpenetrative, over-lapping kind of Succession, which is already, as it were, halfway to the Simultaneity of God. It is this aversion from Clock-Time Succession and even from Duration which gives to Mysticism, as such, its remarkable preference for Spatial images, and its strong bent towards concepts of a Static and Determinist type, profoundly antagonistic though these are

[1] There is a good description of this doctrine in H. Höffding's *Sören Kierkegaard*, Stuttgart, 1896, pp. 100–104.

to the Dynamic and Libertarian character which ever marks the occasions and conditions for the acquiring of religious experience.

And yet, here again, the Mystic is clinging, even one-sidedly, to the more central, more specifically religious, of the two movements. For it is certain that God is indeed Simultaneous and Eternal; that it is right thus to try and apprehend, what appears to us stretched out successively in time, as simultaneously present in the one great Now of God; and that our deepest experiences testify to History itself being ever more than mere process, and to have within it a certain contribution from, a certain approximation to and expression of, Eternity.

(3) And again, the Mystic finds his joy in the sense of a Pure Reception of the Purely Objective; that God should do all and should receive the credit of all, is here a primary requirement.—And yet all penetrating Psychology, Epistemology, and Ethics find this very receptivity, however seemingly only such, to be, where healthy and fruitful, ever an action, a conation of the soul,—an energizing and volition which, as we have seen, are present in its very cognition of anything affirmed by it as trans-subjective, from a grain of sand up to the great God Himself. This antipathy to even a relative, God-willed independence and power of self-excitation, gives Mysticism, as such, its constant bent towards Quietism; and hence, with regard to the means and nature of knowledge, its tendency to speak of such a purely spiritual effect as Grace, and such purely spiritual beings as the Soul and God, as though they were literally sensible objects sensibly impressing themselves upon the Mystic's purely passive senses. This tendency reinforces the Mystic's thirst for pictorial, simultaneous presentation and intuition of the verities apprehended by him, but is in curious contradiction to his even excessive conceptions concerning the utter separateness and difference from all things material of all such spiritual realities.—And yet, here too, it is doubtless deeply important ever to remember, and to act in accordance with, the great truth that God Himself is apprehended by us only if there be action of our own, and that, from elementary moral dispositions right up to consummate sanctity, the whole man has ever to act and will more and more manysidedly, fully, and persistently.

But the corresponding, indeed the anterior and more

centrally religious, truth here is, that all this range of our activity could never begin, and, if it could, would lose itself *in vacuo*, unless there already were Reality around it and within it, as the stimulus and object for all this energizing,—a Reality which, as Prof. Ward has told us with respect to Epistemology, must, for a certain dim but most true experience of ours, be simply given, not sought and found. And indeed the operations of Grace are ever more or less penetrating and soliciting, though nowhere forcing, the free assent of the natural soul : we should be unable to seek God unless He had already found us and had thus, deep down within ourselves, caused us to seek and find Him. And hence thus again the most indispensable, the truest form of experience underlies reasoning, and is a kind of not directly analyzable, but indirectly most operative, intuition or instinct of the soul.

(4) And yet the Mystic, in one of his moods (the corresponding, contradictory mood of a Pantheistic identification of his true self with God shall be considered in our next chapter), finds his joy in so exalting the difference of nature between himself and God, and the incomprehensibility of God for every finite intelligence, as,—were we to press his words,—to cut away all ground for any experience or knowledge sufficient to justify him in even a guess as to what God is like or is not like, and for any attempt at intercourse with, and at becoming like unto, One who is so utterly unlike himself.

4. *Criticism of the fourth pair, mystical " Agnosticism."*

Now this acutely paradoxical position, of an entire certainty as to God's complete difference from ourselves, has been maintained and articulated, with a consistency and vividness beyond that of any Mystic known to me, by that most stimulating, profound, tragically non-mystical, religious ascetic and thinker, the Lutheran Dane, Sören Kierkegaard (1813–1855). His early friend, but philosophical opponent, Prof. Höffding, describes him as insisting that " the suffering incident to the religious life is necessarily involved in the very nature of the religious relation. For the relation of the soul to God is a relation to a Being utterly different from man, a Being which cannot confront man as his Superlative and Ideal, and which nevertheless is to rule within him." " What wonder, then," as Kierkegaard says, " if the Jew held that the vision of God meant death, and if the Heathen believed that to enter upon relations with God was the beginning of insanity ? " For the man who lives for God

" is a fish out of water." [1]—We have here what, if an error, is yet possible only to profoundly religious souls; indeed it would be easy to point out very similar passages in St. Catherine and St. John of the Cross. Yet Höffding is clearly in the right in maintaining that " Qualitative or Absolute difference abolishes all possibility of any positive relation. . . . If religious zeal, in its eagerness to push the Object of religion to the highest height, establishes a yawning abyss between this Object and the life whose ideal It is still to remain,—such zeal contradicts itself. For a God who is not Ideal and Exemplar, is no God." [2]

Berkeley raised similar objections against analogous positions of the Pseudo-Dionysius, in his Alciphron in 1732.[3] Indeed the Belgian Jesuit, Balthazar Corderius, has a very satisfactory note on this matter in his edition, in 1634, of the Areopagite,[4] in which he shows how all the negative propositions of Mystical Theology, e. g. " God is not Being, not Life," presuppose a certain affirmative position, e. g. " God is Being and Life, in a manner infinitely more sublime and perfect than we are able to comprehend "; and gives reasons and authorities, from St. Jerome to St. Thomas inclusive, for holding that some kind and degree of direct confused knowledge (I should prefer, with modern writers, to call it experience) of God's existence and nature is possessed by the human soul, independently of its reasoning from the data of sense.

St. Thomas's admissions are especially striking, as he usually elaborates a position which ignores, and would logically exclude, such " confused knowledge." In his *Exposition and Questions on the Book of Boetius on the Trinity*, after arguments to show that we know indeed *that* God is, but not *what* He is,—at most only what He is not, he says : " We should recognize, however, that it is impossible, with regard to anything, to know whether it exists, unless, in some way or other, we know *what* it is, either with a perfect or with a confused knowledge. . . . Hence also with regard to God,—we could not know whether He exists, unless we somehow knew *what* He is, even though in a confused manner." And this

<hr/>

[1] Höffding's *Kierkegaard*, pp. 119, 120.
[2] *Ibid.* p. 123.
[3] See *Works*, ed. London, 1898, Vol. II, pp. 299–306.
[4] *Quaestio Mystica*, at the end of the notes to Chapter V of Dionysius's *Mystical Theology*, ed. Migne, 1889, Vol. I, pp. 1050–1058.

knowledge of *what* He is, is interestingly, because unconsciously, admitted in one of the passages directed to proving that we can but know *that* He is. " In our earthly state we cannot attain to a knowledge of Himself beyond the fact that He exists. And yet, among those who know *that* He is, the one knows this more perfectly than the other." [1] For it is plain that, even if the knowledge of the existence of something were possible without any knowledge of that thing's nature, no difference or increase in such knowledge of the thing's bare existence would be possible. The different degrees in the knowledge, which is here declared to be one concerning the bare existence of God, can, as a matter of fact, exist only in knowledge concerning His nature. I shall have to return to this great question further on.

Here I would only point out how well Battista Vernazza has, in her *Dialogo*, realized the importance of a modification in such acutely dualistic statements as those occasionally met with in the *Vita*. For, in the *Dialogo*, the utter qualitative difference between God and the Soul, and the Soul and the Body, which find so striking an utterance in one of Catherine's moods, is ever carefully limited to the soul's sinful acts and habits, and to the body's unspiritualized condition; so that the soul, when generous and faithful to God's grace, can and does grow less and less unlike God, and the body can, in its turn, become more and more an instrument and expression of the soul. A pity only that Battista has continued Catherine's occasional over-emphasis in the parallel matter of the knowledge of God : since, even in the *Dialogo*, we get statements which, if pressed, would imply that even the crudest, indeed the most immoral conception of God is, objectively, no farther removed from the reality than is the most spiritual idea that man can attain of Him.

It would indeed be well if the Christian Mystics who, since about 500 A.D., are more and more dependent for their formulations upon the Areopagite, had followed, in this matter, not his more usual and more paradoxical, but his exceptional, thoroughly sober vein of teaching,—that contained in the third chapter of his *Mystical Theology*, where he finds degrees of worth and approximation among the affirmative attributions, and degrees of unfitness and distance among the negative ones. " Are not life and goodness more

---

[1] *In Librum Boetii de Trinitate*, in D. Thomae Aquinatis *Opera*, ed. altera Veneta, Vol. VIII, 1776, pp. 341*b*, 342*a*; 291*a*.

cognate to Him than air and stone? And is He not further removed from debauchery and wrath, than from ineffableness and incomprehensibility "? [1] But such a scale of approximations would be utterly impossible did we not somehow, at least dimly, experience or know *what* He is.

We shall then have to amend the Mystic's apparent Agnosticism on three points. We shall have to drop any hard and fast distinction between knowledge of God's Existence and knowledge of His Nature, since both necessarily more or less stand and fall together. We shall have to replace the terms as to our utter ignorance as to what He is, by terms expressive of an experience which, if not directly and independently clear and analyzable to the reflex, critical reason, can yet be shown to be profoundly real and indefinitely potent in the life of man's whole rational and volitional being. It is this dim, deep experience which ever causes our reflex knowledge of God to appear no knowledge at all. And we shall reject any absolute qualitative difference between the soul's deepest possibilities and ideals, and God; and shall, in its stead, maintain an absolute difference between God, and all our downward inclinations, acts, and habits, and an indefinite difference, in worth and dignity, between God and the very best that, with His help, we can aim at and become. With regard to every truly existent subject-matter, we can trace the indefinitely wider range and the more delicate penetration possessed by our dim yet true direct contact and experience, as contrasted with our reflex analysis concerning all such contacts and experiences; and this surplusage is at its highest in connection with God, Who is not simply a Thing alongside of other things, but the Spirit, our spirit's Origin, Sustainer, and End, " in whom we live and move and have our being."

III. MYSTICISM AND THE QUESTION OF EVIL.

Introductory: Exclusive and Inclusive Mysticism in Relation to Optimism.

The four couples of weaknesses and corresponding strong points characteristic of Mysticism that we have just considered, and the fact that, in each case, they ever spring respectively

[1] *Mystical Theology*, Dr. Parker, pp. 135, 136. I have somewhat modified Parker's rendering.

from an attempt to make Mysticism be the all of religion, and from a readiness to keep it as but one of the elements more or less present in, and necessary for, every degree and form of the full life of the human soul : make one wish for two English terms, as useful as are the German names " Mystik " and "Mystizismus," for briefly indicating respectively "the legitimate share of Feeling in the constitution of the religious life, and the one-sidedness of a religion in which the Understanding and the Will," and indeed also the Memory and the Senses, with their respective variously external occasions, vehicles, and objects, " do not come to their rights," as Prof. Rauwenhoff well defines the matter.[1] I somehow shrink from the term " Mysticality " for his " Mystizismus " ; and must rest content with the three terms—of " Mysticism," as covering both the right and the wrong use of feeling in religion ; and of " True " or " Inclusive Mysticism," and of " Pseudo-" or " Exclusive Mysticism," as denoting respectively the legitimate, and the (quantitatively or qualitatively) mistaken, share of emotion in the religious life.

Now the four matters, which we have just considered, have allowed us to reach an answer not all unlike that of Nicolas of Coes, Leibniz, and Hegel,—one which, if it remained alone or quite final, would, in face of the fulness of real life, strike us all, nowadays, as somewhat superficial, because too Optimistic and Panlogistic in its trend. The fifth set of difficulties and problems now to be faced will seem almost to justify Schopenhauer at his gloomiest. Yet we must bear in mind that our direct business here is not with the problem of Evil in general, but only with the special helps and hindrances, afforded by inclusive and by Exclusive Mysticism respectively, towards apprehending the true nature of Evil and turning even it into an occasion for a deeper good. In this case the special helps and hindrances fall under three heads.

I. *Mysticism too optimistic. Evil positive, but not supreme.*

(1) First of all, I would strongly insist upon the following great fact to which human life and history bear witness, if we but take and test these latter on a large scale and with a patient persistency. It is, that not the smoother, easier times and circumstances in the lives of individuals and of peoples, but, on the contrary, the harder and hardest trials of every

---

[1] *Religions-philosophie*, German tr. ed. 1894, p. 116. His scheme finds three psychological forms and constituents in all religion, Intellectualism, Mysticism, Moralism, each with its own advantages and dangers.

conceivable kind, and the unshrinking, full acceptance of these, as part of the price of conscience and of its growing light, have ever been the occasions of the deepest trust in and love of God to which man has attained. In Jewish History, the Exile called forth a Jeremiah and Ezekiel, and the profound ideal of the Suffering Servant; the persecution of Antiochus Epiphanes raised up a Judas Maccabaeus; and the troubles under the Emperor Hadrian, a Rabbi Akiba. And in Christian History, the persecutions from Nero to Robespierre have each occasioned the formation of heroic lovers of Love Crucified. And such great figures do not simply manage to live, apart from all the turmoil, in some Mystic upper region of their own; but they face and plunge into the very heart of the strife, and get and give spiritual strength on occasion of this closest contact with loneliness, outrage, pain, and death. And this fact can be traced throughout history.

Not as though suffering automatically deepens and widens man into a true spiritual personality,—of itself it does not even tend to this; nor as though there were not souls grown hard or low, or frivolous or bitter, under suffering,—to leave madness and suicide unconsidered,—souls in which it would be difficult to find any avoidable grave fault. But that, wherever there is the fullest, deepest, interiority of human character and influence, *there* can ever be found profound trials and sufferings which have been thus utilized and transfigured. It is doubtless Our Lord's uniquely full and clear proclamation of this mysterious efficacity of all suffering nobly borne; above all it is the supreme exemplification and fecundity of this deepest law of life, afforded and imparted by His own self-immolation, that has given its special power to Christianity, and, in so doing, has, more profoundly than ever before or elsewhere, brought home to us a certain Teleology here also,—the deepest ever discovered to man. For though we fail in our attempts at explaining how or why, with an All-knowing, All-powerful, and All-loving God, there can be Evil at all, we can but recognize the law, which is ever being brought home to us, of a mysterious capacity for purification and development of man's spiritual character, on occasion and with the help of trouble, pain, and death itself.

(2) Now all this, we must admit, is practised and noted directly and in detail, only by the Ascetical and the Outward-going elements in Religion; whereas Mysticism, as such, is optimistic, not only as is Christianity, with respect to the end,

but, in practice, with regard to the actual state of things already encircling it as well. For so careful a selection and so rigorous an abstraction is practised by Mysticism, as such, towards the welter of contingencies around it, that the rough shocks, the bitter tonics, the expansive birth-pangs of the spirit's deeper life, in and by means of the flux of time and sense, of the conflict with hostile fellow-creatures, and of the claimfulness of the lower self, are known by it only in their result, not in their process, or rather only as this process ebbs and fades away, in such recollective moments, into the distance.

No wonder, then, that Mysticism, as such, has ever tended to deny all positive character to Evil. We have already found how strongly this is the case with the prince of Mystic philosophers, Plotinus. But even St. Augustine, with his massive experience, and (in his other mood) even excessive realization, of the destructive force of Evil and of the corrupt inclinations of man's heart, has one whole large current of teaching expressive of the purely negative character of Evil. The two currents, the hot and concrete, and the cold and abstract one, appear alternately in the very *Confessions,* of 397 A.D. There, ten years after his conversion, he can write : " All things that are corrupted, are deprived of good. But, if they are deprived of all good, they will cease to exist. . . . In so far, then, as they exist, they are good. . . . Evil is no substance." Notwithstanding such Neo-Platonist interpretations, he had found Evil a terribly powerful force ; the directly autobiographical chapters of this same great book proclaim this truth with unsurpassable vividness,—he is here fully Christian.[1] And in his unfinished work against the Pelagianizing Monk Julianus, in 429 A.D., he even declares—characteristically, whilst discussing the Origin of Sin : " Such and so great was Adam's sin, that it was able to turn (human) nature itself into this evil." Indeed, already in 418, he had maintained that " this wound " (of Original Sin) " forces all that is born of that human race to be under the Devil, so that the latter, so to speak, plucks the fruit from the fruit-tree of his own planting." [2]

---

[1] *Confessions :* " Evil, Negative," VII, 12, etc. " Evil, Positive," VI, 15 ; VIII, 5, 11, etc.

[2] *Opus Imperfectum,* III, 56, ed. Ben., Vol. X, col. 1750*b*. *De Nuptiis et Concupiscentia,* I, 23, *ibid.* col. 625*a*.—M. L. Grandgeorge, in his memoir *St. Augustin et le Neo-Platonisme,* 1896, gives an interesting collection of such Negative and Positive declarations, and traces the former to their precise sources in Plotinus, pp. 126, 127 ; 130, 131.

Pseudo-Dionysius, writing about 500 A.D., has evidently no such massive personal experience to oppose to the Neo-Platonic influence, an influence which, in the writings of Proclus (who died 485 A.D.), is now at its height. " Evil," he says, " is neither in Demons nor in us, as an existent (positive) evil, but (only) as a failure and dearth of the perfection of our own proper goods." [1] He says this and more of the same kind, but nothing as to the dread power of Evil. St. Thomas Aquinas (who died in 1271 A.D.) is, as we know, largely under the influence of the Negative conception : thus " the stain of sin is not something positive, existent in the soul. . . . It is like a shadow, which is the privation of light." [2]

Catherine, though otherwise much influenced by the Negative conception, as *e. g.* in her definition of a soul possessed by the Evil Spirit as one suffering from a " privation of love," finds the stain of sin, doubtless from her own experience, to be something distinctly positive, with considerable power of resistance and propagation.[3]—Mother Juliana of Norwich had, in 1373, also formulated both conceptions. " I saw not Sin, for I believe it hath no manner of substance, nor no part of being " : Neo-Platonist theory. " Sin is so vile and so mickle for to hate, that it may be likened to no pain. . . . All is good but Sin, and naught is evil but Sin " : Christian experience.[4]

Eckhart had, still further back (he died in 1327 A.D.), insisted much that " Evil is nothing but privation, or falling away from Being; not an effect, but a defect " : [5] yet he also finds much work to do in combating this somehow very powerful " defect."—Not till we get to Spinoza (who died in 1677) do we get the Negative conception pushed home to its only logical conclusion : " By Reality and Perfection, I mean the same thing. . . . All knowledge of Evil is inadequate knowledge. . . . If the human mind had nothing but adequate ideas, it would not form any notion of Evil." [6]

(3) As regards the Christian Mystics, their negative conception of evil, all but completely restricted as it was to cosmolo-

[1] *Divine Names*, ch. iv, sec. xxiv.

[2] *Summa Theol.*, I, ii, qu. 86, art. 1 ad 3.

[3] *Vita*, pp. 39b, 116b.

[4] *Sixteen Revelations*, ed. 1902, pp. 69, 70.

[5] Meister Ekhart's " Lateinische Schriften," published by Denifle, *Archiv f. Litteratur u. Kirchengeschichte des M. A.*, 1886, p. 662.

[6] *Ethica*, II, def. vi; IV, prop. lxiv et coroll.; ed. Van Vloten et Land, 1895, Vol. I, pp. 73, 225.

gical theory, did those Mystics themselves little or no harm; since their tone of feeling and their volitional life, indeed a large part of their very speculation, were determined, not by such Neo-Platonist theories, but by the concrete experiences of Sin, Conscience, and Grace, and by the great Christian historical manifestation of the powers of all three.—It is clear too that our modern alternative : " positive-negative," is not simply identical with the scholastic alternative : " substantial-accidental," which latter alternative is sometimes predominant in the minds of these ancient theorizers; and that, once the question was formulated in the latter way, they were profoundly right in refusing to hypostatize Evil, in denying that there exists any distinct thing or being wholly bad.—Yet it is equally clear how very Greek and how little Christian is such a preoccupation (in face of the question of the nature of Evil) with the concepts of Substance and Accident, rather than with that of Will; and how strangely insufficient, in view of the tragic conflicts and ruins of real life, is all even sporadic, denial, of a certain obstructive and destructive efficacy in the bad will, and of a mysterious, direct perversity and formal, intentional malignity in that will at its worst.

(4) On these two points it is undeniable that Kant (with all his self-contradictions, insufficiencies, and positive errors on other important matters) has adequately formulated the practical dispositions and teachings of the fully awakened Christian consciousness, and hence, pre-eminently, of the great Saints in the past, although, in the matter of the perverse will, the Partial Mystics have, even in their theory, (though usually only as part of the doctrine of Original Sin,) largely forestalled his analysis. " Nowhere in this our world, nowhere even outside it, is anything thinkable as good without any reservation, but the good will alone." " That a corrupt inclination to evil is rooted in man, does not require any formal proof, in view of the clamorous examples furnished to all men by the experience of human behaviour. If you would have such cases from the so-called state of nature, where some philosophers have looked for the chief home of man's natural goodness, you need only compare, with such an hypothesis, the unprovoked cruelties enacted in Tofoa, New Zealand . . . and the ceaseless scenes of murder in the North-Western American deserts, where no human being derives the slightest advantage from them,—and you

will quickly have more than sufficient evidence before you
to induce the abandonment of such a view. But if you
consider that human nature is better studied in a state of
civilization, since there its gifts have a better chance of development,—you will have to listen to a long melancholy
string of accusations : of secret falseness, even among friends ;
of an inclination to hate him to whom we owe much ; of a
cordiality which yet leaves the observation true that ' there
is something in the misfortune of even our best friend which
does not altogether displease us' : so that you will quickly have
enough of the vices of culture, the most offensive of all, and
will prefer to turn away your look from human nature
altogether, lest you fall yourself into another vice,—that of
hatred of mankind." [1]

It is sad to think how completely this virile, poignant
sense of the dread realities of human life again disappeared
from the teachings of such post-Kantians as Hegel and
Schleiermacher,—in other important respects so much more
satisfactory than Kant. As Mr. Tennant has well said, in
a stimulating book which, on this point at least, voices the
unsophisticated, fully awakened conscience and Christian
sense with refreshing directness, " for Jesus Christ and for the
Christian consciousness, sin means something infinitely deeper
and more real than what it can have meant for Spinoza or
the followers of Hegel." [2] Here again we have now in
Prof. Eucken, a philosopher who, free from ultimate Pessimism, lets us hear once more those tones which are alone
adequate to the painful reality. " In great things and in
small, there exists an evil disposition beyond all simple
selfishness : hatred and envy, even where the hater's self-
interest is not touched ; an antipathy to things great and
divine ; a pleasure found in the disfigurement or destruction
of the Good. . . . Indeed the mysterious fact of Evil, as a
positive opposition to Good, has never ceased to occupy the
deepest minds. . . . The concept of moral guilt cannot be got
rid of, try as we may." [3]

(5) And yet even with regard to this matter, Mysticism re-

[1] *Grundlegung zur Metaphysik der Sitten*, 1785, *Werke*, ed. Berlin
Academy, Vol. IV, 1903, p. 393. *Religion innerhalb der Grenzen der
reinen Vernunft*, 1793, *Werke*, ed. Hartenstein, Vol. VI, 1868, pp. 127,
128.

[2] *The Origin and Propagation of Sin*, 1902, p. 125.

[3] *Wahrheits-gehalt der Religion*, 1901, pp. 271, 272.

presents a profound compensating truth and movement, which we cannot, without grave detriment, lose out of the complete religious life. For in life at large, and in human life and history in particular, it would be sheer perversity to deny that there is much immediate, delightful, noble Beauty, Truth, and Goodness; and these also have a right to the soul's careful, ruminating attention. And it is the Mystical element that furnishes this rumination.—Again, " it is part of the essential character of human consciousness, as a Synthesis and an organizing Unity, that, as long as the life of that consciousness lasts at all, not only contrast and tension, but also concentration and equilibrium must manifest themselves. Taking life's standard from life itself, we cannot admit its decisive constituent to lie in tension alone." [1] And it is the Mystical mood that helps to establish this equilibrium.—And finally, deep peace, an overflowing possession and attainment, and a noble joy, are immensely, irreplaceably powerful towards growth in personality and spiritual fruitfulness. Nothing, then, would be more shortsighted than to try and keep the soul from a deep, ample, recollective movement, from feeding upon and relishing, from as it were stretching itself out and bathing in, spiritual air and sunshine, in a rapt admiration, in a deep experience of the greatness, the beauty, the truth, and the goodness of the World, of Life, of God.

2. *Mysticism and the Origin of Evil.*

The second hindrance and help, afforded respectively by Exclusive and by Inclusive Mysticism in the matter of Evil, concerns the question of its Origin.

(1) Now it appears strange at first sight that, instead of first directly realizing and picturing the undeniable, profoundly important facts of man's interior conflict, his continuous lapses from his own deepest standard, and his need of a help not his own to become what he cannot but wish to be, and of leaving the theory as to how man came by this condition to the second place; the Mystics should so largely—witness Catherine— directly express only this theory, and should face what is happening *hic et nunc* all but exclusively under the picture of the prehistoric beginnings of these happenings, in the state of innocence and the lapse of the first man. For men of other religious modalities have held this doctrine as firmly as the Mystics, yet have mostly dwelt directly upon the central core

[1] Prof. Höffding, in his *Sören Kierkegaard*, pp. 130, 131.

of goodness and the weakness and sinfulness to be found in man; whilst the Mystics had even less scruple than other kinds of devout souls in embodying experimental truths in concepts and symbols other than the common ones.

(2) I think that, here again, it was the Neo-Platonist literary influence, so strong also on other points with the Mystics of the past, and a psychological trend characteristic of the Mystical habit of mind, which conjoined thus to concentrate the Mystic's attention upon the doctrines of Original Justice and of a First Lapse, and to give to these doctrines the peculiar form and tone taken on by them here. We have noted, for instance, in the case of Catherine herself, how powerfully her thought and feeling, as to the first human soul's first lapse into sin, is influenced by the idea of each human soul's lapse into a body; and we have found this latter idea to be, notwithstanding its echoes in the Deutero-Canonical Book of Wisdom and in one non-doctrinal passage in St. Paul, not Christian but Neo-Platonist. Yet it is this strongly antibody idea that could not fail to attract Mysticism, as such.— And the conception as to the plenary righteousness of that first soul before its lapse, which she gets from Christian theology, is similarly influenced, in her theorized emotion and thought, by the Neo-Platonist idea of every soul having already existed, perfectly spotless, previous to its incarnation: a view which could not but immensely attract such a high-strung temperament, with its immense requirement of something fixed and picturable on which to rest. Thus here the ideal for each soul's future would have been already real in each soul's past. In this past the soul would have been, as it were, a mirror of a particular fixed size and fixed intensity of lustre; its business here below consists in removing the impurities adhering to this mirror's surface, and in guarding it against fresh stains.

(3) Now it is well known how it was St. Augustine, that mighty and daring, yet at times ponderous, intellect, who, (so long a mental captive of the Manichees and then so profoundly influenced by Plotinus,) was impelled, by the experiences of his own disordered earlier life and by his ardent African nature, to formulate by far the most explicit and influential of the doctrines upon these difficult matters. And if, with the aid of the Abbé Turmel's admirable articles on the subject, we can, with a fairly open mind, study his successive, profoundly varying, speculations and conclusions concerning the Nature and

Origin of Sin,[1] we shall not fail to be deeply impressed with the largely impassable maze of opposite extremes, contradictions and difficulties of every kind, in which that adventurous mind involved itself.—And to these difficulties immanent to the doctrine,—at least, in the form it takes in St. Augustine's hands,—has, of course, to be added the serious moral danger that would at once result, were we, by too emphatic or literal an insistence upon the true guiltiness of Original sin, to weaken the chief axiom of all true morality—that the concurrence of the personality, in a freely-willed assent, is necessarily involved in the idea of sin and guilt.—And now the ever-accumulating number and weight of even the most certain facts and most moderate inductions of Anthropology and Ethnology are abolishing all evidential grounds for holding a primitive high level of human knowledge and innocence, and a single sudden plunge into a fallen estate, as above, apparently against, all our physiological, psychological, historical evidences and analogies, (which all point to a gradual rise from lowly beginnings,) and are reducing such a conception to a pure postulate of Theology.

Yet Anthropology and Ethnology leave in undisturbed possession the great truths of Faith that " man's condition denotes a fall from the Divine intention, a parody of God's purpose in human history," and that "sin is exceedingly sinful for us in whom it is a deliberate grieving of the Holy Spirit " ; and they actually reinforce the profound verities that " the realization of our better self is a stupendously difficult task," and as to " Man's crying need of grace, and his capacity for a gospel of Redemption." [2]   But they point, with a force great in proportion to the highly various, cumulatively operative, immensely interpretative character of the evidence,—to the conclusion that " Sin," as the Anglican Archdeacon Wilson strikingly puts it, "is . . . the survival or misuse of habits and tendencies that were incidental to an earlier stage of development. . . . Their sinfulness would thus lie in their anachronism, in their resistance to the . . . Divine force that makes for moral development and righteousness." Certainly

---

[1] " Le Dogme du Péché Originel dans S. Augustin," *Revue d'Histoire et de Littérature Religieuses*, 1901, 1902. See too F. R. Tennant, *The Sources of the Doctrine of the Fall and Original Sin*, 1903, which, however, descends only to St. Ambrose inclusively.

[2] So F. R. Tennant, *The Origin and Propagation of Sin*, 1902, pp. 131, 110.

"the human infant" appears to careful observers, as Mr. Tennant
notes, " as simply a non-moral animal," with corresponding
impulses and propensities. According to this view " morality
consists in the formation of the non-moral material of nature
into character . . ." ; so that " if goodness consists essentially
in man's steady moralization of the raw material of morality, its
opposite, sin, cannot consist in the material awaiting moralization, but in the will's failure to completely moralize it."
" Evil " would thus be " not the result of a transition from the
good, but good and evil would " both alike " be voluntary
developments from what is ethically neutral." [1] Dr. Wilson
finds, accordingly, that " this conflict of freedom and conscience
is precisely what is related as ' the Fall ' *sub specie historiae*."
Scripture " tells of the fall of a creature from unconscious
innocence to conscious guilt. But this fall from innocence "
would thus be, " in another sense, a rise to a higher grade of
being." [2]

(4) It is, in any case, highly satisfactory for a Catholic
to remember that the acute form, given to the doctrine of
Original Sin by St. Augustine, has never been finally accepted
by the Catholic Roman Church ; indeed, that the Tridentine
Definition expressly declares that Concupiscence does not, in
strictness, possess the nature of Sin, but arises naturally, on
the withdrawal of the *donum superadditum*,—so that Mr.
Tennant can admit, in strictest accuracy, that " in this respect,
the Roman theology is more philosophical than that of the
Symbols of Protestant Christendom." [3] It is true that the
insistence upon " Original Sin " possessing somehow " the true
and proper nature of Sin " remains a grave difficulty, even
in this Tridentine formulation of the doctrine ; whilst the
objections, already referred to as accumulating against the
theory in general, retain some of their cogency against other
parts of this decree.—Yet we have here an impressive proclamation of the profoundest truths : the spiritual greatness
of God's plan for us, the substantial goodness of the material
still ready to our hand for the execution of that plan, and
His necessary help ever ready from the first ; the reality
of our lapse, away from all these, into sin, and of the effects of
such lapse upon the soul ; the abiding conflict between sense
and spirit, the old man and the new, within each one of us ;

---

[1] F. R. Tennant, *The Origin and Propagation of Sin*, 1902, pp. 82, 95 ;
107, 108 ; 115.
[2] *Ibid.* p. 83.   [3] *Ibid.* p. 153.

and the close solidarity of our poor, upward-aspiring, down-ward-plunging race, in evil as well as in good.

(5) And as to the Christian Mystics, their one particular danger here,—that of a Static Conception of man's spirit as somehow constituted, from the first, a substance of a definite, final size and dignity, which but demands the removal of disfiguring impurities, is largely eliminated, even in theory, and all but completely overcome in practice, by the doctrine and the practice of Pure Love. For in " Charity " we get a directly dynamic, expansive conception and experience : man's spirit is, at first, potential rather than actual, and has to be conquered and brought, as it were, to such and such a size and close-knitness of organization, by much fight with, and by the slow transformation of, the animal and selfish nature. Thus Pure Love, Charity, Agape, has to fight it out, inch by inch, with another, still positive force, impure love, concu-piscence, Eros, in all the latter's multiform disguises. Here Purity has become something intensely positive and of bound-less capacities for growth ; as St. Thomas says, " Pure Love has no limit to its increase, for it is a certain participation in the Infinite Love, which is the Holy Spirit." [1]—In this utterly real, deeply Christian way do these Mystics overcome Neo-Platonist static abstractions, and simultaneously regain, in their practical theory and emotional perception, the great truth of the deep, subtle force of Evil, against which Pure Love has to stand, in virile guard, as long as earth's vigil lasts. And the longest and most difficult of these conflicts is found, —here again in utterly Christian fashion,—not in the sensual tendencies proceeding from the body, but in the self-adoration, the solipsism of the spirit. We have found this in Catherine : at her best she ever has something of the large Stoic joy at being but a citizen in a divine Cosmopolis ; yet but Love and Humility, those profoundest of the Christian affections, have indefinitely deepened the truth of the outlook, and the range of the work to be done, in and for herself and others.

(6) Yet even apart from Pure Love, Mysticism can accurately be said to apprehend an important truth when, along its static line of thought and feeling, it sees each soul as, from the first, a substance of a particular, final size. For each soul is doubtless intended, from the first, to express a particular thought and wish of God, to form one, never simply replaceable

---

[1] *Summa Theol.*, II, ii, qu. 24, art. 7, in corp.

member in His Kingdom, to attain to a unique kind and degree of personality : and though it can refuse to endorse and carry out this plan, the plan remains within it, in the form of never entirely suppressible longings. The Mystic, then, sees much here also.

3. *The warfare against Evil. Pseudo-Mysticism.*

The third of the relations between Mysticism and the conception and experience of Evil requires a further elucidation of an important distinction, which we have already found at work all along, more or less consciously, between the higher and the lower Mysticism, and their respective, profoundly divergent, tempers, objects, and range.

(1) Prof. Münsterberg discriminates between these two Mysticisms with a brilliant excessiveness, and ends by reserving the word " Mysticism " for the rejected kind alone. " As soon as we speak of psychical objects,—of ideas, feelings, and volitions,—as subject-matters of our direct consciousness and experience, we have put before ourselves an artificial product, a transformation, to which the categories of real life no longer apply." In this artificial product causal connections have taken the place of final ends. But " History, Practical Life, . . . Morality, Religion have nothing to do with these psychological constructions ; the categories of Psychology," treated by Münsterberg himself as a Natural, Determinist Science, " must not intrude into their teleological domains. But if," on the other hand, " the categories belonging to Reality," which is Spiritual and Libertarian, " are forced on to the psychological system, a system which was framed " by our mind " in the interest of causal explanation, we get a cheap mixture, which satisfies neither the one aim nor the other. Just this is the effect of Mysticism. It is the personal, emotional view applied, not to the world of Reality, where it fits, but to the Physical and Psychological worlds, which are constructed by the human logical will, with a view to gaining an impersonal, unemotional causal system. . . . The ideals of Ethics and Religion . . . have now been projected into the atomistic structure " (of the Causal System), " and have thus become dependent upon this system's nature ; they find their right of existence limited to the regions where ignorance of Nature leaves blanks in the Causal System, and have to tremble at every advance which Science makes." It is to this projection alone that Münsterberg would apply the term " Mysticism," which thus becomes exclusively " the doctrine that the pro-

cesses in the world of physical and psychical objects are not always subject to natural laws, but are influenced, at times, in a manner fundamentally inexplicable from the standpoint of the causal conception of Nature. . . . Yet, the special interest of the Mystic stands and falls here with his conviction that, in these extra-causal combinations," thus operative right within and at the level of this causal system, " we have a " direct, demonstrable " manifestation of a positive system of quite another kind, a System of Values, a system dominated, not by Mechanism, but by Significance." [1]

(2) Now we have been given here a doubtless excessively antithetic and dualistic picture of what, in actual life, is a close-knit variety in unity,—that interaction between, and anticipation of the whole in, the parts, and that indication of the later stages in the earlier,—which is so strikingly operative in the order and organization of the various constituents and stages of the processes and growth of the human mind and character, and which appears again in the Reality apprehended, reproduced, and enriched by man's powers.

Even in the humblest of our Sense-perceptions, there is already a mind perceiving and a Mind perceived ; and, in the most abstract and artificial of our intellectual constructions, there is not only a logical requirement, but also, underlying this requirement as this cause's deepest cause, an ever-growing if unarticulated experience and sense that only by the closest contact with the most impersonal-seeming, impersonally conceived forces of life and nature, and by the deepest recollection within its own interior world of mind and will, can man's soul adequately develop and keep alive, within itself, a solid degree and consciousness of Spirit, Free-will, Personality, Eternity, and God. Thus, in proportion as he comes more deeply to advance in the true occasions of his spirit's growth, does man still further emphasize and differentiate these two levels : the shallower, spatial-temporal, mathematico-physical, quantitative and determinist aspect of reality and level of apprehension ; and the deeper, alone at all adequate, experience of all the fuller degrees of Reality and effectuations of the spirit's life, with their overlapping, interpenetrating Succession, (their Duration), and their Libertarianism, Interiority, and Sense of the Infinite. He thus emphasizes both levels, because the determinist level is found to be, though never the source or

---

[1] *Psychology and Life*, 1899, pp. 267, 268. *Grundzüge der Psychologie*, Vol. I, 1900, pp. 170, 171.

direct cause, yet ever a necessary awakener and purifier of the Libertarian level.

Strictly within the temporal-spatial, quantitative method and level, indeed, we can nowhere find Teleology; but if we look back upon these quantitative superficialities from the qualitative, durational and personal, spiritual level and standpoint, (which alone constitute our direct experience,) we find that the quantitative, causal level and method is everywhere inadequate to exhaust or rightly to picture Reality, in exact proportion to this reality's degree of fulness and of worth. From the simplest Vegetable-Cell up to Orchids and Insectivorous Plants; from these on to Protozoans and up, through Insects, Reptiles, and Birds, to the most intelligent of Domestic Animals; from these on to Man, the Savage, and up to the most cultured or saintly of human personalities: we have everywhere, and increasingly, an inside, an organism, a subject as well as an object,—a series which is, probably from the first, endowed with some kind of dim consciousness, and which increasingly possessed of a more and more definite consciousness, culminates in the full self-consciousness of the most fully human man. And everywhere here, though in indefinitely increasing measure, it is the individualizing and historical, the organic and soul-conceptions and experiences which constitute the most characteristic and important truths and reality about and in these beings. For the higher up we get in this scale of Reality, the more does the Interior determine and express itself in the Exterior, and the more does not only kind differ from kind of being, but even the single individual from the other individuals within each several kind. And yet nowhere, not even in free-willing, most individualized, personal Man do we find the quantitative, determinist envelope simply torn asunder and revealing the qualitative, libertarian spirit perfectly naked and directly testable by chronometer, measuring-rod, or crucible. The spirit is thus ever like unto a gloved hand, which, let it move ever so spontaneously, will ever, in the first instance, present the five senses with a glove which, to their exclusive tests, appears as but dead and motionless leather.

(3) Now we have already in Chapter IX studied the contrasting attitudes of Catherine and her attendants towards one class of such effects,—those attributed to the Divine Spirit,—and hence, in principle, towards this whole question. Yet it is in the matter of phenomena, taken to be directly Diabolic

or Preternatural, that a Pseudo-Mysticism has been specially fruitful in strangely materialistic fantasies. As late as 1774 the *Institutiones Theologiae Mysticae* of Dom Schram, O.S.B., a book which even yet enjoys considerable authority, still solemnly described, as so many facts, cases of Diabolical *Incubi* and *Succubae*. Even in 1836–1842 the layman Joseph Görres could still devote a full half of his widely influential *Mystik* to " Diabolical Mysticism,"— witchcraft, etc. ; a large space to " Natural Mysticism,"—divin-ation, lycanthropy, vampires, etc. ; and a considerable part of the " Divine Mysticism," to various directly miraculous phenomenalisms. The Abbé Ribet could still, in his *La Mystique Divine, distinguée de ses Contrefaçons Diaboliques*, of 1895, give us a similarly uncritical mixture and transposi-tion of tests and levels. But the terrible ravages of the belief in witchcraft in the later Middle Ages, and, only a few years back, the humiliating fraud and craze concerning " Diana Vaughan," are alone abundantly sufficient to warn believers in the positive character of Evil away from all, solidly avoidable, approaches to such dangerous forms of this belief.[1]

(4) Yet the higher and highest Mystical attitude has never ceased to find its fullest, most penetrating expression in the life and teaching of devoted children of the Roman Church,— several of whom have been proclaimed Doctors and Models by that Church herself. And by a conjunction of four characteristics these great normative lives and teachers still point the way, out of and beyond all false or sickly Mysticism, on to the wholesome and the true.

(i) There is, first, the grand trust in and love of God's beautiful, wide world, and in and of the manifold truth and goodness present throughout life,—realities which we have already found rightly to be dwelt on, in certain recollective movements and moments, to the momentary exclusion of their positively operative, yet ever weaker, opposites. " Well I wote," says Mother Juliana, " that heaven and earth, and all that is made, is great, large, fair and good " ; " the full-head of joy is to behold God in all," and " truly to enjoy in Our Lord, is a full

---

[1] Mr. W. R. Inge, in his useful *Christian Mysticism*, 1899, has some sharp expressions of disgust against these long-lived survivals within the Catholic Church. And though his own tone towards Rome in general belongs also, surely, to a more or less barbaric past, he has done good service in drawing forcible attention to the matter.

lovely thanking in His sight." [1] This completely un- Manichaean attitude,—so Christian when held as the ultimate among the divers, sad and joyful, strenuous and contemplative moods of the soul,—is as strongly present in Clement of Alexandria, in the Sts. Catherine of Siena and of Genoa, in St. John of the Cross, and indeed in the recollective moments of all the great Mystics.

(ii) There is, next, a strong insistence upon the soul having to transcend all particular lights and impressions, in precise proportion to their apparently extraordinary character, if it would become strong and truly spiritual. " He that will rely on the letter of the divine locution, or on the intellectual form of the vision, will necessarily fall into delusion. ' The letter killeth, the spirit quickeneth '; we must therefore reject the literal sense, and abide in the obscurity of faith." " One desire only doth God allow in His presence, that of perfectly observing His law and carrying the Cross of Christ. . . . That soul, which has no other aim, will be a true ark containing the true Manna, which is God." " One act of the will, wrought in charity, is more precious in the eyes of God, than that which all the visions and revelations of heaven might effect." " Let men cease to regard these supernatural apprehensions . . . that they may be free." [2] Here the essence of the doctrine lies in the importance attached to this transcendence, and not in the particular views of the Saint concerning the character of this or that miraculous-seeming phenomenon to be transcended.

(iii) And this essential doctrine retains all its cogency, even though we hold the strict necessity of a contrary, alternating movement of definite occupation with the Concrete, Contingent, Historical, Institutional, in thought and action. For this occupation will be with the normal, typical means, duties, and facts of human and religious life; and, whilst fully conscious of the Supernatural working in and with these seemingly but natural materials, will, with St. Augustine, pray God to " grant men to perceive in little things the common-seeming indications of things both small and great," and, with him, will see a greater miracle in the yearly transformation of the vine's watery sap into wine, and in the germination of any single seed, than even in that of Cana. [3]

---

[1] *Sixteen Revelations*, ed. 1902, pp. 23, 84, 101.
[2] *Ascent of Mount Carmel*, tr. Lewis, 1891, pp. 159; 26, 27; 195, 265.
[3] *Confessions*, Bk. XI, ch. xxiii, 1. Tract in Johann. Ev., VIII, 1; XXIV, 1: ed. Ben., Vol. III, 2, coll. 1770 *b*, 1958 *d*.

(iv) And then there is, upon the whole, a tendency to concentrate, at these recollective stages, the soul's attention upon Christ and God alone. " I believe I understand," says Mother Juliana, " the ministration of holy Angels, as Clerks tell; but it was not shewed to me. For Himself is nearest and meekest, highest and lowest, and doeth all. God alone took our nature, and none but He; Christ alone worked our salvation, and none but He." [1] And thus we get a wholesome check upon the Neo-Platonist countless mediations, of which the reflex is still to be found in the Areopagite. God indeed is alone held, with all Catholic theologians, to be capable of penetrating to the soul's centre, and the fight against Evil is simplified to a watch and war against Self, in the form of an ever-increasing engrossment in the thought of God, and in the interests of His Kingdom. " Only a soul in union with God," says St. John of the Cross, " is capable of this profound loving knowledge : for this knowledge is itself that union. . . . The Devil has no power to simulate anything so great." " Self-love," says Père Grou, " is the sole source of all the illusions of the spiritual life. . . . Jesus Christ on one occasion said to St. Catherine of Siena : ' My daughter, think of Me, and I will think of thee ' : a short epitome of all perfection. ' Wheresoever thou findest self,' says the *Imitation*, ' drop that self ' : the soul's degree of fidelity to this precept is the true measure of its advancement." [2] The highly authorized *Manuel de Théologie Mystique* of the Abbé Lejeune, 1897, gives but one-sixth of its three-hundred pages to the discussion of all quasi-miraculous phenomena, puts them all apart from the substance of Contemplation and of the Mystical Life, and dwells much upon the manifold dangers of such, never essential, things. The French Oratorian, Abbé L. Laberthonnière, represents, in the *Annales de Philosophie Chrétienne*, a spirituality as full of a delicate Mysticism as it is free from any attachment to extraordinary phenomena. The same can be said of the Rev. George Tyrrell's *Hard Sayings* and *External Religion*. And the Abbé Sandreau has furnished us with two books of the most solid tradition and discrimination in all these matters.[3]

[1] *Sixteen Revelations*, ed. cit. p. 210.
[2] J. N. Grou, *Méditations sur l'Amour de Dieu*, Nouvelle ed. Perisse, pp. 268, 271.
[3] L. Laberthonnière, *Annales de Philosophie Chrétienne*, 1905, 1906. G. Tyrrell, *Hard Sayings*, 1898; *External Religion*, 1902. A. Sandreau, *La Vie d'Union à Dieu*, 1900; *L'Etat Mystique*, 1903.

(5) And we should, in justice, remember that the Phenomenal-ist Mysticism, objected to by Prof. Münsterberg and so sternly transcended by St. John of the Cross, is precisely what is still hankered after, and treated as of spiritual worth, by present-day Spiritualism. Indeed, even Prof. James's in many respects valuable *Varieties of Religious Experience* is seriously damaged by a cognate tendency to treat Religion, or at least Mysticism, as an abnormal faculty for perceiving phenomena inexplicable by physical and psychical science.

(6) And finally, with respect to the personality of Evil, we must not forget that " there are drawings to evil as to good, which are not mere self-temptations, . . . but which derive from other wills than our own ; strictly, it is only persons that can tempt us." [1]

[1] M. D. Petre, *The Soul's Orbit*, 1904, p. 113.

CHAPTER XIV

THE TWO FINAL PROBLEMS: MYSTICISM AND PANTHEISM,
THE IMMANENCE OF GOD, AND SPIRITUAL PERSONALITY,
HUMAN AND DIVINE

INTRODUCTORY.

*Impossibility of completely abstracting from the theoretical
form in the study of the experimental matter.*

We now come to the last two of our final difficulties and
problems—the supposed or real relations between Inclusive or
Exclusive Mysticism and Pantheism; and the question concerning the Immanence of God and Spiritual Personality,
Human and Divine.

(1) A preliminary difficulty in this, our deepest, task arises
from the fact that, whereas the evidences of a predominantly
individual, personal, directly experimental kind, furnished by
every at all deeply religious soul, have hitherto been all but
completely overlooked by trained historical investigators, in
favour of the study of the theological concepts and formulations accepted and transmitted by such souls, now the
opposite extreme is tending to predominate, as in Prof.
William James's *Varieties of Religious Experience*, 1902, or
in Prof. Weinel's interesting study, *The Effects of the Spirit
and of the Spirits in the Sub-Apostolic Age*, 1899. For
here, as Prof. Bousset points out in connection with the
latter book, we get an all but complete overlooking of the
fact that, even in the most individual experience, there is
always some intellectual framework or conception, some more
or less traditional form, which had previously found lodgment
in, and had been more or less accepted by, that soul; so that,
though the experience itself, where at all deep, is never the
mere precipitate of a conventionally accepted traditional intellectual form, it is nevertheless, even when more or less
in conflict with this form, never completely independent of it.[1]

---

[1] *Göttinger Gelehrte Anzeigen*, 1901, p. 757.

—Yet though we cannot discriminate in full detail, we can show certain peculiarities in the traditional Jewish, Mohammedan, Christian Mysticism to be not intrinsic to the Mystical apprehensions as such, but to come from the then prevalent philosophies which deflected those apprehensions in those particular ways.

(2) In view then of this inevitable interrelation between the experimental, personal matter and the theoretical, traditional form, I shall first consider the Aristotelian and Neo-Platonist conceptions concerning the relations between the General and the Particular, between God and Individual Things, as being the two, partly rival yet largely similar, systems that, between them, have most profoundly influenced the intellectual starting-point, analysis, and formulation of those experiences; and shall try to show the special attraction and danger of these conceptions for the mystically religious temperament. I shall next discuss the conceptions as to the relations between God and the individual personality,—the Noûs, the Spirit, and the Soul,—which, still largely Aristotelian and Neo-Platonist, have even more profoundly commended themselves to those Mystics, since these conceptions so largely met some of those Mystics' requirements, and indeed remain still, in part, the best analysis procurable. I shall, thirdly, face the question as to any intrinsic tendency to Pantheism in Mysticism as such, and as to the significance and the possible utility of any such tendency, keeping all fuller description of the right check upon it for my last chapter. And finally, I shall consider what degree and form of the Divine Immanence in the human soul, of direct Experience or Knowledge of God on the part of man, and of " Personality " in God, appear to result from the most careful analysis of the deepest religious consciousness, and from the requirements of the Sciences and of Life.

I. Relations between the General and the Particular, God and Individual Things, according to Aristotle, the Neo-Platonists, and the Medieval Strict Realists.

   1. *Aristotle, Plato, Plotinus, Proclus.*

(1) With regard to the relations between the General and Particular, we should note Aristotle's final perplexities and contradictions, arising from his failure to harmonize or to

transcend, by means of a new and self-consistent conception, the two currents, the Platonic and the specifically Aristotelian, which make up his thought.   For, with him as with Plato, all Knowledge has to do with Reality : hence Reality alone, in the highest, primary sense of the word, can form the highest, primary object of Knowledge ;   Knowledge will be busy, primarily, with the Essence, the Substance of things.   But with him, as against Plato, every substance is unique, whence it would follow that all knowledge refers, at bottom, to the Individual,—individual beings would form, not only the starting-point, but also the content and object of knowledge. —Yet this is what Aristotle, once more at one with Plato, stoutly denies : Science, even where it penetrates most deeply into the Particular, is never directed to individual things as such, but always to General Concepts ; and this, not because of our human incapacity completely to know the Individual, as such, but because the General, in spite of the Particular being better known to us, is more primitive and more knowable, as alone possessing that Immutability which must characterize all objects of true knowledge.[1]   The true Essence of things consists only in what is thought in their Concept, which concept is always some Universal ; yet this Universal exists only in Individual Beings, which are thus declared true Substances : here are two contentions, the possibility of whose co-existence he fails to explain.   Indeed at one time it is the Form, at another it is the Individual Being, composed of Form and Matter, which appears as real ; and Matter, again, appears both as the Indefinite General and as the Cause of Individual Particularity.[2]

(2) Now Plato had indeed insisted upon ascending to even greater abstraction, unity, and generality, as the sure process for attaining to the truth of things ; and had retained what is, for us, a strangely unpersonal, abstract element, precisely in his highest concept, since God here is hardly personal, but the Idea of Good, a Substance distinct from all other things, yet not, on this account, an Individual.   Yet Plato's profoundly aesthetic, social, ethical, above all religious, consciousness forced him to the inconsistency of proclaiming that, as the Sun is higher than the light and the eye, so the Good is higher than (mere) Being and Knowledge ; and this Supreme Idea of the Good gives to things their Being, and to the under-

---

[1] Zeller, *Philosophie der Griechen*, II, 2, ed. 1879, pp. 309, 312.
[2] *Ibid.* p. 348.

standing its power of Cognition, and is the Cause of all Right-
ness and Beauty, the Source of all Reality and Reason, and
hence, not only a final, but also an efficient Cause,—indeed
the Cause, pure and simple.[1] In the *Philebus* he tells us
explicitly that the Good and the Divine Reason are identical;
and in the *Timaeus* the Demiurge, the World-Former, looks
indeed to the Image of the World, in order to copy it : yet
the Demiurge is also himself this image which he copies.[2]
We thus still have a supreme Multiplicity in Unity as the
characteristic of the deepest Reality; and its chief attribute,
Goodness, is not the most abstract and aloof, but the most
rich in qualities and the most boundlessly self-communicative:
" He was good, so he desired that all things should be as like
unto himself as possible." [3] And Aristotle, (although he places
God altogether outside the visible world, and attributes to
Him there one sole action, the thinking of his own thought,
and one quasi-emotion, intellectual joy at this thinking,) still
maintains, in this shrunken form, the identity of the Good
and of the Supreme Reason, Noûs, and a certain Multiplicity
in Unity, and a true self-consciousness, within Him.

(3) It is Plotinus who is the first expressly to put the Godhead,—in strict obedience to the Abstractive scheme,—beyond
all Multiplicity, hence above the highest Reason itself, for
reason ever contains at least the duality of Subject thinking
and of Object thought; above Being, for all being has ever a
multitude of determinations; and above every part and the
totality of All Things, for it is the cause of them all. The
Cause is here ever outside the effect, the Unity outside the
Multiplicity, what is thought outside of what thinks. The
First is thus purely transcendent,—with one characteristic
exception : although above Being, Energy, Thought, and
Thinking, Beauty, Virtue, Life, It is still the Good ; and because
of this, though utterly self-sufficing and without action of any
kind, It, " as it were," overflows, and this overflow produces a
Second.[4] And only this Second is here the Noûs, possessed
of what Aristotle attributes to the First : it is no sheer

[1] Republic, VI, 508*e*; VII, 517*b*; and Zeller, *ibid.* II, 1, ed. 1889,
pp. 707–710.
[2] *Philebus,* 22*c*; *Timaeus,* 28*a, c*; 92*c* (with the reading ὅδε ὁ κόσμος
. . . εἰκὼν τοῦ ποιητοῦ).
[3] *Timaeus,* 29*e*.
[4] *Enneads,* I, vii, 1, 61*d*; I, viii, 2, 72*e*; VI, viii, 16, end. See, for all
this, Zeller, *Philosophie der Griechen,* III, ii, ed. 1881, pp. 476–480; 483;
510–414.

Unity, " all things are together there, yet are they there discriminated " : it is contemplative Thinking of itself; it is pure and perfect Action.[1]

(4) And Proclus who, through the Pseudo-Dionysius, is the chief mediator between Plato and Plotinus on the one hand, and the Medieval Mystics and Scholastics on the other, is, with his immense thirst for Unity, necessarily absorbed by the question as to the Law according to which all things are conjoined to a whole. And this Law is for him the process of the Many out of the One, and their inclination back to the One; for this process and inclination determine the connection of all things, and the precise place occupied by each thing in that connection. All things move in the circle of procession from their cause, and of return to it; the simplest beings are the most perfect; the most complex are the most imperfect.[2]

2. *The Anti-Proclian current, in the Areopagite's view.*

Now in the Pseudo-Dionysius we find an interesting oscillation between genuine Neo-Platonism, which finds Beings perfect in proportion to the fewness and universality of their attributes, although, with it, he inconsistently holds Goodness, —the deepest but not the most general attribute,—to be the most perfect of all; and Aristotelianism at its richest, when it finds Beings perfect according to the multiplicity and depth of their attributes. Dionysius himself becomes aware of the dead-lock thence ensuing. " The Divine name of the Good is extended to things being and to things not being,"—a statement forced upon him by his keeping, with Plato and Plotinus, Goodness as the supreme attribute, and yet driving home, more completely than they, their first principle that Generality and Perfection rise and sink together. " The Name of Being is extended to all things being " and stretches further than Life. " The name of Life is extended to all things living " and stretches further than Wisdom. " The Name of Wisdom is extended," only, " to all the intellectual, and rational, and sensible."

But if so, " for what reason do we affirm " (as he has been doing in the previous sections), " that Life," the less extended, " is superior to (mere) Being," the more extended? " and that Wisdom," though less extended, " is superior to mere Life," the more extended? And he answers in favour of

---

[1] *Enneads*, VIII, ix, 350*b*; VI, 2317, 610*d*; III, ix, 3, 358*a*, *b*.
[2] Zeller, *op. cit*. III, ii, pp. 787–789.

depth and richness of attributes. " If any one assumed the intellectual to be without being or life, the objection might hold good. But if the Divine Minds," the Angels, " both are above all other beings, and live above all other living creatures, and think and know above sensible perception and reasoning, and aspire beyond all other existent and aspiring beings, to . . . the Beautiful and Good : then they encircle the Good more closely." For " the things that participate more in the one and boundless-giving God, are more . . . divine, than those that come behind them in gifts." [1] And with abiding truth he says : " Those who place attributes on That which is above every attribute, should derive the affirmation from what is more cognate to It; but those who abstract, with regard to That which is above every abstraction, should derive the negation from what is further removed from It. Are not, *e. g.* Life and Goodness more cognate to It than air and stone ? And is It not further removed from debauch and anger than from ineffableness and incomprehensibility ? " [2]

But more usually Dionysius shows little or no preference for any particular attribution or denegation; all are taken to fall short so infinitely as to eliminate any question as to degrees of failure. " The Deity-Above-All . . . is neither Soul nor Mind, neither One nor Oneness, neither Deity nor Goodness." [3] God is thus purely transcendent.

3. *Continuators of the Proclian current.*

The influence of the Areopagite was notoriously immense throughout the Middle Ages,—indeed unchecked,—along its Proclian, Emanational, Ultra-Unitive current,—among the Pantheists from the Christian, Mohammedan and Jewish camps.

(1) Thus Scotus Eriugena (who died in about 877 A.D.) insists : " In strict parlance, the Divine Nature Itself exists alone in all things, and nothing exists which is not that Nature. The Lord and the Creature are one and the same thing." " It is its own Self that the Holy Trinity loves, sees, moves within us." One of his fundamental ideas is the equivalence of the degrees of abstraction and those of existence; he simply hypostatizes the logical table.[4] Eriugena was condemned.

---

[1] *Divine Names,* ch. v, sec. 1 : tr. Parker, pp. 73–75.
[2] *Mystical Theology,* ch. iii : Parker, pp. 135, 136.
[3] *Ibid.,* ch. iv, sec. 2 : Parker, pp. 136, 137.
[4] *De Divisione Naturae,* III, 17; I, 78. Ueberweg-Heinze, *Grundriss der Geschichte der Philosophie,* Vol. II, ed. 1898, p. 159.

(2) But the Pseudo-Aristotelian, really Proclian, *Liber de Causis*, written by a Mohammedan in about 850 A.D., became, from its translation into Latin in about 1180 A.D. onwards, an authority among the orthodox Scholastics. It takes, as " an example of the (*true*) doctrine as to Causes, Being, Living-Being, and Man. Here it is necessary that the thing Being should exist first of all, and next Living-Being, and last Man. Living-Being is the proximate, Being is the remote cause of Man; hence Being is in a higher degree the cause of Man than is Living-Being, since Being is the cause of Living-Being, which latter again is the cause of Man." . . . " Being, (of the kind) which is before Eternity, is the first cause. . . . Being is more general than Eternity. . . . Being of the kind which is with and after Eternity, is the first of created things . . . It is above Sense, and Soul, and Intelligence." [1]

(3) The Mohammedan Avicenna, who died in 1037 A.D., is mostly Aristotelian in philosophy and Orthodox in religious intention, and, translated into Latin, was much used by St. Thomas. Yet he has lapses into pure Pantheism, such as : " The true Being that belongs to God, is not His only, but is the Being of all things, and comes forth abundantly from His Being. That which all things desire is Being : Being is Goodness ; the perfection of Being is the perfection of Goodness." [2]

(4) And the Spanish Jew, Ibn Gebirol (Avicebron), who died about 1070 A.D., is predominantly Proclian, but with a form of Pantheism which, in parts, strikingly foreshadows Spinoza. His masterly *Fons Vitae*, as translated into Latin, exercised a profound influence upon Duns Scotus. " Below the first Maker there is nothing but what is both matter and form." " All things are resolvable into Matter and Form. If all things were resolvable into a single root," (that is, into Form alone,) there would be no difference between that one root and the one Maker." There exists a universal Matter and a universal Form. The first, or universal Matter, is a substance existing by itself, which sustains diversity, and is one in number : it is capable of receiving all the different kinds of forms. The universal Form is a substance which constitutes the essence of all the different kinds of forms. . . . By means of the knowledge of this universal Form, the

<hr />

[1] Secs. 2, 4, ed. Bardenhewer, 1882, pp. 163–166.

[2] Commentarius, in *Aristolelis Metaphysica*, Tract. VIII, cap. 6, quoted by Denifle, *Archiv f. Litteratur-u-Kirchengeschichte*, 1886, p. 520.

knowledge of every (less general) form is acquired,—is deduced from it and resolved into it." " Being falls under four categories, answering to : whether it is, what it is, what is its quality, and why it is : but, of these, the first in order of dignity is the category which inquires whether it is at all." [1] We thus get again the degree of worth strictly identical with the degree of generality.

4. *Inconsistencies of Aquinas and Scotus.*

(I) St. Thomas, the chief of the orthodox Scholastics, has embodied the entire Dionysian writings in his own works, but labours assiduously—and successfully, as far as his own statements are concerned—to guard against the Pantheistic tendencies special to strict Realism. Yet it is clear, from his frequent warnings and difficult distinctions regarding the double sense of the proposition, " God is sheer Being," and from the ease with which we find Eckhart, an entirely consistent Realist, lapse into the Pantheistic sense, how immanent is the danger to any severe form of the system.[2] And he fails to give us a thoroughly understandable and consistent account as to the relations between the General and the Particular, between Form and Matter, and between these two pairs of conceptions. Thus " Materia signata," matter, as bearing certain dimensions, " is the principle of individuation " : [3] yet this *quantum* is already an individually determined quantity, and *this* determination remains unexplained. And certain forms exist separately, without matter, in which case each single form is a separate species; as with the Angels and, pre-eminently, with God.—Yet, as already Duns Scotus insisted, Aquinas' general principle seems to require the non-existence of pure forms as distinct beings, and the partial materiality of all individual beings.[4]

(2) And Duns Scotus teaches, in explicit return to Avicebron, that every created substance consists of matter as well as of form, and that there is but one, First Matter, which is identical in every particular and derivative kind of matter. The world appears to him as a gigantic tree, whose root is this indeterminate matter; whose branches are the transitory substances;

[1] Ibn Gebirol, *Fons Vitae*, ed. Bäumker, 1895 : IV, 6, pp. 225, 224; V, 22, p. 298; II, 20, pp. 60–61; V, 24, p. 301.

[2] *De Ente et Essentia*, c. vi. *Summa Theol.*, I, qu. 3, art. 4 ad 1; and elsewhere.

[3] *De Ente et Essentia*, c. ii.

[4] See Ueberweg-Heinze, *op. cit.* pp. 280, 281.

whose leaves the changeable accidents; whose flowers, the rational souls; whose fruit are the Angels : and which God has planted and which He tends.   Here again the order of Efficacity,—with the tell-tale exception of God,—is identical with that of Generality.[1]

5. *Eckhart's Pantheistic trend.*

But it is Eckhart who consistently develops the Pantheistic trend of a rigorous Intellectualism.   The very competent and strongly Thomistic Father Denifle shows how Eckhart strictly followed the general scholastic doctrine, as enunciated by Avicenna : " In every creature its Being is one thing, and is from another, its Essence is another thing, and is not from another"; whereas in God, Being and Essence are identical.   And Denifle adds :   " Eckhart will have been unable to answer for himself the question as to what, in strictness, the ' Esse ' is, in distinction from the ' Essentia '; indeed no one could have told him, with precision. . . . Eckhart leaves intact the distinction between the Essence of God and that of the creature; but, doubtless in part because of this, he feels himself free,—in starting from an ambiguous text of Boetius,—to break down the careful discriminations established by St. Thomas, in view of this same text, between Universal Being, Common to all things extant, and Divine Being, reserved by Aquinas for God alone."[2] " What things are nearer to each other, than anything that *is* and Being?   There is nothing between them."   " Very Being," the Being of God, " is the actualizing Form of every form, everywhere."   " In one word," adds Denifle, "the Being of God constitutes the formal Being of all things."[3]   The degrees of Generality and Abstract Thinkableness are again also the degrees of Reality and Worth : " the Eternal Word assumed to Itself, not this or that human being, but a human nature which existed bare, unparticularized."   " Being and Knowableness are identical."

When speaking systematically Eckhart is strictly Plotinian: " God and Godhead are as distinct as earth is from heaven." " The Godhead has left all things to God : It owns nought, willsnought, requiresnought, effectsnought, producesnought." " Thou shalt love the Godhead as It truly is : a non-God,

---

[1] *De rerum Principio*, qu. viii.   Ueberweg-Heinze, *op. cit.* pp. 295, 296.

[2] H. S. Denifle, *Meister Eckhart's Lateinische Schriften, loc. cit.* pp. 489, 490; 540, n. 6.

[3] *Ibid.* p. 519.

non-Spirit, non-Person . . . a sheer, pure, clear One, severed from all duality : let us sink down into that One, throughout eternity, from Nothing unto Nothing, so help us God." " The Godhead Itself remains unknown to Itself." " It is God who energizes and speaks one single thing,—His Son, the Holy Ghost, and all creatures. . . . Where God speaks it, there it is all God; here, where man understands it, it is God and creature." [1] No wonder that the following are among the propositions condemned by Pope John XXII in 1329 : " God produces me as His own Being, a Being identical, not merely similar "; and, " I speak as falsely when I call God (the God-head) good, as if I call white, black." [2]

6. *The logical goal of strict Realism.*

This series of facts, which could be indefinitely extended, well illustrates the persistence of " the fundamental doctrine common to all forms of Realism,—of the species as an entity in the individuals, common to all and *identical* in each, an entity to which individual differences adhere as accidents," as Prof. Pringle Pattison accurately defines the matter. "Yet when existence is in question, it is the individual, not the universal, that is real; and the real individual is not a compound of species and accidents, but is individual to the inmost fibre of his being." Not as though Nominalism were in the right. For " each finite individual has its " special " place in the one real universe, with all the parts of which it is inseparably connected. But the universe is itself an individual or real whole, containing all its parts within itself, and not a universal of the logical order, containing its exemplifications under it." [3] And, above all, minds, spirits, persons,—however truly they may approximate more and more to certain great types of rationality, virtue, and religion, which types are thus increasingly expressive of God's self-revealing purpose and nature,— are ever, not merely numerically different, as between one individual and the other, but, both in its potentialities and especially in its spiritual actualization, no one soul can or does take the place of any other.

And if we ask what there is in any strict Realism to attract the Mystical sense, we shall find it, I think, in the insistence of such Realism upon Unity, Universality, and Stability.

[1] *Meister Eckhart*, ed. Pfeiffer, 1857, pp. 158, 1; 99, 8; 180, 15; 532, 30; 320, 27; 288, 26; 207, 27.
[2] Denzinger, *Enchiridion Symbolorum*, ed. 1888, Nos. 437, 455.
[3] *Hegelianism and Personality*, ed. 1893, pp. 230, 231, and note.

Yet in so far as Mysticism, in such a case Exclusive Mysticism, tends to oust the Outgoing movement of the soul, it empties these forms of their Multiple, Individual, and Energizing content.   Inclusive Mysticism may be truly said alone to attain to the true Mystic's desires; for only by the interaction of both movements, and of all the powers of the soul, will the said soul escape the ever-increasing poverty of content characteristic of the strict Realist's pyramid of conceptions; a poverty undoubtedly antagonistic to the secret aspiration of Mysticism, which is essentially an apprehension, admiration, and love of the infinite depths and riches of Reality—of this Reality no doubt present everywhere, yet in indefinitely various, and mutually complementary and stimu-lative forms and degrees.   And the readiness with which Mysticism expressed itself in the Nominalist Categories,—distinctly less adequate to a healthy, Partial Mysticism than the more moderate forms of Realism,—shows how little intrinsic was the link which seemed to bind it to a Realism of the most rigorous kind.

II. Relations between God and the Human Soul.

In taking next the question as to the relations between God and the Human Soul, we shall find our difficulties increased, because, here especially, the Philosophers and even the Biblical Writers have, with regard to religious experience, used expressions and furnished stimulations of a generally complex and unclarified, intermittent, and unharmonized kind; and especially because certain specifically religious experiences and requirements have operated here with a unique intensity, at one time in a Pantheistic, at another in a more or less Deistic, direction.   The reader will specially note the points in the following doctrines which helped on the conception that a certain centre or highest part of the soul is God, or a part of God, Himself.

1. *Plato and Aristotle.   " The Noûs."*

(1) Plato teaches the pre-existence and the post-existence (immortality) of the soul, as two interdependent truths.   In his earlier stage, *e. g.* the *Phaedrus,* he so little discriminates, in his argument for immortality, between the individual soul and the World-Soul, as to argue that " the Self-Moving " Soul generally " is the beginning of motion, and this motion,"

(specially here in connection with the human soul,) " can neither be destroyed nor begotten, since, in that case, the heavens and all generation would collapse." Yet individual souls are not, according to him, emanations of the World-Soul; but, as the particular ideas stand beside the Supreme Idea, so do the particular souls stand beside the Soul of the Whole, in a distinct peculiarity of their own.[1]—And again, since the soul has lapsed from a purer, its appropriate, life into the body, and has thus no original, intrinsic relation to this body, the activity of the senses, indeed in strictness even that of the emotions, cannot form part of its essential nature. Only the highest part of the soul, the Reason, *Noûs*, which, as " sun-like, God-like," can apprehend the sun, God, is one and simple, as are all the ideas, immortal; whereas the soul's lower part consists of two elements,—the nobler, the irascible, and the ignobler, the concupiscible passions. But how the unity of the soul's life can co-exist with this psychical tritomy, is a question no doubt never formulated even to himself by Plato : we certainly have only three beings bound together, not one being active in different directions.[2]

(2) Aristotle, if more sober in his general doctrine, brings some special obscurities and contradictions. For whilst the pre-existence of the soul, taken as a whole, is formally denied, and indeed its very origin is linked to that of the body, its rational part, the Noûs, comes into the physical organism from outside of the matter altogether, and an impersonal pre-existence is distinctly predicated of it,—in strict conformity with his doctrine that the Supreme Noûs does not directly act upon, or produce things in, the world.[3]

2. *St. Paul. The " Spirit."*

But it is St. Paul who, in his Mystical outbursts and in the systematic parts of his doctrine, as against the simply hortatory level of his teaching, gives us the earliest, one of the deepest, and to this hour by far the most influential, among the at all detailed experiences and schemes, accepted by and operative among Christians, as to the relations of the human soul to God. And here again, and with characteristic intensity,

[1] *Phaedrus*, 245*d*; Zeller, *op. cit.* II, 1, ed. 1889, p. 830.

[2] *Ibid.* pp. 843, 844; 849, 850.

[3] Pre-existence of the Noûs : *Gen. Anim.*, II, 3, 736*b*; *de Anima*, III, 5, 430*a*; Zeller, *op. cit.* II, 2, ed. 1879, pp. 593, 595. The Supreme Noûs, purely transcendent : *Metaph.*, XII, 7–10. But see Dr. Edward Caird's admirable pp. 1–30, Vol. II, of his *Evolution of Theology in the Greek Philosophers*, 1904.

certain overlapping double meanings and conceptions, and some vivid descriptions of experiences readily suggestive of the divinity of the soul's highest part, repeatedly appear.

(1) In the systematic passages we not only find the terms *Psyche*, " Soul," for the vital force of the body; and *Noûs*, (" Mind,") " Heart," and " Conscience," for various aspects and functions of man's rational and volitional nature : but a special insistence upon *Pneuma*, " Spirit," mostly in a quite special sense of the word. Thus in 1 Cor. ii, 14, 15, we get an absolute contrast between the psychic or sarkic, the simply natural man, and the Pneumatic, the Spiritual one, all capacity for understanding the Spirit of God being denied to the former. The Spiritual thus appears as itself already the Divine, and the Spirit as the exclusive, characteristic property of God, something which is foreign to man, apart from his Christian renovation and elevation to a higher form of existence. Only with the entrance of faith and its consequences into the mind and will of man, does this transcendent Spirit become an immanent principle : "through His Spirit that dwelleth in you." [1] —Hence, in the more systematic Pauline Anthropology, *Pneuma* cannot be taken as belonging to man's original endowment. Certainly in 1 Cor. ii, 11, the term " the spirit of a man " appears simply because the whole passage is dominated by a comparison between the Divine and the human consciousness, which allows simultaneously of the use of the conversely incorrect term, " the mind of God,"—here, v. 16, and in Rom. xi, 34. And the term " the spirit of the world," 1 Cor. ii. 12, is used in contrast with " the Spirit of God," and as loosely as the term " the God of this world," is applied, in 2 Cor. iv, 4, to Satan.—Only some four passages are difficult to interpret thus : *e.g.* " All defilement of flesh and spirit " (2 Cor. vii, 1); for how can God, Spirit, be defiled? Yet we can " forget that our body is a temple of the Holy Spirit," 1 Cor. vi, 19 ; and its defilement can " grieve the Holy Spirit " (Eph. iv, 30).[2]

And note how parallel to his conception of this immanence of the transcendent Spirit is St. Paul's conception, based upon his personal, mystical experience, of the indwelling of Christ in the regenerate human soul. Saul had indeed been

[1] Rom. viii, 11. See too Rom. viii, 9, 14; 1 Cor. iii, 16; vi, 11; vii, 40; xii, 3.

[2] H. J. Holtzmann, *Lehrbuch der N. T. Theology*, 1897, Vol. II, pp. 9–12; 15–18.

won to Jesus Christ, not by the history of Jesus' earthly life, but by the direct manifestation of the heavenly Spirit-Christ, on the way to Damascus : whence he teaches that only those who know Him as Spirit, can truly " be in Christ,"—an expression formed on the model of " to be in the Spirit," as in Mark xii, 36, and Apoc. i, 10.

(2) And then these terms take on, in specifically Pauline Mystical passages, a suggestion of a local extension and environment, and express, like the corresponding formulae " in God," " in the Spirit," the conception of an abiding within as it were an element,—that of the exalted Christ and His Divine glory. Or Christ is within us, as the Spirit also is said to be, so that the regenerate personality, by its closeness of intercourse with the personality of Christ, can become one single Spirit with Him, 1 Cor. vi, 17. " As the air is the element in which man moves, and yet again the element of life which is present within the man : so the Pneuma-Christ is for St. Paul both the Ocean of the Divine Being, into which the Christian, since his reception of the Spirit, is plunged," and in which he disports himself, " and a stream which, derived from that Ocean, is specially introduced within his individual life." [1] Catherine's profound indebtedness to this Mystical Pauline doctrine has already been studied ; here we are but considering this doctrine in so far as suggestive, to the Mystics, of the identity between the true self and God,—an identity readily reached, if we press such passages as " Christ, our life " ; " to live is Christ " ; " I live, not I, but Christ liveth in me." [2]

3. *Plotinus.*

Some two centuries later, Plotinus brings his profound influence to bear in the direction of such identification. For as the First, the One, which, as we saw, possesses, for him, no Self-consciousness, Life, or Being, produces the Second, the Noûs, which, possessed of all these attributes, exercises them directly in self-contemplation alone ; and yet this Second is so closely like that First as to be " light from light " : so does the Second produce the Third, the Human Psyche, which, though " a thing by itself," is a " god-like (divine) thing," since it possesses " a more divine part, the part which is neighbour to what is above, the Noûs, with which and from

---

[1] H. J. Holtzmann, *op. cit.* Vol. II, pp. 79, 80. Johannes Weiss, *Die Nachfolge Christi*, 1895, p. 95.
[2] Col. iii, 4 ; Phil. i, 21 ; Gal. ii, 20.

which Noûs the Psyche exists."—The Psyche is " an image of the Noûs " : " as outward speech expresses inward thought, so is the Psyche a concept of the Noûs,—a certain energy of the Noûs, as the Noûs itself is an energy of the First Cause." " As with fire, where we distinguish the heat that abides within the fire and the heat that is emitted by it . . . so must we conceive the Psyche not as wholly flowing forth from, but as in part abiding in, in part proceeding from the Noûs." [1]

And towards the end of the great Ninth Book of the Sixth Ennead, he tells how in Ecstasy " the soul sees the Source of Life . . . the Ground of Goodness, the Root of the Soul. . . . For we are not cut off from or outside of It . . . but we breathe and consist in It : since It does not give and then retire, but ever lifts and bears us, so long as It is what It is." " We must stand alone in It and must become It alone, after stripping off all the rest that hangs about us. . . . There we can behold both Him and our own selves,—ourselves, full of intellectual light, or rather as Pure Light Itself, having become God, or rather as being simply He . . . abiding altogether unmoved, having become as it were Stability Itself." " When man has moved out of himself away to God, like the image to its Prototype, he has reached his journey's end." " And this is the life of the Gods and of divine and blessed man . . . a flight of the alone to the Alone." [2]

4. *Eckhart's position. Ruysbroek.*

(1) Eckhart gives us both Plotinian positions—the God-likeness and the downright Divinity of the soul. " The Spark (*das Fünkelein*) of the Soul . . . is a light impressed upon its uppermost part, and an image of the Divine Nature, which is ever at war with all that is not divine. It is not one of the several powers of the soul. . . . Its name is Synteresis,"—*i.e.* conscience. " The nine powers of the soul are all servants of that man of the soul, and help him on to the soul's Source." [3]— But in one of the condemned propositions he says : " There is something in the soul which is Increate and Uncreatable ; if the whole soul were such, it would be (entirely) Increate and Uncreatable. And this is the Intellect,"—standing here exactly for Plotinus's Noûs. [4]

(2) Ruysbroek (who died in 1381) combines a considerable

[1] *Enneads*, V, book 1, cc. 3 and 6.
[2] *Ibid*. VI, book 9, 9 and 11.
[3] *Eckhart*, ed. Pfeiffer, pp. 113, 33 ; 469, 40, 36.
[4] Denzinger, *op. cit.* No. 454.

fundamental sobriety with much of St. Paul's daring and many echoes of Plotinus. " The unity of our spirit with God is of two kinds,—essential and actual. According to its essence, our spirit receives, in its innermost highest part, the visit of Christ, without means and without intermission; for the life which we are in God, in our Eternal Image, and that which we have and are in ourselves, according to the essence of our being . . . are without distinction.—But this essential unity of our spirit with God has no consistency in itself, but abides in God and flows out from and depends on Him." The actual unity of our spirit with God, caused by Grace, confers upon us not His Image, but His Likeness, " and though we cannot lose the Image of God, nor our natural unity with Him,—if we lose His Likeness, His Grace, Christ, who, in this case, comes to us with mediations and intermissions, we shall be damned." [1]

5. *St. Teresa's mediating view.*

St. Teresa's teachings contain interesting faint echoes of the old perplexities and daring doctrines concerning the nature of the Spirit; but articulate a strikingly persistent conviction that the soul holds God Himself as distinct from His graces, possessing thus some direct experience of this His presence. " I cannot understand what the mind is, nor how it differs from the soul or the spirit either : all three seem to me to be but one, though the soul sometimes leaps forth out of itself, like a fire which has become a flame : the flame ascends high above the fire, but it is still the same flame of the same fire." " Something subtle and swift seems to issue from the soul, to ascend to its highest part and to go whither Our Lord will . . . it seems a flight. This little bird of the spirit seems to have escaped out of the prison of the body." Indeed " the soul is then not in itself . . . it seems to me to have its dwelling higher than even the highest part of itself." [2]—" In the beginning I did not know that God is present in all things. . . . Unlearned men used to tell me that He was present only by His grace. I could not believe that . . . A most learned Dominican told me He was present Himself . . . this was a great comfort to me." " To look upon Our Lord as being in the innermost parts of the soul . . . is a much more profitable method, than that of looking upon Him as external to

---

[1] *Vier Schriften von Johannes Ruysbroek*, ed. Ullmann, 1848, pp. 106, 107.

[2] *Life, written by Herself*, tr. D. Lewis, ed. 1888, pp. 124, 421, 146.

us." "The living God was in my soul." And even, "hitherto" up to 1555, " my life was my own; my life, since then, is the life which God lived in me." [1]

6. *Immanence, not Pantheism.*

St. Teresa's teaching as to God's own presence in the soul points plainly, I think, to the truth insisted on by the Catholic theologian Schwab, in his admirable monograph on Gerson. " Neither speculation nor feeling are satisfied with a Pure Transcendence of God; and hence the whole effort of true Mysticism is directed, whilst not abolishing His Transcendence, to embrace and experience God, His living presence, in the innermost soul,—that is, to insist, in some way or other, upon the Immanence of God. Reject all such endeavours as Pantheistic, insist sharply upon the specific eternal difference between God and the Creature : and the Speculative, Mystical depths fade away, with all their fascination." [2] Not in finding Pantheism already here, with the imminent risk of falling into a cold Deism, but in a rigorous insistence, with all the great Inclusive Mystics, upon the spiritual and moral effects, as the tests of the reality and worth of such experiences, and, with the Ascetical and Historical souls, upon also the other movement—an outgoing in some kind of contact with, and labour at, the contingencies and particularities of life and mind—will the true safeguard for this element of the soul's life be found. [3]

III. MYSTICISM AND PANTHEISM : THEIR DIFFERENCES AND POINTS OF LIKENESS.

But does not Mysticism, not only find God in the soul, but the soul to be God? Is it not, as such, already Pantheism? Or, if not, what is their difference?

1. *Plotinus and Spinoza compared.*

Now Dr. Edward Caird, in his fine book, *The Evolution of Theology in the Greek Philosophers*, 1904, tells us that " Mysticism is religion in its most concentrated and exclusive form; it is that attitude of mind in which all other relations

---

[1] *Life, written by Herself*, tr. D. Lewis, ed. 1888, pp. 355, 130, 430; 174.

[2] J. B. Schwab, *Johannes Gerson*, 1858, pp. 361, 362.

[3] I can find but one, secondary Ecclesiastical Censure of the doctrine of God's substantial presence in the soul,—the censure passed by the Paris Sorbonne on Peter Lombard. The same Sorbonne repeatedly censured St. Thomas on other points.

are swallowed up in the relation of the soul to God"; and
that " Plotinus is the Mystic *par excellence.*" [1] And he then
proceeds to contrast Plotinus, the typical Mystic, with Spinoza,
the true Pantheist.

" Whether " or not " Spinoza, in his negation of the limits
of the finite, still leaves it open to himself to admit a reality
in finite things which is *not* negated," and " to conceive of the
absolute substance as manifesting itself in attributes and
modes " : " it is very clear that he does so conceive it, and
that, for all those finite things which he treats as negative
and illusory in themselves, he finds in God a ground of reality
. . . which can be as little destroyed as the divine substance
itself." " God, *Deus sive Natura,* is conceived as the immanent principle of the universe, or perhaps rather the
universe is conceived as immanent in God."—Thus to him
" the movement by which he dissolves the finite in the infinite,
and the movement by which he finds the finite again in the
infinite, are equally essential. If for him the world is nothing
apart from God, God is nothing apart from His realization in
the world." This is true Pantheism.[2]

But in Plotinus the *via negativa* involves a negation of the
finite and determinate in all its forms; hence here it is impossible to find the finite again in the infinite. The Absolute
One is here not immanent but transcendent.[3] " While the
lower always has need of the higher, the higher is regarded as
having no need " for any purpose " of the lower "; and " the
Highest has no need of anything but Itself." " Such a process cannot be reversed": " in ascending, Plotinus has drawn
the ladder after him, and left himself no possibility of descending again. The movement, in which he is guided by definite
and explicit thought, is always upwards; while, in describing
the movement downwards, he has to take refuge in metaphors
and analogies," for the purpose of indicating a purely self-
occupied activity which only accidentally produces an external
effect, *e.g.* "the One as it were overflows, and produces another
than itself." [4] " Thus we have the strange paradox that the
Being who is absolute, is yet conceived as in a sense external to
the relative and finite, and that He leaves the relative and finite
in a kind of unreal independence." " On the one side, we have a

---

[1] Vol. II, pp. 210, 211.
[2] *Ibid.* pp. 230, 231.
[3] *Ibid.* p. 231.
[4] *Ibid.* pp. 253–257. *Enneads,* V, book ii, 1.

life which is nothing apart from God, and which, nevertheless, can never be united to him, except as it loses itself altogether; and, on the other side, an Absolute, which yet is not immanent in the life it originates, but abides in transcendent isolation from it. . . . It is this contradiction which . . . makes the writings of Plotinus the supreme expression of Mysticism." [1]

Now I think, with this admirable critic, that we cannot but take Spinoza as the classical representative of that parallelistic Pantheism to which most of our contemporary systems of psycho-physical parallelism belong. As Prof. Troeltsch well puts it, " we have here a complete parallelism between every single event in the physical world, which event is already entirely explicable from its own antecedents within that physical world, and every event of a psychical kind, which, nevertheless, is itself also entirely explicable from its own psychical antecedents alone." And " this parallelism again is but two sides of the one World-Substance, Which is neither Nature nor Spirit, and Whose law is neither natural nor spiritual law, but Which is Being in general and Law in general." In this one World-Substance, with its parallel self-manifestations as extension and as thought, Spinoza finds the ultimate truth of Religion, as against the Indeterminist, Anthropomorphic elements of all the popular religions,—errors which have sprung, the Anthropomorphic from man's natural inclination to interpret Ultimate Reality, with its complete neutrality towards the distinctions of Psychical and Physical, by the Psychic side, as the one nearest to our own selves; and the Indeterminist from the attribution of that indetermination to the World-Substance which, even in Psychology, is already a simple illusion and analytical blunder.

" It is in the combination," concludes Professor Troeltsch, " of such a recognition of the strict determination of all natural causation, and of such a rejection of materialism (with its denial of the independence of the psychic world), that rests the immense power of Pantheism at the present time." [2] On the other hand, the supposed Pantheistic positions of the later Lessing, of Herder, Goethe and many another predominantly aesthetic thinker, must, although far richer and more nearly adequate conceptions of full reality, be assigned,

[1] Vol. II, pp. 232, 233.
[2] " Religions-philosophie," in *Die Philosophie im Beginn des zwanzigsten Jahrhunderts*, 1904, Vol. I, pp. 115, 117.

qua Pantheism, a secondary place, as inconsistent, because already largely Teleological, indeed Theistic Philosophies.

2. *Complete Pantheism non-religious; why approached by Mysticism.*

Now the former, the full Pantheism, must, I think, be declared, with Rauwenhoff, to be only in name a religious position at all. " In its essence it is simply a complete Monism, a recognition of the *Pan* in its unity and indivisibility, and hence a simple view of the world, not a religious conception." [1]—Yet deeply religious souls can be more or less, indeed profoundly, influenced by such a Monism, so that we can get Mystics with an outlook considerably more Spinozist than Plotinian. There can, *e.g.*, be no doubt as to both the deeply religious temper and the strongly Pantheistic conceptions of Eckhart in the Middle Ages, and of Schleiermacher in modern times; and indeed Spinoza himself is, apart from all questions as to the logical implications and results of his intellectual system, and as to the justice of his attacks upon the historical religions, a soul of massive religious intuition and aspiration.

But further: Mystically tempered souls,—and the typical and complete religious soul will ever possess a mystical element in its composition,—have three special *attraits* which necessarily bring them into an at least apparent proximity to Pantheism.

(1) For one thing Mysticism, like Pantheism, has a great, indeed (if left unchecked by the out-going-movement) an excessive, thirst for Unity, for a Unity less and less possessed of Multiplicity; and the transition from holding the Pure Transcendence of this Unity to a conviction of its Exclusive Immanence becomes easy and insignificant, in proportion to the emptiness of content increasingly characterizing this Oneness.

(2) Then again, like Pantheists, Mystics dwell much upon the strict call to abandon all self-centredness, upon the death to self, the loss of self; and in proportion as they dwell upon this self to be thus rejected, and as they enlarge the range of this petty self, do they approach each other more and more.

(3) And lastly, there is a peculiarity about the Mystical habit of mind, which inevitably approximates it to the Pantheistic mode of thought, and which, if not continuously taken by the Mystic soul itself as an inevitable, but most demonstrable, in-

---

[1] *Religions-philosophie*, Germ. tr., ed. 1894, p. 140.

adequacy, will react upon the substance of this soul's thought in a truly Pantheistic sense. This peculiarity results from the Mystic's ever-present double tendency of absorbing himself, away from the Successive and Temporal, in the Simultaneity and Eternity of God, conceiving thus all reality as partaking, in proportion to its depth and greater likeness to Him, in this *Totum Simul* character of its ultimate Author and End; and of clinging to such vivid picturings of this reality as are within his, this Mystic's reach. Now such a Simultaneity can be pictorially represented to the mind only by the Spatial imagery of co-existent Extensions,—say of air, water, light, or fire: and these representations, if dwelt on as at all adequate, will necessarily suggest a Determinism of a Mathematico-Physical, Extensional type, *i. e.* one, and the dominant, side of Spinozistic Pantheism.—It is here, I think, that we get the double cause for the Pantheistic-seeming trend of almost all the Mystical imagery. For even the marked Emanationism of much in Plotinus, and of still more in Proclus,—the latter still showing through many a phrase in Dionysius,—appears in their images as operating upon a fixed Extensional foundation: and indeed these very over-flowings, owing to the self-centredness and emptiness of content of their Source, the One, and to their accidental yet automatic character, help still further to give to the whole outlook a strikingly materialistic, mechanical, in so far Pantheistic, character.

3. *Points on which Mysticism has usefully approximated to Pantheism.*

And yet we must not overlook the profound, irreplaceable services that are rendered by Mysticism,—provided always it remains but one of two great movements of the living soul,—even on the points in which it thus approximates to Pantheism. These services, I think, are three.

(1) The first of these services has been interestingly illustrated by Prof. A. S. Pringle Pattison, from the case of Dr. James Martineau's writings, and the largely unmediated co-existence there of two different modes of conceiving God. " The first mode represents God simply as another, higher Person; the second represents Him as the soul of souls. The former, Deistic and Hebraic, rests upon an inferential knowledge of God, derived either from the experience of His resistance to our will through the forces of Nature, or from that of His restraint upon us in the voice of Conscience,—

God, in both cases, being regarded as completely separated from the human soul, and His existence and character apprehended and demonstrated by a process of reasoning.—The second mode is distinctly and intensely Christian, and consists in the apprehension of God as the Infinite including all finite existences, as the immanent Absolute who progressively manifests His character in the Ideals of Truth, Beauty, Righteousness, and Love." And Professor Pattison points out, with Professor Upton, that it was Dr. Martineau's almost morbid dread of Pantheism which was responsible for the inadequate expression given to this Mystical, or "Speculative" element in his religious philosophy. For only if we do not resist such Mysticism, do we gain and retain a vivid experience of how " Consciousness of imperfection and the pursuit of perfection are alike possible to man only through the universal life of thought and goodness in which he shares, and which, at once an indwelling presence and an unattainable ideal, draws him on and always on." " Personality is " thus " not ' unitary ' in Martineau's sense, as occupying one side of a relation, and unable to be also on the other. The very capacity of knowledge and morality implies that the person . . . is capable of regarding himself and all other beings from what Martineau well names ' the station of the Father of Spirits.' " [1]

I would, however, guard here against any exclusion of a seeking or finding of God in Nature and in Conscience : only the contrary exclusion of the finding of God within the soul, and the insistence upon a complete separation of Him from that soul, are inacceptable in the " Hebraic " mood. For a coming and a going, a movement inwards and outwards, checks and counter-checks, friction, contrast, battle and storm, are necessary conditions and ingredients of the soul's growth in its sense of appurtenance to Spirit and to Peace.

(2) A further service rendered by this Pantheistic-seeming Mysticism,—though always only so long as it remains not the only or last word of Religion,—is that it alone discovers the truly spiritual function and fruitfulness of Deterministic Science. For only if Man deeply requires a profound de-subjectivizing, a great shifting of the centre of his interest, away from the petty, claimful, animal self, with its " I against all the world," to a great kingdom of souls, in which Man

---

[1] " Martineau's Philosophy," *Hibbert Journal*, Vol. I, 1902, pp. 458, 457.

gains his larger, spiritual, unique personality, with its " I as part of, and for all the world," by accepting to be but one amongst thousands of similar constituents in a system expressive of the thoughts of God; and only if Mathematico-Physical Science is specially fitted to provide such a bath, and hence is so taken, with all its apparently ruinous Determinism and seeming Godlessness: is such Science really safe from apologetic emasculation; or from running, a mere unrelated dilettantism, alongside of the deepest interests of the soul; or from, in its turn, crushing or at least hampering the deepest, the spiritual life of man. Hence all the greater Partial Mystics have got a something about them which indicates that they have indeed passed through fire and water, that their poor selfishness has been purified in a bath of painfully-bracing spiritual air and light, through which they have emerged into a larger, fuller life. And Nicolas of Coes, Pascal, Malebranche are but three men out of many whose Mysticism and whose Mathematico-Physical Science thus interstimulated each other and jointly deepened their souls.

We shall find, further on, that this purificatory power of such Science has been distinctly heightened for us now. Yet, both then and now, there could and can be such purification only for those who realize and practise religion as sufficiently ultimate and wide and deep to englobe, (as one of religion's necessary stimulants), an unweakened, utterly alien-seeming Determinism in the middle regions of the soul's experience and outlook. Such an englobement can most justly be declared to be Christianity driven fully home. For thus is Man purified and saved,—if he already possesses the dominant religious motive and conviction,—by a close contact with Matter; and the Cross is plunged into the very centre of his soul's life, operating there a sure division between the perishing animal Individual and the abiding spiritual Personality: the deathless Incarnational and Redemptive religion becomes thus truly operative there.

(3) And the last service, rendered by such Mysticism, is to keep alive in the soul the profoundly important consciousness of the prerequisites, elements and affinities of a Universally Human kind, which are necessary to, and present in, all Religion, however definitely Concrete, Historical and Institutional it may have become. Such special, characteristic Revelations, Doctrines and Institutions, as we find them in

all the great Historical Religions, and in their full normative substance and form in Christianity and Catholicism, can indeed alone completely develop, preserve and spread Religion in its depth and truth; yet they ever presuppose a general, usually dim but most real, religious sense and experience, indeed a real presence and operation of the Infinite and of God in all men.

It is, then, not an indifferentist blindness to the profound differences, in their degree of truth, between the religions of the world, nor an insufficient realization of man's strict need of historical and institutional lights and aids for the development and direction of that general religious sense and experience, which make the mind revolt from sayings such as those we have already quoted from the strongly Protestant Prof. Wilhelm Hermann, and to which we can add the following. "Everywhere, outside of Christianity, Mysticism will arise, as the very flower of the religious development. But the Christian must declare such Mystical experience of God to be a delusion." For "what is truly Christian is *ipso facto* not Mystical." "We are Christians because, in the Humanity of Jesus, we have struck upon a fact which is of incomparably richer content, than are the feelings that arise within our own selves." Indeed, "I should have failed to recognize the hand of God even in what my own dead father did for me, had not, by means of my Christian education, God appeared to me, in the Historic Christ." [1]—As if it were possible to consider Plato and Plotinus, in those religious intuitions and feelings of theirs which helped to win an Augustine from crass Manichaeism to a deep Spiritualism, and which continue to breathe and burn as part-elements in countless sayings of Christian philosophers and saints, to have been simply deluded, or mere idle subjectivists! As if we could apprehend even Christ, without some most real, however dim and general, sense of religion and presence of God within us to which He could appeal! And as if Jeremiah, Ezekiel and the Maccabaean Martyrs, and many a devoted soul within Mohammedanism or in Brahmanic India, could not and did not apprehend something of God's providence in their earthly father's love towards them!

No wonder that, after all this, Hermann can,—as against Richard Rothe who, in spite of more than one fantastic if not

---

[1] *Der Verkehr des Christen mit Gott*, ed. 1892, pp. 27, 15, 28, 231.

fanatical aberration, had, on some of the deepest religious matters, a rarely penetrating perception,—write in a thoroughly patronizing manner concerning Catholic Mysticism. For this Mysticism necessarily appears to him not as, at its best, the most massive and profound development of one type of the ultimate religion,—a type in which one necessary element of all balanced religious life is at the fullest expansion compatible with a still sufficient amount and healthiness of the other necessary elements of such a life,—but only as " a form of religion which has brought out and rendered visible such a content of interior life as is capable of being produced within the limits of Catholic piety." [1] The true, pure Protestant possesses, according to Hermann, apparently much less, in reality much more,—the Categorical Imperative of Conscience and the Jesus of History, as the double one-and-all of his, the only spiritual religion.—Yet if Christianity is indeed the religion of the Divine Founder, Who declared that he that is not against Him is for Him; or of Paul, who could appeal to the heathen Athenians and to all men for the truth and experience that in God " we live and move and have our being "; or of the great Fourth Gospel, which tells us that Christ, the True Light, enlighteneth every man that cometh into the world, a light which to this hour cannot, for the great majority, be through historic knowledge of the Historic Christ at all; or of Clement of Alexandria and of Justin Martyr, who loved to find deep apprehensions and operations of God scattered about among the Heathen; or of Aquinas, who, in the wake of the Areopagite and others, so warmly dwells upon how Grace does not destroy, but presupposes and perfects Nature: then such an exclusive amalgam of Moralism and History, though doubtless a most honest and intelligible reaction against opposite excesses, is a sad impoverishment of Christianity, in its essential, world-wide, Catholic character.

Indeed, to be fair, there have never been wanting richer and more balanced Protestant thinkers strongly to emphasize this profound many-sidedness and universality of Christianity: so, at present, in Germany, Profs. Eucken, Troeltsch, Class, Siebeck and others; and, in England, Prof. A. S. P. Pattison and Mr. J. R. Illingworth. In all these cases there is ever a strong sympathy with Mysticism properly understood

---

[1] *Der Verkehr des Christen mit Gott*, ed. 1892, pp. 20; 19-25.

as the surest safeguard against such distressing contractions as is this of Hermann, and that of Albrecht Ritschl before him.

4. *Christianity excludes complete and final Pantheism.*

And yet, as we have repeatedly found, Christianity has, in its fundamental Revelation and Experience, ever implied and affirmed such a conception of Unity, of Self-Surrender, and of the Divine Action, as to render any Pantheistic interpretation of these things ever incomplete and transitional.

(1) The Unity here is nowhere, even ultimately, the sheer Oneness of a simply identical Substance, but a Unity deriving its very close-knitness from its perfect organization of not simply identical elements or relations.

The Self-Surrender here is not a simply final resolution, of laboriously constituted centres of human spiritual consciousness and personality, back into a morally indifferent All, but a means and passage, for the soul, from a spiritually worthless self-entrenchment within a merely psycho-physical apartness and lust to live, on to a spiritual devotedness, an incorporation, as one necessary subject, into the Kingdom of souls,—the abiding, living expression of the abiding, living God.

And, above all, God's Action is not a mechanico-physical, determinist, simultaneous Extension, nor even an automatic, accidental, unconscious Emanation, but, as already Plato divined,—an intuition lost again by Aristotle, and, in his logic, denied by Plotinus,—a voluntary outgoing and self-communication of the supreme self-conscious Spirit, God. For Plato tells us that "the reason why Nature and this Universe of things was framed by Him Who framed it, is that God is good . . . and desired that all things should be as like Himself as it was possible for them to be." [1] Yet this pregnant apprehension never attains here to its full significance, because the Divine Intelligence is conceived only as manifesting itself in relation to something given from without, —the pre-existing, chaotic Matter. And for Aristotle God does not love this Givenness; for "the first Mover moves" (all things) only "as desired" by them : He Himself desires, loves, wills nothing whatsoever, and thinks and knows nothing but His own self alone.[2] And in Plotinus this same transcendence is still further emphasized, for the Absolute One here transcends even all thought and self-consciousness.

[1] *Timaeus*, 29e, seq.
[2] *Metaph.*, VII, 1072b; IX, 1074b.

(2) It is in Christianity, after noble preludings in Judaism, that we get the full deliberate proclamation, in the great Life and Teaching, of the profound fact,—the Self-Manifestation of the Loving God, the Spirit-God moving out to the spirit-man, and spirit-man only thus capable of a return movement to the Spirit-God. As Schelling said, "God can only give Himself to His creatures as He gives a self to them," and, with it, the capacity of participating in His life. We thus get a relation begun and rendered possible by God's utterly prevenient, pure, *ecstatic* love of Man, a relation which, in its essence spiritual, personal and libertarian, leaves behind it, as but vain travesties of such ultimate Realities, all Emanational or Parallelistic Pantheism, useful though these latter systems are as symbols of the Mathematico-Physical level and kind of reality and apprehension. Yet this spiritual relation is here, unlike Plotinus's more or less Emanational conception of it, not indeed simply invertible, as Spinoza would have it, (for Man is ontologically dependent upon God, whereas God is not thus dependent upon Man), but nevertheless largely one of true mutuality. And this mutuality of the relation is not simply a positive enactment of God, but is expressive, in its degree and mode, of God's intrinsic moral nature. For God is here the Source as well as the Object of all love; hence He Himself possesses the supreme equivalent for this our noblest emotion, and is moved to free acts of outgoing, in the creation and preservation, the revelation to, and the redemption of finite spirits, as so many sucessive, mutually supplementary, and increasingly fuller expressions and objects of this His nature. "God is Love"; "God so loved the world, that He gave His only-begotten Son"; "Let us love God, for God hath first loved us"; "if any man will do the will of God, he shall know of the doctrine if it be from God": God's Infinity is here, not the negation of the relatively independent life of His creatures, but the very reason and source of their freedom.[1]

In the concluding chapter I hope to give a sketch of the actual operation of the true correctives to any excessive, Plotinian or Spinozistic, tendencies in the Mystical trend, especially when utilizing Mathematico-Physical Science at the soul's middle level; and of History at the ultimate reaches of the soul's life.

[1] See Caird, *op. cit.* II, p. 337.

IV. THE DIVINE IMMANENCE; SPIRITUAL PERSONALITY

1. *Pantheism.*

As to our fourth question, the Divine Immanence and Personality, our last quotations from St. Teresa give us, I think, our true starting-point. For it is evident that, between affirming the simple Divinity of the innermost centre of the soul, and declaring that the soul ever experiences only the Grace of God, *i. e.* certain created effects, sent by Him from the far-away seat of His own full presence, there is room for a middle position which, whilst ever holding the definite creatureliness of the soul, in all its reaches, puts God Himself into the soul and the soul into God, in degrees and with results which vary indeed indefinitely according to its good-will and its call, yet which all involve and constitute a presence ever profoundly real, ever operative before and beyond all the soul's own operations. These latter operations are, indeed, even possible only through all this Divine anticipation, origin-ation, preservation, stimulation, and, at bottom,—in so far as man is enabled and required by God to reach a certain real self-constitution,—through a mysterious Self-Limitation of God's own Action,—a Divine Self-Restraint.

There can be little doubt that such a *Panentheism* is all that many a daring, in strictness Pantheistic, saying of the Christian, perhaps also of the Jewish and Mohammedan, Mystics aimed at. Only the soul's ineradicable capacity, need and desire for its Divine Lodger and Sustainer would constitute, in this conception, the intrinsic characteristic of human nature; and it is rather the too close identification, in feeling and emotional expression, of the desire and the Desired, of the hunger and the Food, and the too exclusive realization of the deep truth that this desire and hunger do not cause, but are themselves preceded and caused by, their Object,—it is the over-vivid perception of this real dynamism, rather than any *a priori* theory of static substances and identities—which, certainly in many cases, has produced the appearance of Pantheism.

And again it is certain that we have to beware of taking the apparent irruption or ingrafting,—in the case of the operations of Grace,—of an entirely heterogeneous Force and Reality into what seems the already completely closed circle of our natural functions and aspirations, as the complete and ultimate truth of the situation. However utterly different that Force may feel to all else that we are aware of within ourselves, however entirely unmeditated may seem its manifestations : it is clear that we should be unable to recognize even this Its difference, to welcome or resist It, above all to find It a response to our deepest cravings, unless we had some natural true affinity to It, and some dim but most real experience of It from the first. Only with such a general religiosity and vague sense, from a certain contact, of the Infinite, is the recognition of definite, historical Religious Facts and Figures as true, significant, binding upon my will and conscience, explicable at all.

affinity to
divin
experience of
God
Sense of
Infinite

2. *Aquinas on our direct semi-consciousness of God's indwelling.*

St. Thomas, along one line of doctrine, has some excellent teachings about all this group of questions. For though he tells us that " the names which we give to God and creatures, are predicated of God " only " according to a certain relation of the creature to God, as its Principle and Cause, in which latter the perfections of all things pre-exist in an excellent manner " : [1] yet he explicitly admits, in one place, that we necessarily have some real, immediate experience of the Nature of God, for that " it is impossible, with regard to anything, to know whether it exists,"—and he has admitted that natural reason can attain to a knowledge of God's bare existence,—" unless we somehow know what is its nature," at least " with a confused knowledge "; whence " also with regard to God, we could not know whether He exists, unless we somehow know, even though confusedly, what He is."— God, though transcendent, is also truly immanent in the human soul : " God is in all things, as the agent is present in that wherein it acts. Created Being is as true an effect of God's Being, as to burn is the true effect of fire. God is above all things,—by the excellence of His nature, and yet He is intimately present within all things, as the cause of the Being of all."—And man has a natural exigency of the face-to-face Vision of God, hence of the Order of Grace, however entirely its attainment may be beyond his natural powers : " There is in man a natural longing to know the cause, when he sees an effect : whence if the intellect of the rational

Aq.

immanence
of God

[1] *Summa Theol.*, I, qu. 13, art. 5, concl. et in corp. (See the interesting note, " The Meaning of Analogy," in Fr. Tyrrell's *Lex Orandi*, 1903, pp. 80–83.) *In Librum Boetii de Trinitate :* D. Thomae Aquinatis *Opera*, ed. Veneta Altera, 1776, p. 341*b*, 342*a*.

creature could not attain to the First Cause of things,"—here in the highest form, that of the Beatific vision of God—" the longing of its nature would remain void and vain." [1]

But it is the great Mystical Saints and writers who continuously have, in the very forefront of their consciousness and assumptions, not a simply moral and aspirational, but an Ontological and Pre-established relation between the soul and God; and not a simply discursive apprehension, but a direct though dim Experience of the Infinite and of God. And these positions really underlie even their most complete-seeming negations, as we have already seen in the case of the Areopagite.

3. *Gradual recognition of the function of subconsciousness.*

Indeed, we can safely affirm that the last four centuries, and even the last four decades, have more and more confirmed the reality and indirect demonstrableness of such a presence and sense of the Infinite; ever more or less obscurely, but none the less profoundly, operative in the innermost normal consciousness of mankind: a presence and sense which, though they can be starved and verbally denied, cannot be completely suppressed; and which, though they do not, if unendorsed, constitute even the most elementary faith, far less a developed Historical or Mystical Religion, are simply necessary prerequisites to all these latter stimulations and consolidations.

(1) As we have already found, it is only since Leibniz that we know, systematically, how great is the range of every man's Obscure Presentations, his dim Experience as against his Clear or distinct Presentations, his explicit Knowledge; and how the Clear depends even more upon the Dim, than the Dim upon the Clear. And further discoveries and proofs in this direction are no older than 1888.[2]

(2) Again, it is the growing experience of the difficulties and complexities of Psychology, History, Epistemology, and of the apparent unescapableness and yet pain of man's mere anthropomorphisms, that makes the persistence of his search for, and sense of, Objective Truth and Reality, and the keen-

---

[1] *Summa Theol.*, I, qu. 12, art. 1, in corp.

[2] For Leibniz, see especially his *Nouveaux Essais*, written in 1701–1709, but not published till 1765: *Die Philosophischen Schriften von G. W. Leibniz*, ed. Gebhardt, Vol. V, 1882, especially pp. 45; 67; 69; 121, 122. For the date 1888, see W. James's *Varieties of Religious Experience*, 1902, p. 233.

ness of his suffering when he appears to himself as imprisoned
in mere subjectivity, deeply impressive.   For the more man
feels, and suffers from feeling himself purely subjective, the
more is it clear that he is not merely subjective : he could
never be conscious of the fact, if he were.   "Suppose that all
your objects in life were realized . . . would this be a great
joy and happiness to you?" John Stuart Mill asked himself;
and "an irrepressible self-consciousness distinctly answered
'No.'" [1]   Whether in bad health just then or not, Mill was
here touching the very depths of the characteristically human
sense.   In all such cases only a certain profound apprehension
of Abiding Reality, the Infinite, adequately explains the keen,
operative sense of contrast and disappointment.

(3) And further, we have before us, with a fulness and
delicate discrimination undreamed of in other ages, the
immense variety, within a certain general psychological
unity, of the great and small Historical Religions, past and
present, of the world.   Facing all this mass of evidence,
Prof. Troeltsch can ask, more confidently than ever : "Are
not our religious requirements, requirements of Something
that one must have somehow first experienced in order
to require It?   Are they not founded upon some kind of
Experience as to the Object, Which Itself first awakens the
thought of an ultimate infinite meaning attaching to existence, and Which, in the conflict with selfishness, sensu-
ality and self-will, draws the nobler part of the human will,
with ever new force, to Itself?"   "All deep and energetic
religion is in a certain state of tension towards Culture, for
the simple reason that it is seeking something else and something higher." [2]   And Prof. C. P. Tiele, so massively learned in
all the great religions, concludes : "'Religion,' says Feuerbach,
'proceeds from man's wishes' . . . ; according to others, it is
the outcome of man's dissatisfaction with the external world.
. . . But why should man torment himself with wishes
which he never sees fulfilled around him, and which the
rationalistic philosopher declares to be illusions?   Why?
surely, because he cannot help it. . . . The Infinite, very
Being as opposed to continual becoming and perishing,—
or call It what you will,—*that* is the Principle which gives
him constant unrest, because It dwells within him."   And

[1] *Autobiography*, ed. 1875, pp. 133, 134.
[2] "Die Selbständigkeit der Religion"; *Zeitschrift f. Theologie u. Kirche*,
1895, pp. 404, 405.

against Prof. Max Müller,—who had, however, on this point, arrived at a position very like Tiele's own,—he impressively insists that " the origin of religion consists," not in a " perception of the Infinite," but " in the fact that Man *has* the Infinite within him."—I would only contend further that the instinct of the Infinite awakens simultaneously with our sense-perceptions and categories of thinking, and passes, together with them and with the deeper, more volitional experiences, through every degree and stage of obscurity and relative clearness. " Whatever name we give it,—instinct; innate, original, or unconscious form of thought; or form of conception,—it is the specifically human element in man." [1] But if all this be true, then the Mystics are amongst the great benefactors of our race : for it is especially this presence of the Infinite in Man, and man's universal subjection to an operative consciousness of it, which are the deepest cause and the constant object of the adoring awe of all truly spiritual Mystics, in all times and places.

[1] *Elements of the Science of Religion,* 1897, Vol. II, pp. 227-231.

CHAPTER XV

SUMMING UP OF THE WHOLE BOOK. BACK THROUGH
ASCETICISM, SOCIAL RELIGION, AND THE SCIENTIFIC
HABIT OF MIND, TO THE MYSTICAL ELEMENT OF
RELIGION.

I NOW propose to conclude, by getting, through three
successively easier matters, back to the starting-point of this
whole book, and, in doing so, to sum up and delimitate, more
and more clearly, the practical lessons learnt during its long
course. These three last matters and points of observation
shall be Asceticism, Institutionalism, and Mental Activity
and Discipline, or the Scientific Habit—all three in their
relation to the Mystical Element of Religion.

I. ASCETICISM AND MYSTICISM.

Now in the matter of Asceticism, we can again conveniently consider three points.

1. *Ordinary Asceticism practised by Mystics.*

There is, first, the (generally severe) Asceticism which is
ever connected with at least some one phase, an early one,
of every genuine Mystic's history, yet which does not differ
essentially from the direct training in self-conquest to which
practically all pre-Protestant, and most of the old Protestant earnest Christians considered themselves obliged.

(1) Now it is deeply interesting to note how marked has been,
off and on throughout the last century and now again quite
ᴿecently, the renewal of comprehension and respect for the
general principle of Asceticism, in quarters certainly free from
all preliminary bias in favour of Medieval Christianity
Schopenhauer wrote in 1843 : " Not only the religions of
the East but also genuine Christianity shows, throughout its
systems, that fundamental characteristic of Asceticism which
my philosophy elucidates. . . . Precisely in its doctrines of

renunciation, self-denial, complete chastity, in a word, of general mortification of the will, lie the deepest truth, the high value, the sublime character of Christianity. It thus belongs to the old, true, and lofty ideal of mankind, in opposition to the false, shallow, and ruinous optimism of Greek Paganism, Judaism and Islam." " Protestantism, by eliminating Asceticism and its central point, the meritoriousness of celibacy, has, by this alone, already abandoned the innermost kernel of Christianity. . . . For Christianity is the doctrine of the deep guilt of the human race . . . and of the heart's thirst after redemption from it, a redemption which can be acquired only through the abnegation of self,—that is, through a complete conversion of human nature." [1]—And the optimistically tempered American Unitarian, the deeply versed Psychologist, Prof. William James, tells us in 1902 : " In its spiritual meaning, Asceticism stands for nothing less than for the essence of the twice-born philosophy." " The Metaphysical mystery, that he who feeds on death, that feeds on men, possesses life supereminently, and meets best the secret demands of the Universe, is the truth of which Asceticism has been the faithful champion. The folly of the cross, so inexplicable by the intellect, has, yet, its indestructible, vital meaning. . . . Naturalistic optimism is mere syllabub and sponge-cake in comparison." [2]

(2) Indeed, the only thing at all special to Mysticism, in its attitude towards this general principle and practice of Asceticism, is that it ever practises Asceticism as a means towards, or at least as the make-weight and safeguard of, Contemplation, which latter is as essentially Synthetic, and, in so far, peaceful and delightful, as the former is Analytic, polemical and painful ; whereas non-Mystical souls will practise Asceticism directly with a view to greater aloofness from sin, and greater readiness and strength to perform the various calls of duty. And hence, if we but grant the legitimacy of the general principle of ordinary Asceticism, we shall find the Mystical form of this Asceticism to be the more easily comprehensible variety of that principle. For the Mystic's practice, as concerns this point, is more varied and inclusive than that of others, since he does not even tend to make the whole of his inner life into a system of checks and of tension.

---

[1] *Die Welt als Wille und Vorstellung*, ed. Griesbach, Vol. II, pp. 725, 734, 736.

[2] *The Varieties of Religious Experience*, 1902, pp. 362, 364.

The expansive, reconciling movement operates in him most strongly also, and, where of the right kind, this expansive movement helps, even more than the restrictive one, to purify humble, and deepen his heart and soul.

2. *God's Transcendence a source of suffering.*

There is, however, a second, essentially different source and kind of suffering in some sorts and degrees of Mysticism, and indeed in other *attraits* of the spiritual life, which is deeply interesting, because based upon a profound Meta-physical apprehension. Although, at bottom, the opposite extreme to Pantheism, it readily expresses itself, for reasons that will presently appear, in terms that have a curiously Pantheistic colour.

(1) St. John of the Cross writes in 1578 : " It is a principle of philosophy, that all means must . . . have a certain resemblance to the end, such as shall be sufficient for the object in view. If therefore the understanding is to be united to God, . . . it must make use of those means which can effect that union, that is, means which are most like unto God. . . . But there is no essential likeness or communion between creatures and Him, the distance between His divine nature and their nature is infinite. No creature therefore . . . nothing that the imagination may conceive or the understanding comprehend . . . in this life . . . can be a proximate means of union with God," for " it is all most unlike God, and most disproportionate to Him." " The understanding . . . must be pure and empty of all sensible objects, all clear intellectual perceptions, resting on faith : for faith is the sole proximate and proportionate means of the soul's union with God." [1]

Now it is certain, as we have already found, that the awakened human soul ever possesses a dim but real experience of the Infinite, and that, in proportion as it is called to the Mystical way, this sense will be deepened into various degrees of the Prayer of Quiet and of Union, and that here, more plainly than elsewhere, will appear the universal necessity of the soul's own response, by acts and the habit of Faith, to all and every experience which otherwise remains but so much unused material for the soul's advance. And it is equally certain that St. John of the Cross is one of the greatest of such contemplatives, and that neither his intuition

---

[1] *Ascent of Mount Carmel*, tr. David Lewis, ed. 1889, pp. 94, 95, 97.

and actual practice, nor even his sayings, (so long as any one
saying belonging to one trend is set off against another
belonging to the other trend,) contravenes the Christian and
Catholic positions.—Yet it cannot be denied that, were we to
press his " negative way " into becoming the only one; and
especially were we to take, without discount, such a virtual
repudiation, as is furnished by any insistence upon the above
words, of any essential, objective difference in value between
our various apprehensions of Him and approaches to Him :
the whole system and *rationale* of External, Sacramental and
Historical Religion, indeed of the Incarnation, in any degree
and form, would have to go, as so many stumbling-blocks to
the soul's advance. For the whole principle of all such
Religion implies the profound importance of the Here and
the Now, the Contingent and the Finite, and of the Immanence
of God, in various degrees and ways, within them.

Indications of this incompatibility, as little systematically
realized here as in the Areopagite, are afforded by various
remarks of his, belonging in reality to another trend. Thus,
immediately before his denial of any essential likeness or
communion between any creature and God, he says : " It is
true that all creatures bear a certain relation to God and are
tokens of His Being, some more, some less, according to the
greater perfection of their nature." And of Our Lord's sacred
Humanity he says : " What a perfect living image was Our
Saviour upon earth : yet those who had no faith, though they
were constantly about Him, and saw His wonderful works,
were not benefited by His presence." [1] But even here the
immense importance, indeed downright necessity for Faith, of
such external and historical stimuli, objects and materials,—
in the latter instance all this at its very deepest,—remains
unemphasized, through his engrossment in the necessity of
Faith for the fructification of all these things.

In other places this Faith appears as though working so
outside of all things imageable, as to have to turn rapidly
away from all picturings, as, at best, only momentary starting-
points for the advanced soul. " Let the faithful soul take
care that, whilst contemplating an image, the senses be not
absorbed in it, whether it be material or in the imagination,
and whether the devotion it excites be spiritual or sensible.
Let him . . . venerate the image as the Church commands

---

[1] *Ascent*, pp. 94; 350.

and lift up his mind at once from the material image to those
whom it represents.   He who shall do this, will never be deluded." [1]   Here, again, along the line of argument absorbing
the saint in this book, there is no fully logical ground left for
the Incarnational, Historical, Sacramental scheme of the Infinite immanent in the finite, and of spirit stimulated in
contact with matter, with everywhere the need of the conde-
scensions of God and of our ascensions by means of careful
attention to them.

Sören Kierkegaard, that deep solitary Dane, with so much
about him like to Pascal the Frenchman, and Hurrell Froude
the Englishman, and who, though Lutheran in all his bringing
up, was so deeply attracted by Catholic Asceticism, has, in
recent times (he died in 1855), pushed the doctrine of the
qualitative, absolute difference between God and all that we
ourselves can think, feel, will or be, to lengths beyond even
the transcendental element,—we must admit this to be the
greatly preponderant one,—in the great Spaniard's formal
teaching.   And it is especially in this non-Mystical Ascetic
that we get an impressive picture of the peculiar kind of
suffering and asceticism, which results from such a conviction
to a profoundly sensitive, absorbedly religious soul; and here
too we can, I think, discover the precise excess and onesidedness involved in this whole tendency.   Professor Höffding,
in his most interesting monograph on his friend, tells us how
" for Kierkegaard, . . . the will gets monopolized by religious
Ethics from the very first; there is no time for Contemplation
or Mysticism."   " To tear the will away," Kierkegaard himself says, " from all finite aims and conditions . . . requires a
painful effort and this effort's ceaseless repetition.   And if, in
addition to this, the soul has, in spite of all its striving, to be
as though it simply were not, it becomes clear that the religious life signifies a dedication to suffering and to self-
destruction.   What wonder, then, that, for the Jew, death was
the price of seeing God; or that, for the Gentile, the soul's
entering into closer relations with the Deity meant the beginning of madness? "   For " the soul's relation to God is a
relation to a Being absolutely different from Man, who cannot
confront him as his Superlative or Ideal, and who, nevertheless, is to rule in his inmost soul.   Hence a necessary division,
ever productive of new pains, is operative within man, as long

[1] *Ascent*, p. 353.

as he perseveres in this spiritual endeavour. . . . A finite being, he is to live in the Infinite and Absolute : he is there like a fish upon dry land." [1]

Now Prof. Höffding applies a double, most cogent criticism to this position.—The one is religious, and has already been quoted. " A God Who is not Ideal and Pattern is no God. Hence the contention that the Nature of the Godhead is, of necessity, qualitatively different from that of Man, has ever occasioned ethical and religious misgivings."—And the other is psychological. " Tension can indeed be necessary for the truth and the force of life. But tension, taken by itself, cannot furnish the true measure of life. For the general nature of consciousness is a synthesis, a comprehensive unity : not only contrast, but also concentration, must make itself felt, as long as the life of consciousness endures." [2]

It is deeply interesting to note how Catherine, and at bottom St. John of the Cross and the Exclusive Mystics generally, escape, through their practice and in some of their most emphatic teachings, from Kierkegaard's excess, no doubt in part precisely because they *are* Mystics, since the exclusive Mystic's contemplative habit is, at bottom, a Synthetic one. Yet we should realize the deep truth which underlies the very exaggerations of this onesidedly Analytic and Ascetical view.

God For if God is the deepest ideal, the ultimate driving force and the true congenital element and environment of Man, such as Man cannot but secretly wish to will deliberately, and which, at his best, Man truly wills to hold and serve : yet God remains ever simply incompatible with that part of each man's condition and volition which does not correspond to the best and deepest which that Man himself sees or could see to be the better, *hic et nunc ;* and, again, He is ever, even as compared with any man's potential best, infinitely more and nobler, and, though here not in simple contradiction, yet at a degree of perfection which enables Him, the Supreme Spirit, to penetrate, as Immanent Sustainer or Stimulator, and to confront, as Transcendent Ideal and End, the little human spirit, so great in precisely this its keen sense of experienced contrast.

Catherine exhibits well this double relation, of true contradiction, and of contrast, both based upon a certain genuine

---

[1] *Sören Kierkegaard*, von Harald Höffding, Germ. tr. 1896, pp. 116, 118, 120.

[2] *Ibid.* pp. 122; 130, 131.

affinity between the human soul and God.   On one side of
herself she is indeed a veritable fish out of water; but, on the
other side of her, she is a fish happily disporting itself in its
very element, in the boundless ocean of God.   On the one
side, snapping after air, in that seemingly over-rarified atmosphere in which the animal man, the mere selfish individual,
cannot live; on the other side, expanding her soul's lungs
and drinking in light, life, and love, in that same truly rich
atmosphere, which, Itself Spirit, feeds and sustains her growing spiritual personality.   And the *Dialogo*, in spite of its
frequently painful abstractness and empty unity, has, upon
the whole, a profound hold upon this great doctrine.

Yet it is in Catherine's own culminating intuition,—of the
soul's free choice of Purgatory, as a joyful relief from the
piercing pain of what otherwise would last for ever,—the
vividly perceived contrast between God's purity and her
soul's impurity, that we get, in the closest combination, indeed mutual causation, this double sense of Man's nearness to
and distance from, of his likeness and unlikeness to God.   For
only if man is, in the deepest instincts of his soul, truly related
to God, and is capable of feeling, (indeed he ever actually,
though mostly dimly, experiences,) God's presence and this,
man's own, in great part but potential, affinity to Him: can
suffering be conceived to arise from the keen realization of
the contrast between God and man's own actual condition at
any one moment; and can any expectation, indeed a swift
vivid instinct, arise within man's soul that the painful, directly
contradictory, discrepancy can and will, gradually though
never simply automatically, be removed.   And though, even
eventually, the creature cannot, doubtless, ever become simply
God, yet it can attain, in an indefinitely higher degree, to
that affinity and union of will with God, which, in its highest
reaches and moments, it already now substantially possesses;
and hence to that full creaturely self-constitution and joy in
which, utterly trusting, giving itself to, and willing God, it
will, through and in Him, form an abidingly specific, unique
constituent and link of His invisible kingdom of souls, on
and on.

3. *Discipline of fleeing and of facing the Multiple and
Contingent.*

But there is a third attitude, peculiar (because of its preponderance) to the Mystics as such, an attitude in a manner
intermediate between that of ordinary Asceticism, and that of

the Suffering just described. The implications and effects of, and the correctives for, this third attitude will occupy us up to the end of this book. I refer to the careful turning-away from all Multiplicity and Contingency, from the Visible and Successive, from all that does or can distract and dissipate, which is so essential and prevailing a feature in all Mysticism, which indeed, in Exclusive Mysticism, is frankly made into the one sole movement towards, and measure of, the soul's perfection.

(1) It is true that to this tendency, when and in so far as it has come so deeply to permeate the habits of a soul as to form a kind of second nature, the name Asceticism cannot, in strictness, be any more applied; since now the pain will lie, not in this turning away from all that dust and friction, but, on the contrary, in any forcing of the soul back into that turmoil. And doubtless many, perhaps most, souls with a pronouncedly mystical *attrait*, are particularly sensitive to all, even partial and momentary, conflict. Yet we can nevertheless appropriately discuss the matter under the general heading of Asceticism, since, as a rule, much practice and sacrifice go to build up this habit; since, in every case, this Abstractive Habit shares with Ordinary Asceticism a pronounced hostility to many influences and forces ever actually operative within and around the undisciplined natural man; and since, above all, the very complements and correctives for this Abstractiveness will have to come from a further, deeper and wider Asceticism, to be described presently.

(2) As to Ordinary Asceticism and this Abstractiveness, the former fights the world and the self directly, and then only in so far as they are discovered to be positively evil or definitely to hinder positive good; it is directly attracted by the clash and friction involved in such fighting; and it has no special desire for even a transitory intense unification of the soul's life: whereas the Abstractiveness turns away from, and rises above, the world and the phenomenal self; their very existence, their contingency, the struggles alive within them, and their (as it seems) inevitably disturbing effect upon the soul, —are all felt as purely dissatisfying; and an innermost longing for a perfect and continuous unification and overflowing harmony of its inner life here possess the spirit.

(3) Now we have just seen how a movement of integration, of synthesizing all the soul's piecemeal, inter-jostling acquisitions, of restful healing of its wounds and rents, of sinking back,

(from the glare and glitter of clear, and then ever fragmentary perception, and from the hurry, strain and rapidly ensuing distraction involved in all lengthy external action), into a peaceful, dim rumination and unification, is absolutely necessary, though in very various degrees and forms, for all in any way complete and mature souls.—And we have, further back, realized that a certain, obscure but profoundly powerful, direct instinct and impression of God in the soul is doubtless at work here, and, indeed, throughout all the deeper and nobler movements of our wondrously various inner life. But what concerns us here, is the question whether the *complete* action of the soul, (if man would grow in accordance with his ineradicable nature, environment, and specific grace and call,) does not as truly involve a corresponding counter-movement to this intensely unitive and intuitive movement which, with most men, and in most moments of even the minority of men, forms but an indirectly willed condition and spontaneous background of the soul.

(4) We have been finding, further, that all the Contingencies, Multiplicities and Mediations which, one and all, tend to appear to the Mystic as so many resistances and distractions, can roughly be grouped under two ultimate heads. These intruders are fellow-souls, or groups of fellow-souls,—some social organism, the Family, Society, the State, the Church, who provoke, in numberless degrees and ways, individual affection, devotion, distraction, jealousy, as from person towards person. Or else the intruders are Things and Mechanical Laws, and these usually leave the Mystic indifferent or irritate or distract him; but they can become for him great opportunities of rest, and occasions for self-discipline.

Yet this distinction between Persons and Things, (although vital for the true apprehension of all deeper, above all of the deepest Reality, and for the delicate discrimination between what are but the means and what are the ends in a truly spiritual life,) does not prevent various gradations within, and continuous interaction between, each of these two great groups. For in proportion as, in the Personal group, the Individual appears as but parcel and expression of one of the social organisms, does the impression of determinist Law, of an impersonal Thing or blind Force, begin to mix with, and gradually to prevail over, that of Personality. And in proportion as, in the Impersonal group, Science comes to include all careful and methodical study, according to the most appropriate methods, of any and every kind of truth and reality; and as it moves away from the conceptions of purely quantitative matter, and of the merely numerically different, entirely interchangeable, physical happenings, (all so many mere automatic illustrations of mechanical Law,) on, through the lowly organisms of plant-life, and the ever higher interiority and richer consciousness of animal life, up to Man, with his ever qualitative Mind, and his ever non-interchangeable, ever " effortful," achievements and elaborations of types of beauty, truth and goodness in Human History,—does Science itself come back, in its very method and subject-matter, ever more nearly, to the great personal starting-point, standard and ultimate motive of all our specifically human activity and worth.

(5) Indeed, the two great continuous facts of man's life, first that he thinks, feels, wills, and acts, in and with the help or hindrance of that profoundly material Thing, his physical body, and on occasion of, with regard to, the materials furnished by the stimulations and impressions of his senses; and again, that these latter awaken within him those, in themselves, highly abstract and Thing-like categories of his mind which penetrate and give form to these materials; are enough to show how close is the pressure, and how continuous the effect, of Things upon the slow upbuilding of Personality.

(6) Fair approximations to these two kinds of Things, with their quite irreplaceable specific functions within the economy of the human mental life,—the intensely concrete and particular Sense-Impressions, and the intensely abstract and general Mental Categories,—reappear within the economy of Characteristic Religion, in its Sacraments and its Doctrine. And conversely, there exists, *in rerum natura*, no Science worth having which is not, ultimately, the resultant of, and which does not require and call forth, on and on, certain special qualities, and combinations of qualities, of the truly ethical, spiritual Personality. Courage, patience, perseverance, candour, simplicity, self-oblivion, continuous generosity towards others and willing correction of even one's own most cherished views,—these things and their like are not the quantitative determinations of Matter, but the qualitative characteristics of Mind.

(7) I shall now, therefore, successively take Mysticism in its attitude towards these two great groups of claimants upon

its attention, the Personal and the Impersonal, even though
any strictly separate discussion of elements which, in practice,
ever appear together, cannot but have some artificiality.   And
an apparent further complication will be caused by our having,
in each case, to contrast what Mysticism would do, if it
became Exclusive, with what it must be restricted to doing, if
it is to remain Inclusive, *i. e.* if it is to be but one element in
the constitution of that multiplicity in unity, the deep spiritual
Personality.   The larger Asceticism will thus turn out to be
a wider and deeper means towards perfection than even
genuine Mysticism itself, since this Asceticism will have to
include both this Mysticism and the counter movement
within the one single, disciplined and purified life of the soul.

II. Social Religion and Mysticism.

Introductory : the ruinousness of Exclusive Mysticism.
Prof. Harnack says in his *Dogmengeschichte* : " An old
fairy tale tells of a man who lived in ignorance, dirt and
wretchedness ; and whom God invited, on a certain day, to
wish whatsoever he might fancy, and it should be given him.
And the man began to wish things, and ever more things, and
ever higher things, and all these things were given him.   At
last he became presumptuous, and desired to become as the
great God Himself : when lo, instantly he was sitting there
again, in his dirt and misery.   Now the history of Religion,—
especially amongst the Greeks and Orientals,—closely resembles this fairy tale.   For they began by wishing for themselves certain sensible goods, and then political, aesthetic,
moral and intellectual goods : and they were given them all.
And then they became Christians and desired perfect knowledge and a super-moral life : they even wished to become,
already here below, as God Himself, in insight, beatitude and
life.   And behold, they fell, not at once indeed, but with a
fall that could not be arrested, down to the lowest level, back
into ignorance, dirt and barbarism. . . . Like unto their
near spiritual relations, the Neo-Platonists, they were at first
over-stimulated, and soon became jaded, and hence required
ever stronger stimulants.   And in the end, all these exquisite
aspirations and enjoyments turned into their opposite
extreme." [1]

[1] *Lehrbuch der Dogmengeschichte*, ed. 1888, Vol. II, pp. 413, 414 ; 417.

However much may want discounting or supplementing here, there is, surely, a formidable amount of truth in this picture. And, if so, is Mysticism, at least in its Dionysian type, not deeply to blame? And where is the safeguard against such terrible abuses?

Now Prof. Harnack has himself shown us elsewhere that there is a sense in which Monasticism should be considered eternal, even among and for Protestants. "Monasticism," he says plaintively, in his account of the first three centuries of Protestantism, "even as it is conceivable and necessary among Evangelical Christians, disappeared altogether. And yet every community requires persons, who live *exclusively* for its purposes; hence the Church too requires volunteers who shall renounce ' the world ' and shall dedicate themselves entirely to the service of their neighbour." [1]—And again, scholars of such breadth of knowledge and independence of judgement as Professor Tiele and his school, insist strongly upon the necessity of Ecclesiastical Institutions and Doctrines. The day of belief in the normality, indeed in the possibility for mankind in general, of a would-be quite individual, entirely spiritual, quite " pure " religion, is certainly over and gone, presumably for good and all, amongst all competent workers.—Nor, once more, can the general Mystical sense of the unsatisfying character of all things finite, and of the Immanence of the Infinite in our poor lives, be, in itself, to blame : for we have found these experiences to mingle with, and to characterize, all the noblest, most fully human acts and personalities.—But, if so, what are the peculiarities in the religion of those times and races, which helped to produce the result pictured in the *Dogmengeschichte* ?

Now here, to get a fairly final answer, we must throw together the question of the ordinary Christian Asceticism and that of the Abstraction peculiar to the Mystics; and we must ask whether the general emotive-volitional attitude towards Man and Life,—the theory and practice as to Transcendence and Immanence, Detachment and Attachment, which, from about 500 A.D. to, say, 1450 A.D., predominantly preceded, accompanied, and both expanded and deflected the specifically Christian and normally human experience in Eastern Christendom, were not (however natural, indeed inevitable, and in part useful for those times and races), the chief of the

---

[1] *Das Wesen des Christenthums*, ed. 1902, pp. 180, 181.

causes which turned so much of the good of Mysticism into downright harm. At bottom this is once more the question as to the one-sided character of Neo-Platonism,—its incapacity to find any descending movement of the Divine into Human life.

1. *True relation of the soul to its fellows.   God's " jealousy."*
Let us take first the relation of the single human soul to its fellow-souls.

(1) Now Kierkegaard tells us : " the Absolute is cruel, for it demands *all*, whilst the Relative ever continues to demand *some* attention from us." [1]   And the Reverend George Tyrrell, in his stimulating paper, *Poet and Mystic*, shows us that, as regards the relations between man's love for man and man's love for God, there are two conceptions and answers in reply to the question as to the precise sense in which God is " a jealous God," and demands to be loved alone.   In the first, easier, more popular conception, He is practically thought of as the First of Creatures, competing with the rest for Man's love, and is here placed alongside of them.   Hence the inference that whatever love they win from us by reason of their inherent goodness, is taken from Him : He is not loved perfectly, till He is loved alone.   But in the second, more difficult and rarer conception, God is placed, not alongside of creatures but behind them, as the light which shines through a crystal and lends it whatever lustre it may have. He is loved here, not apart from, but through and in them. Hence if only the affection be of the right kind as to mode and object, the more the better.   The love of Him is the " form," the principle of order and harmony;   our natural affections are the " matter " harmonized and set in order ; it is the soul, they are the body, of that one Divine Love whose adequate object is God in, and not apart from, His creatures.[2] Thus we have already found that even the immensely abstractive and austere St. John of the Cross tells us : " No one desires to be loved except for his goodness; and when we love in this way, our love is pleasing unto God and in great liberty; and if there be attachment in it, there is greater attachment to God."   And this doctrine he continuously, deliberately practises, half-a-century after his Profession, for he writes to his penitent, Donna Juana de Pedrazas in 1589 : " All that is wanting now, is that I should forget you; but

---

[1] Höffding's *Kierkegaard*, p. 119.
[2] *The Faith of the Million*, 1901, Vol. II, pp. 49, 50; 52, 53.

consider how that is to be forgotten which is ever present to the soul." [1]

But Father Tyrrell rightly observes : " To square this view with the general ascetic tradition of the faithful at large is exceedingly difficult." [2] Yet I cannot help thinking that a somewhat different reconciliation, than the one attempted by him,[3] really meets all the substantial requirements of the case.

(2) I take it, then, that an all-important double law or twin fact, or rather a single law and fact whose unity is composed of two elements, is, to some extent, present throughout all characteristically human life, although its full and balanced realization, even in theory and still more in practice, is ever, necessarily, a more or less unfulfilled ideal : viz. that not only there exist certain objects, acts, and affections that are simply wrong, and others that are simply right or perfect, either for all men or for some men : but that there exist simply no acts and affections which, however right, however obligatory, however essential to the perfection of us all or of some of us, do not require, on our own part, a certain alternation of interior reserve and detachment away from, and of familiarity and attachment to, them and their objects. This general law applies as truly to Contemplation as it does to Marriage.

And next, the element of detachment which has to penetrate and purify simply all attachments,—even the attachment to detachment itself,—is the more difficult, the less obvious, the more profoundly spiritual and human element and movement, although only on condition that ever some amount of the other, of the outgoing element and movement, and of attachment, remains. For here, as everywhere, there is no good and operative yeast except with and in flour ; there can be no purification and unity without a material and a multiplicity to purify and to unite.

And again, given the very limited power of attention and articulation possessed by individual man, and the importance to the human community of having impressive embodiments and examples of this, in various degrees and ways, universally ever all-but-forgotten, universally difficult, universally necessary, universally ennobling renunciation : we get the

[1] *Works*, tr. David Lewis, ed. 1889, 1891, Vol. I, p. 308; Vol. II, p. 541.
[2] *Op. cit.* p. 53. [3] *Ibid.* pp. 55, 56.

reason and justification for the setting apart of men specially drawn and devoted to a maximum, or to the most difficult kinds, of this renunciation.   As the practically universal instinct, or rudimentary capacity, for Art, Science, and Philanthropy finds its full expression in artists, scientists, philanthropists, whose specific glory and ever necessary corrective it is that they but articulate clearly, embody massively and, as it were, precipitate what is dimly and intermittingly present, as it were in solution, throughout the consciousness and requirements of Mankind ; and neither the inarticulate instinct, diffused among all, would completely suffice for any one of the majority, without the full articulation by a few, nor the full articulation by this minority could thrive, even for this minority itself, were it not environed by, and did it not voice, that dumb yearning of the race at large : so, and far more, does the general religiosity and sense of the Infinite, and even its ever-present element and requirement of Transcendence and Detachment, seek and call forth some typical, wholesomely provocative incorporation,—yet, here, with an even subtler and stronger interdependence, between the general demand and the particular supply.

And note that, if the minority will thus represent a maximum of " form," with a minimum of " matter," and the majority a maximum of " matter," with a minimum of " form " : yet some form as well as some matter must be held by each ; and the ideal to which, by their mutual supplementations, antagonisms, and corrections, they will have more and more to approximate our corporate humanity will be a maximum of " matter," permeated and spiritualized by a maximum of " form."   If it is easy for the soul to let itself be invaded and choked by the wrong kind of " matter," or even simply by an excess of the right kind, so that it will be unable to stamp the " matter " with spiritual " form " ; the opposite extreme also, where the spiritual forces have not left to them a sufficiency of material to penetrate or of life-giving friction to overcome, is ever a most real abuse.

2. *Ordinary Ascesis corrected by Social Christianity.*

Now it is very certain that Ordinary Asceticism and Social Christianity are, in their conjunction, far less open to this latter danger than is the Mystical and Contemplative Detachment.   For the former combination possesses the priceless conception of the soul's personality being constituted in and through the organism of the religious society,—the visible and invisible Church. This Society is no mere congeries of severally self-sufficing units, each exclusively and directly dependent upon God alone; but, as in St. Paul's grand figure of the body, an organism, giving their place and dignity to each several organ, each different, each necessary, and each influencing and influenced by all the others. We have here, as it were, a great living Cloth of Gold, with, not only the woof going from God to Man and from Man to God, but also the warp going from Man to Man,—the greatest to the least, and the least back to the greatest. And thus here the primary and full Bride of Christ never is, nor can be, any individual soul, but only this complete organism of all faithful souls throughout time and space; and the single soul is such a Bride only in so far as it forms an operative constituent of this larger whole.—And hence the soul of a Mystical habit will escape the danger of emptiness and inflation if it keeps up some,—as much indeed as it can, without permanent distraction or real violation of its special helps and call,—of that outgoing, social, co-operative action and spirit, which, in the more ordinary Christian life, has to form the all but exclusive occupation of the soul, and which here, indeed, runs the risk of degenerating into mere feverish, distracted " activity."

I take the right scheme for this complex matter to have been all but completely outlined by Plato, in the first plan of his *Republic*, and indeed to have been largely derived by Christian thinkers from this source; and the excessive and one-sided conception to have been largely determined by his later additions and changes in that great book, especially as these have been all but exclusively enforced, and still further exaggerated, by Plotinus and Proclus. As Erwin Rohde finely says of this later teaching of Plato : " It was at the zenith of his life and thinking that Plato completed his ideal picture of the State, according to the requirements of his wisdom. Over the broad foundation of a population discriminated according to classes, (a foundation which, in its totality and organization, was to embody the virtue of justice in a form visible even from afar, and which formerly had seemed to him to fulfil the whole function of the perfect State,) there now soars, pointing up into the super-mundane ether, a highest crown and pinnacle, to which all the lower serves but as a substructure to render possible this life in the highest air. A small handful of citizens, the Philosophers, form this final point of the pyramid of the State. In this

State, ordered throughout according to the ends of ethics, these Philosophers will, it is true, take part in the Government, not joyously, but for duty's sake; as soon, however, as duty permits, they will eagerly return to that super-mundane contemplation, which is the end and true content of their life's activity. Indeed, in reality, the Ideal State is now built up, step by step, for the ' one ultimate ' purpose of preparing an abode for these Contemplatives, of training them in their vocation, the highest extant, and of providing a means for the insertion of Dialectic, as a special form of life and the highest aim of human endeavour, into the general organism of the earthly, civilized life. ' The so-called virtues ' all here sink into the shade before the highest force of the soul, the mystic Contemplation of the Eternal. . . . To bring his own life to ripeness for its own redemption, *that* is now the perfect sage's true, his immediate duty. If, nevertheless, he has still to bethink himself of acting upon and of moulding the world the virtues will spontaneously present themselves to him : for he now possesses Virtue itself; it has become his essential condition." [1]

It is truly impressive to find here, in its most perfect and most influential form, that ruinously untrue doctrine of the separation of any one set of men from the mass of their fellows, and of Contemplation from interest in other souls, taking the place, (in the same great mind, in the same great book,) of the beautifully humble, rich, and true view of a constant, necessary interchange of gifts and duties between the various constituents of a highly articulated organism, a whole which is indefinitely greater than, and is alone the full means, end and measure of, all its several, even its noblest, parts.—Yet the Christian, indeed every at all specifically religious, reader, will have strongly felt that the second scheme possesses, nevertheless, at least one point of advantage over the earlier one. For it alone brings out clearly that element of Transcendence, that sense and thirst of the Infinite, which we have agreed upon as the deepest characteristic of man. And if this point be thus true and important, then another,— the making of Contemplation into a special vocation,—can hardly be altogether incorrect.

But if this is our judgment, how are we to harmonize these two points of Plato's later scheme with the general

positions of the earlier one ? Or, rather, how are we to actuate
and to synthesize our complex present-day requirements and
duties, Christian and yet also Modern, Transcendental and
yet Immanental too ? For if we have any delicately vivid
sense of, and sympathy with, the original, very simple, intensely
transcendental, form and emphasis of the Christian teaching,
and any substantial share in the present complex sense of
obligation to various laws and conceptions immanent in
different this-world organizations and systems : we shall
readily feel how indefinitely more difficult and deep the question has become since Plato's, and indeed since the Schoolmen's time.

3. *Preliminary Pessimism and ultimate Optimism of
Christianity.*

Now I think it is Prof. Ernst Troeltsch who has most
fully explicitated the precise centre of this difficulty, which,
in its acuteness, is a distinctly modern one, and the direction
in which alone the problem's true solution should be sought.

(1) " The chief problem of Christian Ethics," he says, " is
busy," not with the relation between certain subjective means
and dispositions, but " with the relation between certain
objective ends, which have, in some way, to be thought
together by the same mind as so many several objects, and
to be brought by it and within it to the greatest possible
unity. And the difficulty here lies in the fact, that the
sub-lunar among these ends are none the less moral ends,
bearing the full specific character of moral values,—that they
are ends-in-themselves, and necessary for their own sakes,
even at the cost of man's natural happiness; and yet that
they operate in the visible world, and adhere to historical
formations which proceed from man's natural constitution,
and dominate his earthly horizon; whilst the Super-worldly
End cannot share its rule with any other end. Yet the
special characteristic of modern civilization resides precisely
in such a simultaneous insistence upon the Inner-worldly
Ends, as possessing the nature of ends-in-themselves, and
upon the Religious, Super-worldly End : it is indeed from
just this combination that this civilization derives its peculiar
richness, power, and freedom, but also its painful, interior
tension and its difficult problems."

(2) The true solution of the difficulty surely is that " Ethical
life is not, in its beginnings, a unity but a multiplicity : man
grows up amidst a number of moral ends, whose unification is

not his starting-point but his problem. And this multiplicity can be still further defined as the polarity of two poles, inherent in man's nature, of which the two chief types proceed respectively from the religious and from the inner-worldly self-determination of the soul,—the polarity of Religious, and that of Humane Ethics, neither of which can be dispensed with without moral damage, yet which cannot be brought completely under a common formula. On this polarity depends the richness, but also the difficulty, of our life, since the sub-lunar ends remain, to a large extent, conditioned by the necessities and pre-requisites of their own special subject-matters, and since only on condition of being thus recognized as ends in themselves, can they attain to their morally educative power." [1]

(3) Or, to put the same matter from the point of view of definitely Christian experience and conviction : " The formula, for the specific nature of Christianity, can only be a complex conception,—the special Christian form," articulation and correction, " of the fundamental thoughts concerning God, World, Man and Redemption which," with indefinite variations of fulness and worth, " are found existing together in all the religions. And the tension present in this multiplicity of elements thus brought together is of an importance equal to that of the multiplicity itself ; indeed in this tension resides the main driving-force of Religion. Christianity " in particular " embraces a polarity within itself, and its formula must be dualistic ; it resembles, not a circle with one centre, but an ellipse with two focuses. For Christianity is," unchangeably, " an Ethics of Redemption, with a conception of the world both optimistic and pessimistic, both transcendental and immanental, and an apprehension both of a severe antagonism and of a close interior union between the world and God. It is, in principle, a Dualism, and yet a Dualism which is ever in process of abolition by Faith and Action. It is a purely Religious Ethic, which concentrates man's soul, with abrupt exclusiveness, upon the values of the interior life ; and yet, again, it is a Humane Ethic, busy with the moulding and transforming of nature, and through love bringing about an eventual reconciliation with it. At one time the one, at another time the other, of these poles is prominent : but neither of them may be completely absent, if the Christian

[1] " Grundprobleme der Ethik " : *Zeitschrift für Theologie und Kirche,* 1902, pp. 164, 167.

outlook is to be maintained.—And yet the original germ of the whole vast growth and movement ever remains an intensely, abruptly Transcendent Ethic, and can never simply pass over into a purely Immanental Ethic. The Gospel ever remains, with all possible clearness and keenness, a Promise of Redemption, leading us, away from the world, from nature and from sin, from earthly sorrow and earthly error, on and on to God; and which cannot allow the last word to be spoken in this life. Great as are its incentives to Reconciliation, it is never entirely resolvable into them. And the importance of that classical beginning ever consists in continuously calling back the human heart, away from all Culture and Immanence, to that which lies above both." [1]

(4) We thus get at last a conception which really covers, I think, all the chief elements of this complex matter. But the reader will have noted that it does so by treating the whole problem as one of Spiritual Dynamics, and not of Intellectual Statics. For the conception holds and requires the existence and cultivation of three kinds of action and movement in the soul. There are, first, the various centres of human energy and duty of a primarily This-world character, each of which possesses its own kind and degree of autonomy, laws, and obligations. There is, next, the attempt at organizing an increasing interaction between, and at harmonizing, (whilst never emasculating or eliminating,) these various, severally characteristic, systems of life and production into an ever larger ultimate unity. And, lastly, there is as strong a turning away from all this occupation with the Contingent and Finite, to the sense and apprehension of the Infinite and Abiding. And this dynamic system is so rich, even in the amount of it which can claim the practice of the majority of souls, as to require definite alternations in the occupations of such souls, ranging thus, in more or less rhythmic succession, from earth to Heaven and from Heaven back again to earth.

(5) And so great and so inexhaustible is this living system, even by mankind at large, that it has to be more or less parcelled out amongst various groups of men, each group possessing its own predominant *attrait*,—either to work out one of those immanental interests, say Art, Natural Science, Politics; or to fructify one or more of these relatively inde-

---

[1] " Was heisst Wesen des Christenthums ? " *Christliche Welt*, 1903, I, coll. 583, 584. The Abbé Loisy has also dwelt, with rare impressiveness, upon the intensely Other-Worldly character of the first Christian teaching.

pendent interests, by crossing it with one or more of the others; or to attempt to embrace the whole of these intra-mundane interests in one preliminary final system; or to turn away from this whole system and its contents to the Transcendent and Infinite; or finally to strive to combine, as far as possible, this latter Fleeing to the Infinite with all that former Seeking of the Finite.—We shall thus get specialists within one single domain; and more many-sided workers who fertilize one Science by another; and philosophers of Science or of History, or of both, who strive to reach the *rationale* of all knowledge of the Finite and Contingent; and Ascetics and Contemplatives who, respectively, call forth and dwell upon the sense and presence of the Infinite and Abiding, underlying and accompanying all the definite apprehensions of things contingent; and finally, the minds and wills that feel called to attempt as complete a development and organization as possible of all these movements.

4. Subdivision of spiritual labour: its necessity and its dangers.

And yet all the subdivision of labour we have just required can avoid doing harm, directly or indirectly, (by leading to Materialism, Rationalism, or Fanaticism, to one or other of the frequent but ever mischievous " Atomisms,") only on condition that it is felt and worked *as* such a subdivision. In other words, every soul must retain and cultivate some sense of, and respect for, the other chief human activities not primarily its own. For, as a matter of fact, even the least rich or developed individual requires and practises a certain amount, in an inchoate form, of each and all of these energizings; and he can, fruitfully for himself and others, exercise a maximum amount of any one of them, only if he does not altogether and deliberately neglect and exclude the others; and, above all, if, in imagination and in actual practice, he habitually turns to his fellow-men, of the other types and centres, to supplement, and to be supplemented by, them.

It will be found, I think, that the quite undeniable abuses that have been special to the Ascetic and Contemplative methods and states, have all primarily sprung from that most plausible error that, if these energizings are, in a sense, the highest in and for man, then they can, at least in man's ideal action and condition, dispense with other and lower energizings and objects altogether. Yet both for man's practice here and even for his ideal state in the hereafter, this is not so. There is no such thing,—either in human experience or in the human ideal, when both are adequately analyzed and formulated,—as discursive reasoning, without intuitive reason; or clear analysis and sense of contrast, without dim synthesis and a deep consciousness of similarity or continuity; or detachment of the will from evil, without attachment of the higher feelings to things good; or the apprehension and requirements of Multiplicity, without those of Unity; or the vivid experience of Contingency, Mutation, and the Worthlessly Subjective, without the, if obscure yet most powerful, instinct of the Infinite and Abiding, of the true Objective and Valuable Subjective. Thus, for humanity at large entirely, and for each human individual more or less, each member of these couples requires, and is occasioned by, the other, and *vice versa*.

The maxims that follow from this great fact are as plain in reason, and as immensely fruitful in practice, as they are difficult, though ever freshly interesting, to carry out, at all consistently, even in theory and still more in act. For the object of a wise living will now consist in introducing an ever greater unity into the multiplicity of our lives,—up to the point where this unity's constituents would, like the opposing metals in an electric battery, become too much alike still to produce a fruitful interaction, and where the unity would, thus and otherwise, become empty and mechanical; and an ever greater multiplicity into the unity,—up to the point where that multiplicity would, seriously and permanently, break up or weaken true recollection; and in more and more expanding this whole individual organism, by its insertion, as a constituent part, into larger groups and systems of interests. The Family, the Nation, Human Society, the Church,—these are the chief of the larger organizations into which the inchoate, largely only potential, organism of the individual man is at first simply passively born, yet which, if he would grow, (not in spite of them, a hopeless task, but by them,) he will have deliberately to endorse and will, as though they were his own creations.

5. *Mystics and Spiritual Direction.*

It is interesting to note the special characteristics attaching to the one social relation emphasized by the medieval and modern varieties of Western Catholic Mysticism; and the effect which a larger development of the other chief forces and modalities of the Catholic spiritual life necessarily has

upon this relation.   I am thinking of the part played by the
Director, the soul's leader and adviser, in the lives of these
Mystics,—a part which differs, in three respects, from that of
the ordinary Confessor in the life of the more active or
" mixed " type of Catholic.

(1) For one thing, there is here a striking variety and
range, in the ecclesiastical and social position of the persons
thus providentially given and deliberately chosen.   The early
German Franciscan Preacher, Berthold of Regensburg, owes
his initiation into the Interior Life to his Franciscan Novice-
Master, the Partial Mystic, David of Augsburg, whose
writings still give forth for us their steady light and genial
warmth;   the French widowed noblewoman and Religious
Foundress, St. Jane Frances de Chantal, is helped on her
course to high contemplation by the Secular Priest and
Bishop, St. Francis de Sales;   the French Jesuit, Jean
Nicolas Grou, is initiated, after twenty-four years' life and
training in his Order, by the Visitation Nun, Sœur Pélagie,
into that more Mystical spirituality, which constitutes the
special characteristic of his chief spiritual books;   the great
Spaniard, St. Teresa herself, tells us how " a saintly noble-
man . . . a married layman, who had spent nearly forty years
in prayer, seems to me to have been, by the pains he took,
the beginning of salvation to my soul "—" his power was great ";
and the English Anchorite, Mother Juliana of Norwich, " a
simple, unlettered creature," seems to have found no special
leader on to her rarely deep, wide, and tender teachings,
but to have been led and stimulated, beyond and after her
first general Benedictine training, by God's Providence alone,
working through the few and quite ordinary surroundings
and influences of her Anchorage at Norwich.[1]   It would be
difficult to find anything to improve in this noble liberty of
these great children of God; nor would a larger influence of
the other modalities necessarily restrict this ample range.

(2) Again, the souls of this type seem, for the most part, to
realize more fully and continuously than those of the ordinary,
simply active and ascetical kind, that the " blind obedience "
towards such leaders, so often praised in their disciples and

[1] *Deutsche Mystiker des Mittelalters*, ed. Pfeiffer, Vol. I, 1845, pp. xli,
xlii.   Any Life of St. Jane F. de Chantal.   A. Cadrès, *Le P. Jean N.
Grou*, 1866, pp. 13, 14.   St. Teresa's *Life, written by Herself*, tr. David
Lewis, ed. 1888, pp. 176, 177; 186.   *Revelations of Divine Love, showed
to Mother Juliana of Norwich*, ed. 1902, p. 4.

penitents, is, where wholesome and strengthening, essentially a simple, tenacious adherence, during the inevitable times of darkness and perplexity, to the encouragements given by the guide to persevere along the course and towards the truths which this soul itself saw clearly, often through the instrumentality of this leader, when it was in light and capable of a peaceful, deliberate decision. For however much the light may have been given it through this human mediation, (and the most numerous, and generally the most important, of our lights, have been acquired thus through the spoken, written, or acted instrumentality of fellow-souls,)—yet the light was seen, and had (in the first instance) to be seen, by the disciple's own spiritual eye; and it is but to help it in keeping faithful to this light (which, in the first and last instance, is God's light and its own) that the leader stands by and helps. But, given this important condition, there remains the simple, experimental fact that, not only can and do others often see our spiritual whereabouts and God's *attrait* for us more clearly than we do ourselves, but such unselfseeking transmission and such humbly simple reception of light between man and man adds a moral and spiritual security and beauty to the illumination, (all other conditions being equal and appropriate,) not to be found otherwise. It is interesting to note the courageous, balanced, and certainly quite unprejudiced, testimony borne to these important points, by so widely read, and yet upon the whole strongly Protestant, a pair of scholars, as Miss Alice Gardner and her very distinguished brother, Professor Percy Gardner.[1]

(3) And finally, the souls of this type have, (at least for the two purposes of the suscitation of actual insight, and for bearing witness to this, now past, experience during the soul's periods of gloom), often tended,—in Western Christendom and during Medieval and still more in Modern times,—to exalt the office and power of the Director, in the life of the soul of the Mystical type, very markedly beyond the functions, rights and duties of the ordinary Confessor in the spiritual life of the ordinary Catholic.

Indeed they and their interpreters have, in those times and places, often insisted upon the guarantee of safety thus afforded, and upon the necessity of such formal and systematic mediation, with an absoluteness and vehemence

[1] A. Gardner, " Confession and Direction," in *The Conflict of Duties*, 1903, pp. 223–229. P. Gardner, in *The Liberal Churchman*, 1905, p. 266.

impossible to conciliate with any full and balanced, especially with any at all orthodox, reading of Church History. For this feature is as marked in the condemned book of Molinos and of most of the other Quietists, as it is in such thoroughly approved Partial Mysticism as that of Père Lallemant and Père Grou : hence it alone cannot, surely, render a soul completely safe against excesses and delusions. And this feature was markedly in abeyance, often indeed, for aught we know, completely wanting, at least in any frequent and methodic form, in the numerous cases of the Egyptian and other Fathers of the Desert : hence it cannot be strictly essential to all genuine Contemplation in all times and places.

(4) The dominant and quite certain fact here seems to be that, in proportion as the Abstractive movement of the soul is taken as self-sufficient, and a Contemplative life is attempted as something substantially independent of any concrete, social, and devotional helps and duties, the soul gets into a state of danger, which no amount of predominance of the Director can really render safe; whereas, in proportion as the soul takes care to practise, in its own special degree and manner, the outgoing movement towards Multiplicity and Contingency, (particular attention to particular religious facts and particular service of particular persons), does such right, quite ordinary-seeming, active subordination to, and incorporation within, the great sacred organisms of the Family, Society, and the Church, or of any wise and helpful subdivision of these, furnish material, purgation and check for the other movement, and render superfluous any great or universal predominance of Direction. St. Teresa is, here also, wonderfully many-sided and balanced. Just as she comes to regret having ever turned aside from Christ's Sacred Humanity, so too she possesses, indeed she never loses, the sense of the profoundly social character of Christianity : she dies as she had lived, full of an explicit and deep love for the Kingdom of God and the Church.

6. *Mysticism predominantly Individualistic.*

Yet it is clear that the strong point of the Mystics, as such, does not lie in the direction of the great social spirituality which finds God in our neighbour and in the great human organizations, through and in which, after all, man in great part becomes and is truly man. They are, as such, Individualistic; the relation between God and the individual soul here ever tends to appear as constituted by these two forces alone. A fresh proof, if one were still wanting, that Mysticism is but one of the elements of Religion,—for Religion requires both the Social and the Individual, the Corporate and the Lonely movement and life.

It is truly inspiring to note how emphatic is the concurrence of all the deepest and most circumspect contemporary Psychology, Epistemology, Ethics, and History and Philosophy of the Sciences and of Religion, in these general conclusions, which find, within the slow and many-sided growth and upbuilding of the spiritual personality, a true and necessary place and function for all the great and permanent capabilities, aspirations and energizings of the human soul. Thus no system of religion can be complete and deeply fruitful which does not embrace, (in every possible kind of healthy development, proportion and combination), the several souls and the several types of souls who, between them, will afford a maximum of clear apprehension and precise reasoning, *and* of dim experience and intuitive reason; of particular attention to the Contingent (Historical Events and Persons, and Institutional Acts and Means) *and* of General Recollection and Contemplation and Hungering after the Infinite; and of reproductive Admiration and Loving Intellection, *and* of quasi-creative, truly productive Action upon and within Nature and other souls, attaining, by such Action, most nearly to the supreme attribute, the Pure Energizing of God.

Thus Pseudo-Dionysius and St. John of the Cross will, even in their most Negative doctrines, remain right and necessary in all stages of the Church's life,—on condition, however, of being taken as but one of two great movements, of which the other, the Positive movement, must also ever receive careful attention : since only between them is attained that all-important oscillation of the religious pendulum, that interaction between the soul's meal and the soul's yeast, that furnishing of friction for force to overcome, and of force to overcome the friction, that material for the soul to mould, and in moulding which to develop itself, that alternate expiration and inspiration, upon which the soul's mysterious death-in-life and life-in-death so continuously depends.

III. THE SCIENTIFIC HABIT AND MYSTICISM.

Introductory. Difficulty yet Necessity of finding a True Place and Function for Science in the Spiritual Life.

Now it is certain that such an oscillatory movement, such a give-and-take, such a larger Asceticism, built up out of the alternate engrossment in and abstraction from variously, yet in each case really, attractive levels, functions and objects of human life and experience, is still comparatively easy, as long as we restrict it to two out of the three great groups of energizings which are ever, at least potentially, present in the soul, and which ever inevitably help to make or mar, to develop or to stunt, the totality of the soul's life, and hence also of the strictly spiritual life. The Historical-Institutional, and the Mystical-Volitional groups and forces, the High-Church and the Low-Church trend, the Memory- and the Will-energies, do indeed coalesce, in times of peace, with the Reason-energy, though, even then, with some difficulty. But in times of war,—on occasion of any special or excessive action on the part of this third group, the Critical-Speculative, the Broad-Church trend, and the energizing of the Understanding,—they readily combine against every degree of the latter. It is as though the fundamental vowels A and U could not but combine to oust the fundamental vowel I; or as if the primary colours Red and Blue *must* join to crush out the primary colour Yellow.

Indeed, it is undoubtedly just this matter of the full and continuous recognition of, and allocation of a special function to, this third element within the same great spiritual organism which englobes the other two, which is now the great central difficulty and pressing problem of more or less every degree and kind of religious life. For the admission of this third element appears frequently to be ruinous to the other two; yet the other two, when kept away from it, seem to lose their vigour and persuasive power.—And yet it is, I think, exactly at this crucial point that the conception of the spiritual life as essentially a Dynamism, a slow constitution of an ever fuller, deeper, more close-knit unity in, and by means of, the soul's ineradicable trinity of forces, shows all its fruitfulness, if we but work down to a sufficiently large apprehension of the capacities and requirements of human nature, moved and aided by divine grace, and to a very precise delimitation of the special object and function of Mysticism.

1. *Science and Religion: each autonomous at its own level; and, thus, each helpful to the other.*

Erwin Rohde has well described Plato's attitude towards Science and Mysticism respectively, and towards the question of their inter-relation. "The flight from the things of this World is, for Plato, already in itself an acquisition of those of the Beyond, and an assimilation to the Divine. For this poor world, that solicits our senses, the philosopher has, at bottom, nothing but negation. Incapable as it is of furnishing a material that can be truly known, the whole domain of the Transitory and Becoming has no intrinsic significance for Science as understood by him. The perception of things which are ever merely relative, and which simultaneously manifest contradictory qualities, has its sole use in stimulating and inviting the soul to press on to the Absolute." [1]

Here we should frankly admit that the soul's hunger for the Infinite is, as the great Athenian so deeply realized, the very mainspring of Religion; and yet we must maintain that it is precisely this single bound away, instead of the ever-repeated double movement of a coming and a going, which not only helped to suppress, or at least gravely to stunt, the growth of the sciences of external observation and experiment, but (and this is the special point,—the demonstrable other side of the medal,) also, in its degree, prevented religion from attaining to its true depth, by thus cutting off, as far as Plato's conviction prevailed, the very material, stimulation, and in part the instruments, for the soul's outgoing, spiritualizing work, together with this work's profound reflex effect upon the worker, as a unique occasion for the growth and self-detachment of the soul.

Now the necessity for such a first stage and movement, which, as far as possible both immanental and phenomenalist, shall be applied and restricted to the special methods, direct objects, and precise range of each particular Science, and the importance of the safeguarding of this scientific liberty, are now clearly perceived, by the leading men of Religion, Philosophy, Psychology and Physics, in connection with the maintenance and acquisition of sincere and fruitful Science.— It is also increasingly seen that, even short of Religion, a

[1] *Psyche*, ed. 1898, Vol. II, p. 289.

second, an interpretative, an at least Philosophical stage and movement is necessary for the full explicitation of Science's own assumptions and affinities. And the keeping of these two movements clearly distinct or even strongly contrasted, is felt, by some far-sighted Theologians, to be a help towards securing, not only a candid attitude of Science towards its own subject-matters, but also a right independence of Philosophy and Theology towards the other Sciences. Thus Cardinal Newman has brought out, with startling force, the necessarily non-moral, non-religious character of Physico-Mathematical Science, taken simply within its direct subject-matter and method. " Physical science never travels beyond the examination of cause and effect. Its object is to resolve the complexity of phenomena into simple elements and principles; but when it has reached those first elements, principles and laws, its mission is at an end; it keeps within that material system with which it began, and never ventures beyond the ' flammantia moenia mundi.' The physicist as such will never ask himself by what influence, external to the universe, the universe is sustained; simply because he is a physicist. If, indeed, he be a religious man, he will, of course, have a very different view of the subject; . . . and this, not because physical science says anything different, but simply because it says nothing at all on the subject, nor can do by the very undertaking with which it set out." Or, as he elsewhere sympathetically sums up Bacon's method of proceeding : " The inquiry into physical causes passes over for the moment the existence of God. In other words, physical science is, in a certain sense, atheistic, for the very reason that it is not theology." [1]

2. *Science builds up a preliminary world that has to be corrected by Philosophy and Religion, at and for their deeper levels.*

The additional experience and analysis of the last half-century apparently forces us, however, to maintain not only that Physico-Mathematical Science, and all knowledge brought strictly to the type of that Science, does not itself pronounce on the Ultimate Questions; but that this Science, as such, actually presents us with a picture of reality which,

---

[1] " Christianity and Physical Science " (1855), in *Idea of a University*, ed. 1873, pp. 432, 433. " University Teaching " (1852), *ibid.* p. 222. See Mr. R. E. Froude's interesting paper, " Scientific Speculation and the Unity of Truth," *Dublin Review*, Oct. 1900, pp. 353-368.

at the deeper level even of Epistemology and of the more ultimate Psychology, and still more at that of Religion, requires to be taken as more or less artificial, and as demanding, not simply completion, but, except for its own special purposes, correction as well. Thus we have seen how M. Bergson finds Clock-Time to be an artificial, compound concept, which seriously travesties Duration, the reality actually experienced by us; and Space appears as in even a worse predicament. M. Emil Boutroux in France, Dottore Igino Petrone in Italy, Profs. Eucken and Troeltsch in Germany, Profs. James Ward and Pringle Pattison in Great Britain, and Profs. William James, Hugo Münsterberg and Josiah Royce in America are, in spite of differences on other points, united in insistence upon, or have even worked out in much detail, such a distinction between the first stage and level of Determinist, Atomistic, Inorganic Nature and our concepts of it, and the second stage and level of Libertarian, Synthetic, and Organic Spiritual Reality, and our experience of it. And the penetrating labours of Profs. Windelband, Rickert, and others, towards building up a veritable *Organon* of the Historical Sciences, are bringing into the clearest relief these two several degrees of Reality and types of Knowledge, the Historical being the indefinitely deeper and more adequate, and the one which ultimately englobes the other.[1]

A profoundly significant current in modern philosophy will thus be brought, in part at least, to articulate expression and application. This current is well described by Prof. Volkelt. " German philosophy since Kant reveals, in manifold forms and under various disguises, the attempt to recognize, in Epistemology, Metaphysics, and Ethics, such kinds of Certainty, such domains of Being, such human Volitions and Values, as lie beyond reason, constitute a something that it cannot grasp, and are rooted in some other kind of foundation. In variously struggling, indeed stammering utterances, expression is given to the assurance that not everything in the world is resolvable into Logic and Thought, but that mighty resisting remainders are extant, which perhaps even constitute the most important thing in the world. . . . Such a longing after such a Reality can be

---

[1] W. Windelband, *Geschichte und Naturwissenschaft*, 1894. H. Rickert, *Kulturwissenschaft und Naturwissenschaft*, 1899. And, above all, H. Rickert, *Die Grenzen der Naturwissenschaftlichen Begriffsbildung*, 1902.

traced in Hamann, Jacobi, Herder, in Novalis, Friedrich
Schlegel, the youthful Schleiermacher, and Jean Paul. Indeed,
even in Hegel, the adorer of Reason, the movement of
Negation, which is the very soul of his philosophy, is, at
bottom, nothing but the Irrational," the Super-Rational,
" element violently pressed into the form of Reason; and
again the single Thing, the This, the Here and the Now, are
felt by him as . . . a something beyond Reason. And has
not the Irrational found expression in Kant, in his doctrines
of the unconditional Liberty of the Will and of Radical Evil?
In the later Schelling and his spiritual relatives the Irrational
has found far more explicit recognition; whilst Schopenhauer
brings the point to its fullest expression. Yet even Nietzsche
still possesses such an element, in his doctrine of the ' Over-
Man.' " [1] And in England we find this same element, in
various degrees and in two chief divergent forms, in the
Cambridge Platonists, Samuel Taylor Coleridge and Thomas
Hill Green on the one hand; and in Bishop Butler and
Cardinal Newman on the other hand.

We can thus point to much clear recognition, or at least
to a considerable influence, of the profound truth that Science
and Wisdom can each prosper and help and supplement the
other, only if each possesses a certain real autonomy, a power
fully to become and to remain itself, and, in various degrees
and ways, to stimulate, check and thwart the other. And
this truth ever presupposes, what human experience, in the
long run, proves to be a fact,—that the different kinds, spheres,
and levels of man's apprehension, and of the total reality
thus apprehended by him, are already immanently planned
each for the other, within a great, largely dormant system of
the world. Thus Man can and should call this congenital
inter-relatedness into ever more vigorous and more fruitful
play; whereas, if it were not already present deep within
the very nature of things, no amount of human effort or
ingenuity could ever evoke or insert it. Prof. Volkelt has,
as we have seen, illustrated this great fact very strikingly,
with regard to the relation extant between the apparently
sheer contingencies of human History and the requirements
of Philosophy, of normative thought and ideal truth. Yet
a similar interconnection can be traced elsewhere, between
any other two or more levels and spheres of wholesome and
permanent human apprehension and action, in their relation

[1] *Schopenhauer*, 1900, pp. 344, 345.

to various degrees and kinds of reality, as this environs man
or inheres in him.

3. *Necessity of the " Thing-element " in Religion.*

But let us note that the recognition, of an at all emphatic,
systematic kind, of such inter-relatedness is, so far, almost
limited to the moods and persons preoccupied with the right
claims of Science or of Philosophy upon each other or upon
the remainder of Life; and is, as yet, all but wanting, when
Life is approached from the side of the specifically Religious
requirements and of the Spiritual consolidation of man's soul.
Yet here especially, at by far the most important point of
the whole matter, the unique place and significance of Science
can now be very clearly grasped.

Indeed it is deeply interesting to note how largely the
fundamental characteristics of Catholicism really meet, or
rather how they strictly require, some such vivid conception
and vigorous use of the Determinist Thing and of its level for
the full constitution of our true depth, our Spiritual Personality itself. If we take, *e. g.*, the criticisms addressed, by so
earnest and acute a mind as the intensely Protestant Emile
Sulze, to the whole Thing-Element and -Concept, as these
are at work in the Catholic practice and position, we shall
find his sense of the difference between Thing and Spirit to
be as enviably keen, and his idea of the end and ultimate
measure of Religion to be as sound and deep, as his conception of the means towards developing Religion and the
Spirit is curiously inadequate.

(1) " Personality," says Sulze, " is, for Religion and Morality,
the supreme Good, of which the source is in God, and the
end, the fruit, and the manifestation is in Man." [1] This I
take to be profoundly true, especially if we insist upon
Perfect Personality being Supreme and Perfect Spirit; and,
again, upon our imperfect personality and spirit as possessed
of certain profound affinities to, and as penetrable and
actually moved by, that Perfect Spirit.

(2) " The value of Personality nowhere finds a full recognition in Catholicism; Catholicism indeed is Pantheism." Now
this harsh judgment is based upon two sets of allegations,
which, though treated by Sulze as of the same nature, are, I
would submit, essentially different, and this because of their
definitely different places and functions in the Catholic system.

[1] *Wie ist der Kampf um die Bedeutung . . . Jesu zu beendigen?* 1901,
p. 9.

" The Impersonal Godhead, the bond which unites the
three Persons, stands above the Persons. Hence those who
took religion seriously had to lose themselves, pantheistically,
in the abyss of the Divinity. And in Christ the Person was
even looked upon as the product of two Natures, the Divine
and the Human, hence of two Impersonal Forces." [1] Here
two peculiarities in the early Conciliar Definitions are
emphasized, which were doubtless as helpful, indeed necessary,
for the apprehension of the great abiding truths thus conveyed
to the Greco-Roman mind, as they are now in need of
reinterpretation in the light of our greater sensitiveness to the
difference, in character and in value, which obtains between
the concept of Spirit and Personality and that of Substances
and Things.

But Sulze continues, without any change in the kind or
degree of his criticism : " Impersonal miraculous means,
created by the Hierarchy, are put by it in the place of the
sanctifying mutual intercourse of the children of God."
" Christianity, torn away from the religious and moral life,
became thus a special, technical apparatus, without any
religious or spiritual worth. Ecclesiastical Christianity has
become a Pantheism, Materialism, indeed Atheism." [2] We
have so continuously ourselves insisted upon the profound
danger, and frequently operative abuse, of any and all complete apartness between any one means, function, or *attrait* of
the spiritual life and the others, that we can, without any
unfairness, restrict ourselves here to the attack upon the
general acceptation of Impersonal means as helps towards
the constitution of Personality. Now Sulze's principle here,
—that only directly personal means can help to achieve the
end of Personality,—is most undoubtedly false, unless Mathematico-Physical Science is also to be ruled out of life, as
necessarily destructive of, or at least as necessarily non-
conductive to, Personality.

(3) Indeed Sulze himself tells us, most truly, that, " for
Religion also, Science is a bath of purification " ; and that
" Doctrine and the Sacraments are aids, in the hands of Christ
and of the Community, towards representing the riches of their
interior life and offering these to believing hearts." [3] This
latter pronouncement is, however, still clearly insufficient.

[1] *Wie ist der Kampf um die Bedeutung . . . Jesu zu beendigen ?* 1901,
p. 10.
[2] *Ibid.* pp. 10, 11.   [3] *Ibid.* pp. 26, 27.

For if there is a double truth which, at the end of well-nigh five centuries, ought to have burnt itself indelibly into the mind and conscience of us all, it is, surely, the following. On the one hand, Man, unless he develops a vigorous alternating counter-movement, ever grows like to the instruments of his labour and self-development, and hence, whilst busy with Things, (whether these be Natural Happenings and their Sciences, or Religious Institutions and Doctrines,) he inclines to become, quite unawares, limited and assimilated to them,— himself thus a Thing among Things, instead of, through such various Things, winning an ever fuller apprehension of and growth in Spiritual Personality. Yet, on the other hand, without such a movement of close contact with the Thing, (both the intensely concrete, the Here and Now Contingency, and the profoundly Abstract, the stringent Universal Law,) and without the pleasure and pain derived from the accompanying sense of contraction and of expansion, of contrast, conflict, supplementation and renovation,—there is no fullest discipline or most solid growth of the true spiritual Personality.

(4) Thus Science, as Sulze himself clearly sees, not merely aids us to represent and to communicate our personality acquired elsewhere, but the shock, friction, contrast, the slow, continuous discipline, far more, beyond doubt, than any positive content furnished by such science, can and should constitute an essential part of the soul's spiritual fertilization. And similarly, if we move on into the directly religious life, the Sacramental contacts and Doctrinal systems (the former so intensely concrete, the latter often so abstract,) are not simply means towards representing and transmitting spirituality acquired elsewhere : but they are amongst the means, and, in some form and degree, the necessary, indeed actually universal means, towards the awakening and developing and fulfilling of this our spiritual personality.

4. *Three possible relations between Thing and Thought, Determinism and Spirit.*

It remains no doubt profoundly true that, with the awakening of the Mystical sense, will come a more or less acute consciousness of an at least superficial and preliminary, difference between this sense, with its specific habits and informations, and those means and forms, in part so contingent and external, in part so intensely abstract and yet so precise. But it is equally certain that such a soul, and at such a stage, even as it continues to require, in some respects more than ever, for its general balanced development, some of the irreplaceable discipline and manly, bracing humiliation of the close external observation and severe abstract generalization of Science : so also does it continue to require, for the deepening of the spirit and for the growth of creatureliness, the contact with religious Things,—the profoundly concrete Sacraments and the intensely abstract Doctrines of the religious community.

(1) In one of Trendelenburg's most penetrating essays, he shows us how, between blind Force and conscious Thought,—if we presuppose any tendency towards unity to exist between them,—there can be but three possible relations. " Either Force stands before Thought, so that Thought is not the primitive reality, but the result and accident of blind Force : or Thought stands before Force, so that blind Force is not itself the primitive reality, but the effluence of Thought; or finally, Thought and Force are, at bottom, only one and the same thing, and differ only in our mind's conception of them." And only one of these three positions can, by any possibility, be the true one : hence their internecine conflict.[1]

(2) Now Religion, in its normal, central stream, stands most undoubtedly for Thought before Force, the second, the Theistic view. And yet it would be profoundly impoverishing for our outlook and practice, and would but prepare a dangerous reaction in ourselves or others, were we ever to ignore the immense influence, in the history, not only of philosophical speculation, but even of religious feeling and aspiration, not indeed of the first, the Materialist, view, (which owes all its strength to non-religious causes or to a rebound against religious excesses,) but of the third, the Pantheistic, Monistic, view, whose classical exponent Spinoza will probably remain unto all time.

(3) If we examine into what constitutes the religious plausibility and power of this view, we shall find, I think, that it proceeds, above all, from the fact that, only too often, the second, the Theistic view and practice, leaves almost or quite out of sight the purification and slow constitution of the Individual into a Person, by means of the Thing-element, the apparently blind Determinism of Natural Law and Natural Happenings. Yet nothing can be more certain than that we must admit and place this undeniable, increasingly obtrusive,

---

[1] " Ueber den letzten Unterschied der philosophischen Systeme," 1847, in *Beiträge zur Philosophie*, 1855, Vol. II, p. 10.

element and power *somewhere* in our lives : if we will not own it as a means, it will grip us as our end. The unpurified, all but merely natural, animal, lustful and selfish individual man, is far too like to the brutes and plants, indeed even to the inorganic substances that so palpably surround him, for it not to be a fantastic thought to such thinkers as Spinoza, (and indeed it would be an excessive effort to himself,) to believe that he is likely, taken simply in this condition, to outlast, and is capable of dominating, the huge framework of the visible world, into which his whole bodily and psychical mechanism is placed, and to which it is bound by a thousand ties and closest similarities : his little selfish thinkings cannot but seem mere bubbles on a boundless expanse of mere matter; all creation cannot, surely, originate in, depend from, and move up to, a Mind and Spirit in any way like unto this trivial ingenuity.

(4) It is true, of course, that Spinoza ended,—as far as the logic of his system went,—by " purifying " away not only this animal Individualism, but Spiritual Personality as well, and this because he takes Mathematico-Physical concepts to be as directly applicable and as adequate to Ultimate Reality as are the Ethico-Spiritual categories. We have then to admit that even so rich and rare, so deeply religious a spirit as Spinoza could insist upon purification by the " preliminary Pantheism," and yet could remain, in theory, the eager exponent of an ultimate Pantheism. Like the Greeks, he not only passes through a middle distance, a range of experience which appears dominated by austere Fate and blind Fortune, but finds Fate even in ultimate Reality. Whilst, however, the Greeks often thought of Fate as superior even to the Gods, Spinoza finds Ultimate Reality to be neither Nature nor Spirit, but simply Being in General, with a Law which is neither Natural nor Spiritual Law, but Law in general. This General Being and General Law then bifurcate, with the most rigorous determinism and complete impartiality, step by step, into parallel and ever co-present manifestations of Nature and of Spirit, and of their respective laws, which, though different, are also each strictly determined within their own series.[1]

(5) But Spinoza's error here undoubtedly lies in his *de facto*

[1] See the admirably lucid analysis in Prof. Troeltsch's " Religions-philosophie," in *Die Philosophie im Beginn des zwanzigsten Jahrhunderts*, 1904, Vol. I. p. 116. already referred to further back.

violent bending (in spite of this theoretical Parallelism) of all Knowledge, Reality, and Life, under the sole Mathematico-Physical categories and method; and in the insistence upon attaining to ultimate Truth by one single bound and with complete adequacy and clearness. And the greatness here consists in the keen and massive sense of three profound truths. He never forgets that Mathematico-Physical Science is rigidly determinist, and that it stands for a certain important truth and penetrates to a certain depth of reality. He never ceases to feel how impure, selfish, petty is the natural man, and how pure, disinterested, noble, can and should be the spiritual personality. And he never lets go the sense that, somehow, that science must be able to help towards this purification.

(6) Now these three truths must be preserved, whilst the Mathematico-Physical one-sidedness and the " one-step " error must be carefully eliminated. And indeed it is plain that only by such elimination can those truths operate within a fully congenial system. For only thus, with a dissimilarity between the Ultimate, Libertarian, Spiritual Reality, and the Intermediate, Determinist, Physico-Mathematical Range, can we explain and maintain the pain, not only of the selfish but also of the true self, in face the Mere Thing; and only thus is all such pain and trouble worth having, since only thus it leads to the fuller development and the solid constitution of an abiding, interior, mental and volitional Personality.

5. *Purification of the Personality by the impersonal.*

Prof. H. J. Holtzmann has got an eloquent page concerning the kind of Dualism which is more than ever desirable for souls, if they would achieve a full and virile personality in this our day. " It would appear to be the wiser course for us to recognize the incompatibility between merely natural existence and truly personal life, just as it is, in its whole acute non-reconciliation; to insert this conflict into our complete outlook on to Life in its full breadth and depth, and to find the harmonization in God the Infinite, in whom alone such parallels can meet, and not deliberately to blind our right eye or our left, in order to force that outlook into one single aspect,—a degree of unification which, when achieved in this violent manner, would mean for us, at the same time, a point of absolute inertia, of eternal stagnation." And he then shows how it is precisely the interaction within our minds, feelings, and volitions, of, on the one hand, the boundless world of nature, with its majestic impersonality, and on the other hand, the inexhaustible, indefinitely deeper realm of personal life, as it appears within the stream of human history, which is best adapted to give us some fuller glimpses of the greatness of God and of the specific character of religion.[1]

The religious imagination, mind, heart, and will,—that is to say, the complete, fully normal human being at his deepest,—has thus been more and more forced, by an increasingly articulated experience of the forces and requirements of actual life, to hold and to practise, with ever-renewed attempts at their most perfect interstimulation and mutual supplementation, a profoundly costing, yet immensely fruitful, trinity in unity of convictions on this point.

In every time, place, and race, man will continue to be or to become religious, in proportion to his efficacious faith in, and love of, the overflowing reality and worth of the great direct objects of religion,—God and the soul, and their inter-relation in and through the Kingdom of God, the Church, and its Divine-Human Head,—the whole constituting God's condescension towards and immanence in man, and man's response and orientation towards the transcendent God.

And again, in every age, place, and race, man will be or will become deeply religious, in proportion to the keenness with which he realizes the immense need of spiritual growth and purification for his, at best, but inchoate personality.

But,—and this third point we must admit, in the precise extension and application given to it here, to be character-istically modern,—man will, (if he belongs to our time and to our Western races, and is determined fully to utilize our special circumstances, lights and trials, as so many means towards his own spiritualization,) have carefully to keep in living touch with that secondary and preliminary reality, the Thing-world, the Impersonal Element, Physical Science and Determinist Law. He will have to pass and repass beneath these Caudine forks; to plunge and to replunge into and through this fiery torrent; and, almost a merely animal individual at the beginning and on this side of such docile bendings and such courageous plungings, he will, (if he com-bines them with, and effects them through, those two other, abiding and ultimate, directly religious convictions,) straighten himself up again to greater heights, and will come forth from the torrent each time a somewhat purer and more developed

[1] *Richard Rothe's Spekulatives System*, 1899, pp. 205, 206.

spiritual person than he was before such contraction and purgation.

6. *This position new for Science, not for Religion.*

Yet even this third point has, if we will but look to its substantial significance and religious function, been equivalently held and practised ever since the Twice-Born life, the deeper religion, has been lived at all.

(1) The Ascetic's self-thwarting, and the Mystic's self-oblivion and seeking after Pure Love, what are they but the expressions of the very same necessities and motives which we would wish to see fully operative here? For we are not, of course, here thinking of anything simply intellectual, and fit only for the educated few. Any poor laundry-girl, who carefully studies and carries out the laws of successful washing, who moves, in alternation, away from this concentration on the Thing, to recollection and increasingly affective prayer and rudimentary contemplation, and who seeks the fuller growth of her spirit and of its union with God, in this coming and going, to and from the Visible and Contingent, to and from the Spiritual and Infinite, and in what these several levels have of contrast and of conflict; or any lowly farm-labourer or blacksmith or miner, who would proceed similarly with his external determinist mechanical work, and with his deeply internal requirements and spiritual growth and consolidation : would all be carrying out precisely what is here intended.

(2) As a matter of fact, the source of such novelty, as may be found here, is not on the side of religion, but on that of science. For the conception of Nature of the ancient Greek Physicists, and indeed that of Aristotle, required to be profoundly de-humanized, de-sentimentalized : a rigorous mathematical Determinism and soulless Mechanism became the right and necessary ideal of Physical Science. But, long before the elaboration of this concept of the ruthless Thing and of its blind Force, Our Lord had, by His Life and Teaching, brought to man, with abidingly unforgettable, divine depth and vividness, the sense of Spirit and Personality, with its liberty and interiority, its far-looking wisdom and its regenerating, creative power of love. And for some thirteen centuries after this supreme spiritual revelation and discovery, that old anthropomorphic and anthropocentric conception of the Physical Universe continued, well-nigh unchanged, even among the earlier and middle schoolmen,

and was readily harmonized with that Spiritual world. Yet they were harmonized, upon the whole, by a juxtaposition which, in proportion as the conception of Nature became Determinist and Mechanical, has turned out more and more untenable; and which, like all simple juxtapositions, could not, as such, have any spiritually educative force. But Spiritual Reality has now,—for those who have become thoroughly awake to the great changes operated, for good and all, in man's conception of the Physical Universe during now three centuries,—to be found under, behind, across these Physical Phenomena and Laws, which both check and beckon on the mind and soul of man, in quest of their ultimate mainstay and motivation.

(3) And let us note how much some such discipline and asceticism is required by the whole Christian temper and tradition, and the weakening of some older forms of it.

During the first three generations Christians were profoundly sobered by the keen expectation of Our Lord's proximate Second Coming, and of the end of the entire earthly order of things, to which all their natural affections spontaneously clung; and again and again, up to wellnigh the Crusading Age, this poignant and yet exultant expectation seized upon the hearts of Christians. And then, especially from St. Augustine's teaching onwards, an all-pervading, frequently very severe, conviction as to the profound effects of Original Sin, a pessimistic turning away from the future of this sub-lunar world, as leading up to the great Apostacy, and a concentration upon Man's pre-historic beginnings, as incomparably eclipsing all that mankind would ever achieve here below, came and largely took the place, as the sobering, detaching element in Christianity, of the vivid expectation of the Parousia which had characterized the earlier Christian times.

Clearly, the Parousia and the Original Sin conception have ceased to exercise their old, poignantly detaching power upon us. Yet we much require some such special channel and instrument for the preservation and acquisition of the absolutely essential temper of Detachment and Other-Worldliness. I think that this instrument and channel of purification and detachment—if we have that thirst for the More and the Other than all things visible can give to our souls, (a thirst which the religious sense alone can supply and without which we are religiously but half-awake,)—is offered to us now by Science, in the sense and for the reasons already described.

7. *Three kinds of occupation with Science.*

Let the reader note that thus, and, I submit, thus only, we can and do enlist the religious passion itself on the side of disinterested, rightly autonomous science. For thus the harmony between the different aspects and levels of life is not, (except for our general faith in its already present latent reality, and in its capacity for ultimate full realization and manifestation,) the static starting-point or automatically persisting fact in man's life; but it is, on the contrary, his ever difficult, never completely realized goal,—a goal which can be reached only by an even greater transformation within the worker than within the materials worked upon by him,—a transformation in great part effected by the enlargement and purification, incidental to the inclusion of that large range of Determinist Thing-laws and experiences within the Spirit's Libertarian, Personal life.

It is plain that there are three kinds and degrees of occupation with Things and Science, and with their special level of truth and reality; and that in proportion as their practice within, and in aid of, the spiritual life is difficult, in the same proportion, (given the soul's adequacy to this particular amount of differentiation and pressure,)—is this practice purifying. And though but few souls will be called to any appreciable amount of activity within the third degree, all souls can be proved, I think, to require a considerable amount of the first two kinds, whilst mankind at large most undoubtedly demands careful, thorough work of all three sorts.

The first kind is that of the man with a hobby. His directly religious acts and his toilsome bread-winning will thus get relieved and alternated by, say, a little Botany or a little Numismatics, or by any other " safe " science, taken in a " safe " dose, in an easy, *dilettante* fashion, for purposes of such recreation. This kind is already in fairly general operation, and is clearly useful in its degree and way, but it has, of course, no purificatory force at all.

The second kind is that of the man whose profession is some kind of science which has, by now, achieved a more or less secure place alongside of, or even within, religious doctrines and feelings,—such as Astronomy or Greek Archaeology. Here the purification will be in proportion to the loyal thoroughness with which he fully maintains, indeed develops, the special characteristics and autonomy both of these Sciences, as the foreground, part-material and stimulation, and of Religion, as the groundwork, background and ultimate interpreter and moulder of his complete and organized life; and with which he makes each contribute to the development of the other and of the entire personality, its apprehensions and its work. This second kind is still comparatively rare, doubtless, in great part, because of the considerable cost and the lifelong practice and training involved in what readily looks like a deliberate complicating and endangering of things, otherwise, each severally, simple and safe.

And the third kind is that of him whose systematic mental activity is devoted to some science or research, which is still in process of winning full and peaceful recognition by official Theology,—say, Biological Evolution or Biblical Criticism. Here the purification will, for a soul capable of such a strain, be at its fullest, provided such a soul is deeply moved by, and keeps devotedly faithful to, the love of God, and of man, of humble labour and of self-renouncing purification, and, within this great ideal and determination, maintains and ameliorates with care the methods, categories and tests special both to these sciences and investigations, and to their ultimate interpretation and utilization in the philosophy and life of religion. For here there will, as yet, be no possibility of so shunting the scientific activity on to one side, or of limiting it to a carefully pegged-out region, as to let Religion and Science energize as forces of the same kind and same level, the same clearness and same finality; but the Science will here have to be passed through, as the surface-level, on the way to Religion as underlying all. What would otherwise readily tend to become, as it were, a mental Geography, would thus here give way to what might be pictured as a spiritual Geology.

8. *Historical Science, Religion's present, but not ultimate, problem.*

The reader will have noted that, for each of these three stages, I have taken an Historico-Cultural as well as a Mathematico-Physical Science, though I am well aware of the profound difference between them, both as to their pre-requisites and method, and their aim and depth. And, again, I know well that, for the present, the chief intellectual difficulty of Religion, or at least the main conflict or friction between the Sciences and Theology, seems to proceed, not from Physical Science but from Historical Criticism, especially as applied to the New Testament, so that, on this ground also, I ought, apparently, to keep these two types of Science separate.—Yet it is clear, I think, that, however distinct, indeed different, should be the methods of these two sorts of Science, they are in so far alike, if taken as a means of purification for the soul bent upon its own deepening, that both require a slow, orderly, disinterested procedure, capable of fruitfulness only by the recurring sacrifice of endless petty self-seekings and obstinate fancies, and this in face of that natural eagerness and absoluteness of mind which strong religious emotions will, unless they too be disciplined and purified, only tend to increase and stereotype.

The matters brought up by Historical Criticism for the study and readjustment of Theology, and for utilization by Religion, are indeed numerous and in part difficult. Yet the still more general and fundamental alternatives lie not here, but with the questions as to the nature and range of Science taken in its narrower sense,—as concerned with Quantity, Mechanism, and Determinism alone.

If Science of this Thing-type be all that, in any manner or degree, we can apprehend in conformity with reality or can live by fruitfully : then History and Religion of every kind must be capable of a strict assimilation to it, or they must go. But if such Science constitute only one kind, and, though the clearest and most easily transferable, yet the least deep, and the least adequate to the ultimate and spiritual reality, among the chief levels of apprehension and of life which can be truly experienced and fruitfully lived by man ; and if the Historical and Spiritual level can be shown to find room for, indeed to require, the Natural and Mechanical level, whilst this latter, taken as ultimate, cannot accommodate, but is forced to crush or to deny, the former : then a refusal to accept more than can be expressed and analyzed by such Physico-Mathematical Science would be an uprooting and a discrowning of the fuller life, and would ignore the complete human personality, from one of whose wants the entire impulse to such Science took its rise.

As a matter of fact, we find the following three alternatives.

Level all down to Mathematico-Physical Science, and you deny the specific constituents of Spirituality, and you render impossible the growth of the Person out of, and at the expense of, the Individual. Proclaim the Person and its Religion, as though they were static substances adequately present from the first, and ignore, evade or thwart that Thing-level and method as far as ever you can, and you will, in so far, keep back the all but simply animal Individual from attaining to his full spiritual Personality. But let grace wake up, in such an Individual, the sense of the specific characteristics of Spirituality and the thirst to become a full and ever fuller Person, and this in contact and conflict with, as well as in recollective abstraction from, the apparently chance contingencies of History and Criticism, and the seemingly fatalistic mechanisms of Physics and Mathematics : and you will be able, by humility, generosity, and an ever-renewed alternation of such outgoing, dispersive efforts and of such incoming recollection and affective prayer, gradually to push out and to fill in the outlines of your better nature, and to reorganize it all according to the Spirit and to Grace, becoming thus a deep man, a true personality.

Once again : take the intermediate, the Thing-level as final, and you yourself sink down more and more into a casual Thing, a soulless Law; Materialism, or, at best, some kind of Pantheism, must become your practice and your creed.—Take the anterior, the Individual-level as final, and you will remain something all but stationary, and if not merely a Thing yet not fully a Person ; and if brought face to face with many an Agnostic or Pantheist of the nobler sort, who is in process of purification from such childish self-centredness by means of the persistently frank and vivid apprehension of the Mechanical, Determinist, Thing-and-Fate level of experience and degree of truth, you will, even if you have acquired certain fragmentary convictions and practices of religion, appear strangely less, instead of more, than your adversary, to any one capable of equitably comparing that Agnostic and yourself—you who, if Faith be right, ought surely to be not less but more of a personality than that non-believing soul.

But take the last, the Spiritual, Personal level as alone ultimate, and yet as necessarily requiring, to be truly reached and maintained, that the little, selfish, predominantly animal-minded, human being should ever pass and repass from this, his Individualistic plane and attitude, through the Thing-and-Fate region, out and on to the " shining table-land, whereof our God Himself is sun and moon " : and you will, in time, gain a depth and an expansion, a persuasive force, an harmoniousness and intelligibleness with which, everything else being equal, the Pantheistic or Agnostic self-renunciation cannot truly compare. For, in these circumstances, the latter type will, at best, but prophesy and prepare the consummation actually reached by the integrational, dynamic religiousness, the Individual transformed more and more into Spirit and Person, by the help of the Thing and of Determinist Law. Freedom, Interiority, Intelligence, Will, Grace, and Love, the profoundest Personality, a reality out of all proportion more worthy and more ultimate than the most utterly unbounded universe of a simply material kind could ever be, thus appear here, in full contradiction of Pantheism, as ultimate and abiding; and yet all that is great and legitimate in Pantheism has been retained, as an intermediate element and stage, of a deeply purifying kind.

9. *Return to Saints John of the Cross and Catherine of Genoa.*

And thus we come back to the old, sublime wisdom of St. John of the Cross, in all that it has of continuous thirst after the soul's purification and expansion, and of a longing to lose itself, its every pettiness and egoistic separateness, in an abstract, universal, quasi-impersonal disposition and reality, such as God here seems to require and to offer as the means to Himself. Only that now we have been furnished, by the ever-clearer self-differentiation of Mathematico-Physical Science, with a zone of pure, sheer Thing, mere soulless Law, a zone capable of absorbing all those elements from out of our thought and feeling which, if left freely to mingle with the deeper level of the growing Spiritual Personality, would give to this an unmistakably Pantheistic tinge and trend. Hence, now the soul will have, in one of its two latter movements, to give a close attention to contingent facts and happenings and to abstract laws, possessed of no direct religious significance or interpretableness which, precisely because of this, will, if practised as part of the larger whole of the purificatory, spiritual upbuilding of the soul, in no way weaken, but stimulate and furnish materials for the other movement, the one specially propounded by the great Spaniard, in which the soul turns away, from all this particularity, to a general recollection and contemplative prayer.

And we are thus, perhaps, in even closer touch with Catherine's central idea,—the soul's voluntary plunge into a painful yet joyous purgation, into a state, and as it were an element, which purges away, (since the soul itself freely accepts the process,) all that deflects, stunts, or weakens the realization of the soul's deepest longings,—the hard self-centredness, petty self-mirrorings, and jealous claimfulness, above all. For though, in Catherine's conception, this at first both painful and joyful, and then more and more, and at last entirely, joyful, ocean of light and fire is directly God and His effects upon the increasingly responsive and unresisting soul : yet the apparent Thing-quality here, the seemingly ruthless Determinism of Law, in which the little individual is lost for good and all, and which only the spiritual personality can survive, are impressively prominent throughout this great scheme. And though we cannot, of course, take the element and zone of the sheer Thing and of Determinist Law as God, or as directly expressive of His nature, yet we can and must hold it, (in what it is in itself, in what it is as a construction of our minds, and in its purificatory function and influence upon our unpurified but purifiable souls,) to come from God and to lead to Him. And thus here also we escape any touch of ultimate Pantheism, without falling into any cold Deism or shallow Optimism. For just because we retain, at the shallower level, the ruthlessly impersonal element, can we, by freely willed, repeated passing through such fatalistic-seeming law, become, from individuals, persons; from semi-things, spirits,—spirits more and more penetrated by and apprehensive of the Spirit, God, the source and sustainer of all this growth and reality.

And yet, let us remember once more, the foreground and preliminary stage to even the sublimest of such lives will never, here below at least, be abidingly transcended, or completely harmonized with the groundwork and ultimate stage, by the human personality. Indeed our whole contention has been that, with every conceivable variation of degree, of kind, and of mutual relation, these two stages, and some sort of friction between them, are necessary, throughout this life, for the full development, the self-discipline, and the adequate consolidation, at the expense of the childish, sophistic individual, of the true spiritual Personality.

IV. Final Summary and Return to the Starting-
point of the Whole Inquiry: the Necessity,
and yet the Almost Inevitable Mutual Hostility, of the Three Great Forces of the Soul
and of the Three Corresponding Elements of
Religion.

Our introductory position as to the three great forces of
the soul, with the corresponding three great elements of
religion, appears, then, to have stood the test of our detailed
investigation. For each of these forces and corresponding
elements has turned out to be necessary to religion, and yet
to become destructive of itself and of religion in general
where this soul-force and religious element is allowed gravely
to cripple, or all but to exclude, the other forces and elements,
and their vigorous and normal action and influence.

1. *Each of these three forces and elements is indeed necessary,
but ruinously destructive where it more or less ousts the other
two.*

(1) The psychic force or faculty by which we remember
and picture things and scenes; the law of our being which
requires that sense-impressions should stimulate our thinking
and feeling into action, and that symbols, woven by the
picturing faculty out of these impressions, should then express
these our thoughts and feelings; and the need we have, for
the due awakening, discipline and supplementation of every
kind and degree of experience and action, that social tradition,
social environment, social succession should ever be before
and around and after our single lives: correspond to and
demand the Institutional and Historical Element of Religion.
This element is as strictly necessary as are that force and
that law.

Yet if this force and need of the soul, and this religious
element are allowed to emasculate the other two primary
soul-forces and needs and the religious elements corresponding
to them, it will inevitably degenerate into more or less of a
Superstition,—an oppressive materialization and dangerous
would-be absolute fixation of even quite secondary and temporary expressions and analyses of religion; a ruinous belief
in the direct transferableness of religious conviction; and a
predominance of political, legal, physically coercive concepts
and practices with regard to those most interior, strong yet

delicate, readily thwarted or weakened, springs of all moral and religious character,—spiritual sincerity and spontaneity and the liberty of the children of God. We thus get too great a preponderance of the " Objective," of Law and Thing, as against Conviction and Person; of Priest as against Prophet; of the movement from without inwards, as against the movements from within outwards.

The Spanish Inquisition we found to be probably the most striking example and warning here. Yet the Eastern Christian Churches have doubtless exhibited these symptoms, if less acutely, yet more extensively and persistently. And the Protestant Reformation-Movement, (even in the later lives of its protagonists, Luther, Zwingli, and Calvin,) much of orthodox Lutheranism and Calvinism, and some forms and phases of Anglican Highchurchism and of Scotch Presbyterianism, show various degrees and forms of a similar onesidedness. In Judaism the excesses in the Priestly type of Old Testament religion, especially as traceable after the Exile, and their partial continuation in Rabbinism, furnish other, instructive instances of such more or less partial growth,— the Pharisees and the Jerusalem Sanhedrin being here the fullest representatives of the spirit in question. The classical Heathen Roman religion was, throughout, too Naturalistic for its, all but exclusive, externalism and legalism to be felt as seriously oppressive of any other, considerable element of that religion. And much the same could doubtless be said of Indian Brahmanism to this day. But in orthodox Mohammedanism we get the truly classical instance of such a predominance, in all its imposing strength and terrible, because all but irremediable, weakness—with its utterly unanalytic, unspeculative, unmystical, thing-like, rock-solid faith; its detailed rigidity and exhaustive fixity; its stringent unity of organization and military spirit of entirely blind obedience; its direct, quite unambiguous intolerance, and ever ready appeal to the sword, as the normal and chief instrument for the propagation of the spirit; and its entirely inadequate apprehension of man's need of purification and regeneration in all his untutored loves, fears, hopes and hates.

(2) Then there is the soul-force by which we analyze and synthesize, and the law of our being which requires us to weigh, compare, combine, transfer, or ignore the details and the evidential worth of what has been brought home to us

through the stimulation of our senses, by our picturing faculty and memory, and by means of our Social, Historical, and Institutional environment, and which orders us to harmonize all these findings into as much as may be of an intelligible whole of religion, and to integrate this religious whole within some kind of, at least rough, general conception as to our entire life's experience. And this force and law are answered by the Critical-Historical and Synthetic-Philosophical element of religion. We thus get Positive and Dogmatic Theology. And this element is as humanly inevitable and religiously necessary as is that soul-force and law.

Yet here again, if this force, law, and element are allowed superciliously to ignore, or violently to explain away, the other kinds of approaches and contributions to religious truth and experience, special to the other two soul-forces and religious elements, we shall get another destructive one-sidedness, a Rationalistic Fanaticism, only too often followed by a lengthy Agnosticism and Indifference. Whilst the Rationalist Fanaticism lasts, everything will doubtless appear clear and simple to the soul, but then this " everything " will but represent the merest skimmings upon the face of the mighty deep of living, complete religion,—a petty, artificial arrangement by the human mind of the little which, there and then, it can easily harmonize into a whole, or even simply a direct hypostatizing of the mind's own bare categories.

The worship of the Goddess of Reason at Notre-Dame of Paris we found to be here, perhaps, the most striking instance. Yet Rationalist excesses, varying from a cold Deism down to an ever short-lived formal Atheism, and the lassitude of a worldly-wise Indifferentism, are traceable within all the great religions. Thus a large proportion of the educated members of the ancient Greco-Roman world were, from the Sophists and the Second Punic War onward, stricken with such a blight. The Sadducees are typical of this tendency among the Jews for some two centuries. The tough persistence of a mostly obscure current of destructive free-thought throughout Western Europe in the Middle Ages shows well the difficulty and importance of a mental and spiritual victory over these forces of radical negation, and of not simply driving them beneath the surface of society. And the ready lapse of the most daring and intense of the Medieval, Jewish and Christian, Scholastics into a thoroughly Pantheistic Panlogism, points to the prevalence, among these circles, of a certain tyranny of the abstractive and logical faculty over the other powers and intimations of the soul.—Unitarianism again is, in its origins and older form, notwithstanding its even excessive anti-Pantheism, strongly Scholastic in its whole temper and method, and this without the important correctives and supplementations brought to that method by the largely Mystical and Immanental Angel of the Schools. The greater part of the " Aufklärung"-Movement was vitiated by an often even severer, impoverishment of the whole conception of religion. And, in our day, the Liberal movements within the various Christian bodies, and again among Brahmanic religionists in India, rarely escape altogether from ignoring or explaining away the dark and toilsome aspects of life, and the inevitable excess of all deep reality, and indeed of our very experience of it, above our clear, methodical, intellectual analysis and synthesis of it. Too often and for too long all such groups have inclined to assimilate all Experience to clear Knowledge, all clear Knowledge to Physico-Mathematical Science, all Religion to Ethics, and all Ethics to a simple belief in the ultimacy of Determinist, Atomistic Science. The situation is decidedly improving now; History and Culture are being found to have other, more ultimate categories, than are those of Mathematics and Physics, and to bring us a larger amount of reality, and Ethics and Religion are discovered to be as truly distinct as they are closely allied and necessary, each to the deepest development of the other.

(3) The faculty and action of the soul, finally, by which we have an however dim yet direct and (in its general effects) immensely potent, sense and feeling, an immediate experience of Objective Reality, of the Infinite and Abiding, of a Spirit not all unlike yet distinct from our own, Which penetrates and works within these our finite spirits and in the world at large, especially in human history; and by which we will and give a definite result and expression to, our various memories, thinkings, feelings, and intuitions, as waked up by their various special stimulants and by the influence of each upon all the others; is met by the Mystical and the directly Operative element of Religion. And here again we have a force and law of the human spirit, and a corresponding element of religion, which can indeed be starved or driven

into a most dangerous isolation and revolt, but which are simply indestructible.

The Apocalyptic Orgies of the Münster Anabaptists we found to be perhaps the most striking illustration of the dire mischief that can spring from this third group of elemental soul-forces, when they ignore or dominate the other two. Yet some such Emotional Fanaticism can be traced, in various degrees and forms, throughout all such religious groups, schools, and individuals as seriously attempt to practise Pure Mysticism,—that is, religious Intuition and Emotion unchecked by the other two soul-forces and religious elements, or by the alternation of external action and careful contact with human Society and its needs and helps, Art and Science, and the rest.

Thus we find that, after the immense, luxuriant prevalence of an intensely intuitive, emotional, tumultuously various apprehension and manifestation of religion during the first two generations of Christians, and even after the deep, wise supplementation and spiritualization of this element by St. Paul, who in his own person so strikingly combined the Institutional, Rational and Intuitive-Emotional forces and elements, this whole force and element rapidly all but disappeared for long from Western Christian orthodoxy. And Montanism in still early times, and, during the very height of the Middle Ages, the Waldensian and Albigensian movements—all predominantly intuitive, enthusiastic, individualist —appear as so many revolutionary explosions, threatening the whole fabric of Christendom with dissolution. The "Eternal Gospel" movement of Abbot Joachim, on the other hand, gives us the intuitional-emotive element in a more purified, institutionally and rationally supplemented form.

Again we find that, for a while, in reaction from an all but hopelessly corrupt civilization, the Fathers of the Desert attained in many cases, by means of an all but Exclusive Mysticism, to a type of sanctity and to the inculcation of a lesson which the Church has gratefully recognized. We have to admit that many of the Italian, French and Spanish Quietists of the seventeenth century were no doubt excessively, or even quite unjustly, suspected or pursued, as far at least as their own personal motives and the effect of their doctrines upon their own characters were concerned : and that the general reaction against even the proved, grave excesses

of some of these men and women, went often dangerously far
in the contrary direction. Indeed even the fierce fanaticism
of the Dutch-Westphalian Apocalyptic Intuitionists can but
excuse, not justify, the policy of quite indiscriminately ruthless
extermination pursued by Luther, Zwingli and Calvin, and by
their official churches after their deaths, towards any and all
Illuminism, however ethically pure and socially operative.
The " Society of Friends " which, measured by the smallness
of its numbers, has given to the world an astonishingly large
band of devoted lovers of humankind, is a living witness to
the possibility of such an Illuminism.

And we can note how the sane and solid, deep and delicate
constituents, which had existed, mixed up with all kinds of
fantastic, often hysterical and anti-moral exaltations, within
most of those all but purely Intuitionist circles, gradually
found their escape away into all sorts of unlikely quarters,
helping to give much of their interiority and religious warmth,
not only to various, now fairly sober-minded, Nonconformist
Protestant bodies on the Continent, in England and America,
but also to the more religious-tempered and more spiritually
perceptive among modern philosophers—such as Spinoza,
Kant, Fichte, Schleiermacher, Schelling and Fechner.

Within the Jewish world, we get much of this element at
its noblest and at its worst, in the true and false Prophets
respectively; then among the Essenes, for the times between
the Maccabean resistance and the revolt of Bar Cochba; and
later on in the Kabbala. The Mohammedans still furnish the
example of the Sufi-movement. The Classical Heathen world
produced the Neo-Platonist and the Mithraic movements;
and we can still study, as a living thing, the Buddhist
Mysticism of Thibet.

We have then, here too, something thoroughly elemental,
which requires both persistent operative recognition and a
continuous and profound purification and supplementation
by becoming incorporated within a large living system of
all the fundamental forces of the soul, each operating and
operated upon according to the intrinsic nature and legitimate
range of each.

2. *Each element double ; endless combinations and conflicts.*
We have also found that these three forces and elements
are each double, and that collisions, but also most fruitful
interactions, can and do obtain between even these yoke-
fellows : between Institutionalism and History,—the Present

and the Past, a direct Sense-Impression and Picture and a Memory; between Criticism and Construction,—Analysis and acuteness of mind, and Synthesis and richness and balance of imagination, head, heart, and will; and between Mysticism and Action, as respectively Intuitive and quiescent and Volitional and effortful.

And both the three forces and elements as a whole, and the single members of each pair, can and do appear in every possible variety of combination with, and of opposition against, the others, although there is a special affinity between the Critical-Speculative- and the Intuitive-Volitional pairs (in combination against the Sense-and-Memory pair); between the Sense-and-Memory pair and the single member of Action; and between the single members of Speculation and of Intuition. Yet, ultimately, not any one pair or member can bear its fullest fruit, without the aid of all the others; and there is not one that, in actual human nature, does not tend to emasculate, or to oust as much as possible from the soul, the other pairs or single members.

3. *Our entire religious activity but one element of our complete spirit-life.*

And we have noted further, how even the fullest development in any one soul of all these three couples of specifically religious activities—even supposing that they could be developed to their fullest, without any participation in and conflict with other degrees and kinds of life and reality—do not, by any means, exhaust the range of even the simplest soul's actual energizings.

(1) For over and beyond the specifically religious life—though this, where genuine, is ever the deepest, the central life—every soul lives, and has to live, various other lives. And indeed— and this is the point which specially concerns religion—the soul cannot attain to its fullest possible spiritual development, without the vigorous specific action and differentiation of forces and functions of a not directly religious character, which will have to energize, each according to its own intrinsic nature, within the ever ampler, and ever more closely-knit, organization of the complete life of the soul.

(2) And within this complete life, the three pairs of religious forces and elements each possess their own special affinities and antipathies for certain of the forces and elements which constitute the other, less central organizations of man's marvellously rich activity. The Historical-Institutional

element of Religion has necessarily a special affinity for, and borrows much of its form from, social, legal, political history and institutions of a general kind. The Critical-Speculative element of religion is necessarily cognate to, and in a state of interchange with, the general historical criticism and philosophical insight attained during the ages and amongst the races in which any particular religion is intellectually systematized. And the Mystical-Operative element is necessarily influenced by, and largely utilizes the general emotive and volitional gifts and habits, peculiar to the various ages and peoples within which this double religious element is in operation.

(3) It is thus abundantly clear how greatly a work so manifold in its means, and so harmonious in its end, requires, if it is to come to a considerable degree of realization, that single souls, and single classes and types of souls, should have around them a large and varied Historical and Institutional, a Social life both of a specifically religious and of a general kind, and that, within this large ambit of the actualized religion of others and of the still largely potential religion of their own souls, they shall develop and be helped to realize their own deepest spiritual capacities and *attrait*. They will have to develop these special capabilities to the utmost degree compatible with some practice of the other chief elements of religion, with a continuous respect for and belief in the necessity of the other types of soul, and with a profound belief in, and love of, the full, organized community of all devoted souls, which builds up, and is built up by, all this variety in unity. The Kingdom of God, the Church, will thus be more and more found and made to be the means of an ever more distinct articulation, within an ever more fruitful interaction, of the various *attraits*, gifts, vocations, and types of souls which constitute its society. And these souls in return will, precisely by this their articulation within this ampler system, bring to this society an ever richer content of variety in harmony, of action and warfare within an ever deeper fruitfulness and peace.

4. *Two conditions of the fruitfulness of the entire process.*

Yet even the simplest effort, within this innumerable sequence and simultaneity of activities, will lack the fullest truth and religious depth and fruitfulness, unless two experiences, convictions and motives are in operation throughout the whole, and penetrate its every part, as salt and yeast,

atmosphere and light penetrate, and purify and preserve our
physical food and bodily senses.

The vivid, continuous sense that God, the Spirit upholding
our poor little spirits, is the true originator and the true end
of the whole movement, in all it may have of spiritual beauty,
truth, goodness and vitality; that all the various levels and
kinds of reality and action are, in whatever they have of
worth, already immanently fitted to stimulate, supplement
and purify each other by Him Who, an Infinite Spiritual
Interiority Himself, gives thus to each one of us indefinite
opportunities for actualizing our own degree and kind of
spiritual possibility and ideal; and that He it is Who, however
dimly yet directly, touches our souls and awakens them, in
and through all those minor stimulations and apprehensions,
to that noblest, incurable discontent with our own petty self
and to that sense of and thirst for the Infinite and Abiding,
which articulates man's deepest requirement and characteristic:
this is the first experience and conviction, without which all
life, and life's centre, religion, are flat and dreary, vain and
philistine.

And the second conviction is the continuous sense of the
ever necessary, ever fruitful, ever bliss-producing Cross of
Christ—the great law and fact that only through self-
renunciation and suffering can the soul win its true self, its
abiding joy in union with the Source of Life, with God Who
has left to us, human souls, the choice between two things
alone : the noble pangs of spiritual child-birth, of painful-
joyous expansion and growth; and the shameful ache of
spiritual death, of dreary contraction and decay.

Now it is especially these two, ever primary and supreme,
ever deepest and simplest yet most easily forgotten, bracing
yet costing, supremely virile truths and experiences—facts
which increasingly can and ever should waken up, and
themselves be vivified by, all the other activities and gifts
of God which we have studied—these two eyes of religion
and twin pulse-beats of its very heart, that have been realized,
with magnificent persistence and intensity, by the greatest
of the Inclusive Mystics.

And amongst these Mystics, Caterinetta Fiesca Adorna,
the Saint of Genoa, has appeared to us as one who, in spite
of not a little obscurity and uncertainty and vagueness in the
historical evidences for her life and teaching, of not a few
limitations of natural character and of opportunity, and of

several peculiarities which, wonderful to her *entourage*, can but perplex or repel us now, shines forth, in precisely these two central matters, with a penetrating attractiveness, rarely matched, hardly surpassed, by Saints and Heroes of far more varied, humorous, readily understandable, massive gifts and actions. And these very limits and defects of her natural character and opportunities, of her contemporary disciples and later panegyrists, and of our means for studying and ascertaining the facts and precise value of the life she lived, and of the legend which it occasioned, may, we can hope, but help to give a richer articulation and wider applicability to our study of the character and necessity, the limits, dangers and helpfulness of the Mystic Element of Religion.

INDEX

(Some corrections of mistakes in names and references, as given in the foregoing work, have been silently effected in the following Index)

I. OF SUBJECT-MATTERS

II. OF LITERARY REFERENCES

(The more general literary references given under names of authors in Part I)